Shakespeare

and the

English Romantic Imagination

SHAKESPEARE
and the
English
Romantic Imagination

JONATHAN BATE

CLARENDON PRESS · OXFORD

Oxford University Press, Walton Street, Oxford OX2 6DP

Oxford New York Toronto
Delhi Bombay Calcutta Madras Karachi
Kuala Lumpur Singapore Hong Kong Tokyo
Nairobi Dar es Salaam Cape Town
Melbourne Auckland

and associated companies in
Berlin Ibadan

Oxford is a trade mark of Oxford University Press

Published in the United States
by Oxford University Press, New York

British Library Cataloguing in Publication Data

Bate, Jonathan
Shakespeare and the English Romantic imagination.
1. Shakespeare, William—Influence 2. English
poetry—19th century—History and criticism
I. Title
821'.7'09   PR590

ISBN 0–19–812994–7 (Pbk)

Library of Congress Cataloging in Publication Data

Bate, Jonathan.
Shakespeare and the English romantic imagination.
Bibliography: p
Includes index.
1. English literature—19th century—History and
criticism.   2. Romanticism—England.   3. Shakespeare,
William, 1564–1616—Influence.   4. Influence (Literary,
artistic, etc.)   I. Title.
PR457.B28 1986   822.3'3   86-691

ISBN 0–19–812994–7 (Pbk)

Printed in Great Britain by
J. W. Arrowsmith Ltd, Bristol

In memory
of my
father

Preface

A PREFACE is a good place for saying what a book is not. This one is not a survey of Shakespearean criticism in the late eighteenth and early nineteenth centuries; nor is it an assessment of the value and validity of Romantic readings of Shakespeare. The reader will not find what might first be expected from the title, chapters about Coleridge's lectures and Hazlitt's essays on Shakespeare. Nor is this an account of Shakespeare's pervasive presence in English cultural life during the Romantic age, though I am writing such an account to complement this book.

This is a contribution to the history of poetic influence, not that of Shakespearean criticism. It is a study of Shakespeare's influence on the minds and works of the major English Romantic poets. I approach their poetry by way of their poetics—Wordsworth's prefaces and Keats's letters are considered before their respective poems—but I am concerned more with practice than with theory. There are both pragmatic and polemical reasons for this emphasis. I have tried to answer a need: astonishingly, no one has yet undertaken a wide-ranging study of Shakespeare and Romantic poetry; there are not even single articles or chapters devoted to Shakespeare's influence on the poetry (as opposed to the plays) of Blake, Wordsworth, and Coleridge. I have also sought to redress a balance: recent work on Romanticism and 'influence' has emphasized the theoretical at the expense of the particular, just as it has emphasized Milton at the expense of Shakespeare.

My concern with particular influences on particular poems does not, however, mean that the general has been eschewed. Local observations have frequently led to central questions about the nature both of poetic influence and of that loose set of shared assumptions and procedures which we call the 'Romantic imagination'. Some of those questions are raised in the first two chapters; in the rest of the book they are developed and explored empirically. The whole is necessarily selective: each chapter could form the substance of a book in itself. Within each chapter, there is variation of emphasis: I have discussed at length those allusions which I find especially significant, but recorded other analogues more briefly, leaving the reader to consider what effect they may have. The book advances an argument, but it is also a presentation of material from which the reader may develop other arguments. The final two chapters, on Shelley and Byron, are the most selective; this is not because Shakespeare was any less important to these poets than he was to the other four, but because further examples of Shakespearean echoes in lyric poetry would only have confirmed the argument of the preceding chapters. It seemed best to end by considering what was distinctive about the two poets— the comparative success of Shelley's Shakespearean play, Byron's assaults on uncritical Bardolatry—so as to avoid giving the impression of neatly summing up a subject that is by its nature too various, too large and important, to be summed up neatly.

This book would not have been possible without the work of the Romantic poets' editors, annotators, and commentators. But I have not noted every coincidence of local observation: it is encouraging to know that many Shakespearean allusions have been discerned by other readers and therefore cannot be said to exist solely in the mind of a reader who is looking especially for them, but such encouragement seemed to me insufficient to merit a profusion of footnotes to other people's footnotes. Substantial debts to other scholars are, of course, noted; my principal obligations are to those who have written about influence and allusion, but not specifically with regard to the Romantics or Shakespeare. The presiders are Walter Jackson Bate (a teacher, not a relation) and Christopher Ricks; the *éminence grise* is Harold Bloom.

Parts of chapters four and five formed a paper read at the Wordsworth Summer Conference, Grasmere, 1984, and published in the issue of *The Wordsworth Circle* devoted to that conference. A short section of chapter nine first appeared in *English*, Summer 1982.

I am grateful to the Commonwealth Fund of New York for a Harkness Fellowship which enabled me to start this work at Harvard and to St Catharine's College for a Research Fellowship which enabled me to finish it in Cambridge. I would like to thank the students on whom I tried out various ideas, and the many friends, colleagues, and teachers who read drafts of individual chapters, in particular John Beer, Stephen Clark, Geoffrey Day, Heather Glen, Paul Hartle, and Richard Luckett. Christopher Ridgway generously read the entire typescript; Lucy Newlyn offered valuable suggestions. Kim Scott Walwyn at Oxford University Press provided encouragement and

advice from an early stage. For answers to inquiries, I am grateful to
Professors R. A. Foakes, H. S. Reiss, and Helen Vendler, Mrs C. M.
Gee of the Keats House Library, Mrs Eileen Jay of the Armitt Library
Trust, Ambleside, Kai Kin Yung of the National Portrait Gallery,
and the late Peter Laver of the Wordsworth Library, Dove Cottage.
My debts to Hilary Gaskin are multitudinous. Inaccuracies, inele-
gancies, and solecisms I acknowledge mine.

Preface to Paperback Edition

Alterations for this edition have been confined to the correction of a
handful of minor errors. The complementary book referred to in the
preface is entitled *Shakespearean Constitutions: Politics, Theatre, Criticism
1730–1830*; it will be published by Oxford University Press later in
1989. Also relevant is my essay, 'Shakespeare and Original Genius',
in which the Romantic version of Shakespeare is traced further back
in the eighteenth century than it is here; the essay is forthcoming in
Genius: The History of an Idea, edited by Penelope Murray (Blackwell).

Jonathan Bate
Trinity Hall, Cambridge

Contents

List of Illustrations

Abbreviations

Unless otherwise stated, all works are published in London.

BL   *Biographia Literaria*, ed. James Engell and W. J. Bate, Collected Works of Samuel Taylor Coleridge vii (2 vols., Princeton, 1983).

BPW   Lord Byron, *The Complete Poetical Works*, ed. J. J. McGann (5 vols. so far, Oxford, 1980–); Byron's plays are quoted from his *Poetical Works*, ed. Frederick Page, new edn., corr. John Jump (1970).

CCC   Charles and Mary Cowden Clarke, *Recollections of Writers* (1878).

CH   *Shakespeare: The Critical Heritage 1623–1801*, ed. Brian Vickers (6 vols., 1974–81).

CL   *Collected Letters of Samuel Taylor Coleridge*, ed. E. L. Griggs (6 vols., Oxford, 1956–71).

CN   *The Notebooks of Samuel Taylor Coleridge*, ed. Kathleen Coburn (3 double vols. so far, Princeton and New York, 1957–), cited by entry no.

CPW   *The Complete Poetical Works of Samuel Taylor Coleridge*, ed. E. H. Coleridge (2 vols., Oxford, 1912).

DJ   *Don Juan*, ed. T. G. Steffan, E. Steffan and W. W. Pratt (Harmondsworth, 1973, repr. 1982).

DQW   *Collected Writings of Thomas De Quincey*, ed. David Masson (14 vols., Edinburgh, 1889–90).

EY   *The Letters of William and Dorothy Wordsworth: The Early Years*, ed. E. de Selincourt, 2nd edn., rev. C. L. Shaver (Oxford, 1967).

HCR   *Henry Crabb Robinson on Books and their Writers*, ed. E. J. Morley (3 vols., through pagination, 1938).

HVSV   *His Very Self and Voice: Collected Conversations of Lord Byron*, ed. E. J. Lovell Jr (New York, 1954).

HW   *The Complete Works of William Hazlitt*, ed. P. P. Howe (21 vols., 1930–4).

K   *Blake: Complete Writings*, ed. Geoffrey Keynes (1966, repr. 1969), quotations from *Songs of Innocence and of Experience* silently altered to conform to facsimile edn. with introduction and commentary by Keynes (New York and London, 1967, repr. 1970).

KC   *The Keats Circle*, ed. H. E. Rollins (2nd edn., 2 vols., Cambridge, Mass., 1965).

KL   *The Letters of John Keats 1814–1821*, ed. H. E. Rollins (2 vols., Cambridge, Mass., 1958).

KS   Caroline Spurgeon, *Keats's Shakespeare: A Descriptive Study* (1928).

LJ   *Byron's Letters and Journals*, ed. Leslie Marchand (12 vols., 1973–82).

LY   *The Letters of William and Dorothy Wordsworth: The Later Years*, ed. E. de Selincourt, 2nd edn., rev. A. G. Hill (3 vols. so far, Oxford, 1978–).

MC   *Coleridge's Miscellaneous Criticism*, ed. T. M. Raysor (1936).
MY   *The Letters of William and Dorothy Wordsworth: The Middle Years*, ed. E. de Selincourt, 2nd edn., rev. Mary Moorman and A. G. Hill (2 vols., Oxford, 1969–70).
PL   *Paradise Lost*, ed. Alastair Fowler (1968, repr. 1971).
Prel.   *The Prelude*, unless otherwise stated in 1805 text in edn. of Jonathan Wordsworth, M. H. Abrams and Stephen Gill (New York, 1979).
SC   *Coleridge's Shakespearean Criticism*, ed. T. M. Raysor (2nd edn., 2 vols., 1960).
SJS   *Johnson on Shakespeare*, ed. Arthur Sherbo, Yale edn. of the Works of Samuel Johnson, vii–viii, through pagination (New Haven, 1968).
SL   *The Letters of Percy Bysshe Shelley*, ed. F. L. Jones (2 vols., Oxford, 1964).
SPW   *Shelley: Poetical Works*, ed. Thomas Hutchinson, new edn., corr. G. M. Matthews (1970).
TT   *Specimens of the Table Talk of Samuel Taylor Coleridge*, ed. H. N. Coleridge (2 vols., 1835), cited by date of entry.
WPr   *The Prose Works of William Wordsworth*, ed. W. J. B. Owen and J. W. Smyser (3 vols., Oxford, 1974).
WPW   *Wordsworth's Poetical Works*, ed. Ernest de Selincourt and Helen Darbishire (5 vols., Oxford, 1940–9; 2nd edn. of vols. ii–iii, 1952–4; corr. edn. of iv, 1958), quotations silently altered to conform to earliest published text in book form; cf. *The Oxford Authors: William Wordsworth*, ed. Stephen Gill (Oxford, 1984).

Quotations from poems by Keats are followed by line reference only; I have used the text of *The Poems of John Keats*, ed. Jack Stillinger (Cambridge, Mass., 1978). All quotations from Shakespeare are followed by line reference to *The Riverside Shakespeare*, textual ed. G. Blakemore Evans (Boston, 1974); abbreviations of titles follow C. T. Onions, *A Shakespeare Glossary* (2nd edn., Oxford, 1919). Titles of periodicals are abbreviated according to standard practice.

Shine forth, thou Starre of Poets, *and with rage,*
  Or influence, chide, or cheere the drooping Stage

Ben Jonson

Shakespeares Universalität ist wie der Mittelpunkt der
romantischen Kunst.

Friedrich Schlegel, *Athenäums-Fragmente,* 247

1

Shakespeare, Imagination, Romanticism

> After dinner, and when the rest of the party had departed, I remained sitting with Goethe.
>
> We discoursed upon English literature, on the greatness of Shakespeare; and on the unfavourable position held by all English dramatic authors who had appeared after that poetical giant.
>
> 'A dramatic talent of any importance,' said Goethe, 'could not forbear to notice Shakespeare's works; nay, could not forbear to study them. Having studied them, he must be aware that Shakespeare has already exhausted the whole of human nature in all its tendencies, in all its heights and depths, and that in fact there remains for him, the aftercomer, nothing more to do. And how get courage only to put pen to paper, if conscious, in an earnest appreciating spirit, that such unfathomable and unattainable excellences were already in existence!'[1]

WHAT is the English poet to do when he realizes that he is *der Nachkömmling*, an 'aftercomer'? The rise in Shakespeare's cultural status between the age of Dryden and the age of Coleridge was such that no English poet of the late eighteenth or early nineteenth century could be without a sense of Shakespeare's superiority, a feeling that his plays had exhausted the whole of human nature. The complaint of Goethe, who was thankful that he did not have to write in the language which Shakespeare had wrought to its uttermost, must have been felt even more acutely by his English contemporaries: 'Shakespeare gives us golden apples in silver dishes. We get, indeed, the silver dishes by studying his works; but, unfortunately, we have only potatoes to put into them' (Eckermann, 123).

W. Jackson Bate cites these passages from Eckermann's *Conversations with Goethe* early in *The Burden of the Past* to support his contention that the major difficulty facing the English poet from the mid-eighteenth century onwards has been the anxiety instilled by the thought, '*What is there left to do?*'.[2] Harold Bloom alighted on that word 'anxiety' and propounded his Oedipal theory of influence, in which the history of poetry becomes a series of desperate encounters between 'strong poets' and their even stronger fathers or 'precursors'.[3] For the Freudian, post-modernist Bloom belatedness is a problem; the precursor has to be confronted aggressively, he cannot be acknowledged and accepted. This theory omits one half of the equation. The word *Nachkömmling*, which lies at the heart of Goethe's remark to Eckermann, means not only 'one who comes later', perhaps too late, but also 'a descendant'. The hope that one might be a descendant of a great poet may bring confidence instead of anxiety. The two halves of the equation are seen in Keats: on the one hand, he feared that 'the count/Of mighty Poets is made up', that 'the sun of poesy is set' (*Endymion*, ii. 723–9), but on the other, he comforted himself with the fancy that Shakespeare was a 'Presider', and indeed a precedent, watching benignly over his poetic endeavour. Romantic artists from Fuseli to Berlioz stood in awe of Shakespeare's genius, yet held on to his achievement, daring to hope that they might be worthy of him, might even attain an immortality like his.

There is another respect in which Harold Bloom only tells half the story. Coleridge placed Shakespeare and Milton as 'compeers not rivals' on 'the two glory-smitten summits of the poetic mountain' (*BL* ii. 27). Bloom, however, ignores Goethe on the repressive power of Shakespeare and argues instead that 'if one examines the dozen or so major poetic influencers before this century, one discovers quickly who among them ranks as the great Inhibitor, the Sphinx who strangles even strong imaginations in their cradles: Milton' (*Anxiety*, 32). Perhaps as a result of Bloom's claim that Milton is the central problem in any theory and history of poetic influence in English, recent critical discussion of Romanticism's self-consciously problematic relationship with the tradition has concentrated on Milton.[4] Even before the publication of *The Anxiety of Influence*, we encounter such assertions as the following:

Shakespeare proved to possess too much 'philosophic impartiality'—to be too much of a chameleon—to bring the Romantics out philosophically, to prod them into taking a definite stance that clearly revealed their critical attitudes and theory. . . . it was Milton who provided them with their basic analogies for the poet and his poem and with the main tenets of their poetical theory.[5]

I shall argue that while Milton was profoundly important, especially in matters of politics and prophecy, it was above all Shakespeare who provided the Romantics (though we will need to distinguish between them) with 'basic analogies for the poet and his poem', with crucial 'tenets of poetical theory' and, most importantly, with raw materials for poetic practice. The plays were summoned through allusion in the Romantics' own poems as authority on the question of what it was to be a poet; the echoing of Shakespeare's language provided a way of creatively and modestly acknowledging his priority. It is a commonplace—though one that stands in need of qualification—that the Romantics worshipped Shakespeare, but little consideration has been given to how this idolatry affected their creative practice. I will show that a network of quotations, allusions, and echoes, many of them hitherto unrecognized or uncollected, establishes Shakespeare's presence in the major poems as well as the writings on poetry of the English Romantics.

The contrast between Shakespeare and Milton, an antinomy that is central to both Coleridge's and Hazlitt's criticism, is a creative tension out of which each Romantic finds his own voice. It is as if his lyrical genius is forged from the clash of dramatic and epic as his two mighty forebears are pitted against each other. Just as the Romantic is at his worst when attempting surface imitation of the Shakespearean or Miltonic styles, so he can be at his best when entering into a richer, more intuitive relationship with the two poets.

Miltonists have moved away from the study of specific verbal echoes and parallels—the unmistakable Miltonic cadence—towards a theoretical approach to influence. But with Shakespeare, not even the groundwork has been covered; there is no equivalent of R. D. Havens's survey of verbal borrowings, *The Influence of Milton on English Poetry*.[6] We have editorial footnotes pointing out local verbal parallels and idiosyncratic full-length studies of individual authors, which emphasize spiritual affinities at the expense of particular effects,[7] but little between the two. This book is an attempt to fill that gap. It is a discussion of Shakespearean 'influence' in the largest sense of the word but, mindful of Blake's castigation of Reynolds—'To Generalize is to be an Idiot. To Particularize is the Alone Distinction of Merit' (K 451)—the argument is grounded in the details of verbal borrowings and transformations.

A study of this sort has to steer a careful course between the Scylla of loose rhapsodizing—the old saw that Keats is somehow, indefinably, the most 'Shakespearean' of later poets—and the Charybdis of attaching too much weight to slight parallels, thereby incurring the wrath of Tennyson:

There is, I fear, a prosaic set growing up among us, editors of booklets, bookworms, index-hunters, or men of great memories and no imagination, who *impute themselves* to the poet, and so believe that *he*, too, has no imagination, but is for ever poking his nose between the pages of some old volume in order to see what he can appropriate. They will not allow one to say 'Ring the bell' without finding that we have taken it from Sir P. Sidney, or even to use such a simple expression as the ocean 'roars,' without finding out the precise verse in Homer or Horace from which we have plagiarised it.[8]

But we should not allow Tennyson's disapprobation to make us lose sight of the fact that the borrowing of phrases from Shakespeare was a much discussed issue in the late eighteenth and early nineteenth centuries. In Sheridan's *The Critic*, Puff says of his line 'Perdition catch my soul but I do love thee', that 'two people happened to hit on the same thought—And Shakespeare made use of it first, that's all.'[9] And in *England and the English*, Lord Lytton complained that contemporary playwrights were 'the very Autolycus of plagiarists', robbing phrases from Elizabethan drama while claiming to catch its spirit.[10] I devote chapter two to the questions raised by such remarks.

Nowadays it is unfashionable to dwell on particular verbal parallels. Harold Bloom is not interested in 'the transmission of ideas and images from earlier to later poets'; he says that this is 'just "something that happens," . . . . These are fair materials for source-hunters and biographers, and have little to do with my concern' (*Anxiety*, 71). Materials, he implies, for the scholar and the antiquarian, not the literary critic and the man of strong imagination. But if inherited ideas and images are prominent among the materials of the poet, they should also be prominent among those of the critic. If a Romantic poet were to use the phrase *strong imagination*, he would do so in the knowledge that it occurs twice in Shakespeare—once when Theseus is describing the poetic imagination in *A Midsummer Night's Dream* (V. i. 18), and again in the play that more than any other enacts the power of imagination, *The Tempest* (II. i. 208). Imagination is defined through the recollection of these Shakespearean contexts. Thus when Keats took exception to Dr Johnson's strictures on *A Midsummer Night's Dream* he wrote underneath them in his edition of Shakespeare, 'Such tricks hath *weak* imagination' (*KS* 30).

Bloom's own brilliant 'Revisionary Ratios' could well be revised themselves and applied to this process whereby later poets appropriate images and half-lines from Shakespeare into the texture of their own prose or verse. Provided we remove the final clause, with its antagonistic overtones, his '*Tessera*' offers an excellent description of the Romantics' allusive relationship with Shakespeare: 'A poet antithetically "completes" his precursor, by so reading the parent-poem as to retain its terms but to mean them in another sense, as though the precursor had failed to go far enough' (*Anxiety*, 14). It is a simple—and, *pace* Bloom, not necessarily antipathetic—version of *Tessera* merely to quote a line of Shakespeare in some personal or social context, as happens so often in Byron's letters and Hazlitt's essays. One does not even have to go to Bloom to borrow the term: De Quincey attacked Hazlitt's constant use of quotation on the grounds that it reduced his essays to 'a series of mosaics, a *tessellation* made up from borrowed fragments' (*DQW* v. 238, my italics).

Equally, Bloom's notion of '*Apophrades*, or the return of the dead' may be revised to suggest that allusion offers the later poet a relationship with his predecessors that is not anxious and oppressive, but generous and life-giving.[11] Keats may have said of Milton, 'Life to him would be death to me', but in a letter where he speaks of and quotes from Shakespeare, he finds another image, 'cowering under the Wings of great Poets'—seeking protection in them, not protection from them (*KL* ii. 212, i. 239).

The exploration and definition of a writer's conceptions and various uses of Shakespeare provide a way of defining that writer's 'Romanticism'—hence my use of a capital 'R' throughout this book. The English Romantics did not propound a 'theory' of Romanticism, as the Schlegel brothers and their circle did in Germany, but such a theory—although it is more like a series of working principles, which are often violated—may be evinced from their responses to Shakespeare. In one of the few contemporary attempts to isolate the quintessence of English Romanticism, Leigh Hunt pointed to three things: 'the political convulsions' of the last years of the eighteenth century; the coming together of Wordsworth, Coleridge, and that inveterate Shakespearean, Charles Lamb; and 'the revived inclination for our older and great school of poetry, chiefly produced, I have no doubt, by the commentators on Shakspeare, though they were certainly not aware what fine countries they were laying open.' Similarly, Thomas Babington Macaulay argued that the Romantic revolution consisted of the dethroning of the Augustan poetical dynasty (who had themselves dethroned the successors of Shakespeare and Spenser) by 'a race who represented themselves as heirs of the ancient line, so long dispossessed by usurpers'; the seeds of the revolution, he contends, lay in the revival of 'our fine ancient ballads' and the fact that 'The plays of Shakspeare were better acted, better edited, and better known than they had ever been.'[12]

If we had to pick out a single premiss at the core of English Romanticism, it would probably be the ascription of a central place to the power of the creative imagination, a belief that imagination, genius, and poetry are closely associated with each other.[13] Like the movement in which it plays so large a part, the Romantic approach to Shakespeare has its roots deep in the eighteenth century. Those critics and aestheticians of the second half of the eighteenth century who laid the groundwork for the Romantics by exploring the creative power of imagination turned again and again to Shakespeare for examples of that power. The rise of Romanticism and the growth of Shakespeare idolatry are parallel phenomena.

The predominant image of Shakespeare in the eighteenth century was that of Milton in 'L'Allegro': he was 'fancy's child', warbling 'his native wood-notes wild'. In other words, he was a natural genius, the great poet of imagination (there is no differentiation here between imagination and fancy). Milton's lines are also seminal in that they characterize Shakespeare by means of Shakespearean allusion, a device that will become widespread; 'fancy's child' echoes 'child of fancy' in *Love's Labour's Lost* (I. i. 170). Milton is merely picking up a Shakespearean phrase; contextually, the parallel is singularly inappropriate since the child of fancy in question is Don Armado, with his fantastical learning and affectation, his constant appeals to classical authority and precedent. It was Shakespeare's apparent lack of learning, his much vaunted small Latin and less Greek, that exercised many eighteenth-century critics.

To generalize about the eighteenth century is to be an idiot. Within the apparent homogeneity of neo-classical criticism, there are notable exceptions, isolated voices that sound as if they come from a later age. And there is no straightforward march of progress in the history of critical ideas: in the 1790s and early 1800s, the age of Bardolatry, there will be isolated voices that sound as if they come from an earlier age. Reading Archibald Alison in 1790, one would have thought that nothing had changed since the beginning of the century: 'Had the taste of SHAKESPEARE been equal to his genius, or had his knowledge of the laws of the Drama corresponded to his knowledge of the human heart, the effect of his compositions would not only have been greater than it now is, but greater perhaps than we can well imagine.' This is identical to John Dennis writing in 1712: 'If *Shakespeare* had these great Qualities by Nature, what would he not have been if he had join'd to so happy a Genius Learning and the Poetical Art?'.[14]

The distinction between nature and genius on the one hand, art and learning on the other, had already been made by John Dryden. The best of English neo-classical criticism follows in the tradition of his measured panegyric:

> To begin, then, with Shakespeare: he was the man who of all modern, and perhaps ancient poets, had the largest and most comprehensive soul. All the images of nature were still present to him, and he drew them not laboriously, but luckily; when he describes any thing, you more than see it, you feel it too. Those who accuse him to have wanted learning give him the greater commendation: he was naturally learned; he needed not the spectacles of books to read nature; he looked inwards, and found her there. I cannot say he is every where alike; were he so, I should do him injury to compare him with the greatest of mankind. He is many times flat, insipid; his comic wit degenerating into clenches, his serious swelling into bombast. But he is always great when some great occasion is presented to him . . . .[15]

'You more than see it, you feel it too' foreshadows two crucial later developments, the idea that Shakespeare expresses the passions where other writers merely describe them, and that of the audience's or reader's fellow-feeling, sympathetic identification with the action and emotions of the play. But in the first half of the eighteenth century, other elements of Dryden's appraisal held sway: Shakespeare as a poet notable for his soul rather than his art, and for naturalness not learning; the tempering of praise with a list of faults, such as punning and bombast; the emphasis on decorum ('great when some great occasion').

This is no strict 'French' neo-classicism. When Thomas Rymer attacked Shakespeare for lack of verisimilitude, particularly over the handkerchief business in *Othello*, he did so from an embattled minority position. A critic such as Charles Gildon would censure Shakespeare for neglecting the classical unities but then admit that the 'witchery in him' caused all rules to 'vanish away'.[16] And the theatre-going public were not neo-classical critics, despite the attempts of the literary establishment to refine their taste by rewriting Shakespeare's plays in a more classical style with more decorous action. As Nicholas Rowe acknowledged in his account of Shakespeare, prefixed to the first edited text of the plays, published in 1709, 'That way of Tragi-Comedy was the common Mistake of [the Elizabethan] Age, and is indeed become so agreeable to the *English* Tast that tho' the severer

Critiques among us cannot bear it yet the generality of our Audiences seem to be better pleas'd with it than with an exact Tragedy.'[17]

The weakness of academic histories of criticism is that they concentrate on Shakespeare's place in the minds of the critics, not the hearts of the people. The demand for editions, the prevalence of casual quotation from the plays and the assimilation of phrases into everyday speech, and the success of production after production, especially once Garrick took control at Drury Lane in 1747, are testimony to Shakespeare's real place in the eighteenth century. Garrick's Jubilee at Stratford in 1769, fiasco that it was in itself (in typically English fashion, largely because of the weather), may have marked the beginning of a new age of Bardolatry, but it was also the summation of a hundred years in which Shakespeare's supremacy as the poet of the English people remained unquestioned.

Dr Johnson's preface to his edition of the plays, published in 1765, acknowledges Shakespeare's canonic, monumental status: he 'may now begin to assume the dignity of an ancient, and claim the privilege of established fame and prescriptive veneration'. But critically, the preface is a conservative document; it ends, after all, by quoting and in no way dissenting from Dryden's balanced summary. For Johnson, Shakespeare is 'above all writers, at least above all modern writers, the poet of nature; the poet that holds up to his readers a faithful mirrour of manners and of life'; he may disobey the rules of criticism, but those rules are of limited value since 'there is always an appeal open from criticism to nature.' This is the characteristic English neo-classical position: precisely because of the example of Shakespeare, French codification is rejected in favour of 'nature'. Shakespeare is not, however, set up as an ideal; for all his excellences, he has 'faults sufficient to obscure and overwhelm any other merit' (*SJS* 61–71). In Johnson, then, there are still vestiges of the argument that Shakespeare is the great exception, the genius who broke the rules, who snatched a grace beyond the reach of art. The shift from Johnson to Coleridge, from classic to Romantic, is not a matter of condemnation giving way to commendation but of the great exception becoming the great *exemplum*.

That shift is bound up with a changing conception of nature and with the movement, discerned by M. H. Abrams, from mimetic to expressive models of art, from 'mirror' to 'lamp'. Johnson praised Shakespeare because his drama was 'the mirrour of life'; for Thomas Carlyle, influenced by Coleridge and German Romanticism, Shake-

speare was 'an eye to us all; a blessed heaven-sent Bringer of Light'.[18]
In the age of Johnson, Shakespeare was admired for his truth to created
nature (*natura naturata*); in that of Coleridge, for his grasp of the living
principle at the heart of nature (*natura naturans*, or to use a key
Shakespearean phrase, 'great creating Nature'). The Latin terms are
used by Coleridge himself in the essay in which he is most influenced
by Friedrich Schelling, 'On Poesy or Art':

If the artist copies the mere nature, the *natura naturata*, what idle rivalry! If he
proceeds only from a given form, which is supposed to answer to the notion of
beauty, what an emptiness, what an unreality there always is in his productions, as in Cipriani's pictures! Believe me, you must master the essence, the
natura naturans, which presupposes a bond between nature in the higher sense
and the soul of man.[19]

In a lecture of the same year, 1818, Coleridge applied this distinction
to Shakespeare, arguing that he created not out of 'a *natura naturata*,
an effect, a product' but out of 'a *power* . . . the *universal* which is
potentially in each *particular* . . . the substance capable of endless
modifications' (*MC* 43–4).

German idealism permeated the spirit of the English Romantic
age. Reality came to be located in the interplay of mind and world
through imagination, no longer in a fixed exterior 'general nature'; it
was because of this philosophical development that Romantic poets,
even those who did not know the works of Kant and Schelling as
Coleridge did, dwelt persistently on the perceiving self and the
creative imagination. The close correlation between the rise of
Shakespeare and the rise of Romanticism in Germany is beyond the
scope of this study, but it should not be forgotten that Shakespeare
was the stick with which the *Sturm und Drang* beat off French cultural
hegemony and initiated the Romantic revolution. And it is worth
noting here that works such as Edward Young's *Conjectures on Original
Composition* and Alexander Gerard's *Essay on Genius*, those crucial
discussions of genius and the imagination which advanced Shakespeare
as their exemplar, had enormous influence in Germany.[20] Coleridge
did not always import German ideas; sometimes, he re-imported native
ones. His debt to A. W. Schlegel is a debt at one remove to the British
pre-romantics.

Discussion of nature and perception in German idealistic philosophy
may seem to be taking us some way from Shakespeare, but Schlegel
has a succinct remark suggesting that poetry, especially poetry of the

supernatural, is intimately associated with the organic principle of 'the inward life of nature':

> In general we find in *The Midsummer Night's Dream*, in *The Tempest*, in the magical part of *Macbeth*, and wherever Shakspeare avails himself of the popular belief in the invisible presence of spirits, and the possibility of coming in contact with them, a profound view of the inward life of nature and her mysterious springs, which, it is true, can never be altogether unknown to the genuine poet, as poetry is altogether incompatible with mechanic physics.[21]

Many eighteenth-century critics had seen the supernatural plays as Shakespeare's special achievement, and recognized the close connection between these plays and the imagination (see, for example, Addison in *The Spectator*, Nos. 279 and 419). But the imagination was often treated as slightly suspect; Johnson called it 'a licentious and vagrant faculty, unsusceptible of limitations, and impatient of restraint' (*Rambler*, cxxv). Rowe's tone when writing of Shakespeare's supernatural plays is representative: 'But certainly the greatness of this Author's genius do's nowhere so much appear as where he gives his Imagination an entire Loose, and raises his Fancy to a flight above Mankind and the Limits of the visible World. Such are his Attempts in *The Tempest, Midsummer-Night's Dream, Macbeth* and *Hamlet*' (*CH* ii. 197). For Schlegel and Coleridge, the 'faery way of writing', to use Dryden's phrase, led not to the fringes of experience, away from general nature, but to the imaginative principle without which nature could not be perceived and organized.

Formative influences in this respect are Joseph Warton, who published a series of papers on Shakespeare in *The Adventurer* in 1753–4, and Richard Hurd, in his *Letters on Chivalry and Romance*, first published in 1762. Warton takes Shakespeare's particular excellences to be 'his lively creative imagination; his strokes of nature and passion; and his preservation of the consistency of his characters.' The creative imagination, characterization, and the passions: these are the topics which will preoccupy those critics of the second half of the century in whom there is a gradual ascendancy of what we now consider the 'Romantic' reading of Shakespeare. The choice of plays to which Warton devotes his four essays is significant. *The Tempest* is chosen because it is the most striking instance of Shakespeare's 'creative power'; it is characterized in terms of 'boundless imagination', 'the romantic, the wonderful, and the wild' (*CH* iv. 61). *Lear* is discussed in terms of its intense passions, with particular attention to the power of the single line to convey intense emotion. Warton is very good on the particular, arguing that Shakespeare paints the passions more truly than any other writer by means of 'little and almost imperceptible circumstances' (iv. 67). Coleridge will carry this mode of analysis further, showing how minute particulars are combined in order to produce an organic whole.

Hurd's *Letters* repossessed Spenser for the later eighteenth century by suggesting that 'Gothic' manners were inherently more poetical than classical ones, and that a 'Gothic' poem like *The Faerie Queene* does have a unity of design although it may not answer to classical ideals. Shakespeare is incorporated into this argument in the second (1765) edition, when Hurd adds a passage arguing that his best plays are those that treat Gothic or magical subjects. In the tenth letter it is argued that the 'trite maxim of *following Nature*' should not be applied 'indiscriminately to all sorts of poetry'; 'the more sublime and creative poetry' addresses itself 'solely or principally to the Imagination' and therefore has no need of 'cautious rules of credibility' but can rather concern itself with wonder and magic, ranging freely in the 'supernatural world'. 'In the poet's world, all is marvellous and extraordinary', Hurd continues; poetical truth is perceived by the eye 'when rolling in *a fine frenzy*'.[22] The allusion to Theseus' speech in *A Midsummer Night's Dream* is cardinal, for 'The poet's eye, in a fine frenzy rolling' was being deployed more and more frequently as a proof text in discussions of the imagination. The popularity of the allusion may derive from Akenside's use of it in his immensely influential poem, *The Pleasures of Imagination*. In a passage concerning 'the plastic powers' of imagination, the poet is described as a 'child of Fancy'; the words of Shakespeare, Fancy's eldest child, are then adapted: 'with loveliest frenzy caught,/From earth to heaven he rolls his daring eye,/From heaven to earth' (1744 edn., iii. 373–85).

The poet's eye rolls from heaven to earth, informing other existences, giving them a local habitation and a name. In the mid-eighteenth century, the idea of original genius became increasingly important; a chief characteristic of genius was taken to be its capacity to go outside the self: 'The genius, forgetting that he is a poet, wraps himself up in the person he designs; he becomes him . . . he breathes his soul; he catches his fire; he flames with his resentments' (*CH* iii. 197). This remark prefigures some of the key Romantic statements about Shakespeare, yet it comes from William Guthrie's *Essay upon English Tragedy* of 1747, most of which is devoted to Shakespeare's irregularity. Again and again, we find 'Romantic' fragments buried amidst arguments that are essentially neo-classical. Thus Hurd was not as revolutionary as the passages I have extracted suggest: his main concern was to show that the end of poetry was a Horatian *dulce et utile*. Similarly, Warton never questioned the assumption that poetry should imitate general nature.

Evolutionary narrative is misleading in the history of critical ideas. A book such as R. W. Babcock's *The Genesis of Shakespeare Idolatry*[23] extracts the chief Romantic premises of Shakespearean criticism from eighteenth-century sources, and argues that Coleridge and Hazlitt therefore contributed nothing new. But this is to miss the point that it is the combination of ideas, the arguments into which they are built, that matter most. To take an example. Maurice Morgann's *Essay on the Dramatic Character of Sir John Falstaff*, published in 1777, includes a very Coleridgean passage which employs the metaphor of organic growth, and argues that Shakespeare follows 'certain first principles of *being*' rather than the 'accidents' of character; then in another passage Morgann asserts that Shakespeare is often at his best when not imitating 'nature', since 'True Poesy is *magic*, not *nature*' (*CH* vi. 168 n., 172). This does not, however, mean that Morgann is rejecting classical premises of art: both passages occur in footnotes which are incidental to his main argument, that Falstaff is a realistic character, a reflection of nature. 'Romantic' conceptions do not suddenly appear in the 1790s, nor is there a consistent linear progression towards them. It is rather a case of ideas being available in the *milieu* of the late eighteenth century and critics changing their emphasis. Morgann's organic image emerges in the context of a study of character; at the time, it seems comparatively unimportant. Only when Coleridge uses it with respect to dramatic structure and brings it to the centre of a unified theory of Shakespeare's art does it take on its true significance.

Coleridge's achievement was to combine English empiricism with German systematic rigour, to follow in the tradition both of eighteenth-century critics such as Morgann who began to pay detailed attention to Shakespeare's characters, and of the Germans, A. W. Schlegel especially, who placed Shakespeare at the centre of a theory of art. As I have said, Morgann does not develop at length his organic metaphor and the idea that Shakespeare followed the principles of being, not the accidents of character. But Schlegel constructs his theory of artistic form around organicism:

Form is mechanical when, through external force, it is imparted to any material merely as an accidental addition without reference to its quality . . .

Organical form, again, is innate; it unfolds itself from within, and acquires its determination contemporaneously with the perfect development of the germ. We everywhere discover such forms in nature throughout the whole range of living powers . . . In the fine arts, as well as in the domain of nature—the supreme artist—all genuine forms are organical, that is, determined by the quality of the work. (*Lectures*, 340)

Much has been written about Coleridge's debt to Schlegel on the matter of organic form.[24] What has been ignored is the manner in which he applies this passage. In the fragment headed 'Lecture', Coleridge writes 'The true ground of the mistake, as has been well remarked by a continental critic, lies in the confounding mechanical regularity with organic form'; he then translates the passage. But his final sentence is *not* from Schlegel: 'And even such is the appropriate excellence of her [Nature's] chosen poet, of our own Shakespeare, himself a nature humanized, a genial understanding directing self-consciously a power and an implicit wisdom deeper than consciousness' (*SC* i. 198). 'As has been well remarked by a continental critic' alerts the audience to the fact that Schlegel is about to be quoted or paraphrased; Coleridge may have looked down at his lectern as he read the ensuing sentences, then looked out over the audience to deliver the final sentence, his own application of the theoretical principle quoted. The possessive, patriotic 'our own Shakespeare' stresses the fact that he has now departed from his German source.

If there is a German influence on the final sentence, it is that of Schelling, not Schlegel; as T. M. Raysor notes, 'this statement of the relations of unconscious inspiration to the directing intellectual consciousness is, without verbal parallels, essentially based on Schelling's treatment of the creative process in art' (*SC* i. 198 n.). The Germans provide theory, Coleridge its application to Shakespeare. Furthermore, Coleridge simultaneously engages with the traditional English neo-classical view of the Bard as a genius unconscious of his powers; Shakespeare is envisaged here as a conscious artist, but one who works according to an organic principle that is 'deeper than consciousness'.

Coleridge did not owe his idea of Shakespeare's organic art to Schlegel; he merely found in Schlegel's formulation a concise description of the art which he had been analysing for years in the margins of his copies of Shakespeare's plays. Schlegel's lectures rarely descended to particulars;[25] Coleridge's most signal contribution to the history of Shakespearean criticism was to show how particulars, minutiae, are combined to produce the unified whole that is a Shakespearean drama. He analysed opening scenes in detail, as no one had before, because it was in openings that the germ of the whole could be discerned; and it was because of his contention that each part was essential to the whole that he drew attention to individual words, as few had done before: the '*credibilizing* effect' of the word 'again' in the first scene of *Hamlet*, 'honest' as a key word in *Othello*, the 'single happy epithet' *crying* in Prospero's account of his flight from Milan with the infant Miranda (*SC* i. 18, i. 46–7, ii. 135).[26]

Romantic Shakespearean criticism synthesizes and refines what has gone before. Coleridge makes specific what was general in Germany and makes central what was incidental in late eighteenth-century British criticism. His version of an image first applied to Shakespeare in Elizabeth Montagu's very popular *Essay on the Writings and Genius of Shakespear*, which appeared in 1769 and went through six editions by 1785, provides another case in point. Most of the book is whole-heartedly Johnsonian, often uncritically dependent on the 1765 preface, yet every now and then we come across a passage like the following, which taken in isolation might seem to have been written a generation later: 'Shakespeare seems to have had the art of the Dervise in the Arabian tales, who could throw his soul into the body of another man, and be at once possessed of his sentiments, adopt his passions, and rise to all the functions and feelings of his situation' (*CH* v. 330).

In the introduction to his 1768 edition of the plays, Edward Capell called Shakespeare 'this *Proteus*, who could put on any shape that either serv'd his interest or suited his inclination' (*CH* v. 320). Capell coined the metaphor while discussing Shakespeare's capacity to write in whatever genre the public demanded; six years later William Richardson used it in a context similar to that of Mrs Montagu's Dervise. Early in his *Philosophical Analysis and Illustration of some of Shakespeare's Remarkable Characters*, one of the first pieces of detailed character criticism in the language,[27] he called Shakespeare 'the Proteus of the drama': 'he changes himself into every character, and enters easily into every condition of human nature' (*CH* vi. 118–19).

The image was subsequently used by the chief Romantic Shakespearean critics in both England and Germany. A. W. Schlegel said 'Rather is he, such is the diversity of tone and colour, which varies according to the quality of his subjects he assumes, a very Proteus' (*Lectures*, 378), and in a crucial passage on the sympathetic imagination William Hazlitt wrote that Shakespeare had 'a perfect sympathy with all things' yet was 'alike indifferent to all', that he was characterized by 'the faculty of transforming himself at will into whatever he chose: his originality was the power of seeing every object from the exact point of view in which others would see it. He was the Proteus of the human intellect' (*HW* viii. 42). Hazlitt was the intellectual mentor of Keats; we will see that remarks such as this lie behind Keats's belief that men of genius 'have not any individuality, any determined Character' (*KL* i. 184).

Hazlitt is marked off from his eighteenth-century predecessors by the argument that Shakespeare not only has a perfect sympathy with all things but is also indifferent to all; he enters into his characters but also stands apart from them. This is a position shared with, and probably derived from, that of Coleridge. The latter uses the image of Proteus with more precision than did William Richardson. Coleridge's protean poet is not the same as Mrs Montagu's Dervise; he would have characterized the latter as a 'mere ventriloquist', who 'distributes his own insipidity among the characters' (*SC* ii. 124). The distinction is first made in a letter to William Sotheby, written in July 1802: 'It is easy to cloathe Imaginary Beings with our own Thoughts and Feelings; but to send ourselves out of ourselves, to *think* ourselves in to the Thoughts and Feelings of Beings in circumstances wholly and strangely different from our own / hoc labor, hoc opus / and who has atchieved it? Perhaps only Shakespere' (*CL* ii. 810). Proteus is introduced in a notebook entry made some two years later, in conjunction with another crucial Coleridgean distinction, that between creative imitation and slavish copy: 'the *imitation* instead of *copy* which is illustrated in very nature *shakespearianized* / —that Proteus Essence that could assume the very form, but yet known and felt not to be the Thing by that difference of the Substance which made every atom of the Form another thing / —that likeness not identity' (*CN* ii. 2274).

The idea of Shakespeare's simultaneous participation in and detachment from his characters had been stated most forcefully in a slightly earlier notebook entry, where *Lear* and *Othello* are described as 'a divine Dream / all Shakespere, and nothing Shakespere' (*CN* ii. 2086). The image of Proteus recurs most centrally in some lecture notes on *Venus and Adonis*, probably written in spring 1808 (still prior to the publication of Schlegel's lectures, that is): 'to become by power of Imagination another Thing—Proteus, a river, a lion, yet still the God felt to be there' (*CN* iii. 3247). The context here is a discussion of fancy as an aggregative power, imagination a modifying one; Shakespeare thus occupies a crucial place in an early formulation of a critical distinction that will be at the heart of the *Biographia Literaria*.

Similarly, the climactic use of the Proteus image in chapter fifteen of the *Biographia* is anticipated by the lectures on Shakespeare of 1811–12. In the third lecture of that course, Shakespeare is compared to Proteus (*SC* ii. 54); in the fourth, he is contrasted to Milton. According to Tomalin's report, which closely follows Coleridge's notebook, the fourth lecture included a reference to two thrones on the English Parnassus, 'Milton on the one and Shakespeare on the first': 'He, darting himself forth, and passing into all the forms of human character and human passion; the other attracted all forms and all things to himself into the unity of his own grand ideal'; 'Shakespeare became all things well into which he infused himself, while all forms, all things became Milton—the poet ever present to our minds' (*SC* ii. 66).[28] 'Into which he infused himself' may be Tomalin's interpolation; the notebook entry from which Coleridge was working has in its place 'yet for ever remaining himself', one of those clauses that differentiates Shakespeare from the mere 'ventriloquist' (*CN* iii. 4115). The passage is repeated almost verbatim in the *Biographia*, but with one important change: the image of Proteus is incorporated from the previous lecture, and thus given its richest context.

> While the former [Shakespeare] darts himself forth, and passes into all the forms of human character and passion, the one Proteus of the fire and the flood; the other attracts all forms and things to himself, into the unity of his own IDEAL. All things and modes of action shape themselves anew in the being of MILTON; while SHAKSPEARE becomes all things, yet for ever remaining himself. (*BL* ii. 27–8).

Shakespeare was central not only to much eighteenth-century thinking about the sympathetic power of imagination but also to many aestheticians who concentrated on the theory of association. Shakespearean quotation was a favourite device of Alexander Gerard in his *Essay on Genius* (1774), a key work on imagination, genius, and the associative principle. The major chapters in part two of the book on 'the Sources of the Varieties of Genius in the Imagination' and 'the Influence of the Passions on Association' constantly move from philosophical generalization to the analysis of specific Shakespearean examples. The chapter 'Of the Predominance of the associating Principles' hinges on a demonstration of that principle at work in the language of certain Shakespearean characters, such as Mistress Quickly.

Gerard was not the first to proceed from Shakespeare's 'trifling relations of ideas' (*Essay on Genius*, 226) to a Lockean theory which posited that the association of ideas was the principle ruling the imagination. Mistress Quickly and her kind had already featured in Lord Kames's *Elements of Criticism*. First published in Edinburgh in 1762, it went through seven editions by 1788; an explanation for the book's popularity is provided by one Dr John Gregory in a letter to James Beattie, who had himself written on the plastic power of Shakespeare's imagination: 'What has made Lord Kaims's "Elements of Criticism" so popular in England is his numerous illustrations and quotations from Shakespeare. If his book had wanted these illustrations, or if they had been taken from ancient or foreign authors, it would not have been so generally read in England.'[29] The Romantic poets proceeded in a similar way: when they wrote about imagination, whether in verse or in prose, they referred to (and borrowed) the language of the poet who embodied the creative imagination.

Coleridge, then, is working within a well-established tradition when he begins his essays on the principles of method in the 1818 *Friend* with specific Shakespearean examples. By referring to certain characters he substantiates his argument that *method* constitutes the difference between a well-disciplined, superior mind and an un-cultivated one. Hamlet is immethodical 'from the excess, Mrs Quickley from the want, of reflection and generalization'; method 'must result from the due mean or balance between our passive impressions and the mind's own re-action on the same'.[30] Here Coleridge's characteristic reconciliation of opposites—active and passive, mind and nature, the particular and the general, the parts and the whole—is approached via a consideration of characters who fail to make that reconciliation. Hamlet and Mistress Quickly are paradigmatic in this negative way, but Shakespeare's works are positive exemplars: 'we may define the excellence of *their* method as consisting in that just proportion, that union and interpenetration of the universal and the particular, which must ever pervade all works of decided genius and true science' (*Friend*, i. 457).

The essays on method move from the particular to the general, from a reading of dramatic poetry to an extended philosophical discourse. The first of them ends with praise of Shakespeare's method, the third begins 'From Shakspeare to Plato, from the philosophic poet to the poetic philosopher, the transition is easy' (i. 472). For Coleridge, the reading of Shakespeare leads straight to the central questions of philosophy. Hamlet, Shakespeare's most philosophical tragic creation, is especially important in this respect; he plays as crucial a role for Coleridge as he does for Goethe's Wilhelm Meister. Crabb Robinson summarizes Coleridge's interpretation: 'Hamlet he considered in a point of view which seems to agree very well with the representation given in *Wilhelm Meister*. He is a man whose *ideal* and internal images are so vivid that all real objects are faint and dead to him' (*SC* ii. 165). On another occasion, Robinson noted wryly, 'I doubt whether he did not design that an application should be made to himself' (*HCR* 57); he is anticipating the famous remark in *Table Talk*, 'Hamlet's character is the prevalence of the abstracting and generalizing habit over the practical. . . . I have a smack of Hamlet myself, if I may say so' (24 June 1827).

Coleridge's reading of Hamlet is closely related to his wider philosophical development. '*Hamlet* was the play,' he records in 1819, 'or rather Hamlet himself was the character in the intuition and exposition of which I first made my turn for philosophical criticism, and especially for insight into the genius of Shakespeare, *noticed*' (*SC* i. 16). Coleridge does not study the prince at the expense of the play; he argues that the scene where Claudius faces Laertes is 'Proof, as indeed all else is, that Shakespeare never intended us to see the king with Hamlet's eyes, tho', I suspect, the managers have long done so' (*SC* i. 31). But it is the character of Hamlet which becomes intimately associated with Coleridge's philosophy. Crabb Robinson's use of the words '*ideal* and internal' alerts us to the relationship between this Hamlet and German idealism: the mind alone is knowable, action in the external world is problematic. Hamlet's knowledge is derived from ideas, not impressions; 'an Idea, or, if you like, a Principle, carries knowledge within itself, and is prospective'. Polonius, in contrast, lives according to maxims; 'A Maxim is a conclusion upon observation of matters of fact, and is merely retrospective' (*TT* 24 June 1827). For Coleridge, the 'moral' of the play is the vanity of philosophizing and the necessity of action in the world, concerns that bore weightily on his own life. It is as if Hamlet has a mind in tune with the transcendentalism of Kant's *Critique of Pure Reason*, but cannot until the end of the play muster the moral courage to live according to the ethical imperative of the *Critique of Practical Reason*.

Analogously, Coleridge's endeavour as philosopher was to unify an idealist epistemology with the moral demands of his Christianity.[31]

Hamlet enabled the Romantics to create a Shakespeare who was both objective and subjective. Friedrich Schiller argued in his essay *Über naive und sentimentalische Dichtung* that Shakespeare was a 'naive' poet who could never be seen in his works, that he apprehended nature directly like the ancients, not reflectively like the moderns. Yet Friedrich Schlegel, despite being profoundly influenced by Schiller's essay, maintained that the spirit of Shakespeare was visible in the character of Hamlet. Similarly, John Keats would speak again and again of Shakespeare's invisibility in his works, yet also assert that Hamlet was 'perhaps more like Shakspeare himself in his common every day Life than any other of his Characters' (*KL* ii. 116).

The presence of Hamlet in Romantic discourse usually indicates that the artist is examining his own self; the presence of Hamlet's creator is often indicative of an attempt to 'annihilate' the self (the term is Keats's). The self was a central problem for the Romantics; Shakespeare was thus brought to the centre of their thinking, a position he had not occupied in the eighteenth century when, though universally admired, he exercised little influence on poetic practice and was marginalized by critics who embraced neo-classical principles. There is a kernel of truth in Coleridge's caricature: Shakespeare had too long been treated as 'a sort of Tartarian Dalai Lama, adored indeed, and his very excrescences prized as relics, but with no authority, no real influence' (*SC* i. 195, cf. *CN* iii. 3288). Authority and influence are the keys to Romantic Shakespeare.

Coleridge departs from his eighteenth-century predecessors in adducing philosophical principles from the character of Hamlet and illustrating 'the principles of poetry', as he put it in the prospectus to his 1811–12 lectures, from Shakespeare and his mighty opposite, Milton, rather than from the ancients. The fourth lecture of that series, in which he formulates his image of Milton and Shakespeare on the two golden thrones of the English Parnassus, ends with a definition of the poet: 'a person who balances sameness with difference, and triteness with novelty; who reconciles judgement with enthusiasm, and vehemence with feeling, art with nature, the manner with the matter, and our admiration of the poet with the sympathy with the characters and incidents of the poem' (*SC* ii. 69; cf. *CN* iii. 4112). This becomes part of the 'Philosophic definitions of a poem with poetry' in chapter fourteen of the *Biographia Literaria*; a generalization about poetry is thus built out of a lecture on Shake-speare's poetry. So with the structure of the *Biographia*: chapter four-teen offers its definitions, then chapter fifteen elucidates 'the specific symptoms of poetic power' in an analysis of Shakespeare's narrative poems, one of the first pieces of 'practical criticism'—Coleridge uses the term—in the language. Literary theory is inseparable from the practical criticism of Shakespeare's verse.

Coleridge says that from *Venus and Adonis* and *The Rape of Lucrece* he 'abstracted the following marks, as characteristics of original poetic genius in general'. His verb is telling: the abstract is extrapolated from Shakespeare, it is not imposed on him. The first mark of original poetic genius is said to be musical versification together with the power that reduces 'multitude into unity of effect'. The second is 'choice of subjects very remote from the private interests and circum-stances of the writer himself'; it was this capacity to transcend self-interest that impelled Shakespeare to the drama: Coleridge here uses such phrases as 'himself meanwhile unparticipating in the passions' and 'the utter *aloofness* of the poet's own feelings'. The key word 'un-participating' is a Coleridgean coinage. Third, the genius moulds his images to the circumstances in which they are used or to the pre-dominant passion of the whole. And fourth, he is characterized by depth and energy of thought, for 'No man was ever yet a great poet, without being at the same time a profound philosopher' (*BL* ii. 19–26). The ideals of sympathy and impersonality; the importance of internal unity, of every part being related to the whole; the desire not to detach poetry from philosophy: these are the essentials of Coleridge's aesthetics. Individual ideas may be derived from German and English predecessors, but the whole is derived from a reading of Shakespeare.

It is not enough to say that the laying open of Shakespeare in the later eighteenth century, which was discerned by Leigh Hunt and Macaulay, paved the way for Coleridge's aesthetic theory. More than this, as traditional beliefs and certainties, what Earl Wasserman calls the 'cosmic syntaxes' of the Enlightenment, were questioned and undermined, the imagination came to be seen as a 'means of grace'.[32] By the time we reach Keats, Shakespeare, archetype of imaginative power, has become a fixed point in the turbulent universe, not merely an exemplary poet who shapes aesthetic theory. A letter of March 1818 to Benjamin Bailey refers to 'Things real—such as existences of Sun Moon and Stars and passages of Shakspeare' (*KL* i. 243). The Bard is placed beside the forces of nature; for Keats, he is in a very literal sense a 'cosmic syntax'.

But if Shakespeare is the 'star of poets', what is the later poet to do in the face of his brightness? We are brought back to the anxiety of influence, to the burden of the past which poets began to feel acutely in the eighteenth century:

> Few Moderns in the List with these may stand,
> For in those Days were Giants in the Land.
> Suffice it now by Lineal Right to claim,
> And bow with Filial Awe to *Shakespeare's* Fame,
> The second Honours are a glorious Name.[33]

How could the modern writer accommodate the giant race from before the flood?[34] By appropriating Shakespeare into his own world-view, as Henry Mackenzie did when he made Hamlet into an exquisitely sensibilitous Man of Feeling?[35] By following the example of John O'Keefe in *Wild Oats* (1791) and inventing a world where one lives, breathes, and quotes Shakespeare—so that, as the protagonist Rover puts it in the final lines of this highly successful comedy, 'a spark from Shakespeare's muse of fire was the star that guided me through my desolate and bewildered maze of life'? Could the English Romantics establish their 'Lineal Right' by allowing Shakespeare to guide them through the desolate and bewildered mazes of their own lives? Could they honour his 'glorious Name' by expressing 'Filial Awe' without descending into Oedipal anxiety?

2

'The Eighth Commandment was not Made for Bards': Coleridge and the Problem of Inherited Language

THE rediscovery and increasing influence of *Peri Hupsous*, the discussion of sublimity probably written in the first century AD by 'Longinus', was vital to the rise of Romanticism.[1] In his thirteenth chapter, Longinus, citing Plato as an authority, argues that sublimity may be achieved by imitating and emulating great writers of the past. 'Many are possessed by a spirit not their own', he writes; as the Pythian priestess at Delphi prophesies as one inspired having been impregnated by the supernatural power, so 'the genius of the ancients acts as a kind of oracular cavern, and effluences flow from it into the minds of their imitators.' Plato 'diverted to himself countless rills from the Homeric spring'; his strength derived from his attempt 'to compete for the prize against Homer, like a young aspirant challenging an admired master.' The contest is necessary if the aspirant is to develop his artistic might, but it is no disgrace for him to be defeated by his elders. Furthermore, 'In all this process there is no plagiarism'.[2]

We usually take Longinus' importance for Romanticism to be his emphasis on inspiration, on the poet not as a craftsman who learns his trade but as a madman invested with divine spirit. This passage suggests that inspiration need not be incompatible with imitation; the spirit which possesses the poet may be that of his predecessors. Longinus' metaphors will recur: the figure of authority, the poet possessed by the language of his forebears, influence as literally a flowing into the consciousness of particular phrases and effects, the element of competition between poet and master, the knowledge that the latter must be confronted although he cannot be outdone.

Effluence and influence are especially relevant tropes in the context of this study. The metaphor of Shakespeare as a heavenly body has a long history, going back to Ben Jonson's commendatory verses prefixed to the First Folio: 'Shine forth, thou Starre of *Poets*, and with rage, / Or influence, chide, or cheere the drooping Stage' (*CH* i. 25).

The word 'influence' originally referred to the ethereal fluid flowing from the stars which was believed to control a man's destiny; there is consequently a peculiar and powerful propriety about the metaphor of Shakespeare as star, 'influencing' the development of English literature. The distinctively 'Romantic' apprehension of Shakespeare turns on responsiveness to the pressure of his influence. He is read in a particular way—as original genius, master of the sympathetic imagination, creator of supernatural beings—and this reading shapes the ideals and aspirations of later creative life. Jonson's poem licenses this investiture of power upon the Bard: since Shakespeare remains alive through his 'Booke', his significance is 'not of an age, but for all time'. He will be revivified, reinterpreted, rewritten even, in each subsequent age.

Coleridge uses an image analogous to that of Plato diverting rills from the Homeric spring when, in the preface to 'Christabel', he endeavours to preclude 'charges of plagiarism or servile imitation' from his own work: 'For there is amongst us a set of critics, who seem to hold, that every possible thought and image is traditional; who have no notion that there are such things as fountains in the world, small as well as great; and who would therefore charitably derive every rill they behold flowing, from a perforation in some other man's tank' (*CPW* i. 214). The fountain suggests a spontaneous out-flowing; a poet who views his art as self-expression and wishes to be self-begotten and original has particular problems when he inherits thoughts and images. This is one reason why Coleridge is so defensive about his borrowings. The images of fountain and rill are traditional; there is a side of Coleridge that realizes how difficult it is to say anything new. The more one has read—and few English poets read more than Coleridge—the more one is forced to acknowledge that most thoughts and images are the property of one's predecessors. Almost everything Coleridge wrote is at some level an engagement with the traditional and the inherited. Early in the *Biographia* he implicitly acknowledges how difficult it is for the poet to make successful use of material inherited from the great: 'referring various lines in Gray to their original in Shakspeare and Milton', he had 'the clear perception how completely all the propriety was lost in the transfer' (*BL* i. 20).

A glance through the contents of Coleridge's complete poems yields many titles like the following: 'An Ode in the Manner of Anacreon', 'Imitated from Ossian', 'Imitations: Ad Lyram', 'Elegy:

Imitated from one of Akenside's Blank-verse Inscriptions', 'Lines in the Manner of Spenser', 'Sonnets attempted in the Manner of Contemporary Writers', 'Paraphrase of Psalm xlvi'. There is even the occasional imitation of an imitation, such as 'Translation of a Passage in Ottfried's Metrical Paraphrase of the Gospel'.[3] Many of Coleridge's epigraphs and mottos are also imitations, creative misquotations occasionally subscribed 'Adapted from an elder Poet'.[4]

It might be pointed out that the titles I have quoted are mere exercises, that they do not have the centrality to Coleridge that the imitations of Horace do to Pope. But many of Coleridge's more considerable works are also in an imitative tradition. The 'Monody on the Death of Chatterton', on which he expended such effort in his early years, is an attempt to engage with the Pindaric ode; *Zapolya: A Christmas Tale* is written 'in humble imitation of the *Winter's Tale* of Shakspeare' (*CPW* ii. 883); 'The Rime of the Ancyent Marinere' is, in the words of the Advertisement to *Lyrical Ballads*, 'professedly written in imitation of the *style*, as well as of the spirit of the elder poets'; even the conversation poems, in which Coleridge finds a poetic voice truly his own, are indebted to earlier works, such as the meditative verse of Cowper.[5]

'Kubla Khan' is the most extraordinary case of all. On the one hand, Coleridge attempted to characterize it as the ultimate example of spontaneity and originality, an opium-dream of pure imagination; on the other, he acknowledged that its opening at least was a version of a passage in an Elizabethan prose work, *Purchas his Pilgrimage*. Both common reader and academic critic are justified in their assessments of the poem: it is a lyric in the purest sense, unprecedented in English verse, but it is also richly textured with verbal echoes and resonances from a wide range of sources.[6]

More than any other English writer Coleridge is master of a synthetic mode of composition. This is true of both his prose and his verse. Nearly all his published works combine 'imitation' and original production; they all move between the two poles of close translation (or transcription) and original vision. Procedures such as paraphrase and adaptation lie on a continuum between these poles. Even in the prose works for which he has been vilified as a plagiarist, borrowed materials are constantly transformed and combined in new ways—and it is the power of organization and combination that for Coleridge *is* imagination. Tellingly, he praises Southey for his art of 'compilation' in *The Chronicle of the Cid* and argues that genius is shown in 'various excellencies of translation, selection, and arrange-ment' (*BL* i. 60 n.). The mind which appropriates and reconstitutes an insight of Schlegel on Shakespeare, or Schelling on the imagi-nation, is the same as that which creates 'In Xanadu did Kubla Khan / A stately pleasure-dome decree' out of '*In Xamdu did Cublai Can* build *a stately* Palace'. Coleridge almost always does something new with the material he takes over; to use the terms of his essay 'On Poesy or Art', itself a version of Schelling, his works are not copies but imitations. Set beside their originals they produce a combination of 'likeness and unlikeness, or sameness and difference'.[7]

To plagiarize is to sympathize. Coleridge writes in the *Biographia* of the 'pleasure of sympathy' he feels when his thought coincides with that of Boehme and Schelling (i. 147). In a late notebook entry he alludes to the ideal of imagination as a sympathetic faculty: 'The first lesson, that innocent Childhood affords me, is—that it is an instinct of my Nature to pass out of myself, and to exist in the form of others.'[8] Coleridge's instinct to use the words of others, though it may not be innocent, is a part of this sympathy.

Thomas McFarland's is the sanest summary of the problem of Col-eridge's plagiarisms: every writer steals the ideas and words of his predecessors, but Coleridge does so more extensively and creatively than others, to the extent that plagiarisms 'so honeycomb his work as to form virtually a mode of composition' (*Pantheist Tradition*, 28). Why then has the question of plagiarism led to virulent attacks on Coleridge by critics from Ferrier in the 1840s to Fruman in the 1970s?[9] One reason is that Coleridge was so often disingenuous or defensive about his sources—most famously when he was questioned after his Shakespeare lectures and produced a tissue of misinformation about copies of Schlegel.

The opening of 'Kubla Khan' provides a case in point; in the pre-fatory note to the poem Coleridge says that he 'was reading the fol-lowing sentence, or words of the same substance, in "Purchas's Pilgrimage": "Here the Khan Kubla commanded a palace to be built, and a stately garden thereunto . . ."' (*CPW* i. 296). The substance may be the same but it is the words that matter: Coleridge's misquotation of Purchas removes 'In Xamdu' and 'did'; he changes the order of the emperor's names and moves 'stately' into the second half of the sentence. The effect is to make the lines in the poem appear to be a transformation when they are in fact closer to a transcription. It was not necessary for Coleridge to cover his tracks.

Taken out of context and put at the beginning of a poem, prepared for only by the title, the image has a magical power it altogether lacks in Purchas. And to turn it into verse—metrically, 'In Xanadu did Kubla Khan' is a superbly balanced line—was to bring about a radical enough transformation. It is the partial covering of tracks, the half-admission, that has got Coleridge into trouble.

Why could he not always have simply proclaimed his practice with the brazenness of Vida in a sixteenth-century *De Arte Poetica*?

Come then, all ye youths! and, careless of censure, give yourselves up to STEAL. . . . Unhappy is he . . . who, rashly trusting to his own strength and art, as though in need of no external help, in his audacity refuses to follow the trustworthy footsteps of the ancients, abstaining, alas! unwisely from plunder . . . How [deeply] could they wish to have spared their idle labour and to have learnt other arts from their parents! Often I love to play on ancient phrase, and utter some far other thought in the same words. Nor will any wise man care to blame my self-confessing thefts—thefts open and to be praised and approved. [10]

To some extent the explanation for Coleridge's defensive strategies lay in his own troubled psyche, but it was also bound up with the fact that, although he and his contemporaries wrote many imitations, Romanticism strove in many respects to depart from classical mimetic norms. After all, had the spirit of the age not been perceived as antipathetic to traditional models and procedures, Byron would not have made allegiance to Pope and Horatian imitation a central plank of his attack on contemporary culture.

Attitudes towards literary borrowing hardened during Coleridge's working life. In 1793 one John Ferriar published a descriptive account of the borrowings in *Tristram Shandy*; he treated his subject sympathetically, arguing that Sterne usually borrowed creatively, but his article led many readers to write to periodicals such as *The Gentleman's Magazine*, denouncing Sterne as an unscrupulous plagiarist. Ferriar seems to have been so influenced by public opinion that in 1798 he published an expanded version of his essay, entitled *Illustrations of Sterne*, which adopted a much more admonitory tone. [11] This controversy marks a turning-point in the history of the reading public's response to plagiarism. That other great literary scandal of the 1790s, the Ireland family's Shakespeare forgeries, had its forebears in Lauder, Ossian, and Chatterton; this was the first time there was a public outcry about unacknowledged literary borrowing. The shift of emphasis from forgery, a matter of making money out of the literary tradition, to plagiarism, more to do with illicitly making personal artistic capital out of the tradition, is symptomatic of the change from 'eighteenth-century' to 'Romantic' values. A brief sketch of the history of literary imitation will show why the whole area was especially problematic for the Romantics.

Longinus was only one of many ancient critics to discuss imitation. Dionysus of Halicarnassus, Quintilian, Seneca, and Macrobius all argued that poetry could advance if writers ranged freely among the best models and combined their distinctive qualities.[12] What we might condemn as plagiarism, classical culture would have praised as imitation. Macrobius' account in the preface to his *Saturnalia* of how works should bear a physiognomic resemblance to their forebears was borrowed unacknowledged from one of Seneca's moral epistles: his argument thus performed itself. Imitation was not merely a theory in classical times; nearly all Roman poetry was written in response to Greek exemplars, in a conscious attempt to recover Greek ideals and give them new life in Roman contexts.

As the idea of a rebirth implies, imitation and revivification of the ancients was a central Renaissance endeavour. In *Le familiari* Petrarch picked up the metaphor of physiognomic resemblance. He stressed that imitation should not be sterile reproduction, but part of a march of progress from generation to generation. 'He who imitates must have a care that what he writes be similar, not identical [with his model], and that the similarity should not be of the kind that obtains between a portrait and a sitter, where the artist earns the more praise the greater the likeness, but rather of the kind that obtains between a son and his father.'[13] In England, poets from Ben Jonson to Alexander Pope engaged in the classical, imitative task of seeking to establish a new Augustan age; creative imitation was Pope's most characteristic mode of composition. Dryden and Pope make exquisite use of the metaphor of father and son; Christopher Ricks has shown that the words inherited by Augustan poets from their predecessors become their strongest allusions, and that many such allusions are self-performing in that they turn on images of succession and inheritance.[14]

Not even at the height of the English neo-classical age was the relationship between present and past poetic achievement taken to be straightforward. Dryden had faith in the progress of literature—'poetry may not go backward, when all other arts and sciences are advancing'[15]—but despite his belief that his own age was civilized

where that of Elizabeth had been barbaric, and his consequent support for and participation in the practice of adapting plays to suit
contemporary taste, his admiration for Shakespeare's genius was un-
bounded. And when Pope appealed to the '*Bards Triumphant*' of
earlier days, it was with a distinctly Bloomian smack of the inferiority
of the belated poet: 'Oh may some Spark of *your* Coelestial Fire / The
last, the meanest of your Sons inspire' (*Essay on Criticism*, 195–6).
Nevertheless, Pope embraced the traditional mimetic model of artistic production, with its assumption that the imitation of great models
was co-ordinate with mimesis in its largest sense, the imitation of
nature. In the *Essay on Criticism*, itself a creative imitation of Boileau
and Horace, he wrote of how Virgil intended to draw from nature but
'when t'examine ev'ry Part he came, / *Nature* and *Homer* were, he
found, the *same*' (134–5).

A number of related developments in eighteenth-century taste
meant that imitation gradually became more problematic. At the
heart of the matter was the cult of original genius. Works such as
William Duff's *Essay on Original Genius* (1767) argued that the greatest
writers were originals in both senses of the word; not only were they
independent and self-begetting rather than derivative and imitative,
they also lived near the origins of their culture. Duff took Homer,
Shakespeare, and Ossian to be the three great original geniuses. His
argument makes the questionable supposition that Homer and
Shakespeare were in no way dependent on their predecessors, and is
somewhat undermined by the fact that 'Ossian' was written in the
eighteenth century, but the model of decline it employed became
widespread. Thomas Love Peacock's *Four Ages of Poetry* (iron, gold,
silver, brass) arose out of this tradition and led Shelley to make his
impassioned defence of the originality of poets in his own age. Shelley
evaded a temporal scheme by using the neo-platonic argument that
all true poets participate in the One, but the growing 'burden of the
past' was such that in 1825 Macaulay could take up a position diametrically opposed to Dryden's: 'as civilisation advances, poetry
almost necessarily declines'.[16]

If the new model of decline posited that imitations would inevitably
be vastly inferior to their originals, the cult of genius questioned the
very value of the practice. It was no longer thought of as an ideal to
borrow the best from the artists of the past; 'eclecticism' was transformed from a term of praise to one of condemnation.[17] Edward
Young, in his *Conjectures on Original Composition* of 1759, which Dr

Johnson thought consisted of maxims by then common,[18] reversed the traditional assumption and said that imitation of earlier authors was not an element of the imitation of nature but the antithesis of it: 'Imitations are of two kinds: one of nature, one of authors. The first we call originals, and confine the term imitation to the second.'[19]

Longinus did not differentiate between imitation and emulation. He did not argue that *imitatio* (Greek *mimesis*) was servile, *aemulatio* (*zelosis*) creative; both were seen as essential to the writer's relationship with his forebears. But Young makes the distinction sharply: 'Imitation is inferiority confessed; emulation is superiority contested, or denied; imitation is servile, emulation generous; that fetters, this fires'. According to Young, the moderns have produced few original works because 'illustrious examples engross, prejudice, and intimidate' —the *Conjectures* are central to Jackson Bate's argument in *The Burden of the Past*. Great works of the past will only 'nourish' rather than 'annihilate' if direct imitation is eschewed: 'The less we copy the renowned ancients, we shall resemble them the more.' For Young 'learning', knowledge of the classics, must be subservient to genius; imitation of Homer must give way to emulation of the 'creative power' of Homer. Young contrasts the scholarship, the translations and imitations, of his own age with the inspiration and genius of Shakespeare.

Young's essay provides an entry into a discussion of the particular problems encountered by the Romantic as he faced up to his Shakespearean heritage. If one were to emulate Shakespeare, one would have to avoid imitating him, since his strength lay in his capacity to create without imitating others. The distinction between imitation and emulation implies that the letter killeth, the spirit giveth life. The weakness not only of the Romantics' neo-Elizabethan plays but also of much eighteenth-century blank verse tragedy, beginning with Nicholas Rowe's *Jane Shore* (1714), professedly written in imitation of the style of Shakespeare,[20] and ironically enough including Young's own *Othello*-influenced *The Revenge* (1721), demonstrated that Shakespearean drama was inimitable. But it was from Shakespeare's language, his metaphoric power above all, that later poets had most to learn; in this respect, the letter would give life. How was the poet to emulate, to make his own, particular Shakespearean verbal effects? That was the problem, the task.

Young's citation of Shakespeare as an ideal is telling. In a sense it was easy for Pope to imitate Horace, for the Augustans to reincarnate but also to set themselves apart from the classics, because they were writing in a different language. But where Augustan authorities were ancient, the Romantics looked to the *English* classics. Between Pope's time and that of the Romantics, Shakespeare's plays were transformed into 'classics', edited, annotated, and made the object of scholarly disputation—to the extent that in his satire of 1794, *The Pursuits of Literature*, T. J. Mathias could cast Shakespeare as Actaeon, hunted down by his own commentators.

In the second half of the eighteenth century, Shakespeare gradually took on the authoritative status previously accorded only to the Bible and the ancients. Popular collections such as William Dodd's *The Beauties of Shakespear* (1752) and Elizabeth Griffith's *The Morality of Shakespeare's Drama Illustrated* (1775) used passages from the plays to illustrate such subjects as 'Affectation', 'Cheerfulness', and 'A Father's Advice to his Son, going to travel'. These are headings in Dodd's index; the last of them indicates a major fault of such collections, the way they ignore contexts: Dodd forgets the element of parody when Shakespeare puts 'A Father's Advice' into the mouth of Polonius. Moralists who dwelt on choice extracts accordingly found themselves in deep waters; Paul Hiffernan deduced a programme of 'Ethics for Young Gentlemen' from Polonius's advice to Laertes, which inevitably led him to a critical examination of Polonius's character and the somewhat dubious conclusion that Shakespeare intended him as an exemplary father, not the bumbling idiot he was portrayed as on the eighteenth-century stage.[21] The most effective appropriations of earlier works into later writing are usually those that invoke the full force of a passage's original context.

The influence of Dodd and his followers was such that in the first number of Leigh Hunt's *Reflector*, Barron Field could look back on the developments of the previous forty years and conclude that 'next to the sacred volume, Shakspeare may be said to be the Bible of England.' Like the Bible, the plays have been made the object of concordances and commentaries—other points of contact could be added, such as the discussion of canon and apocrypha—all that is lacking is a 'Shakspeare Sermon', which Field ironically provides, using the Coleridgean defensive strategy of saying that it is written by a 'friend'.[22] The notorious Scottish preacher Edward Irving really did take texts for sermons from Shakespeare; according to Hazlitt in *The Spirit of the Age*, 'He has held a play-book in one hand, and a Bible in the other, and quoted Shakespeare and Melancthon in the same breath' (*HW* xi. 44).

These parallels suggest an important analogy for the phenomenon that is the subject of this book: as hymn-writers of the period wove biblical phrases into their works, so poets wove Shakespearean phrases into theirs.

Quotation and allusion are to the local and the specific what imitation is to the work as a whole. As an imitation may merely seek to reproduce the effect of an original, a quotation or allusion may merely invoke a canonized text as authority. As more sophisticated forms of imitation transform their originals by establishing an interplay between the old and the new which will involve difference as well as sameness, more sophisticated forms of quotation and allusion establish creative tension between the original and the new contexts of an admired text.

A writer imitating a complete work or a poetic form will often introduce specific allusions in order to support and give substance to his relationship with his forebear. Such allusions make a number of assumptions characteristic of neo-classical poetics: that the literary tradition is a source of value, that the reader is sufficiently educated to recognize the allusion, that a combination of new with old is enriching. Classical allusion as used by Dryden and Pope at their best is, in Reuben Brower's words, 'a resource equivalent to symbolic metaphor and elaborate imagery in other poets': 'Through allusion, often in combination with subdued metaphor and exquisite images, Pope gets his purchase on larger meanings and evokes the finer resonances by which poetry (in Johnson's phrase) "penetrates the recesses of the mind" '.[23]

We usually think of allusion as an Augustan device, because it is an assertion of continuity with the classical tradition (it is out of a desire to salvage the classical tradition in the modern age that Eliot and Pound allude so obsessively). But there is no a priori reason why it should be the exclusive preserve of the neo-classical poet. I believe that for the Romantics allusion offered one solution to the problem of how to emulate earlier writers without being servile to them and how to make use of their words other than by plagiarism. If one avoided formal imitation of earlier writers, but brought them into play when writing in a different form, one would be seen to accommodate them, even to proclaim one's filiation from them. And if one quoted, one could not be accused of plagiarism; this distinction is made well by Horace Walpole in 1780 in a defence of Sir Joshua Reynolds's paintings:

Sir J. Reynolds has been accused of plagiarism for having borrowed attitudes from ancient masters. Not only candour but criticism must deny the *force* of the charge. When a single posture is imitated from an historic picture and applied to a portrait in a different dress and with new attributes, this is not plagiarism, but quotation: and a quotation from a great author, with a novel application of the sense, has always been allowed to be an instance of parts and taste; and may have more merit than the original.[24]

Walpole proposes a parallel between the painter's borrowing of an attitude and the writer's borrowing of a phrase. A visual quotation cannot be signalled by inverted commas or italics: a better literary parallel is therefore the allusion, which is generally thought of as something less overt than a quotation. In his stimulating book *The Figure of Echo*, John Hollander distinguishes between quotation and allusion, fitting them into a 'rhetorical hierarchy of allusive modes' consisting of *quotation*, 'the literal presence of a body of text', *allusion*, sometimes fragmentary or periphrastic, but always intended to conjure up some text in 'the portable library shared by the author and his ideal audience', and *echo*, altogether more elusive, audible only to well-tuned ears, a metaphor for alluding that does not depend on conscious intention.[25]

I agree with much of what Hollander says, for example that certain echoes are only heard by readers who know the earlier text especially well, but I do not find his hierarchy especially useful. The argument that quotations are 'literal', and by implication accurate, is questionable: a quotation taken from memory, as Romantic Shakespearean references nearly always are, will often be inaccurate; besides, in centuries before our own, departure from the wording, to say nothing of the spelling or punctuation, of an original was not thought of as error.[26] The metaphor of bodily presence is valuable for all forms of verbal appropriation, not merely direct quotation. An allusion *may* summon up the context and connotations of an earlier writer's words, but sometimes it will serve simply to give authority to the later writer's utterance, not to establish any broader intertextual relationship. Hollander asserts that 'a pointing to, or figuration of, a text recognized by the audience is not the point' of echo, while it is of allusion (p. 64); but aural and rhythmic correspondences are best defined as *echoes* and they may well be figurations of a recognizable text. Although quotation, allusion, and echo are progressively less open, less demonstrable, forms of citation, particular verbal effects often derive their richness from a combination of the attributes which Hollander treats as alternatives.

We do, however, need to distinguish between 'sources' or 'borrowings' and those allusions or echoes which contribute to the reader's possible understanding of a poem. The classic study of borrowings is *The Road to Xanadu*. John Livingston Lowes proves, in so far as such a thing can be proved, that Bartram's *Travels* is among the sources of 'Kubla Khan', but this knowledge is not relevant to the meaning—or the being—of the poem; it is merely a piece of information about Coleridge's reading and the synthetic nature of his (the) imagination. I will sometimes adduce possible Shakespearean sources, parallel passages, in the poems and plays I examine; they will serve to show how the Romantics were steeped in Shakespeare, and which parts of Shakespeare were especially important to them, but they will contribute little to my argument about intertextual relationships. As Herman Meyer puts it, 'the borrowing is distinguished from the quotation'—from all forms of allusiveness, I would say—'by the fact that it has no referential character. . . . the return to the source may bring about a certain philological clarification, but no enrichment of the meaning and no added aesthetic value.'[27]

An allusion is more significant than a borrowing because it fulfils a purpose, acts as a kind of shorthand. In writing 'the meaning—or the being—of the poem' above, I was alluding to Archibald MacLeish's 'A poem should not mean / But be', in order to show that I was aware of the danger of implying that a poem has a 'meaning'. My allusion was dependent on the assumption that the reader of a book such as this would be familiar with MacLeish's lines, or at least the critical principle they express. This brings us to a question that is crucial to my argument: would Shakespearean allusions—whether clearly signalled quotations or quieter echoes—have been recognized by readers in the Romantic period? The first major piece of evidence to suggest that they would have been is the fact that Shakespeare was so much better known than he is today. The banker Coutts was not an unusually literary figure, yet at the age of seventy-four, 'he has Shakespere by [he]art; and can repeat the following line to almost any that can be quoted'.[28] The idea of completing a quotation by providing the following line is an example of simple 'Tessera'; if a line were to be quoted and then capped with an invented conclusion, that would constitute my version of Bloom's 'completion and *antithesis*'.

It might be argued that Coutts was mentioned in Joseph Farington's diary because his feat was exceptional. But a continental visitor to England in the 1780s clearly thought that detailed knowledge of Shakespeare was widespread: 'The English national authors are in all hands, and read by all people, of which the innumerable editions they have gone through, are a sufficient proof.'[29] Those editions were not merely available to the wealthy; Moritz also speaks of odd volumes of Shakespeare on sale in the streets for a penny or even a halfpenny. Shakespeare was also by far the most performed dramatist in the late eighteenth and early nineteenth centuries, so the theatre-going public would have had the chance to familiarize themselves with the plays by hearing as well as reading them (thus people would sometimes think they were alluding to Shakespeare when in fact they were quoting from Cibber or another adapter of the plays for the stage).

To prove that Coutts's knowledge of Shakespeare by heart was a norm not an exception, one would have to write a history of Shakespeare's cultural presence in the Romantic age. Four areas in particular might be singled out as evidence. The most popular and socially influential art of the age was caricature; an enormous number of satirical engravings make use of Shakespearean allusions, many of them extremely subtle; if Gillray and his contemporaries expected their lowbrow public to recognize these, more demanding literary artists would surely have expected their audience to have the same capacity. A second area is that of parody: from the 1790s onwards the poetry columns of periodicals such as *The Gentleman's Magazine* published 'parodies' that adapted a wide range of Shakespearean speeches and applied them to contemporary political and social affairs; their effectiveness depends on the assumption that readers will know their Shakespeare well enough to enjoy clever departures from the original.[30]

Thirdly, closer to the Romantic poets themselves, there is the extraordinary frequency with which writers in the age weave Shakespearean quotations into their prose, again with the expectation that the original will be recognized and the felicity of its adaptation noticed; I have shown elsewhere that Shakespearean quotation is particularly important in the essays of William Hazlitt.[31] Fourthly, there is the assumption that the novel-reading public will know their Shakespeare, seen at its clearest in the use of epigraph. Scott's novels are full of Shakespearean epigraphs, as are many of the most popular Gothic novels of the period. To take one example: the first chapter of M. G. Lewis's best-selling *The Monk* (1796) portrays Ambrosio as a chaste and scrupulous spiritual leader; but the epigraph to the chapter is 'Lord Angelo is precise . . .'—the quotation from *Measure for Measure* thus places him for the reader, providing the only indication at this stage of his hypocritical, debauched nature, which will later be fully revealed.

Audience recognition, then, is not a problem in a study of Romantic Shakespearean allusion; the plays occupy the most prominent place in the portable library shared by poet and reader. A much more vexed question is that of authorial intention. For Hollander, 'an inadvertent allusion is a kind of solecism' (p. 64). That allusions are intentional is an axiom shared by most theorists of the subject: 'allusions in the proper sense of the word are intentional'; 'an allusion is an intentional echo of an earlier text: it not only reminds us; it means to remind us.'[32] But no poet consciously intends all the effects that readers and critics find in his poems. As long as we can show that a writer is familiar with an earlier text, there is no reason to suppose that the text has not worked its way from his memory into his composition. This idea of a power of mind over which the poet does not have conscious control is one that exercised considerable influence in the late eighteenth century; the possibility of unconscious allusion is therefore of special relevance to the Romantic age.

In 1794 Walter Whiter published his *Specimen of a Commentary on Shakspeare* which, although it had no influence on immediately subsequent criticism,[33] is symptomatic of thinking in the 1790s about unconscious poetic power. The second part of the book is entitled 'An Attempt to explain and illustrate various passages of Shakspeare, on a New Principle of Criticism, derived from Mr Locke's doctrine of the Association of Ideas'. Whiter claims that he is the first to 'unfold the secret and subtle operations of genius from the most indubitable doctrine in the theory of metaphysics'.[34] Others had discussed the close connection between genius and the associative powers of the imagination, but Whiter was the first to draw a distinction between 'that active power, which passes rapidly through a variety of successive images, which discovers with so wonderful an acuteness their relations and dependencies; and which combines them with such exquisite effect in all the pleasing forms of fiction and invention' and the more authentically Lockean notion of 'the combination of those ideas, which have *no* natural alliance or relation to each other, but which have been united only by chance, or by custom' (*Specimen*, 60–1). He is interested, he says, in those associations which 'contain no *intentional* allusion to the source from whence they are derived'; he numbers 'The remembrance of a familiar phraseology' among these '*indirect* and *involuntary* allusions' (63–6). J. K. Chandler concludes that Whiter has been 'forced into predicating the oxymoronic notion of an unintentional allusion',[35] but it seems to me that Whiter has in fact defined the most successful sort of Romantic Shakespearean allusion. The kind of allusion about which Whiter writes is a process in the imagination, even an emblem of the power of imagination, not a consciously contrived artistic effect. An unconscious allusion shows that the precursor-text has literally penetrated the recesses of the later writer's mind; it enables him to derive support from that text without becoming a plagiarist or ape, to speak words that are both his own and another's. Furthermore, an unconscious allusion is especially appropriate when the Romantic alludes to Shakespeare, whom he takes to be an unselfconscious artist, just as it is the best sort of allusion in any poem that seeks to make the poet into an unselfconscious bird singing in full-throated ease.

My use of the word 'text' to refer to phrases from earlier works in the mouths of later writers carries the implication that the process of allusion is analogous to that of a preacher citing a biblical text as authority for his own beliefs. Wordsworth writes of 'fellowship with venerable books / To sanction the proud workings of the soul' (*Prel.* ix. 240). Coleridge frequently speaks of his 'authorities'. The first footnote in the *Biographia* begins 'The authority of Milton and Shakspeare may be usefully pointed out to young authors' (*BL* i. 6 n.). There are subsequent references in the same book to the 'authority' of the seventeenth-century English divines, Milton, Bacon, and works of fame that have endured down the ages (*BL* i. 173, 174, 290, ii. 88). When used as a verb, the word is italicized: 'I appeal to the practice of the best poets, of all countries and in all ages, as *authorizing* the opinion . . .' (*BL* ii. 73).

Allusion serves the rhetorical function of *auctoritas*, the appeal to a sanctioning—and sanctified—authority. The various senses of the Latin word *auctor* provide a wide range of apposite metaphors: authority, example, model, pattern; creator, maker, inventor, one who originates or proposes anything; father, progenitor, ancestor; security, guarantor, spokesman, champion. The best general definition of *auctor* is 'one who enlarges, confirms, or gives to a thing its complete form'.[36] These figures of completion, fathering, and support suggest many of the roles played by authors invoked through allusion.

But authority is also associated with authoritarian and, by implication, with the ascription of a central place to authorial voice. These images are singularly inappropriate to Romantic conceptions of

Shakespearean magnanimity and impersonality. In this sense, a Shakespearean allusion is much more problematic than a Miltonic one. The latter is the ideal allusion in that Milton himself was a learned, allusive poet, an original yet a writer who constantly fed off the tradition. Equally, he cut a figure and was visible in his own works. He also provided an example of a poet who was successful yet conscious of being born an age too late. Beside Milton's 'unless an age too late' in the invocation to book nine of *Paradise Lost* (ix. 44), Keats wrote an emphatic 'Had not Shakespeare liv'd?' (*Romantics on Milton*, 560). Hazlitt asserted in his essay 'Why the Arts are not Progressive?' that 'Milton alone was of a later age, and not the worse for it' (*HW* iv. 161); the context of Macaulay's argument that poetry declines as civilization advances was his essay in the *Edinburgh Review* of August 1825 in which he argued that Milton's special distinction was to have produced a great poem in a civilized rather than a primitive age.

Shakespeare, however, was taken to be an ideal poet because he was a chameleon not an authoritarian. Paradoxically, he provided the authoritative example of Romantic irony, that kind of writing in which the authority of the author is undermined.[37] If Shakespeare was invisible in his own works, was it right for him to be invoked as a presence in later works? That he wrote plays led to a further complication: allusion summons an author as authority, but an allusion to a play may summon the character who speaks the lines, not the author who wrote them. Some Shakespearean allusions go badly wrong for this reason. On other occasions, however, it is a source of strength: by alluding to a line of Richard III or Iago, Romantic poets could indulge their fascination with the psychology of evil, but also implicitly distance themselves from the sentiment expressed.[38]

Although unconscious allusion, as I have defined it, provided a partial solution to the particular difficulties of Shakespearean citation, authority remained a major problem for the Romantics. On the one hand, there was a revolutionary impulse behind most of their best writings; the quest for originality, the desire to throw off the burden of tradition, was fundamentally radical. On the other hand, they were all obsessed with the literary tradition, with entering into a line of descent that ran from Chaucer to Spenser to Shakespeare to Milton. Thus at the very time Wordsworth and Coleridge were supporting the French Revolution, their literary position was a version of the politics of Burke, the leading spokesman against the Revolution. Many of Burke's remarks in his *Reflections on the Revolution in France* concerning English tradition, continuity, heredity, and 'canonized forefathers' would, if transferred from the political to the literary sphere, have appealed deeply to Wordsworth and Coleridge. Equally, the commitment to authority and tradition of the later, conservative Coleridge who wrote *On the Constitution of the Church and State*, was implicit in his earlier commitment to literary authorities. The connection between these different kinds of authority was seen by Peacock in *The Four Ages of Poetry*: 'The silver age was the reign of authority'—of deference to the examples of the golden age, that is—'but authority now began to be shaken, not only in poetry but in the whole sphere of its dominion'.[39]

It therefore became imperative to separate the literary sphere from the political. No one saw this more clearly than Hazlitt. He recognized in his essay on *Coriolanus* that despite Shakespeare's capacity to present both sides of a political argument, 'The language of poetry naturally falls in with the language of power' (*HW* iv. 214). Hazlitt turns the relationship between poetry and power to advantage by distinguishing between an 'aristocracy of rank' and an 'aristocracy of letters'.[40] His *Table Talk* essay 'On the Aristocracy of Letters' attacks the idea that there is any connection between the social and the literary élite, between political and artistic authorities. In 'On the Jealousy and Spleen of Party', Tom Moore is upbraided for compromising with 'patrician' society:

It might be some increasing consciousness of the frail tenure by which he holds his rank among the great heirs of Fame, that urged our Bard to pawn his reversion of immortality for an indulgent smile of patrician approbation, as he raised his puny arm against 'the mighty dead,' to lower by a flourish of his pen the aristocracy of letters nearer to the level of the aristocracy of rank. (*HW* xii. 365)

The allusion to Thomson ('hold high converse with the mighty dead', *Winter*, 432) makes it clear that Hazlitt's 'aristocrats' are the great writers of the past. There is little doubt as to who is foremost among them: in his sonnet prefixed to the Second Folio, Milton described Shakespeare as the 'great heir of fame'. Furthermore, the juxtaposition of 'immortality' and 'the great heirs of Fame' also evokes the opening of *Love's Labour's Lost*, where the King speaks of 'fame' and being made 'heirs of all eternity' (i. i. 1–7). For Hazlitt Shakespeare is a king, ruling over the aristocracy of the mighty dead. And in sharp contrast to the French *ancien régime*, this aristocracy is both benevolent and immortal.

These reflections on writers' citations of authoritative 'texts' may seem to be rather naïve and pre-lapsarian; in our post-structuralist critical world, all writings are 'texts' and my distinctions risk being swept away by the wholesale 'intertextuality' of Kristeva or Barthes:

> Every text, being itself the intertext of another text, belongs to the intertextual, which is not to be confused with some origin of the text: to search for the 'sources of', the 'influences upon' a work, is to fall in with the myth of filiation; the quotations which go to make up a text are anonymous, untraceable, and yet *already read*; they are quotations without quotation marks.[41]

There is a sense in which all words are quotations with lost origins and in which all texts are dependent upon shared discursive codes that cannot be understood in terms of direct influence. As so often, the post-structuralist position has a Romantic precedent. Emerson pointed out that Plato's contemporaries taxed him with plagiarism, 'but the inventor only knows how to borrow': 'Every book is a quotation; and every house is a quotation out of all forests, and mines, and stone-quarries; and every man is a quotation from all his ancestors.'[42]

But certain words and phrases are associated with specific origins. To write 'skyey' or to use 'incarnadine' as a verb is to proclaim a 'filiation'—an affiliation with Shakespeare that exists within the text itself, that is not a myth created by the source-hunting critic. The word 'skyey' seems to have been coined by Shakespeare and then dropped out of the language (except in allusions to its original context in *Measure for Measure*) until it reappeared in poems by Coleridge, Southey, Keats, and Shelley, all of whom were in some way 'Servile to all the skyey influences' (*Meas* III. i. 9) of Shakespeare's genius.[43] Perhaps 'servile' is an exaggeration: the phrase is more apt if we misquote it as Hazlitt always did, 'subject to all the skyey influences'.[44]

We need to reconstruct, not deconstruct, the history of influence and the metaphors in which poets think about influence. Writers—both poets and critics—are both inheritors and guardians of the words of their predecessors. The 'transmission of the torch', to use a phrase of De Quincey's (*DQW* iv. 29), from poetic father to poetic son is a matter of more than scholarly interest. It is by the operation of 'skyey influences' that both the works of dead poets and indeed language itself is kept alive. A remark in the *Biographia Literaria* comes to the heart of my enterprise: 'language is the armoury of the human mind; and at once contains the trophies of its past, and the weapons of its future conquests' (ii. 30). This book seeks to show how the trophies of Shakespeare are the weapons of the Romantics.

Influence, imitation, emulation, plagiarism, quotation, allusion, echo, authority, text: it would need a book to explore any one of these terms adequately. My soundings have been provisional, crude, selective. Definition is of limited value: there was no simple linear progression from 'neo-classical' to 'Romantic' models; different writers, even in the same period, use the same terms to mean different things. It is only through an empirical approach, through the multiplication of specific instances, that I will be able to clarify and substantiate my argument. The best way to conclude this preliminary discussion will be with some working examples.

In a late light-hearted poem called 'The Reproof and Reply', Coleridge is unusually candid about the art of borrowing. Perhaps it is because he is writing a none too serious poem long after he has ceased to think of himself as a poet by his own definition of the term that he feels able to be so open. The poem's subtitle is 'The Flower-Thief's Apology, for a robbery committed in Mr and Mrs —'s garden, on Sunday morning, 25th of May, 1823, between the hours of eleven and twelve' (*CPW* i. 441–3). The stealing of flowers acts as a metaphor for the stealing of fine phrases, flowers of language, from other poets. Thus when Coleridge uses the language of flowers he alludes to Wordsworth, inverting the end of the 'Immortality' ode— 'the meanest flower that blows' is changed to 'each flower that *sweetest* blows'. Then in the final stanza he makes an assertion similar to that of Vida back in 1527: 'The Eighth Commandment was not made for Bards!' The line enacts what it proclaims, for it is itself stolen from the first of Southey's popular 'Love Elegies of Abel Shufflebottom', a poem about stealing a lady's handkerchief which concludes ' *The Eighth Commandment* WAS NOT MADE FOR LOVE'. There may be a further level of allusion in that Southey's pseudonym echoes that used by Coleridge in his parodic 'Sonnets attempted in the manner of contemporary writers': they were published in the *Monthly Magazine* in 1797 with the signature 'Nehemiah Higginbottom'.

Coleridge's demonstration in 'The Reproof and Reply' that poets are flower-thieves provides proof of Walpole's argument that allusion obviates plagiarism. The adaptation of Wordsworth is signalled by quotation marks, that of Southey by a footnote. An examination of Coleridge's conversation poem 'The Nightingale' (*CPW* i. 264–7) will reveal the difference between overt references of this sort and the less obvious kind of intertextual resonance that takes place in the imagination, and that does not stand out on the surface of a text.

As Coleridge contemplates the nightingale, the epithets of 'Il Penseroso' come to his mind: '"Most musical, most melancholy" bird!' The phrase is given the appearance of having come to the poet spontaneously; when he thinks about it, he questions it: 'A melancholy bird? Oh! Idle thought! / In Nature there is nothing melancholy.' The poem argues that Milton's melancholy man 'First named these notes a melancholy strain' and then 'many a poet echoes the conceit' (here echoing is seen as a slavish activity); for Coleridge, however, it is 'the merry Nightingale'. Milton has been invoked only to be questioned, but Coleridge does not want to appear to be criticizing him, so in a footnote he distinguishes between the poet and his melancholy persona:

This passage in Milton possesses an excellence far superior to that of mere description; it is spoken in the character of the melancholy Man, and has therefore a *dramatic* propriety. The Author makes this remark, to rescue himself from the charge of having alluded with levity to a line in Milton; a charge than which none could be more painful to him, except perhaps that of having ridiculed his Bible. (*CPW* i. 264 n.)

Milton himself thus retains his quasi-biblical authoritative status.

Coleridge then moves from an overt dialogue with Milton to a muted encounter with Shakespeare. Rather than struggle to build up his rhyme, he argues, the young poet would do better to stretch his limbs 'Beside a brook in mossy forest-dell', to surrender himself 'to the influxes / Of shapes and sounds and shifting elements', forgetful 'of his song / And of his fame'. This way he will share in 'Nature's immortality' and his song will itself 'Be loved like Nature'. This sounds remarkably like a description of the protean Shakespeare, open to all impressions, not interested in posthumous fame but now an immortal who is synonymous with Nature. The progression from Milton to Shakespeare is clarified if we recall the companion poem to 'Il Penseroso': in 'L'Allegro' there is a movement from the 'youthful poet' dreaming 'On summer eves by haunted stream' (compare Coleridge's 'Beside a brook in mossy forest-dell') to the famous lines 'Or sweetest Shakespeare fancy's child, / Warble his native wood-notes wild'. As we will find in Keats's ode, Shakespeare and the nightingale have become one.

Thus when Coleridge bids farewell to the nightingale at the end of the poem he says 'That strain again!' This is the best sort of Shakespearean appropriation. It is not an overt quotation, like the earlier line from Milton, but it is a summoning of the music of *Twelfth Night*, an instance of the strain of Shakespearean music that runs through English Romantic poetry. Such resonances are quieter than the Miltonic cadences we all recognize, and for that reason many of them have gone unnoticed, but because below the surface they are all the more intimately associated with, to use Whiter's phrase, the 'secret and subtle operations of genius' that are the distinctive power of the Romantic imagination.

3

Shakespearean Voices in Coleridge's Poetry

THE Reverend James Boyer made his pupils at Christ's Hospital learn passages of Shakespeare and Milton by heart. He demanded that they should be recited accurately: according to Coleridge, these were the lessons 'which required most time and trouble to *bring up*, so as to escape his censure' (*BL* i. 9). The language of Shakespeare was ingrained upon Coleridge's memory at school; it inevitably emerged in his poetry.

But although he knew Shakespeare from his schooldays, Coleridge did not immediately profess strong allegiance to him. His first poetic love, he tells us in the *Biographia*, was the sonneteer William Lisle Bowles. In a letter to John Thelwall written in 1796, he even adapted Garrick's famous characterization of Shakespeare as 'the god of our idolatry' into 'Bowles (the bard of my idolatry)' (*CL* i. 259). Yet to use this phrase, which ultimately goes back to *Romeo and Juliet* (ii. ii. 114), is to acknowledge tacitly that Shakespeare is the real god. Shrewdly, Coleridge sensed even as a young man that Shakespeare would prove inimitable; Bowles provided a more manageable model.

In his early poems Coleridge encounters Shakespeare at one remove. A section in his undergraduate 'Lines on an Autumnal Evening' begins 'O (have I sigh'd) were mine the wizard's rod, / Or mine the power of Proteus, changeful God!' (*CPW* i. 52). In view of his subsequent remarks about Shakespeare as Proteus and Prospero as 'the very Shakspeare himself, as it were, of the tempest' (*SC* i. 119), this sounds like a plea for Shakespeare's creative power. But Coleridge's apologetic footnote to the lines points elsewhere—'They have not the merit even of originality: as every thought is to be found in the Greek Epigrams.' We are familiar from Coleridge's prose with the tactic of acknowledging a debt that obscures the most important influence; thus when, in the *Biographia*, he mentions the German contribution to Shakespearean criticism, Lessing is given disproportionate emphasis while Schlegel is not mentioned. Whether out of awe or deviousness, Coleridge is similarly indirect in his poetic appropriations of Shakespeare.

In the *Morning Chronicle* of 23 September 1794, and then *The Watchman* of 17 March 1796, Coleridge published a rhymed imitation of one of Akenside's blank-verse inscriptions. He could have used this as an opportunity to confront the genius of Shakespeare by choosing the fourth inscription, 'For a Statue of Shakespeare'. In fact, he chose the third, but included in it a Shakespearean quotation for which there was no precedent in Akenside's original: 'Where "sleeps the moonlight" on yon verdant bed' (*CPW* i. 70). The implication is that, however much Akenside may be admired, the best description of moonlight remains that of Shakespeare in the lyrical scene which opens the final act of *The Merchant of Venice*.

Coleridge also used Thomas Chatterton as an intermediary between himself and Shakespeare, as Wordsworth would later do in 'Resolution and Independence' and Keats in 'To Autumn'. The 1794 version of 'Monody on the Death of Chatterton' explicitly sets the marvellous boy in the tradition of Spenser and Otway. But Shakespeare is again quoted without being mentioned by name: 'While "mid the pelting of that pitiless storm," / Sunk to the cold earth Otway's famish'd form!' (*CPW* i. 126). The line is taken away from *King Lear* and applied to the Restoration tragedian who gave hope to the Romantics because his *Venice Preserved* seemed to them to be the only tragedy worthy of Shakespeare written in a later age. It must have been a source of considerable satisfaction to Coleridge that when his play *Remorse* was produced at Drury Lane in 1813, Leigh Hunt said in a review that it was the 'only tragedy touched with real poetry for the last fifty years' and that there had been 'no complete production of the kind since the time of Otway'.[1] Coleridge's drama is seen to revive a line that began with Shakespeare and expired with Otway. The link between Chatterton and Shakespeare is made in a footnote to the name of a river mentioned in the 'Monody': 'Avon, a river near Bristol, the birth-place of Chatterton.' The mention of Avon and birth-place in the same sentence cannot but make the reader think of Shakespeare.

Certain touches in the monody suggest a parallel between Chatterton, the archetypal youthful poet, and Hamlet, the Romantics' archetypal poet-figure. Although Coleridge does not allude directly to *Hamlet* in his early poems, he cannot escape the play. His sonnet on the Polish freedom fighter Koskiusko begins 'O what a loud and fearful shriek was there', a rhythmic echo of the first line of Hamlet's soliloquy (in a play during which an army goes to fight for Poland),

'O, what a rogue and peasant slave am I!' (*CPW* i. 82, *Ham* II. ii. 550).[2] The sonnet on Mrs Siddons which Coleridge took over from Lamb alludes principally to *Macbeth*, since Lady Macbeth was the actress's greatest role, but it also incorporates a version of the most *Macbeth*-like line in *Hamlet*, ' 'Tis now the very witching time of night' (*CPW* i. 86, *Ham* III. ii. 388). The ground is prepared for Coleridge's subsequent identification of himself as Hamlet.

The Shakespeare of the terrible, the sublime, and the supernatural —of *Macbeth* and *King Lear*—was possibly even more important for Coleridge's poetry than was the introspective, self-doubting Hamlet. Coleridge was quick to recognize that his admired Bowles had failed in the encounter with this Shakespeare. He admitted to a college friend in 1794 that 'The "Shakespeare" is sadly unequal to the rest' of Bowles's poems (*CL* i. 94). The poem in question is an apostrophe to Shakespeare of the sort that abounded in the late eighteenth century. It is Bowles at his most conventional:

> O Sovereign Master! who with lonely state
> Dost rule as in some isle's enchanted land,
> On whom soft airs and shadowy spirits wait,
> Whilst scenes of 'faerie' bloom at thy command,
> On thy wild shores forgetful could I lie,
> And list, till earth dissolved to thy sweet minstrelsy![3]

(That image of the poet lying 'forgetful' on Shakespeare's 'wild shores' surfaces again in the passage of Coleridge's 'The Nightingale' which was discussed at the end of chapter two.) The rest of Bowles's poem consists largely of a cento of quotations from the plays, some of them marked by italics or footnotes, strung together with the stock vocabulary of faerie (' 'Mid rude romantic woods, and glens forlorn'). In the second stanza Shakespeare is given his traditional characterization as a magician conjuring up 'a wondrous masque'. More specifically, he conjures up a series of images from five of his plays. Thus the remaining five stanzas set out to evoke Lear on the heath, the forest of *As You Like it*, the fairies of *A Midsummer Night's Dream*, Prospero with his wand and Ariel with his song, and finally the weird sisters.

Certain minor poems of the mid–late 1790s reveal Coleridge struggling as Bowles had done with the language of Shakespearean romance. 'Pity' is a farrago of images out of the middle acts of *King Lear*.[4] The 'Ode to the Departing Year' includes a network of rhythmic and verbal allusions to the violent world of *Macbeth*. 'Fire,

Famine, and Slaughter: A War Eclogue', despite the strong emphasis on Milton in the apologetic preface Coleridge added to it when it was published in *Sibylline Leaves*, is as obvious an imitation of the witch-scenes in *Macbeth* as anything in the language. 'Lines written at Shurton Bars' is slightly more successful in its quiet allusions to the heath-scenes of *King Lear* (*CPW* i. 99, lines 73–8; the tears, kisses, and pity of the following stanza also suggest Lear and Cordelia). The poem's more prominent allusion, however, is to Wordsworth. In a footnote to line five, Coleridge makes his first published statement of admiration for his new acquaintance: 'The expression "green radiance" is borrowed from Mr Wordsworth, a Poet whose versification is occasionally harsh and his diction too frequently obscure; but whom I deem unrivalled among the writers of the present day in manly sentiment, novel imagery, and vivid colouring' (*CPW* i. 97 n.).

The Shakespearean influence on Coleridge in the mid-1790s is subordinate to those of Wordsworth and, above all, Milton. Pseudo-Miltonic diction is the bane of Coleridge's blank verse. The more sublime and exclamatory parts of 'Religious Musings', 'Ode to the Departing Year', 'France: An Ode', and 'Fears in Solitude' are testimony to Coleridge's struggle with Milton, as indeed is his desire to write an epic on 'The Fall of Jerusalem'.[5] Wordsworth continued both to inspire and to inhibit throughout Coleridge's poetic career.[6] 'To William Wordsworth', dated January 1807, is probably Coleridge's last major poetic achievement: it is Wordsworth who has led him to write a substantial poem again after four barren years, but the resulting poem argues that Wordsworth's *Prelude* is the true poetic achievement. Significantly, the language of 'To William Wordsworth' implies that *The Prelude* has caught the spirit of both great English poets: phrases such as 'high theme by thee first sung aright' are unashamedly Miltonic, while a line like 'Not learnt, but native, her own natural notes!' suggests the traditional characterization of Shakespeare (*CPW* i. 403–8).

Because they are egotists who stamp their distinctive tone and diction on every line of their work, Milton and Wordsworth cannot but be faced frontally; the encounter with Shakespeare is more muted, as hard to pin down as the protean poet himself. On the one hand, Shakespeare is more easily assimilable than Milton and Wordsworth: a line like 'The stilly murmur of the distant Sea' in 'The Eolian Harp' (*CPW* i. 100) sounds Shakespearean—what is masterly is the syntactic flexibility that creates 'stilly'—but it is not obtrusively pseudo-Elizabethan in the way that Coleridge's latinisms are so often cumbersomely pseudo-Miltonic. On the other hand, Shakespeare's elusiveness demands something other than overt imitation. In 1797–8 both Coleridge and Wordsworth attempted to imitate Shakespeare. They both failed, but then went on to write their best and most distinctive poetry—poetry that was responsive to Shakespeare without being in thrall to him.

I think that Shakespeare was peculiarly important to the poetic conjunction of Wordsworth and Coleridge. An essential part of the later poet's approach to Shakespeare was the attempt to write blank-verse drama. It is telling that several of Coleridge's early references to Shakespeare also mention Schiller, whose *Robbers* was seen as the most successful neo-Shakespearean drama of the age. For Coleridge, one aspect of Shakespeare lacking in Schiller was the supernatural,[7] but this did not stop him according the German dramatist high praise in a note to his sonnet 'To the Author of "The Robbers"', first published in 1796: 'Schiller introduces no supernatural beings; yet his human beings agitate and astonish more than all the *goblin* rout—even of Shakespeare' (*CPW* i. 73 n.). Schiller, however, had the advantage of not writing in Shakespeare's language, not being in constant danger of merely copying his words. One weakness of Coleridge's translations of *The Piccolomini* and *The Death of Wallenstein* is that he cannot resist introducing Shakespearean phrases, which detract from the stronger Shakespearean influence of character and action on the German originals. Schiller catches the bustle and energy of the history plays; Coleridge distracts from this by introducing phrases like 'in my mind's eye' which make us think of very different parts of Shakespeare (see *Piccolomini*, I. i. 28).

Translation of Schiller was a compromise in which Coleridge engaged at the turn of the century; before this, he had expressed the hope that an English poet might revive Shakespearean drama without going through a German interpreter. In March 1797, he wrote enthusiastically to Joseph Cottle:

I have heard from Sheridan, desiring me to write a Tragedy—I have no genius that way—Robert Southey has—and highly as I think of his Joan of Arc, I cannot help prophesying, that he will be known to posterity as Shakespear's great Grandson, and only as Milton's great great grand nephew-in-law.—I think, that he will write a Tragedy; and Tragedies. (*CL* i. 313)

The familial images are revealing: the epic *Joan of Arc* is supposed to make Southey into a descendant, albeit a collateral one, of Milton. Coleridge gives no evidence for his claim that Southey is in a direct line of descent from Shakespeare. He can hardly be thinking of *The Fall of Robespierre*, the historical drama on which, while an undergraduate at Cambridge, he collaborated with Southey, for its static rhetorical encounters resemble not so much a Shakespearean drama as the debate of the fallen angels in *Paradise Lost*. Coleridge is probably thinking of Southey's *Wat Tyler*; he does not mention it by name because it was then unpublished and potentially treasonable (when a pirated edition appeared in 1817 it caused considerable embarrassment to Southey, who was by then the reactionary Poet Laureate).

The principal Shakespearean influence on Southey's dramas is *Julius Caesar*. *The Fall of Robespierre* is a special case because literary influence intersects with historical fact. To us, 'I do repent me much / That I kill'd Caesar and spar'd Antony' and 'I invoke thy shade, / Immortal Brutus' (II. 166, 272, *CPW* ii. 507, 510) will suggest Shakespeare's play, but in the early 1790s there is an additional, more immediate context: the French revolutionaries themselves enacted a series of allusions—rhetorical, architectural, iconographic, sartorial—to the Roman republic. As Burke implied by means of his persistent use of theatrical metaphor in *Reflections on the Revolution in France*, drama had been transferred from the realm of fiction to the political stage in Europe.[8]

Wat Tyler is more crudely indebted to *Julius Caesar*. The emphasis on civil unrest and the vicissitudes of the mob, Tyler's address beginning 'Friends and Countrymen': these are unimaginative Shakespearean posturings. Southey's borrowings from other plays are equally flat. 'Must we lie tamely at our tyrant's feet, / And, like your spaniels, lick the hand that beats us?' mimics a favourite Shakespearean locution, but trivializes it through excessive alliteration. A contrast between the 'proud palace' and a 'hut of poverty', in the context of lines like 'Came ye not / As helpless to the world?' and 'Do ye not feel / The self-same winds as keenly parch ye?', glances at those questions in which Lear reveals that he is beginning to feel as his people feel, but Southey does not explore the conflicts that lead to such questionings. And a phrase like 'Alas, poor Tyler!' is merely embarrassing.[9]

Still, *Wat Tyler* has a certain dramatic life that is absent from the statuesque *Fall of Robespierre*. Its theatricality suggests that stagings of

Shakespeare may have influenced Southey, a possibility confirmed by some touches that smack of Colley Cibber's dynamic version of *Richard III*, which held the stage throughout the eighteenth century.[10] Most Romantic plays lack the dramatic vitality of Cibber, let alone that of Shakespeare. Coleridge had to write a complete play himself before recognizing this; having done so, he would have seen the limitations of Southey's play, as he did not in the letter to Cottle. Politically attractive as *Julius Caesar* might have been, the real challenge lay in confronting the four great tragedies; perhaps that is why phrases from *Lear* enter *Wat Tyler* even though there are no parallels of plot or character.

Despite his protestation 'I have no genius that way', Coleridge did write a tragedy for Sheridan. This is where the conjunction of Wordsworth, Coleridge, and neo-Shakespearean drama took place. As James Butler remarks, the *annus mirabilis* of English Romanticism began in early June 1797 when Coleridge leapt over a gate and bounded down a pathless field to the Wordsworths' cottage at Racedown:

In the year to come was the writing of *The Rime of the Ancient Mariner, Christabel, Kubla Khan*, and Wordsworth's contributions to *Lyrical Ballads* (1798), as well as the fruitful exchange of ideas that developed when the Wordsworths moved to Alfoxden to be close to Coleridge at Nether Stowey. As Hazlitt remembered after visiting Alfoxden in 1798, it was a time when one felt 'the sense of a new style and a new spirit in poetry'.[11]

Butler's point is that this *annus mirabilis* began with a reading of *The Ruined Cottage*. But without in any way diminishing the significance of Wordsworth's tragic poem, the relevant passage from a letter of Dorothy Wordsworth to Mary Hutchinson, when quoted more fully, reveals the equal importance of tragic drama: 'The first thing that was read after he came was William's new poem *The Ruined Cottage* with which he was much delighted; and after tea he repeated to us two acts and a half of his tragedy *Osorio*. The next morning William read his tragedy *The Borderers*' (*EY* 189).

Coleridge thought of the two plays as a pair. Soon after his arrival at Racedown he wrote again to Cottle: 'Wordsworth admires my Tragedy—which gives me great hopes. Wordsworth has written a Tragedy himself.' Comparison, however, leads to a sense of his own inferiority—'I feel myself a *little man by his* side'—and of Wordsworth's place in, or even above, the tradition of Shakespeare and Schiller: 'There are in the piece those *profound* touches of the human heart, which

I find three or four times in "The Robbers" of Schiller, and often in Shakespere—but in Wordsworth there are no *inequalities*' (*CL* i. 325). Drury Lane rejected Coleridge's play and Covent Garden Wordsworth's, in each case on grounds of 'obscurity'; the theatre managers presumably thought, with some justification, that metaphysical generalization swamped dramatic action. Coleridge then proposed publishing *Osorio* and *The Borderers* in a single volume, accompanied by 'small prefaces containing an analysis of our principal characters' (*CL* i. 400). But comparison still discouraged him: 'As to the Tragedy, when I consider it [in] reference to Shakespear's and to *one* other Tragedy, it seems a poor thing; and I care little what becomes of it' (*CL* i. 412).

Coleridge continues in a more positive vein: 'when I consider [it] in comparison with modern Dramatists, it *rises*'. He did not like to be compared unfavourably with the hacks who wrote for the contemporary stage; his 'Critique of *Bertram*' reprinted in *Biographia Literaria*, with its attack on Charles Maturin's 'senseless plagiarism' from Shakespeare (*BL* ii. 232), was motivated by pique at the Drury Lane managerial committee's opinion that his own *Zapolya* was not so Shakespearean and therefore would not be so successful as *Bertram*.[12] In fact, there is little to choose between the two plays; they are equally unreadable. *Bertram* is, as Coleridge recognized in his critique, a poor imitation of Shakespearean tragedy at one remove—that is to say, Shakespeare mediated through what Wordsworth called 'sickly and stupid German Tragedies'. *Zapolya* is a poor imitation of Shakespeare's last plays, crudely indebted to the temporal structure of *The Winter's Tale* and the plot of *Cymbeline*. *Bertram* was melodramatic enough to be a box-office success; *Zapolya* at least has the merit of going to a group of Shakespearean plays that were less frequently ransacked by derivative dramatists.

Much later, Coleridge accounted for his dissatisfaction with *Osorio*, even after it had been rewritten as *Remorse* and, thanks to the good offices of Lord Byron, enjoyed a successful run at Drury Lane:

There's such a divinity doth hedge our Shakspeare round, that we cannot even imitate his style. I tried to imitate his manner in the Remorse, and, when I had done, I found I had been tracking Beaumont and Fletcher, and Massinger instead. It is really very curious. At first sight, Shakspeare and his contemporary dramatists seem to write in styles much alike: nothing so easy as to fall into that of Massinger and the others; whilst no one has ever yet produced one scene conceived and expressed in the Shakspearian idiom. (*TT* 17 February 1833)

The last clause in this passage suggests that he has forgotten or thought better of his high praise of Wordsworth's tragedy (a sign of the estrangement between the two poets?); the first image echoes 'There's such divinity doth hedge a king' (*Ham* IV. v. 124) and thus neatly implies that Shakespeare is king of poets. Keats used an analogous image when in a marginal annotation to *Troilus and Cressida* on the subject of Shakespeare's 'innate universality' he wrote of his 'kingly gaze' (*KS* 151). Coleridge's verb 'tracking' echoes Dryden's remark on Ben Jonson and the ancients, 'you track him every where in their snow' (*Of Dramatic Poesy*, i. 31): again, one sees that the Elizabethan and Jacobean dramatists have the kind of authority for the Romantic that the ancients had for the neo-classical writer.

Coleridge's attempt at self-criticism is applicable to both *Remorse* and *Zapolya*; neither of his plays holds our attention as Shakespeare's do. The comparison with the lesser Jacobeans is, I think, just: so often when reading Massinger or Beaumont and Fletcher our attention wanders. Their verse is always fluid, but often slack; we are not continually engaged by coinages, rhetorical twists, bold metaphors, and sustained image-clusters, as we are when reading Shakespeare. Coleridge made the distinction beautifully in one of his 1818 lectures, and in so doing, produced a version of his favourite contrast between mechanic and organic form.

[Beaumont and Fletcher] took from the ear and eye, unchecked by any intuition of an inward impossibility, just as a man might fit together a quarter of an orange, a quarter of an apple, and the like of a lemon and of a pomegranate, and make it look like one round diverse colored fruit. But nature, who works from within by evolution and assimilation according to a law, cannot do it. Nor could Shakespeare, for he too worked in the spirit of nature, by evolving the germ within by the imaginative power according to an idea (*MC* 42–3).

In his plays Coleridge frequently took a quarter of a Hamlet, a quarter of a Lear, and the like of a Macbeth and of an Othello, and tried to make it look like one round diverse Shakespearean fruit. Consider, for example, a representative speech from *Osorio*, of which Coleridge thought sufficiently well not to revise in *Remorse*:

> O this unutterable dying away here,
> This sickness of the heart!
>   What if I went
> And liv'd in a hollow tomb, and fed on weeds?

> Ay! that's the road to heaven! O fool! fool! fool!
> What have I done but that which nature destin'd
> Or the blind elements stirr'd up within me?
> If good were meant, why were we made these beings?
> And if not meant—
>
> (II. 110, *CPW* ii. 539)

Osorio's gallimaufry begins in the manner of Hamlet, then shifts to the tone of Timon, glances at Lear or Othello with the repetition of 'fool!', and ends with something of Macbeth's equivocation—'If good were meant, why . . .? And if not meant . . .' mimics the structure of Macbeth's 'This supernatural soliciting / Cannot be ill; cannot be good' (I. iii. 130), with its 'If ill, Why . . .? If good, why . . .?'. Furthermore, Osorio is interrupted with Ferdinand's 'How feel you now, my lord?', as Banquo's reaction to the speech in *Macbeth* is 'Look how our partner's rapt' (the correspondence is slightly closer in *Remorse*, where Coleridge changes the interjection to 'You are disturbed, my lord!'). Though there is this similarity in content, there is none in effect. Osorio is only going through the motions of describing passion; Coleridge is unable to imitate the way that Shakespeare *expresses* passion by showing us the intricate processes of his characters' mental operations.

Moments of action present Coleridge with as many problems as those of contemplation. The following exchange, a little earlier in the same scene, was also left substantively unchanged in *Remorse*:

> *Ferdinand.* But listen to me now. I pray you, listen!
> *Osorio.* Villain! no more! I'll hear no more of it.
> *Ferdinand.* My lord! it much imports your future safety
>   That you should hear it.
> *Osorio.*   Am I not a man?
>   'Tis as it should be! Tut—the deed itself
>   Was idle—and these after-pangs still idler!
>
> (II. 72, *CPW* ii. 538)

Contextually, there are certain parallels with Iago's feeding of false information to Othello; perhaps that is why the phrase ' 'Tis as it should be' is adapted from those first words spoken by Othello, which tell us so much about his character, ' 'Tis better as it is' (I. ii. 6). But the language of this exchange is under the sway of *Macbeth*. Coleridge said that *Macbeth* was 'the most rapid' of Shakespeare's tragedies in its movement (*SC* i. 49), and it is the cut and thrust of dialogue in that play which he sought to emulate in order to give pace to his own play. As a reader of Shakespeare, Coleridge was acutely sensitive to the organic relationship between speeches. In a fine marginal note to the lines early in *Macbeth* where Banquo and Macbeth are reunited with Duncan, he draws attention to the sustained image of planting, growth, and harvest that binds the sequence together—Shakespeare does not write as if for the actor who will learn his own lines in isolation from the rest (*SC* i. 63). But as a dramatist, Coleridge apes the language and rhythms of Shakespeare without making each speech part of a unified linguistic pattern.

Thus the repetition in 'no more! I'll hear no more of it' is merely a piece of filling designed to give a sense of Osorio urgently trying to stem Ferdinand's provocations. But Lady Macbeth's 'No more o' that, my lord, no more o' that' in the sleep-walking scene (v. i. 44) is the climactic use of the words 'no more' which have recurred at several key moments throughout the play. The phrase is first heard in the mouth of Duncan: 'No more that Thane of Cawdor shall deceive / Our bosom interest' (i. ii. 63); Macbeth reproduces the internally rhyming pair 'no more' and 'Cawdor' when he says in the next scene 'No more than to be Cawdor' (i. iii. 75). Then there is the terrible 'Sleep no more!' (ii. ii. 32), a voice that rings out in Wordsworth's consciousness in the French Revolution part of *The Prelude* and will also be of considerable importance in Coleridge's non-dramatic poetry. The conjunction with Macbeth's names is compounded in 'Glamis hath murther'd sleep, and therefore Cawdor / Shall sleep no more' (ii. ii. 39). A few lines later Macbeth says of returning to the bed-chamber, 'I'll go no more' (ii. ii. 47); then in act four scene one, a scene that appealed deeply to the Romantic taste for supernatural apparitions, the weird sisters' 'Seek to know no more' (iv. i. 103, 'no' is heightened by the homonym) elicits Macbeth's 'I'll see no more' (118) and 'no more sights!' (155). Ironically, it is Lady Macbeth who sleeps no more: her repetition of 'no more o' that' links her own sleeplessness with her husband's earlier fears of sleeplessness. And finally Macbeth makes his conclusive comparison of life to a poor player 'That struts and frets his hour upon the stage, / And then is heard *no more*' (v. v. 25, my italics). It is hardly an exaggeration to say that the germ of the whole play is contained in the single phrase. Coleridge discerned some of these connections, particularly with regard to Macbeth's names; he was the first critic to point to the dramatic irony in the way that the king's 'presentimental' remark about Cawdor,

> There's no art
> To find the mind's construction in the face:
> He was a gentleman on whom I built
> An absolute trust . . .

(see *SC* i. 63), is made at the precise moment of entry of the new Cawdor on whom he builds even greater trust. But Coleridge failed to carry such critical intuitions over into dramatic practice.

Again, 'Am I not a man?' is reminiscent of *Macbeth* but diminished in effect because Osorio's manhood is not consistently questioned in the way that Macbeth's is. Shakespeare plays persistently on the idea of Macbeth's manhood and its relation to Lady Macbeth's unsexing.[13] Macbeth says 'I dare do all that may become a man; / Who dares do more is none' (I. vii. 46, note the conjunction with 'more'); Lady Macbeth throws his words back in his face:

> When you durst do it, then you were a man;
> And to be more than what you were, you would
> Be so much more the man.

> (I. vii. 49)

Later, she taunts her husband with 'Are you a man?' (III. iv. 57). This links Macbeth to the murderers, since they have said earlier in the act 'We are men, my liege', provoking his 'Ay, in the catalogue ye go for men' (III. i. 91)—his reply to his wife begins with the same word, 'Ay, and a bold one'. Then at a vital moment during the scene in England, true manhood is seen to reside not in manliness but in humanity, as Macduff answers Malcolm's immature 'Dispute it like a man' with 'But I must also feel it as a man' (IV. iii. 220–1).

A third network of lines in *Macbeth* is suggested by Osorio's 'the deed itself'. In the lines on 'pity' that so influenced Blake, Macbeth refers to 'the horrid deed' (I. vii. 24); subsequently, the murder of Duncan is reified as 'the deed'—'I have done the deed', 'A little water clears us of this deed' (II. ii. 14, 64). 'A deed of dreadful note' (III. ii. 44), 'We are yet but young in deed' (III. iv. 143: here a wonderful compression that incorporates 'indeed'), and 'A deed without a name' (IV. i. 49) are only the most memorable instances of the word. Coleridge saw that the soliloquy 'If it were done, when 'tis done', in which 'deed' first occurs, was answered by Macbeth's 'To know my deed, 'twere best not know myself' (II. ii. 70), a line which occurs immediately before the knocking at the gate that so fascinated De Quincey. But Coleridge did not write plays with the sensitivity with which he read them. Osorio's 'idle' and 'idler' lack the pace and energy of *Macbeth*; his line approximates more to Hamlet's 'I must be idle' (III. ii. 90) or to the world of *Antony and Cleopatra*, where the 'idleness' of Egypt is so important. In fact, 'idle' could not be further from the world of *Macbeth*; it is no coincidence that this is the only one of Shakespeare's ten tragedies in which the word does not appear.

Coleridge would no doubt have countered the foregoing analysis of Osorio's 'no more', 'Am I not a man?', and 'the deed itself Was idle' as he countered Hazlitt's accusation in *The Morning Chronicle* that 'the contrast between the pictures of the brothers' earlier in the play was 'too evidently copied from the well-known passage in Shakespeare' (*HW* xviii. 465). In a letter to Rickman, he wrote

I hear that Hazlitt i[n the] M. C. has sneered at my presumption in [entering] the Lists with Shakespear's Hamlet in Teresa's Description of the two Brothers: when (so help me the Muses) that Passage never once occurred to my conscious recollection, however it may, unknown to myself, have been the working Idea within me. But mercy on us! is there no such thing as two men's having similar Thoughts on similar Occasions—? (*CL* iii. 429).

But Puff's defence is not relevant here: what matters is not 'conscious recollection' but 'the working Idea' within the poet's mind. Plagiarism is not at stake; it would be ludicrous to accuse Coleridge of stealing such phrases as 'no more' from Shakespeare. The point at issue is that small words are put to work in Shakespeare, while in Coleridge's play only concepts and abstracts carry weight; this accounts in large measure for the lack of dramatic vitality. None of these key words in *Macbeth*—no more, man, deed—has a recurring, organic place in *Osorio*. The one word in the passage that is crucial to the play as a whole is the very unshakespearean 'after-pangs'. Not only is that word suggestive of 'remorse'—the matter of both this play and 'The Ancient Mariner'—but it is probably a Coleridgean coinage. It is not recorded at all in OED and its structure is similar to those other Coleridgean coinages 'possible *after-perversion* of the natural feelings', 'beneficial *after-effects* of verbal precision', and 'The sense of a disproportion of certain *after-harm* to present gratification' (*BL* ii. 61 n., ii. 143, *Friend*, i. 105, my italics). The association between 'pangs' and the eponymous theme of *Remorse* is further suggested by 'High minds, of native pride and force, / Most deeply feel thy pangs, Remorse!', a couplet in Scott's *Marmion* (III. xiii), which, like Coleridge's play, has at its centre a villain-hero whose nature is at once noble and fallen.

To turn from the failures of verbal detail to the mechanism of the plot: one major difference between *Macbeth* and *Osorio* is that the latter has no equivalent of the witches. Much as Coleridge admired the supernatural in Shakespeare, he realized that to present apparitions on stage in his own play would have been to risk melodrama or lurid theatricality, as Maturin's *Bertram* was to show. Coleridge's scepticism about the staging of Shakespeare usually occurs in contexts of unusual imaginative vision. He worried about the staging of the weird sisters, considering at one point that the way to embody them successfully might be to depart from the conventions of the contemporary theatre and have John Flaxman sculpture character-masks like those of Greek tragedy (*SC* i. 60). In an annotation to a passage on the subject of dramatic illusion in Richard Payne Knight's *Analytical Inquiry into the Principles of Taste*, probably made in preparation for the 1808 lectures on Shakespeare, Coleridge argued that Shakespearean drama could be staged effectively, if handled by good actors, but that the 'imaginative Tragedies'—*Lear*, *Macbeth*, and *Hamlet*—presented special problems because 'there is such a disproportion betw[een] the Powers of Nature, Storms etc., and the means employed to represent them and in like manner, with respect to the supernatural agencies'.[14] For a simple mind, Coleridge argues, the scenery and machinery of the modern theatre heighten the effect of dramatic illusion; for a more cultivated audience, they destroy it. Shakespeare, he frequently reminds us, wrote for a bare stage and invited our imagination to realize the scene (*SC* ii. 57, 68). Coleridge also saw particular dangers in attempts to embody Shakespeare's most magical creations in the cumbersome early nineteenth-century theatre. He said that *The Tempest* addressed itself 'entirely to the imaginative faculty', arguing that although complicated scenery and decorations might assist the illusion by appealing to the senses, the effect was dangerous,

For the principal and only genuine excitement ought to come from within,—from the moved and sympathetic imagination; whereas, where so much is addressed to the mere external senses of seeing and hearing, the spiritual vision is apt to languish, and the attraction from without will

withdraw the mind from the proper and only legitimate interest which is
intended to spring from within. (*SC* i. 118)

It is also with regard to *The Tempest* that Coleridge treats the subject
of dramatic illusion at greatest length. As on so many other occasions, he
synthesizes English and German sources; both Lord Kames and A. W.
Schlegel had used the image of a 'waking dream' to account for what
Coleridge called our 'willing illusion' in the theatre. In the words of
Black's translation of Schlegel, 'the theatrical as well as every other
poetical illusion, is a waking dream, to which we voluntarily surrender
ourselves'.[15] Coleridge discusses the subject briefly in the third lecture of his course of 1811–12, and at greater length when lecturing on
The Tempest in the course of 1818–19. In the longer passage, he compares dramatic illusion to dream but argues that the difference is that
in the theatre 'We *choose* to be deceived' (*SC* i. 116). Modern dream-
theory might question the assumption that we do not choose to be
deceived in our dreams, but Coleridge's argument falls in with the
dream-theory of his own time, particularly that of Erasmus Darwin.
Elisabeth Schneider has noted that in the section on dreams in *The
Botanic Garden*, Darwin refers to Kames's argument for the 'ideal
presence' of dramatic characters, and coins the phrase 'theatric
reverie'.[16]

Coleridge's most succinct statement concerning dramatic illusion
occurs in a lecture note, possibly of 1808: 'These and all other stage
presentations are to produce a sort of temporary half-faith, which the
spectator encourages in himself and supports by a voluntary contribution on his own part, because he knows that it is at all times in his
power to see the thing as it really is' (*SC* i. 178). The idea has a long
history, going back to a fragment of Gorgias concerning responsiveness in the Greek theatre, 'the man who is deceived has more wisdom
than he who is not'.[17] But for Coleridge the relationship between
poetry and willing illusion is not confined to the specific matter of
personation in the theatre. In that notebook entry on *Lear* and *Othello*
as divine dreams, 'all Shakespere, and nothing Shakespere', he
makes the broad assertion that poetry is 'rationalized dreaming'. All
poetry is rationalized dreaming, but in certain forms the relationship
with dream is especially apparent. Dramatic poetry is one of them,
but given Shakespeare's insuperability in this genre and Coleridge's
unease in the contemporary theatre, some other form had to be
found. One possibility is suggested by a famous passage in the

Biographia which is extremely close to that on 'temporary half-faith' in the theatre. We are told that in the *Lyrical Ballads* Coleridge directed himself to persons and characters supernatural, or at least romantic, 'so as to transfer from our inward nature a human interest and a semblance of truth sufficient to procure for these shadows of imagination that willing suspension of disbelief for the moment, which constitutes poetic faith' (*BL* ii. 6). Coleridge hoped to induce in the readers of his supernatural poems a state of voluntary dreaming analogous to the willing illusion of the spectator of Shakespeare's plays.

As revealing as the general parallel between the passage on poetic faith and that on 'temporary half-faith' in the theatre is the particular phrase 'shadows of imagination'. It suggests the language of Theseus in that scene of *A Midsummer Night's Dream* from which it is impossible to escape when considering eighteenth- and early nineteenth-century writings on imagination. In this context it is decisive that Coleridge alludes to Shakespeare's *dream* play ('I am convinced', he wrote in a marginal annotation, 'that Shakespeare availed himself of the title of the play in his own mind [as] a *dream* throughout', *SC* i. 90). The connection with theatrical illusion is intensified by the fact that it is of *actors* that Theseus says 'The best in this kind are but shadows; and the worst are no worse, if imagination amend them' (v. i. 211).

The practical effect of this theoretical connection is that certain Shakespearean voices, particularly from the magical plays, are to be heard in Coleridge's supernatural poems. Wilson Knight draws parallels between 'Christabel' and *Macbeth*: 'There is darkness (though moon-lit), the owl, the restless mastiff. There is sleep and silence broken by fearsome sounds. The mastiff's howl is touched with deathly horror: "some say she sees my lady's shroud". Opposed to the nightmarish are images of religious grace.'[18] Apart from 'the owlet's scritch' ('Christabel', 152), Wilson Knight's instances are not especially convincing—the mastiff is not numbered among the many breeds of dog mentioned in *Macbeth*. But his sense of atmospheric correspondence is just. It is borne out by certain verbal recollections, most notably at the moment when Geraldine seems to see Christabel's dead mother acting as a guardian spirit:

> But soon with altered voice, said she—
> 'Off, wandering mother! Peak and pine!
> I have power to bid thee flee.'

Alas! what ails poor Geraldine?
Why stares she with unsettled eye?
Can she the bodiless dead espy?

(204)

Geraldine's loss of confidence is not the only change of tone: the poem's voice is altered too, in that it is now Shakespearean. The final two lines are strongly reminiscent of Macbeth and the ghost of Banquo. In Coleridge's poem, as in John Philip Kemble's 1794 production of *Macbeth*, the ghost does not actually appear; it is confined to the troubled imagination of the protagonist.[19] Geraldine is, however, no Macbeth. The exclamation 'Peak and pine!' alerts the reader to her true ancestors, the witches: 'Weary sev'nnights, nine times nine, / Shall he dwindle, peak, and pine' (I. iii. 22).[20] She is like the weird sisters in that she communicates part of her knowledge and then disappears. Coleridge actually drew a direct comparison when he outlined to Gillman a possible conclusion to the poem, 'Geraldine being acquainted with all that is passing, like the Weird Sisters in Macbeth, vanishes.'[21]

The original context of 'peak and pine' is an account by one of the witches of what she will do to a mariner, the master of the *Tiger*:

I'll drain him dry as hay:
Sleep shall neither night nor day
Hang upon his penthouse lid;
He shall live a man forbid;
Weary sev'nnights, nine times nine,
Shall he dwindle, peak, and pine;
Though his bark cannot be lost,
Yet it shall be tempest-toss'd.

(I. iii. 18)

This is the fate of Coleridge's Mariner. He is drained hideously dry ('With throats unslaked, with black lips baked'); his bark is 'tempest-toss'd', an epithet Coleridge had used in an earlier poem to describe a restless soul;[22] he comes to live as an outsider, 'a man forbid'. John Livingston Lowes[23] noted a connection between 'The Ancient Mariner' and *Macbeth* when he explained the choice of simile in the following stanza by pointing out that the phrase 'About, about' belongs to the witches:

About, about, in reel and rout
The death-fires danced at night;

> The water, like a witch's oils,
> Burnt green, and blue and white.

(127)

Lowes refers to the occurrence of 'about, about' a few lines after the passage concerning the master of the Tiger (I. iii. 34) and proceeds to compare the two mariners. He ignores the occurrence in the theatrically popular song (written by Middleton) in the fourth act of the play, which was surely Coleridge's immediate inspiration. The cauldron scene is not only more contextually relevant to the images of dancing and witch's oils, it also provides a spectrum of colours: 'Black Spirits and white, / Red Spirits and gray . . . A round, a round, a round, about, about' (IV. i. 44 t.a.).

Nevertheless, the parallels with the master of the Tiger are extremely powerful. 'Sleep shall neither night nor day / Hang upon his pent-house lid' is especially important. The Mariner is unable to sleep until he is released from the albatross; he then speaks of the gentleness and restorative power of sleep. In *Macbeth* it is not only the ship-master who is condemned to sleeplessness; as was seen in connection with the phrase 'no more', the idea of sleeplessness recurs throughout the play, culminating in the sleep-walking scene. Two poles are marked by 'Duncan is in his grave; / After life's fitful fever he sleeps well' (III. ii. 22) and Macbeth's series of 'sleep no more's. The images of sleep in that outburst worked profoundly on Coleridge's consciousness:

> the innocent sleep,
> Sleep that knits up the ravell'd sleave of care,
> The death of each day's life, sore labour's bath,
> Balm of hurt minds, great nature's second course,
> Chief nourisher in life's feast.

(II. ii. 33)

The influence of these lines is apparent in several poems, including 'Dejection' ('Cover her, gentle Sleep! with wings of Healing').[24] Macbeth's sleeplessness comes across most vividly in 'The Pains of Sleep', where 'Sleep, the wide blessing, seemed to me / Distemper's worst calamity'. That poem's slide into the matter of *Macbeth* reaches a climax with its lines on 'natures deepliest stained with sin', which employ the image of a tempest-tossed mind and then a number of the play's key words, 'hell', 'horror', 'deed':

For aye entempesting anew
The unfathomable hell within
The horror of their deeds to view.

(*CPW* i. 390)

The master of the Tiger resembles the Ancient Mariner as well as Macbeth. Given this similarity, and a number of other verbal echoes,[25] we may propose broader comparisons between the respective protagonists of playwright and poet of the supernatural. Coleridge, who was all too familiar with 'terrible dreams / That shake us nightly' (*Mac* III. ii. 18), wrote of the passage in which this phrase occurs, 'Ever and ever mistaking the anguish of conscience for fears of selfishness, and thus, as a punishment of that selfishness, plunging deeper in guilt and ruin' (*SC* i. 68). It could as well have been written of his own mariner. One could imagine the poem's marginal gloss reading 'The Mariner hath murther'd the Albatross, the innocent Albatross, and therefore he shall sleep no more'. Both Macbeth and the Mariner pay the price of deliberately committing a crime that upsets the order of nature. A marginal note on Macbeth's lines about how blood will have blood enunciates a principle at the heart of 'The Ancient Mariner': 'Who by guilt tears himself live-asunder from nature is himself in a preternatural state; no wonder, therefore, if [he is] inclined to all superstition and faith in the preternatural' (*SC* i. 68).

Both Macbeth and the Mariner are men of strong imagination. To the Romantic way of reading, each of them images the poetic consciousness. The correspondence goes some way towards explaining Macbeth's presence in 'Kubla Khan', Coleridge's most compressed expression and embodiment of creativity. A nexus of verbal details establishes an analogy between Macbeth and the poet-figure of the second section of 'Kubla Khan'. The style of 'Fire, Famine, and Slaughter' shows that Coleridge was eminently aware of the role of repetition in the language of the weird sisters. In 'Kubla Khan', the general admonition 'Beware! Beware!' replaces those specific warnings 'beware Macduff, / Beware the Thane of Fife' (IV. i. 71). 'Weave a circle round him thrice' suggests witches bringing a man under their spell. Magic traditionally does things three times; the word thrice begins and sets the tone of the cauldron scene in *Macbeth*.[26] But if one is to think of the figure in the circle as a Macbeth, one should also recognize that the weaver of the circle may be a Prospero—'They all enter the circle which Prospero had made, and there stand charm'd'

(*Tp* v. i. 57 s.d.)! The combination of *Macbeth* and *The Tempest* suggests that the poet has a quasi-magical power which may be malign or benign.

That the inspired figure is an image of the poet is shown by his 'flashing eyes' and 'floating hair'. Livingston Lowes argues that Coleridge's image combines descriptions of the fanatic devotees of Aloadine the Mahometan in *Purchas his Pilgrimage* and the Abyssinian king Tecla Haimanout in James Bruce's *Travels to Discover the Source of the Nile* (*Road to Xanadu*, 345). These may be *sources* for the image, but we cannot suppose that Coleridge is *alluding* to Purchas and Bruce, bringing them into play in his poem. For Coleridge's reader, the picture that would immediately be conjured up is that of an inspired poet, as visualized in the *Ion* of Plato (where, as in 'Kubla Khan', he is associated with milk and honey: *Ion*, 534a–b), in countless eighteenth-century poems on poesy (Gray's 'Bard' has 'haggard eyes' and 'hoary hair' that 'Stream'd, like a meteor'), and most famously in Theseus' 'The poet's eye, in a fine frenzy rolling'. The allusion enables the reader to identify the figure as a poet and the subject of the second section of 'Kubla Khan' as that of building a paradise like Kubla's through the creative power of poetic imagination. But to build a paradise through poetry instead of religion is potentially to engage with the daemonic.[27] This accounts for the parallel with Macbeth. We are to view the inspired poet with 'holy dread'; he is a special kind of man, marked off from the rest of humanity—'And all should cry, Beware! Beware!'

Coleridge's poems of intense imaginative vision consistently move towards the supernatural and in so doing move towards the supernatural parts of Shakespeare. By invoking the plays as authorities, using them as props, Coleridge avoids the problems inherent in their inimitability. The only stylistic and metrical comparisons that might be made would be between the four-stress lines of the songs in the magical plays and the rhythms of, say, the conclusion to part two of 'Christabel' and the second section of 'Kubla Khan'. Coleridge much admired Shakespeare's songs: he undertook a metrical analysis of the fairy's song, 'Over hill, over dale', in the second act of *A Midsummer Night's Dream* and extravagantly praised Puck's 'Now the hungry lion roars . . .' (*SC* i. 91–2). But the songs cannot be said to constitute Shakespeare's major achievement in verse. That achievement was to give to iambic pentameter the fluency, flexibility, and variety of the speaking voice. It was in the conversation poems, not the supernatural ones, that Coleridge found a truly Shakespearean idiom.

So it is that in 'This Lime-tree Bower my Prison' there is a very different transformation of *Macbeth*. The poem ends with one of Coleridge's loveliest images:

> when the last rook
> Beat its straight path along the dusky air
> Homewards, I blest it! deeming its black wing
> (Now a dim speck, now vanishing in light)
> Had crossed the mighty Orb's dilated glory,
> While thou stood'st gazing; or, when all was still,
> Flew creeking o'er thy head, and had a charm
> For thee, my gentle-hearted Charles, to whom
> No sound is dissonant which tells of Life.

> (*CPW* i. 181)

The rook is traditionally a gregarious bird, unlike the solitary crow. It acts here as an image for the poet, freeing himself from his isolation in the lime-tree bower and flying to his friends on the wings of his own poetry. The imaginative process of the poem has joined him to his friends, transformed him from crow to rook. The distinction between rook and crow is made by William Empson in his brilliant analysis of the image on which Coleridge is writing a variation, Macbeth's 'Light thickens, and the crow / Makes wing to th' rooky wood' (III. ii. 50):

Rooks live in a crowd and are mainly vegetarian; *crow* may be either another name for a *rook*, especially when seen alone, or it may mean the solitary Carrion crow. This subdued pun is made to imply here that Macbeth, looking out of the window, is trying to see himself as a murderer, and can only see himself as in the position of the *crow* . . . that he is anxious, at bottom, to be at one with the other *rooks*, not to murder them; that he can no longer, or that he may yet, be united with the rookery; and that he is murdering Banquo in a·forlorn attempt to obtain peace of mind.[28]

Coleridge has learnt from Shakespeare precision in his handling of an image of the bird's flight across the evening sky. 'Now a dim speck, now vanishing in light' is extremely delicate, while the more Miltonic tone of the following line, with its 'mighty Orb's dilated glory', is singularly inappropriate. But Coleridge does not copy Shakespeare's effect; he translates a sinister image into a benign one. *Macbeth* is a play of curses; Coleridge blesses the rook.

There is a further rich variation. Rooks are creatures of foreboding—slightly later in *Macbeth* they are invoked in the context of
augury. They are thus associated with another large black bird of
foreboding, that mentioned by Lady Macbeth early in the play,

> The raven himself is hoarse
> That croaks the fatal entrance of Duncan
> Under my battlements.
>
> (I. v. 38)

Coleridge's rook does not croak: it 'creeks'. To 'creek' can mean to
turn or wind; it was once synonymous with 'to croak'; but Coleridge's
primary reference is to the sound of the bird's wingbeat. He observes
in a footnote that Bartram had noted the same circumstance of the
Savanna Crane, ' "When these Birds move their wings in flight, their
strokes are slow, moderate and regular; and even when at a considerable distance or high above us, we plainly hear the quill-feathers:
their shafts and webs upon one another creek as the joints or working
of a vessel in a tempestuous sea" ' (*CPW* i. 181 n.). The rook has a
'charm' in two senses. It exerts a benign not a malign spell because it
tells of life, and it is charming—delightful—in its imperfection, its
laboured movement, its effortfulness that is somehow human.

There may be another Shakespearean charm in 'This Lime-tree
Bower'.[29] The word 'tempestuous' in Coleridge's footnote is suggestive: Ariel tells Prospero that thanks to his magic Alonso, Sebas-
tian, and Antonio are

> all prisoners, sir,
> In the lime-grove which weather-fends your cell;
> They cannot boudge till your release.
>
> (*Tp* v. i. 9)

(Modern texts print the Folio's 'line-grove' but eighteenth-century
editions, including those owned by Coleridge, follow Rowe's emen-
dation to 'lime-grove'.) Coleridge seems to have scrutinized this
passage carefully: in 'Dejection', a poem much concerned with
weather, protection, and isolation, we find the phrase 'weather-
fended Wood'. 'Weather-fends' is a Shakespearean coinage, used on
this one occasion alone. It does not seem to have appeared again until
William Crowe borrowed it in his topographical poem, *Lewesdon Hill*
(1788); Coleridge was the next to take possession of it. The presence
in his mind of *The Tempest*, act five, scene one, as he was writing

'This Lime-tree Bower' is further suggested by the possible echo of Ariel's 'Where the bee sucks, there suck I, / In a cowslip's bell I lie' (v. i. 88 ff.) in 'Yet still the solitary humble-bee / Sings in the bean-flower' (58). In this instance, the borrowings exercise strong variations on their originals, for Prospero's rough magic is inverted: Coleridge is imprisoned, not the group; art sets the poet free.

Both the speech in which Macbeth watches the rook and the final lines of 'This Lime-tree Bower' are notable for their enjambement; the unfolding of clauses and images reveals the working of the character's (or the poet's) imagination. Shakespearean blank verse enacts movements of mind and inner voice. The term 'conversation poem', Coleridge's description of 'The Nightingale' which applies as well to his other blank verse meditations of the late 1790s, is valuable: Coleridge addresses the reader as Shakespearean characters in soliloquy address their audience.

'Frost at Midnight' is like a Shakespearean soliloquy; Coleridge's silent babe acts as an audience on stage of the sort that is frequent in the plays. The poem is a triumph of unallusiveness; its assimilation of a Shakespearean manner is such that terms like imitation, allusion, and even echo are not relevant. As in many other poems, an essentially Shakespearean tone is masked by other intertextual references— to the sooty film upon the grate in Cowper's 'The Winter Evening' (*The Task*, iv. 291 ff.) and to a Miltonic simile, 'in populous city pent' (*PL* ix. 445). But if the poem is juxtaposed with Bolingbroke's monologue in the third act of *2 Henry IV*, the more profound resemblance will be felt:

> The inmates of my cottage, all at rest,
> Have left me to that solitude, which suits
> Abstruser musings: save that at my side
> My cradled infant slumbers peacefully.
> 'Tis calm indeed! so calm, that it disturbs
> And vexes meditation with its strange
> And extreme silentness;

> (*CPW* i. 240)

> How many thousand of my poorest subjects
> Are at this hour asleep! O sleep! O gentle sleep!
> Nature's soft nurse, how have I frighted thee,
> That thou no more wilt weigh my eyelids down,
> And steep my senses in forgetfulness?

> Why rather, sleep, liest thou in smoky cribs,
> Upon uneasy pallets stretching thee,
> And hush'd with buzzing night-flies to thy slumber . . .

(III. i. 4)

Although Coleridge frequently went to Shakespeare for images connected with sleep and waking, it should be repeated that this is a matter not of influence or allusion—Coleridge's thatch that 'Smokes in
the sun-thaw' is an observation of nature, not a direct reference to
Shakespeare's 'smoky cribs'—but of tonal similarity, of each poet's
capacity to evoke the meditativeness of a man who muses while others
sleep, to move between the mind within and the world without.
Coleridge's language is, as usual, more abstract than Shakespeare's,
though in turning to the particular—the child, the film on the
grate—he succeeds in saving his poem from abstruseness, in grounding it, as Shakespeare grounds Bolingbroke's soliloquy by means of
references to poor man and ship-boy. The best effects in each piece
are those that are both intense and new. ' 'Tis calm indeed!', a mere
assertion, is weaker than Shakespeare's 'calmest and most stillest
night' (III. i. 28), which gains much of its force from the double
superlative that is, strictly speaking, tautological. Coleridge is at his
strongest with 'extreme silentness', another image intensified beyond
the demands of logic (silence is silence and cannot strictly be
extreme).

What joins the two passages is a shared sense of the speaking voice
and of process, of the mind at work. Bolingbroke proceeds from
'asleep' to 'sleep' to 'gentle sleep' to the metaphor of 'Nature's soft
nurse'; Coleridge moves from 'slumbers peacefully' to 'calm indeed'
to 'so calm', then introduces another vein of repetition and expan-
sion in

> sea, hill, and wood,
> This populous village! Sea, and hill, and wood,
> With all the numberless goings on of life,
> Inaudible as dreams!

Bolingbroke is concerned with the self in relation to office, Coleridge
with the self. By making the poet the protagonist he is marking himself
off from the selfless Shakespeare even as he finds a manner that is
worthy of him. 'Dejection' is Shakespearean in terms of both its verbal
intensity and its quiet assimilation of certain moments and images

from the plays that were special to the Romantic imagination. But it is desperately unshakespearean in its introspection and lack of self-confidence. Since the poem's relationship with Shakespeare works in the poet's creative processes, not on the surface of the text, I shall quote from its original version, a verse-letter to Sara Hutchinson (*CL* ii. 790–8). When it is published as 'Dejection: An Ode', first in the *Morning Post*, then much later in *Sibylline Leaves*, its literariness becomes a matter of more observable relationships—with the ode tradition, with the ballad (the final text begins with an extract from, not merely a reference to, 'The grand old Ballad of Sir Patrick Spence'). The removal of an allusion to 'Peter Bell' ('dear William's Sky Canoe') and the change from 'William' to 'Otway' as author of the 'tender Lay' of an infant in the wild are symptomatic of how Coleridge replaces personal poetic relationships with those that have meaning in the public domain.[30] Even in the private 'Letter' form of the poem, Shakespeare's participation is veiled and internalized; as in so many Romantic poems, the overt allusion, signalled by quotation marks, is to Milton: 'sky-gazing in "ecstatic fit"' (cf. Milton's 'The Passion', 42).

Coleridge watches the sunset's 'peculiar Tint of Yellow Green' with an exquisite eye for colour. But his own judgement on his visual powers contrasts sharply with what would be supposed from his fine observation: 'And still I gaze—and with how blank an eye!' (34). 'See better,' Kent says to Lear, 'and let me still remain / The true blank of thine eye' (I. i. 158). Coleridge adapts the theme of sight and feeling which reaches its climax in *Lear* with Gloucester's 'I see it feelingly' (IV. vi. 149), a line as powerful in its effect on the Romantics as was Milton's 'darkness visible'. In 'Dejection', sight and feeling are divided: 'I see, not feel, how beautiful they are' (43). What is physical as well as mental in *Lear*—Gloucester literally feels because he can no longer see—is a matter of mood in 'Dejection'. Shakespeare is more tactile than Coleridge in that Kent's 'blank' is a technical term meaning the centre of a target. Both eye and target take the form of concentric circles. The image is part of a sequence of references to archery ('The bow is bent and drawn, make from the shaft', 'Let it fall rather, though the fork invade / The region of my heart') which darkly foreshadows the blinding of Gloucester—behind the exchange there lurks an image, never explicitly brought forward, of an arrow in the eye. Coleridge's blank eye does not do so much work; it evokes a state of mind and nothing more.

Later in the poem, Coleridge recalls a time when his blankness was tempered:

> Yes, dearest Sara! yes!
> There *was* a time when tho' my path was rough,
> The Joy within me dallied with Distress;
> And all Misfortunes were but as the Stuff
> Whence Fancy made me Dreams of Happiness.
>
> (231)

'There was a time' is a fairly obvious way of introducing nostalgia. 'Time was when . . .' is a frequent locution in Cowper's evocations in *The Task* of a better rural past; 'A time there was, ere England's griefs began' is a typical line in Goldsmith's *The Deserted Village*. Two years before writing 'Dejection', Coleridge used the phrase in a gothic pastiche of Wordsworth entitled 'The Mad Monk'.[31] Wordsworth appears to have taken the pastiche as a compliment, for the lines in question provide material for the first stanza of his 'Ode: Intimations of Immortality'. The following will sound familiar to readers of Wordsworth's ode:

> 'There was a time when earth, and sea, and skies,
>   The bright green vale, and forest's dark recess,
> With all things, lay before mine eyes
>   In steady loveliness:
> But now I feel, on earth's uneasy scene,
>   Such sorrows as will never cease;—
>   I only ask for peace;
> If I must live to know that such a time has been!'
>
> (*CPW* i. 348)

The monk is mad because he murdered a maiden; he harps persistently on the colour red and comes out with such exclamations as '*I struck the wound,*—this hand of mine!' He is another of Coleridge's Macbeth-figures. This suggests that the source of 'There was a time . . . such a time has been' is Macbeth's 'The time has been, my senses would have cool'd / To hear a night-shriek . . .' (V. v. 10), which occurs immediately before what might be termed his 'mortality ode', 'To-morrow, and to-morrow, and to-morrow . . .'. 'The Mad Monk' thus acts as an intermediary between Macbeth's mortality ode, Coleridge's dejection ode ('There *was* a time') and Wordsworth's more optimistic immortality ode ('There was a time when meadow, grove, and stream . . .').

In 'Dejection' Coleridge then makes one of his leaps from *Macbeth* to *The Tempest.*[32] With his juxtaposition of 'Stuff' and 'Dreams' he is playing Prospero. A moment in Peacock's *Nightmare Abbey* is apposite here: Flosky, the Coleridge-character, says (presumably with reference to 'The Ancient Mariner' and Coleridge's explanation of how 'Kubla Khan' was composed) 'I am writing a ballad which is all mystery; it is "such stuff as dreams are made of," and is, indeed, stuff made of a dream' (ch. 8). In 'Dejection' it is 'Fancy' that used to make misfortune into the stuff of dreams, but now, Coleridge laments, the 'shaping Spirit of Imagination' is suspended (242–3). Having played Prospero, Coleridge is now Hamlet, who complains of having more offences than he has 'imagination to give them shape' (III. i. 125).[33] Hamlet's self-abnegation in act three scene one is partly ironic; Coleridge's is wholly serious, even morbid. The very echoes of Shakespeare in 'Dejection' reveal the poem to be profoundly un-shakespearean. The absence of irony and comedy are severely limiting. Coleridge's gestures are grand, but sometimes empty—the wind is addressed as an 'Actor, perfect in all tragic Sounds' (198), an image wholly at odds with that of man as a poor player in Macbeth's valediction, and indeed with Wordsworth's version of Jaques's seven ages in 'Immortality'.

Coleridge would have liked to be a Prospero as he took Shakespeare to be ('Prospero, the mighty wizard, whose potent art could not only call up all the spirits of the deep, but the characters as they were and are and will be, seems a portrait of the bard himself': *SC* ii. 253). He succeeds in playing his role when he manipulates the supernatural in 'The Ancient Mariner' and to a lesser extent 'Christabel', when he conjures up a dream-like imaginative creation in 'Kubla Khan', and when his control of voice gives him artistic freedom in 'This Lime-tree Bower' and 'Frost at Midnight'. But ultimately, as he recognized himself, he was a Hamlet—or rather, a part of Hamlet, the introspective part. Bound within the self, restricted to the poetry of self-expression, he could not attain Shakespeare's variety and impersonality. It was not possible to be both Hamlet and Hamlet's creator. The only solution was to stop thinking of oneself as a poet and become the servant of Shakespeare.

Hereafter Coleridge wrote far less poetry and very little enduring poetry. His sense of his own inadequacies as a poet cannot be separated from the enriched awareness of Shakespeare that made him into the most acute critic of the early nineteenth century. On 6

December 1800 he wrote to William Godwin of 'the divinity of Shakespere'; eleven days later he confided to John Thelwall, 'As to Poetry, I have altogether abandoned it, being convinced that I never had the essentials of poetic Genius, and that I mistook a strong desire for original power' (*CL* i. 653, 656). Originality and verbal power were, of course, what he took to be the special qualities of Shakespeare.

As a philosopher, Coleridge began to be exercised by the theory of mind that could be extrapolated from Shakespeare's characters; he dated his turn for philosophical criticism arising from consideration of Hamlet to that crucial year, 1798. As a critic, he began to analyse in more and more detail the ways in which each Shakespearean drama was organized through a structure of language, character, and action into a unified whole—a unity he had rarely achieved in his own poems, so frequently fragmented and, in sharp distinction to Shakespeare's works, egotistic. As a poet, he began to lose confidence and enter into a rapid decline; in 1814 he warned an aspiring poet, one Thomas Curnick, that it was 'scarcely practicable' for a man to write poetry on any subject 'without finding his poem, against his will and without his previous consciousness, a cento of lines that had pre-existed in other works; and this it is which makes poetry so very difficult, because so very easy, in the present day. I myself have for many years past given it up in despair' (*CL* iii. 469–70). In the face of this impasse, Coleridge became a commentator instead of an aspirant: we have Shakespeare's inimitability to thank for some of our best Shakespearean criticism.

4

Wordsworth on Shakespeare

IN his own time, Wordsworth had a reputation for being antipathetic to Shakespeare. There could be no more symbolic starting-point than the occasion recorded by both Leigh Hunt and Charles Cowden Clarke when Wordsworth criticized the repetition of the present participle in a line from *Henry V*, 'The singing masons building roofs of gold' (I. ii. 198): 'This, he said, was a line which Milton would never have written. Mr Keats thought, on the other hand, that the repetition was in harmony with the continued note of the singers, and that Shakspeare's negligence (if negligence it was) had instinctively felt the thing in the best manner.'[1] Not only does this imply that Keats was sympathetic to Shakespeare, Wordsworth to Milton, but it also shows the two poets reconstituting their forebears in their own image. Wordsworth conceives of Milton as a meticulous poet, rejecting cacophonous or awkward lines as he sought to do himself by obsessively revising his own work; Keats's phrase for Shakespeare's manner of composition, 'instinctively felt the thing in the best manner', could as well be Keats writing about himself in one of the letters.

Cowden Clarke describes the incident, then goes on to generalize: 'more than once it has been said that Wordsworth had not a genuine love of Shakespeare: that, when he could, he always accompanied a "*pro*" with his "*con.*," and, Atticus-like, would "just hint a fault and hesitate dislike"' (CCC 150). The balancing of beauties and faults, the belief that 'even Shakspeare himself had his blind sides, his limitations',[2] is indicative of an eighteenth-century strain that runs through Wordsworth's criticism.

The idea that Wordsworth imagined himself to be in the line of Milton rather than Shakespeare is stated most forcefully by Hazlitt. 'Milton is his great idol, and he sometimes dares to compare himself with him', he writes in the *Spirit of the Age* essay on Wordsworth, then continues 'We do not think our author has any very cordial sympathy with Shakespear. How should he? Shakespear was the least of an egotist of any body in the world. [Wordsworth] does not much relish the variety and scope of dramatic composition. "He hates those

interlocutions between Lucius and Caius" ' (*HW* xi. 92). The last
phrase is in quotation marks because Hazlitt believed that Wordsworth
made such a remark at some time; Hazlitt adverts to it on several
occasions, using it as shorthand for Wordsworth's supposed anti-
Shakespearean sentiments.[3] Hazlitt's argument turns on the opposition between Wordsworthian egotism and dramatic impersonality, an
issue that I will discuss when I consider Wordsworth's own remarks
on the relative demands of self-expression and dramatic character.
But at this point we need to ask whether Wordsworth really did hold
the beliefs ascribed to him.

Here it is difficult to weigh the evidence. Many of Wordsworth's
remarks about Shakespeare take the form of *ex cathedra* pronouncements
reverently recorded by men and women who made the pilgrimage to
visit the aged poet at Rydal Mount; they are therefore of less value
than the sharp insights of Hazlitt. The latter had both personal and
intellectual reasons for being critical of Wordsworth, and in this
respect may have used Shakespeare as a weapon, but he was nevertheless closer to the poet's most fertile years. The Wordsworth described in 'My First Acquaintance with Poets', a Macbeth-figure
(' "his face was as a book where men might read strange matters" ')[4]
reading the supernatural *Peter Bell* in the open air, is of more interest
to us than the elderly moralist who complained to Aubrey de Vere
that in his delineations of character Shakespeare 'does not assign as
large a place to religious sentiments as enters into the constitution of
human nature under normal circumstances.'[5]

There are, however, insights to be gleaned from the *obiter dicta* of
the later Wordsworth. J. J. Tayler had tea with him in 1826 and discovered that 'Spenser, Shakspeare, and Milton are his favourites
among the English poets, especially the latter, whom he almost idolises'
(Grosart, iii. 502). Even if ranked below Shakespeare, Milton seems
to have been the poet to whom Wordsworth owed special allegiance:
'To Shakespeare he paid cordial and reverent homage, styling him,
as I remember, the unapproached first of poets. Homer, whose
Odyssey he oftenest quoted, he placed second, and Dante, I think,
third. For Milton he had a special sympathy and admiration.'[6] In
contrast to Keats and Hazlitt, who frequently viewed Milton with
awe but Shakespeare with affection, Wordsworth here imagines
Shakespeare to be the more distant, the less recoverable of the
two—in another version of this reminiscence, the epithet is changed
to 'unapproachable'.[7]

As far as the chronology of preference is concerned, a Mrs Davy recorded in 1847 that Wordsworth said Milton's poetry 'was earlier a favourite with him than that of Shakspeare' (Grosart, iii. 457). But Wordsworth's memory was hazy by this time (in the Fenwick notes he misdated many of his own poems) and, besides, such statements of preference are not necessarily borne out by poetic practice: we will see that although Blake claimed that Milton loved him in childhood while Shakespeare in riper years gave him his hand, his early songs are steeped in the language of Shakespeare. Despite his subsequent professions of allegiance to Milton, in 1812 Wordsworth associated himself with Shakespeare on the matter of '*intense* poetical feeling'. More equivocally, he claimed later that he 'could write like Shakespeare if he had a mind'; 'So you see nothing is wanting but the mind', was Lamb's wry comment on this (*HCR* 93, 466–7).

Wordsworth's strongest rebuttal of the commonplace that he had little sympathy with Shakespeare has often been overlooked, perhaps because until recently it has only been available in manuscript. Barron Field wrote, but did not publish, a memoir of Wordsworth; the latter looked through it and found Hazlitt's judgement in *The Spirit of the Age* quoted at length. He replied in the margin: 'This is monstrous! I extol Chaucer and others because the world at large knows little or nothing of their merits. Modesty and deep feeling [—] how superfluous a thing it is to praise Shakespere [—] have kept me often and almost habitually silent upon that subject. Who thinks it necessary to praise the Sun?'[8] 'Deep feeling' suggests that there was an intensity about Wordsworth's response to Shakespeare, 'modesty' that it may not at first be apparent. If it is a subject about which he was habitually reticent, unusual weight may have to be attached to slight hints and covert allusions. The metaphor of the sun converts the belief (voiced by critics from Dryden onwards) that Shakespeare has the force of nature into the bold claim that he *is* a force of nature. Here, in sharp contrast to the occasion recorded by Leigh Hunt and Cowden Clarke, Wordsworth comes close to Keats's yoking of 'Sun Moon and Stars and passages of Shakspeare'.

Two letters to John Britton, an antiquarian and devoted Shakespearean, reinforce the evidence provided by the Field manuscript. In March 1816 Wordsworth refused a request by Britton for a poem commemorating the birth of Shakespeare; he gave as one of his reasons that 'I should have before me the tender exclamation of Milton, "Dear Son of Memory, great Heir of Fame, / What need'st

Thou such *weak* witness of thy Name" ' (*MY* ii. 289). (Milton's sonnet
on Shakespeare is also used powerfully at the end of the first *Essay on
Epitaphs*, when Wordsworth is considering the difficulty of paying
adequate tribute to 'the mighty benefactors of mankind': *WPr* ii. 61.)
Some months later the persistent Britton sent Wordsworth a print of
Shakespeare, which prompted him to ask 'who could shape out to
himself features and a countenance that would appear worthy of such
a mind'? (*MY* ii. 339). One begins to see that a recurring Wordsworthian theme is the impossibility of articulating any conception
that does justice to Shakespeare's genius.

For Hazlitt, Keats, and Byron quotation provided a solution to this
problem, a way of assimilating Shakespeare into one's own discourse.
To a lesser extent, this is also true of Wordsworth. Although Shakespearean and other quotations are only occasionally woven into his
letters and prose works, as they are so persistently in those of the
younger writers, Wordsworth was quick to deny the allegation that
'he never quotes other poems than his own' (*HCR* 486). In another
annotation to Field he claimed that he 'could repeat with a little previous rummaging of [his] memory several 1000 lines of Pope' (Field,
37 n.). In the early years he could apparently do the same with the
three poets whom, according to Tayler, he most admired. Not merely
were the names of Shakespearean characters 'household term[s]' in
his childhood (see *Prel.* vii. 527–9), but according to Wordsworth's
nephew, 'the Poet's father set him very early to learn portions of the
works of the best English poets by heart, so that at an early age he
could repeat large portions of Shakspeare, Milton, and Spenser.'[9]

Such facility in the art of quotation sets Wordsworth and his readers
apart from us; this, along with our way of reading texts in themselves
rather than in the context of a received body of commonly possessed
earlier texts, is why modern readers often overlook significant allusions and echoes. Another of R. P. Graves's reminiscences is helpful
here; he writes of an Irishman who spent much time with Wordsworth
and was 'the object to him of a peculiar psychological interest and
admiration':

I refer to Mr Archer, son of a citizen of Dublin, who with no mean amount of
original power, had a passion for poetic literature, and possessed so remarkable a memory, that he knew by heart the works of all the classical English
poets, and on the prompting of a phrase from Wordsworth, could take up the
passage on the instant, and recite it in continuation *ad libitum*. (*Afternoon
Lectures*, 282)

I think that Archer was of 'peculiar psychological interest' to Wordsworth because he represented a certain kind of ideal reader; the game where Wordsworth provides 'the prompting of a phrase' and Archer picks up its context is analogous to the process in many of his poems whereby a phrase is quoted from Milton or Shakespeare, and the reader is asked to bring the context of the original to bear on the passage into which it is appropriated.

Wordsworth owned copies of Enfield's *The Speaker*, Knox's *Elegant Extracts*, and Bysshe's *Art of English Poetry*, each of which contains a large number of Shakespearean purple passages designed by the compilers to be learned and quoted readily.[10] Anybody likely to read Wordsworth would have encountered these books in school or at home; the poet could expect his readers to have the best-known parts of the English classics at their fingertips. Since such crucial passages as 'The Poet's eye', 'The cloud-capt towers', Macbeth's dagger, the *Hamlet* ghost scenes, and Queen Mab were included in both Enfield and Knox, they would be easily recognized by nearly all readers.

It is hard to determine precisely when and in what form Wordsworth got to know his Shakespeare. He owned four editions of the plays, two of the poems, and one of the sonnets.[11] Since his library included editions of the plays dated 1767, 1790, and 1796, it is fair to assume that a lot of his reading was done before and during the 'great decade', and from original texts as well as books of extracts. Dorothy read extensively in Shakespeare, particularly at times in 1800 and 1802 when William was away.[12] Brother and sister may have talked about the plays, though there are few direct references to Wordsworth reading Shakespeare. On 5 May 1802 Dorothy 'read The Lover's Complaint to Wm in bed', and three days later she read *Henry V* in the orchard at Dove Cottage while 'William lay on his back on the seat' (*Journals*, 121, 123). Early in 1804 William read *Hamlet* and Dorothy wrote to Coleridge, 'I am about to read Shakespeare through, and have read many of the plays' (*EY* 451).

Did Wordsworth also get to know Shakespeare in the theatre? There is little evidence in this area. A reference in a notebook poem to Hamlet 'in a barn', along with a recollection in *The Prelude* of going as a child to 'a country-playhouse, some rude barn / Tricked out for that proud use' (*1850* vii. 449), imply that strolling players visited Hawkshead during Wordsworth's schooldays, but no record exists to provide details of their repertory. As an adult, Wordsworth probably went with Dorothy to see Mrs Siddons in *The Merchant of Venice* at

Drury Lane in December 1797 and seems to have attended productions of *Julius Caesar*, *Romeo and Juliet*, and *Richard II* in London between 1812 and 1815.[13]

One thing we do know, however, is that Wordsworth expressed
considerable interest in the phenomenon of Master Betty, the child
actor who became the nine days' wonder of the London stage in the
early years of the new century. On Christmas Day 1804—the year,
that is, in which he completed his 'Ode: Intimations of Immortality
from Recollections of Early Childhood', with its 'little Actor'—
Wordsworth wrote to ask Sir George Beaumont's opinion of Betty.
He was sceptical of the Young Roscius's capacity to 'manage a
Character of Shakespear', but hoped that the boy might 'rescue the
English theatre from the infamy that has fallen upon it' (*EY* 519). On
the same day, Dorothy wrote in almost identical terms to Lady Beaumont (*EY* 520).

Beaumont sent back an 'excellent Letter about the young Roscius'
but it arrived at the worst possible time, shortly after the death of
Wordsworth's beloved brother, John (*EY* 548). It was not until May
1805 that he felt able to write again to Beaumont about Betty; when
he did so, he produced his fullest statement about his (lack of)
knowledge of Shakespeare on the stage. The passage may be allowed
to speak for itself, though we should note in particular the emphasis
on the 'spirit' of Shakespeare and on *Hamlet*, especially act one scene
five—and the opinion that Shakespeare sometimes writes badly:

I wish much to hear your further opinion of the young Roscius, above all of
his Hamlet it is certainly impossible that he should understand the character,
that is the composition of the character. But many of the sentiments that are
put into Hamlet's mouth, he may be supposed to be capable of feeling, and to
a certain degree of entering into the spirit of some of the situations. I never
saw Hamlet acted my self nor do I know what kind of play they make of it. I
think I have heard that some parts which I consider as among the finest are
omitted; in particular, Hamlet's wild language after the Ghost has dis-
appeared. The Players have taken intolerable Liberties with Shakespear's
Plays, especially with Richard the Third, which though a character admirably
conceived, and drawn, is in some scenes bad enough in Shakespear himself,
but the play, as it is now acted, has always appeared to me a disgrace to the
English stage. Hamlet I suppose is treated by them with more reverence; they
are both characters far, far above the abilities of any actor whom I have ever
seen. Henderson was before my time, and of course Garrick. (*EY* 587)

This is not an attack on the principle of acting Shakespeare, but on
particular contemporary conditions. Wordsworth might not have

made it after the advent of Kean or if Shakespeare had been acted in texts closer to the original. But, given the ignorance of and antipathy to the stage expressed here, any conclusions about Wordsworth's Shakespeare must be based firmly on his reading of the plays.

Wordsworth gained a thorough grounding in the plays in his early years—not only did his father make him learn extensive passages, but in *The Prelude* we see him reading poetry for pleasure as both a boy and a young man—then probably re-read and discussed them with Dorothy in the early 1800s. It is clear from Dorothy's *Journal* that in the years 1800 to 1803 William was also reading Chaucer, Spenser, and Milton.[14] Having written the very contemporary—though surprisingly allusive—*Lyrical Ballads*, he turned to the national classics in order to school himself for the completion of his epic task, the philosophical *Recluse* and its supporting poem on the growth of the poet's mind.

The importance which Wordsworth attached to the English classics at this time is clear from his first letter to De Quincey in which he says that, gratified as he may be by the young man's 'high admiration' of his writings, he would be sorry indeed 'to stand in the way of the proper influence of other writers': 'You will know that I allude to the great names of past times, and above all to those of our own Country' (29 July 1803, *EY* 400). In the 1820s Wordsworth associated four poets in particular with England and also recommended to an aspiring poet that he should study them in detail (*LY* i. 402, 284). They are, naturally enough, the four with whom he schooled himself: 'When I began to give myself up to the profession of a poet for life, I was impressed with a conviction, that there were four English poets whom I must have continually before me as examples—Chaucer, Shakspeare, Spenser, and Milton. These I must study, and equal *if I could*; and I need not think of the rest' (*Memoirs*, ii. 470). When I turn to Wordsworth's poems, I shall discuss some of the effects of Shakespeare being 'continually before' him as one of his examples. Despite—or because of—one attempt to 'equal' him in formal terms, Wordsworth came to realize that he was indeed right to 'fear competition' (*HCR* 776) with Shakespeare, and in most of his approaches to the plays used allusion to turn competition into implied collaboration.

The influence of Milton on Wordsworth has been discussed at length by both conventional 'source-hunting' scholars and psychologically oriented 'Bloomian' critics. But the other three mighty examples remain neglected. This is especially surprising in the case of Shakespeare, for not only is his supremacy unquestioned in the 1800

preface to the *Lyrical Ballads*, but in the major addition of 1802 his
authority is of considerable importance. Furthermore, in the essay supplementary to the preface of 1815, Wordsworth answers those critics
who imagined he was wholly hostile to poetic tradition, concerned only
with rustic life and his own feelings. A reading of the prefaces with
Shakespeare in view provides both new insights into Wordsworth's
poetic theory and an approach to the question of literary allusion and
verbal echo in his poetic practice.

I have pointed out that many of the major late eighteenth- and early
nineteenth-century discussions of poetry, from Kames's *Elements of
Criticism* to Coleridge's *Biographia*, make extensive use of Shakespeare,
adducing passages from the plays as authoritative examples to substantiate general arguments. Wordsworth's 1800 preface, in contrast,
only mentions Shakespeare three times. Two of these references set
Shakespeare up as an ideal, but they do so in a way that is no more
than conventional: he can command pathos without being 'pathetic
beyond the bounds of pleasure'; the strongest indictment of contemporary taste is that his works have been almost displaced by 'sickly
and stupid German Tragedies' (*WPr* i. 146, 128).
   Perhaps because the Wordsworths were reading and thinking about
Shakespeare between 1800 and 1802, he has a more central, though
still unobtrusive (and infrequently remarked upon), place in the 1802
version of the preface. The principal addition is the long passage concerning the question 'What is a Poet?' As Coleridge and Hazlitt will
do when asking similar questions in the *Biographia* and the lecture 'On
Poetry in General', Wordsworth answers by invoking Shakespeare.
But he only does so implicitly, possibly because the kind of poetry he
is writing is on the surface so very different from Shakespeare's. A
poet, says Wordsworth, 'has a greater knowledge of human nature,
and a more comprehensive soul, than are supposed to be common
among mankind' (*WPr* i. 138). His readers would surely have recognized the allusion to that most famous of all paragraphs on Shakespeare, Dryden's 'To begin, then, with Shakespeare: he was the man
who of all modern, and perhaps ancient poets, had the largest and
most comprehensive soul.' Where Dryden begins with Shakespeare,
Wordsworth proceeds to the poet in general, but in alluding to Dryden
brings Shakespeare to the fore of his reader's mind. He is thus able to
say towards the end of his discussion, 'Emphatically may it be said of
the Poet, as Shakspeare hath said of man, "that he looks before and

after" ' (i. 141). The quotation is from *Hamlet* (IV. iv. 37). For Wordsworth, the poet is a special kind of man; Shakespeare is a special kind of poet, so what he says of man may fittingly be said of the poet, especially as he says it through the mouth of Hamlet, his 'type' of the Romantic poet.

Wordsworth goes on to characterize the poet by his 'disposition to be affected more than other men by absent things as if they were present' (i. 138). In this respect Shakespeare is the exemplary poet; Wordsworth may be recalling Johnson's famous remark in the preface about Shakespeare's capacity to approximate the remote; he may also have discussed the matter with Coleridge, who, as we have seen, was to list 'the choice of subjects very remote from the private interests and circumstances of the writer himself' among the specific symptoms of poetic power elucidated in his analysis of Shakespeare's *Venus and Adonis*.

It is also in the addition of 1802 that Wordsworth discusses 'the dramatic parts of composition' (*WPr* i. 142). Here his relationship with Shakespeare is more problematic; not being a dramatist himself, he cannot simply set up Shakespeare as the exemplary poet. The passage in question needs to be set in the context of Wordsworth's other remarks about Shakespeare and dramatic form.

Wordsworth admired each of his four presiding geniuses in the English pantheon for different reasons. Although we must not forget the *caveat* that the opinions of the aged laureate may have had little to do with the practice of the radical young poet, two late remarks reveal the quality for which Shakespeare was particularly valued. In 1841 Wordsworth classified the poets for Lady Richardson, 'At the head of the first class I would place Homer and Shakspeare, whose universal minds are able to reach every variety of thought and feeling without bringing their own individuality before the reader. They infuse, they breathe life into every object they approach, but you never find *themselves*' (Grosart, iii. 435). Then two years later he said something similar to Crabb Robinson: 'In Shakespeare and ·Homer we are astonished at the universality of their penetration. They seem to embrace the whole world. Every form and variety of humanity they represent with equal truth' (*HCR* 628). In 1830 Wordsworth said that Homer was 'second to Shakespeare' (*LY* ii. 319) and back in about 1808 he annotated Knight's *Taste* to the effect that the writings of Shakespeare and Milton 'infinitely transcend those of the Greeks'.[15] For the earlier Wordsworth, then, Homer was of secondary importance;

the late *obiter dicta* to which he came closest were the following,
one recorded by John Park and the other by Aubrey de Vere: 'No
writer has ever come near Shakespeare in that highest power, by
which he exhibits Human Nature, apart from any mixture of the
writer's personal feelings' and 'It was well for Shakspeare that he
gave himself to the drama. It was that which forced him to be sufficiently human.'[16] The variety, impersonality, and humanity afforded
by dramatic form were for Wordsworth Shakespeare's greatest
qualities.

These attitudes were commonplace enough. As early as 1753,
Joseph Warton had asserted that only Homer and Shakespeare knew
the heart of man intimately enough to portray all kinds of character
consistently (*CH* iv. 61); Hazlitt and Keats attached enormous
importance to Shakespeare's capacity to 'infuse' himself into his
characters, to annihilate his own being. What is significant in the context of Wordsworth's preface is their implications for the argument
that poetry expresses the self, that 'all good poetry is the spontaneous
overflow of powerful feelings' (*WPr* i. 126).

Hazlitt's remarks in *The Spirit of the Age* and elsewhere show that he
took the Wordsworthian poetic to be incompatible with Shakespeare's
dramatic variety and lack of egotism. Late in life, Wordsworth
himself drew a distinction between the characters in his poems and
those of dramatic authors, arguing that he was distinguished by having 'drawn out into notice' the points in which men *resemble* each
other, while the drama necessarily has to dwell on the differences between them (*LY* iii. 44). It is true that, say, Wordsworth's solitaries
are all very similar and, further, that many poems establish a common ground of sympathy between them and superficially very different figures (Wordsworth and the Leech Gatherer, the Pedlar and
Margaret). This is one of the keys to the humanity of Wordsworth's
poetry. But it is equally true that his characters sometimes seem to be
created in his own image. In this sense, if we accept Coleridge's
terms—Milton 'attracts all forms and things to himself' while Shakespeare 'becomes all things, yet for ever remaining himself'—Wordsworth's is a Miltonic rather than a Shakespearean genius. In a letter to
Lamb about the *Lyrical Ballads*, which is unfortunately lost (we only
have Lamb's paraphrase of it), Wordsworth said that the kind of
'Imagination' to which he aspired 'was not the characteristic of
Shakespeare' but that 'which Milton possessed in a degree far exceed-
ing other Poets' (*EY* 316).

In the 1802 preface Wordsworth asserts that 'it will be the wish of the Poet to bring his feelings near to those of the persons whose feelings he describes, nay, for short spaces of time, perhaps, to let himself slip into an entire delusion, and even confound and identify his own feelings with theirs' (*WPr* i. 138). In this formulation, the poet remains conspicuous by his presence; although he allows himself to be modified by his characters, he does not transform himself into them as Coleridge, Keats, and others imagined the protean Shakespeare to do. This is true of Wordsworth's practice as well as his theory. Coleridge discerned that even in the poems 'in which he purposes to be most dramatic' Wordsworth himself is still speaking; there are few poems in which his own voice 'does not occasionally burst forth' (*BL* ii. 100). For Coleridge, Wordsworth's attempts to be dramatic are often no more than a form of 'ventriloquism' in which 'two [the poet and his character] are represented as talking, while in truth one man only speaks' (*BL* ii. 135). Shakespeare, on the other hand, seems 'characterless, because characteristic': 'The poet lost in his portraits contrasted with the poet as a mere ventriloquist; wonderful union of both in Shakespeare' (*SC* i. 73). Coleridge praises both Shakespeare and Wordsworth for creating characters whose words, even when taken in isolation, are recognizably their author's; the difference is that Wordsworth's characters are sometimes only mouthpieces for their author, while Shakespeare's are never that.

This distinctiveness of voice is a matter of tone and attitude rather than diction; Wordsworth stresses that the dramatic parts of composition should not be 'coloured by a diction of the Poet's own' (*WPr* i. 142). Perhaps he wished to combine a Miltonic tone of moral weightiness with a natural Shakespearean language, English and flexible. During the year in which he made his additions to the preface, he associated Shakespeare with language and Milton with morality in one of his sonnets 'Dedicated to National Independence and Liberty',

> We must be free or die, who speak the tongue
> That Shakespeare spake; the faith and morals hold
> Which Milton held.

> (*WPW* iii. 117)

There are different ways of attempting to achieve Shakespearean language. In the 1800 preface Wordsworth rejects 'phrases and figures of speech which from father to son have long been regarded as the common inheritance of Poets' (*WPr* i. 132), but we will see that he is sometimes guilty of sterile imitation of Shakespearean phraseology; the more valuable 'inheritance' is of a language of sympathy, while the more effective use of 'phrases and figures of speech' is an allusive one which does not attempt to obscure but rather proclaims the progression 'from father to son'.

This metaphor is consistent with Wordsworth's further reflections, in the 1802 version of his appendix on poetic diction, on the use of earlier poets' language. There he complains of poets who 'with the spirit of a fraternity' arrogate 'to themselves as their own' the 'modes of expression' of their predecessors (*WPr* i. 161). The attempt to establish a brotherhood of poets, past and present, means that the language of later poets becomes merely 'poetic' and moves away from the language of men. Wordsworth seeks instead a language 'such as men do use'; Ben Jonson's phrase serves to remind Wordsworth and his readers that this kind of language is to be found in the seventeenth not the eighteenth century, and, further, that the later poet must acknowledge the achievement of his predecessors who, in this sense, are fathers not brothers. Allusion proclaims filiation: by introducing the phrase 'a selection of language really used by men' in the 1802 version of the preface, Wordsworth is alluding to Jonson's 'language, such as men do use' and, in so doing, proclaiming his descent from the Elizabethans.[17]

The importance attached by Wordsworth to the great tradition of English poets is made even clearer by his essays of 1815. In the preface to the edition of his poems published that year, he adopts the strategy of defining the imagination by alluding to Shakespeare. He argues that W. Taylor's definitions in *English Synonyms Discriminated* reduce both imagination and fancy to mere modes of memory, leaving no term to designate 'that faculty of which the Poet is "all compact;" he whose eye glances from earth to heaven, whose spiritual attributes body forth what his pen is prompt in turning to shape' (*WPr* iii. 30). Theseus' lines on 'The poet's eye' were included in *Elegant Extracts* with the heading 'The Power of Imagination' (ii. 25 in 1791 edn.): being virtually Shakespeare's only statement on the subject, they were almost universally treated in the Romantic age as the Bard's own, and therefore the most compelling, definition of the poetic imagination.

Wordsworth then goes on to exemplify the imagination through Shakespeare and Milton (in addition to Virgil). He refers to the

Dover cliff passage in *King Lear*, which has peculiar importance for the Romantics, not only because it offers a sublime precipice but also because it is an example of the power of the poetic imagination—the cliff is not a stage-location, it is created in Gloucester's imagination through the vividness of Edgar's poetry. The particular image quoted by Wordsworth in his 1815 preface is 'half way down / *Hangs* one who gathers samphire' (*WPr* iii. 31). This provides a model for the many precipices in Wordsworth's own poems; that emphasis on the word '*Hangs*' at the beginning of the line is altogether characteristic of the poet who so finely suspends 'hung' at the end of a line in the bird's-nesting scene early in *The Prelude* (i. 341).

It is again important to see Shakespeare and Milton as complementary exemplars; from *Lear* Wordsworth proceeds to a passage in *Paradise Lost* where he finds 'the full strength of the imagination involved in the word *hangs*' (*WPr* iii. 31). Similarly, in discussing Fancy, although his primary example is Shakespeare's Queen Mab, Wordsworth also introduces images from *Paradise Lost*. But Shakespeare is seen as unique in a way that Milton is not. The latter may be a 'grand store-house' of 'enthusiastic and meditative Imagination', but then so are Spenser and the 'prophetic and lyrical parts' of the Bible; when it comes to 'the human and dramatic Imagination', on the other hand, Shakespeare stands alone (iii. 34–7). The quotation used to support this assertion is Lear's 'I tax not you, ye Elements, with unkindness'; Coleridge found in this same passage 'undoubted proof' of Shakespeare's 'Imagination or the power by which one image or feeling is made to modify many others, and by a sort of *fusion to force many into one*' (*CN* iii. 3290, *SC* i. 188). Wordsworth's choice of passage to exemplify fancy also seems to have been influenced by Coleridge's Shakespearean criticism: in one of his 1811–12 lectures he had argued that in Queen Mab 'is to be noted all the fancy of the poet' (*SC* ii. 86). In a looser sense, Shakespeare is the prime figure behind the preface of 1815 in that its fundamental premise, the integral relationship between genius and imagination, is ultimately derived from such works as Gerard's *Essay on Genius* and Duff's *Essay on Original Genius*, which base their arguments on the example of Shakespeare above all other writers.

While the preface to *Lyrical Ballads* emphasizes the poet himself and his use of the language of men, and the 1815 preface sets out to define the poetic imagination, the supplementary essay focuses directly on the literary tradition. Here (*WPr* iii. 68–9) Wordsworth covers his material briskly, almost perfunctorily, uttering a series of common-places: 'Shakspeare stooped to accommodate himself to the People' (an example of the eighteenth-century strain of criticism); Shake-speare's judgement was equal to his genius, he was not ' "a wild irregular genius, in whom great faults are compensated by great beauties" ' (Wordsworth attacks a view that was common in the eighteenth century, but by no means as widespread as he implies); only the Germans have done justice to Shakespeare. Coleridge was understandably annoyed at the last of these claims (*CL* iv. 839). These opinions confirm that Shakespeare was paramount in Words-worth's understanding of the English poetic tradition, and that the accusations of antipathy made by Hazlitt and others were unfounded.

That they are conventional opinions does not mean that Words-worth was incapable of producing original insights into Shakespeare. He spoke perceptively to Klopstock about the dramatic effectiveness of the Fool in *Lear* (*BL* ii. 203) and, in contrast to A. W. Schlegel's wild judgements on the apocryphal plays, judged shrewdly that *Pericles* should be admitted to the canon on 'internal evidence alone' (*LY* i. 648). And only a sensitive reader of the plays could have remarked that Shakespeare avoids excessive passion and pathos by means of tight metrical control (1800 Preface, *WPr* i. 146).

Hazlitt's belief that Wordsworth's egotism sat uneasily with Shake-speare's self-effacing power is, nevertheless, astute. One senses a cer-tain bafflement about a remark of Wordsworth's like 'I cannot account for Shakspeare's low estimate of his own writings' (*Memoirs*, ii. 470), and in the following statement a definite desire to recast the Bard in one's own image: 'Grand thoughts (and Shakspeare must often have sighed over this truth), as they are most naturally and most fitly con-ceived in solitude, so can they not be brought forth in the midst of plaudits, without some violation of their sanctity' (*WPr* iii. 83). It is most unlikely that Shakespeare conceived 'grand thoughts' in solitude (not, at least, the kind of mountain solitude Wordsworth has in mind) and even if he did, one doubts that he lost much sleep over the players' manhandling of them. The parenthesis is a rhetorical trick: it is Words-worth who is sighing.

Hazlitt's and Wordsworth's conceptions of Shakespeare were partly shaped by their own preoccupations. Thus Hazlitt's desire for a wholly impersonal Shakespeare led him to dismiss the sonnets. Wordsworth, however, admired them—in the 'Essay, Supplementary' he gave a long list of those he thought were best—precisely because he imagined they showed a certain self-interest. 'Scorn not the Sonnet', he wrote in one of his own sonnets, 'with this Key / Shakespeare unlocked his heart' (*WPW* iii. 20). As one who saw poetry as the unlocking of the poet's heart, Wordsworth was relieved to find 'evidence' in Shakespeare's sonnets to support his conviction. The result was that he treated as literal what for Shakespeare was primarily literary. 'Scorn not the Sonnet' was first published in 1827; eleven years later, Keats's friend Charles Brown would publish the first full-length book on the subject of *Shakespeare's Autobiographical Poems*. We still have not escaped from wrong-headed biographical readings of the sonnets.

Wordsworth's admiration was, however, qualified: in some marginalia to Anderson's *British Poets* he described the Dark Lady sonnets as 'worse than a puzzle-peg', 'abominably harsh obscure and worthless', but he thought that the others were 'for the most part much better', that they contained 'many fine lines very fine lines and passages' and were 'in many places warm with passion'—but they still had the 'heavy' faults of 'sameness, tediousness, quaintness, and elaborate obscurity'.[18] As on many other occasions, one is acutely conscious of the eighteenth-century Wordsworth. Coleridge initiated a dialogue in the margin to Anderson, replying 'I see no elaborate obscurity and very little quaintness—nor do I know any Sonnets that will bear such frequent reperusal: so rich in metre, so full of Thought and *exquisitest* Diction.' He also used Wordsworth's comments as pretext for a marginal note addressed to his son: 'These Sonnets then, I trust, if God preserve thy Life, Hartley! thou wilt read with a deep Interest, having learnt to love the Plays of Shakespere, co-ordinate with Milton, and subordinate only to thy Bible' (*Marginalia*, 42–3). Co-ordinate with Milton and subordinate only to thy Bible: these last phrases capture beautifully the place held by Shakespeare's plays in the minds of Coleridge and Wordsworth.

As far as influence on Wordsworth's own poetry is concerned, Shakespeare's sonnets are less important than Milton's. There are elements of Shakespearean language in the three sonnets 'To Sleep' published in 1807 (*WPW* iii. 7–9), but the great majority of Wordsworth's many sonnets are Miltonic in both form and tone. Indeed, in the Fenwick notes he says that it was Milton who inspired him to start writing sonnets in 1801: Shakespeare's sonnets are 'fine' but it was from Milton's that he 'took fire' (Grosart, iii. 52–3). Only with Keats did Shakespeare's sonnets have a profound effect on the poetic practice of an English Romantic.

This may be the case with respect to sonnets, but what of Wordsworth's other poems? Though Wordsworth venerated Shakespeare and implicitly built many of his principles around him, any influence on the poems remains hard to detect, especially in comparison with their frequent Miltonic diction. I shall now unravel the Shakespearean thread in the major poems.

5

Shakespeare in Wordsworth

WHEN Sir Walter Scott was editing Dryden, Wordsworth wrote to him advising that the scholar should point out 'passages or authors to which the Poet has been indebted, not in the piddling way of [a] phrase here and phrase there (which is detestable as a general practice) but where the Poet has really had essential obligations either as to matter or manner' (*EY* 642). Perhaps because Wordsworth's own debts to Milton are so manifest and have been so much discussed,[1] his obligations to Shakespeare, both in the way of phrase here and phrase there and as to matter or manner, have generally been ignored. In this chapter I shall consider Shakespeare's presence in Wordsworth's poetry, concentrating on the 'great decade'. Far more echoes are to be found in the first half of Wordsworth's career than in the work of the 1820s and thereafter, when he was less concerned with the poetic imagination. Shakespeare was no great exemplar when it came to the chief preoccupations of the later Wordsworth; one recalls his complaint that characterization in the plays did not sufficiently emphasize 'religious sentiments'. I attach weight to specific echoes because Wordsworth's claim that the borrowing of phrases is a piddling matter should not divert us from the scrutiny of verbal detail. Like Tennyson's indignant remark about source-hunters, it may well be a defensive gesture that unwittingly reveals where the essential obligations lie.

Different preoccupations drew Wordsworth to different plays. *Macbeth* was particularly important to him in the revolutionary and Godwinian 1790s; an allusion woven into a letter of November 1794 shows that he knew the play well by then and saw its political potential (*EY* 135). *Othello* provided him with a model of pathos. Graves records that Wordsworth pronounced 'the most pathetic of human compositions' to be *Othello*, Plato's record of the last days of Socrates, and Walton's life of George Herbert (Grosart, iii. 468); the poem 'Personal Talk', published in 1807, reveals his special affection for the 'personal themes' in the play of 'The gentle Lady, married to the Moor' (*WPW* iv. 74).

King Lear, like *Macbeth*, is a play that influenced the young Wordsworth. Two passages in his first long poem, 'The Vale of Esthwaite',
written before he left Hawkshead, belie the claim made sixty years later
that Milton's poetry was earlier a favourite with him than
Shakespeare's. The following lines, redolent of the Gothic strain in the
early Wordsworth, reveal a potent, if confused, recollection of *Lear*:

> I saw the ghosts and heard the yell
> Of every Briton [   ] who fell
> When Edmund deaf to horror's cries
> Trod out the cruel Brother's eyes
> With [   ] heel and savage scowl

> (*WPW* i. 278).

'The Vale of Esthwaite' also contains an early Wordsworthian precipice
that evokes the cliff-edges of Dover and Elsinore: 'I lov'd to haunt the
giddy steep / That hung loose trembling o'er the deep' (i. 276).
Wordsworth seems to have been led to his Shakespearean vertigo by
the preceding couplet to this, which reads 'But these were poor and
puny joys / Fond sickly Fancy's idle toys'—'idle toys' is a phrase from
Love's Labour's Lost (IV. iii. 168). In the *Descriptive Sketches* there are
'rocks that *tremble o'er the steep*', a 'dizzy' larch, and '*joys* / To mock the
mind with "desperation's *toys*"' (i. 70, my italics)—an overt, clearly
signalled allusion to Horatio's 'toys of desperation' on Elsinore cliff
(*Ham* I. iv. 75).

The possible echo of Elsinore cliff in 'Esthwaite' and the direct
quotation in *Descriptive Sketches* show that as a young man Wordsworth
was also familiar with the first act of *Hamlet*: the ghost scenes will
subsequently be of major importance. In fact, the *Sketches* and *An
Evening Walk*, the first of his substantial poems to be published,
establish Shakespearean allusion as a characteristic Wordsworthian
device. 'Alluding' is the term Wordsworth uses himself with respect
to his appropriations of the language of Spenser and of Horace in *An
Evening Walk* (*WPW* i. 32, 10). Some lines on discord near the end of
the *Sketches* allude self-consciously to the prologue of *Henry V* in that
Wordsworth quotes Shakespeare's 'Famine, Sword, and Fire' in a
footnote to his own 'havoc, Fire and Sword' (*WPW* i. 88; 'havoc' has
slipped in from another passage about the dogs of war, *Caes* III. i.
273). Wordsworth's footnote quotes not merely the words he has
taken from Shakespeare, but the sentence in which they originally

occur; his allusion explicitly activates a Shakespearean *context* as well as Shakespearean language.

There are three notable Shakespearean echoes in *An Evening Walk*. Of the disappearance of the vision of spirits at twilight, Wordsworth writes 'The pomp is fled, and mute the wondrous strains, / No wrack of all the pageant scene remains' (*WPW* i. 32). This is his first allusion to Prospero's lines after the masque of Ceres; this part of *The Tempest* held peculiar sway over the Romantics because it was so intimately bound up with the imagination, the supernatural, and human transience. Another favourite passage, Theseus on the poet's eye, is used in one of the additions to *An Evening Walk* made at Windy Brow in 1794, but not included in the published text. Wordsworth writes of men endowed with special powers of vision, 'To whom a burning energy has given / That other eye which darts thro' earth and heaven' (*WPW* i. 13 t.a.). This is not the only Shakespearean allusion in the Windy Brow additions. In some lines on youth and death we find the phrase 'sensible warm motion': the parallel, both verbal and contextual, to Claudio's speech on death in *Measure for Measure* would not have been missed by Wordsworth's readers had he published the passage (*WPW* i. 7 t.a.; *Meas* III. i. 119).

It may not be coincidental that two of the three noteworthy Shakespearean allusions in *An Evening Walk* occur in rejected passages. The use of words belonging to earlier poets troubled Wordsworth throughout his life. Many 'poetic' phrases in the early works are defensively placed between inverted commas. Editors have failed to trace sources for a number of these; this could be because sometimes there was no source—Wordsworth was merely attempting to disclaim embarrassing poeticisms.

A good illustration of Wordsworth's uncertainty is provided by a slightly later poem, 'O Nightingale'. As we saw with Coleridge, nightingale poems provide the Romantic with peculiar problems regarding the relationship between inherited language and original observation of the natural world. Wordsworth's poem, composed in 1807, begins 'O Nightingale! thou surely art / A Creature of a fiery heart' (*WPW* ii. 214). When the parodic *Simpliciad* was published and jibed at Wordsworth's 'drunken larks and fiery nightingales', he changed the phrase to 'ebullient heart' (see *WPW* ii. 506). This is how it appeared in the edition of 1815, but it was hardly an improvement so he reverted to the original adjective in the editions of 1820–36, then finally found a compromise in 1845 by placing 'fiery heart' in quotation marks to point out that if anybody were to be criticized for the epithet it should be Shakespeare, for it is a phrase from *3 Henry VI* (I. iv. 87).

The quotation marks in the second line of 'O Nightingale' provide an example in miniature of a major problem. A poet with ambitions of originality and spontaneity finds himself in difficulty when using the language of an earlier poet. This difficulty is especially apparent in the medium of blank verse drama—one recalls Goethe's relief at not having to write poetic drama in English.

The close relationship between Shakespeare and *The Borderers*, Wordsworth's only play, immediately becomes apparent from the prefatory essay prefixed to the manuscript version of 1796–7. Not only is there an explicit reference to Iago, but the essay as a whole is an attempt to explain Rivers, the villain, in psychological terms, precisely as critics of the second half of the eighteenth century had attempted to explain Shakespeare's characters. As the play itself is an imitation of Shakespeare, so the prefatory essay is an imitation of Richardson's *Philosophical Analysis and Illustration of some of Shakespeare's Remarkable Characters* or Whately's *Remarks on some of the Characters of Shakespeare.*[2]

The character described in the preface is a 'moral sceptic' who seeks relief from his own dark nature through 'action and meditation'; 'his energies are most impressively manifested in works of devastation', he has realized that 'power is much more easily manifested in destroying than in creating'. This could well have come from an account of one of Shakespeare's machiavels, such as Edmund or Richard III. The idea of making 'the non-existence of a common motive itself a motive to action' is very close to Coleridge's account of Iago—'the motive-hunting of motiveless malignity' (*SC* i. 44). Aspects of Wordsworth's exploration of criminal psychology are also applicable to Macbeth: 'In this morbid state of mind he cannot exist without occupation, he requires constant provocatives, all his pleasures are prospective, he is perpetually chasing a phantom, he commits new crimes to drive away the memory of the past'. Indeed, Wordsworth is probably thinking explicitly of Macbeth here, for shortly afterwards he echoes one of Lady Macbeth's most memorable phrases, 'the milk of human kindness' (I. v. 17): 'The *mild* effusions of thought, the milk of human reason, are unknown to him'.[3]

In the play itself Rivers,[4] like Iago, plots the ruin of a noble but gullible warrior who trusts him implicitly. Like Iago, he does so by undermining his faith in those he loves, using as unwitting instrument a woman who later plays a central part in his own undoing. The Shakespearean influence is not, however, exclusive: Rivers is also descended from Franz Moor and Spiegelberg in Schiller's *Robbers* (like *The Borderers*, a play about a band of outlaws), from a variety of gothic villains, and perhaps even from Milton's Satan.[5]

The hero, Mortimer (Marmaduke in the later version), bears more resemblance to Hamlet than Othello. 'Like Hamlet, Marmaduke is a noble, idealistic young man, like Hamlet he procrastinates endlessly, putting off his act of "justice" for one reason after another, like Hamlet he is full of world-weariness, disgust at the lust and greed of others'.[6] Mortimer's beloved, Matilda (later Idonea), and her father are shaped by the fourth of Shakespeare's 'great tragedies'. Like Edgar, Matilda leads her blinded father; like Lear, Herbert endures a storm on an exposed heath and dies old and feeble, but purified and devoted to his daughter.[7]

But it is the influence of Shakespeare's language, often in scenes that have obvious parallels in the four tragedies, that is most prominent and, ultimately, a major factor contributing to the play's lack of vitality. Not only are there scores of borrowings, but again and again Wordsworth, like Coleridge in his contemporaneous play, echoes a Shakespearean phrase while failing to reproduce the effect it has in the original. Mortimer's 'Oh thou poor Matilda, / Now I *do* love thee' is a pale shadow of Othello's 'Excellent wretch! Perdition catch my soul / But I do love thee!'[8] Wordsworth fails to match the powerful emotional effect of the oxymoron, 'Excellent wretch', and the implications of 'Perdition'. What is delicately ambivalent in Shakespeare ('O villain, villain, *smiling*, damned villain!', *Ham* I. v. 106, my italics) frequently becomes undistinguished and conventional in Wordsworth ('Oh, villain! damned villain!', III. iii. 51). When Mortimer comes on stage having failed to kill Herbert, he says that the reason was that 'There was something in his face the very counterpart of Matilda. . . . Her very looks smiling in sleep' (II. iii. 272–6). The debt to Lady Macbeth's 'Had he not resembled / My father as he slept, I had done 't' (II. ii. 12) is manifest, but while Shakespeare introduces a new psychological dimension, the fact that Lady Macbeth once loved a father, Wordsworth merely has a resemblance to a character we already know to be beloved of the potential murderer. Equally, an image like 'The hell-hound' (v. iii. 261) is a mere interjection in *The Borderers*, where in *Macbeth* 'Turn, hell-hound, turn!' (v. viii. 3) is the culmination of the strands of infernal and canine imagery that run through the play.

There are many echoes of *Lear* in the scenes between father and daughter, and those when the dispossessed old man is subjected to human and elemental violence in the stormy night: 'We should deserve to wear a cap and bells / Three good round years for playing the fool here / In such a night as this'; 'I am a poor and useless man'; ''Tis a cold night'; 'The heavens are just'; 'The storm beats hard.—A mercy to the wretches / Who have no roof to shelter their poor heads / Such nights as these' (II. iii. 49, 106, 115, 119; IV. iii. 1). But there is no organized pattern of imagery that illuminates the meaning of the play; Wordsworth's dramatic language seeks to be Shakespearean but becomes merely archaic, arbitrary, and even incongruous—the 'cap and bells' intrude uneasily without a Fool to wear them.

The best lines in the play are the best-known ones, 'Action is transitory . . .' (III. v. 60–5), to which Wordsworth later gave new life as part of an epigraph to *The White Doe of Rylstone*. One reason for their unusual power is that they are essentially rather than superficially Shakespearean. The progression from 'Action' through 'motion' to 'vacancy', followed by the introduction of 'Suffering', may be derived from a similar sequence in *Julius Caesar*: 'acting', 'motion', 'interim', 'suffers' (II. i. 63–9). Not only is there a possible verbal echo, but Wordsworth has achieved the fluidity and poetic intensity that mark Brutus's lines. 'Poetic intensity' is a loose phrase, though it is the one that Wordsworth used in comparing himself with Shakespeare. Here, as we will sometimes find with Blake and Keats, critical vocabulary is limited: a locution such as 'in the after vacancy / We wonder at ourselves like men betray'd' strikes me as profoundly Shakespearean, but in a way that is difficult to pin down (is it to do with saying something rather unexceptionable in a highly original manner?). Despite the tonal similarity, Oswald's proposition is a much more general one than Brutus's. The concept of 'suffering' has replaced the verb 'suffers'. This generalizing tendency—abstract nouns lead to static meditation, verbs to dramatic activity—marks most Romantic drama off from its Shakespearean prototype and makes it moribund.

Precisely because it has so many surface parallels, *The Borderers* is not genuinely Shakespearean. It demonstrates the incompatibility of

servile imitation and creative emulation. Wordsworth himself may
have been aware of the weaknesses of his play; the lessons it taught
him perhaps contributed to his attack in the 1800 preface on servile
use of the language of poetic forefathers, his rejection of 'a large por-
tion of phrases and figures of speech which from father to son have
long been regarded as the common inheritance of Poets'. When he
did eventually publish *The Borderers* in 1842, he removed many of the
more glaring examples of figures inherited from Shakespeare, such as
'In the torrent hard by there is water enough to wash all the blood in
the universe' and 'Howl, howl, poor dog! Thou'lt never find him
more' (II. iii. 257, V. iii. 203).

Geoffrey Hartman argues that *The Borderers* is 'written in a
Shakespearean verse the poet had to purge before developing his
own'.[9] I agree, though it says much for Shakespeare's centrality to
Wordsworth that the experiment with his verse comes on the brink of
that most fertile period, 1798–1805. *The Borderers* taught Wordsworth
the essential art of writing dialogue, of creating an easy blank verse
that rendered the speaking voice. And to purge oneself of
Shakespeare's style is not to purge his influence altogether. From *The
Borderers* Wordsworth turned to *Home at Grasmere* and *The Ruined
Cottage*, which Shakespeare influenced in different ways.

Two crucial allusions show Wordsworth suggesting that *The Ruined
Cottage*, his greatest tragic poem, both is and is not Shakespearean.
The pedlar describes the story of Margaret as follows:

> 'Tis a common tale,
> By moving accidents uncharacterted,
> A tale of silent suffering, hardly clothed
> In bodily form, and to the grosser sense
> But ill adapted, scarcely palpable
> To him who does not think.[10]

Othello's account of his courtship is characterized by 'moving
accidents'; he makes his speech to defend himself against Brabantio's
claim that witchcraft has been used to seduce Desdemona;
Brabantio's accusation in the previous scene includes the phrases
'gross in sense' and 'palpable to thinking' (*Oth* I. iii. 135; I. ii. 72, 76).
The echoes suggest that Wordsworth wished to define the tragedy of
Margaret in the terms of Shakespeare's most 'pathetic' and domestic
tragedy; his tale, however, is 'of silent suffering': it eschews the
grander aspect of *Othello*, the high drama implicit in 'moving

accidents'.[11] Silent suffering may incidentally have made Wordsworth think of Cordelia; 'Her voice was low' (MS B, 418; D, 379)
associates Margaret with Lear's 'Her voice was ever soft, / Gentle,
and low, an excellent thing in woman' (v. iii. 273).

In bringing together Margaret, a poor woman, and the Pedlar, a
man who has *felt* his faith alone in the mountains, Wordsworth over-
comes the problem he always faces of the tension between human,
social sympathy and solitary communion with nature. The later
manuscripts and the version included in *The Excursion* show that for
Wordsworth the two stories were intimately bound up with each
other. The pedlar mediates sympathetically between Margaret's
tragedy and the audience (the Wordsworth figure, the reader). This is
one respect in which the poem is profoundly Shakespearean; we have
seen that from the later eighteenth century onwards Shakespeare
came to be considered as the greatest poet of sympathy, that concept
which would form the foundation of Hazlitt's and Keats's poetics
of tragedy. When Wordsworth says that the pedlar 'could afford to
suffer / With them whom he saw suffer' (MS E, 328; MS M, 376:
Cornell, 410–11), he conjures up a moment of quintessential sympathy in Shakespeare, Miranda responding to the shipwreck with the
words, 'O! I have suffered / With those that I saw suffer' (*Tp* I. ii. 5).
Again, however, Wordsworth has his own distinctive perspective;
here it is his belief that only the happy man is capable of profound
sympathy. He felt himself to be 'A happy man, and therefore bold to
look / On painful things' (*Prel.* x. 870) but said that Coleridge, being
afflicted with personal discontent, 'could not "afford to suffer / With
those whom he saw suffer"' (Field, 100).

Shakespeare's influence on *The Ruined Cottage*, then, is a part of
Wordsworth's thinking about the type of tragedy he is writing and the
sympathy it induces. The influence on *Home at Grasmere* is more local,
a matter of certain specific tonal effects. Thus in writing of his retreat
to Grasmere, Wordsworth finds himself falling in with the cadence of
Othello:

> Then farewell to the Warrior's deeds, farewell
> All hope, which once and long was mine, to fill
> The heroic trumpet with the muse's breath![12]

The echo does not, however, ring true: 'Othello's occupation's
gone', but Wordsworth's is just beginning, for his farewell to 'heroic'
verse heralds a new kind of meditative verse, 'On Man, on Nature,

and on human Life, / Thinking [Musing] in solitude . . .'.[13] The best allusions, like the best metaphors, combine similarity with difference; here the complete contrareity destroys the effect. An even less felicitous echo is that of *Lear* (IV. i. 36) in the comparison of wheeling birds to 'plaything fire-works, which on festal nights / Hiss hiss about the feet of wanton boys' (B, 780, Cornell, 86).

The passage beginning 'On Man, on Nature', so fundamental to Wordsworth's poetic endeavour, was published with *The Excursion* in 1814 as 'Prospectus' to *The Recluse*. It is crucial in any consideration of Wordsworth's relationship with his forebears because of the claim to pass the region of Miltonic themes 'unalarmed' and proceed 'into the mind of Man, / My haunt and the main region of my song' (Cornell, 102–3). 'Unalarmed', perhaps, but certainly not uninfluenced, for the whole passage is steeped in Miltonic rhetoric. This should not, however, let us lose sight of Wordsworth's emphasis in the invocation towards the end of the passage:

> Come, thou prophetic Spirit, Soul of Man,
> Thou human Soul of the wide earth that hast
> Thy metropolitan Temple in the hearts
> Of mighty Poets.
>
> (MS B, 1026, Cornell, 104)

The allusion to one of Shakespeare's sonnets on his own personal destiny as a poet, 'Not mine own fears, nor the prophetic soul / Of the wide world, dreaming on things to come' (*Sonn* 107), proclaims Shakespeare to be the exemplary poet of the 'human Soul' and, by implication, Wordsworth's own presiding spirit. It was clearly important to Wordsworth that readers should recognize the Shakespearean allusion, for in the 'Prospectus' published in 1814 he made it more explicit by adding in the phrase 'Dreaming on things to come' (*WPW* v. 5; MS D, 838, Cornell, 105). Behind the Miltonizing is a quiet but compelling hint that Shakespeare holds a central place among the 'mighty Poets' whom Wordsworth here acknowledges as his presiders. He asks that the 'prophetic Spirit' will vouchsafe to his own poetry 'star-like virtue' so that it will shed 'benignant influence' (*WPW* v. 6; Cornell, 107). Coming immediately after an allusion to one of Shakespeare's sonnets on how his poetry will live on after his death, this establishes a reciprocal effect whereby, in order to influence, Wordsworth himself must be influenced by Shakespeare.

The *Lyrical Ballads* do not immediately strike one as especially allusive or especially Shakespearean. But in a perceptive list of what he took to be their principal qualities, Crabb Robinson denoted them Shakespearean:

His repetition of simple phrases, and his dwelling on simple but touching Incidents, his Skill in drawing the deepest moral, and tenderest interest out of trifles evince a great Master, a Talent truely Shakespearean.[14]

A general comparison of this sort is, however, of limited value; Wordsworth and Shakespeare are not the only poets marked by the qualities listed, and 'Shakespearean' may be intended merely as synonymous with excellence.

Would Wordsworth's readers have found more specific Shakespearean resonances in the *Lyrical Ballads*? The Advertisement to the first edition, published in 1798 (*WPr* i. 116–17), suggests that readers might take exception to particular 'lines and phrases', but that 'the more conversant the reader is with our elder writers', the less likely this is to be the case. The best readers, claim Wordsworth and Coleridge on the authority of Sir Joshua Reynolds, are those who have had 'a long continued intercourse with the best models of composition'. There are, then, a number of hints that ask us to read the *Lyrical Ballads* with an ear prepared to hear lines and phrases that answer to the best models among the elder writers.

Wordsworth's conviction that phrases are associated with the way in which they have been used by previous poets is also apparent from the 1800 Preface, though here he concentrates on the possible detrimental effect: he speaks of 'expressions, in themselves proper and beautiful, but which have been foolishly repeated by bad Poets till such feelings of disgust are connected with them as it is scarcely possible by any art of association to overpower' (*WPr* i. 132). Sometimes associations will be of a personal nature, 'particular instead of general' (*WPr* i. 152). As Wordsworth may make a private allusion, for the benefit of an individual reader such as Coleridge, so a particular association in the mind of a reader may impose an allusive pattern that will not generally be noticed. 'Louisa', probably composed in January 1802, provides an illustration of this problem.

In this lyric, Wordsworth puts the phrase 'beneath the moon' in quotation marks (*WPW* ii. 28). Presumably he does so in order to tell the reader that he is aware of having lifted the phrase from the Dover cliff scene of *King Lear* (IV. vi. 26). May we therefore suppose that

Wordsworth associates 'beneath the moon' with *Lear* on other occasions? If we may, it becomes attractive to imagine that when 'The Idiot Boy' rides 'Beneath the moon' (349, *WPW* ii. 77) we can associate him with a play that is like Wordsworth's poem in that the fool and the madman have a kind of wisdom not granted to normal people. The phrase also occurs in 'Goody Blake and Harry Gill', a poem about a curse: can *Lear* then be brought into play again? After all, the line 'Poor Harry Gill is very cold' followed immediately by the word 'A-bed' would seem to be derived from 'Poor Tom's a-cold' (*WPW* iv. 173–6; *Lr* III. iv. 147, IV. i. 52). But these are slight suggestions on which to build a theory of intertextual reference; the possible allusions in the two *Lyrical Ballads* do not have quotation marks or other clear signalling devices. In these cases the associations are probably subconscious; it is legitimate for the critic to point them out, but whether they are to the fore of the reader's mind is doubtful. One is made to think about many things when reading 'The Idiot Boy'; a possible parallel with the idiot vision of *King Lear* is only one of them.

Similarly, in 'Tintern Abbey' there are several Shakespearean echoes that have not been remarked upon, but their presence constitutes only one thread in the rich texture of the poem. Vagrants dwelt in the ruins of Tintern Abbey; before his poem turns inward, Wordsworth glances at them in the image of 'vagrant dwellers in the houseless woods' (20, *WPW* ii. 260). The unusual word 'houseless', which does not occur in Milton, is used twice by Shakespeare—twice in the same speech, at one of the most politically potent moments in tragedy. 'You houseless poverty', begins Lear, responding for the first time to the nakedness and suffering of his people, from which a king is shielded by his court, by robes and furred gowns which hide all,

> Poor naked wretches, wheresoe'er you are,
> That bide the pelting of this pitiless storm,
> How shall your houseless heads and unfed sides,
> Your loop'd and window'd raggedness, defend you
> From seasons such as these?
>
> (III. iv. 26–32)

When Wordsworth wrote 'Tintern Abbey', he had recently extracted 'The Female Vagrant' from 'Salisbury Plain', his early poem of social protest. That poem has a heath and a hovel, such phrases as 'robbed of my perfect mind' (borrowed from Lear's 'I fear I am not in my perfect mind'), and the opening line 'Hard is the life when *naked* and *unhouzed*' (my italics).[15] 'Tintern Abbey', then, has the potential to be another poem about social conditions, to be peopled by houseless vagrants. But, in a move characteristic of his development in the late 1790s, Wordsworth turns away from political engagement and writes a poem about the self in relation to landscape. 'The still, sad music of humanity' leads him to his sister, not to a female vagrant. So it is that the allusive pattern shifts from the socially incisive moment in *Lear* to the introspection of *Hamlet*.

Wordsworth writes that the memory of the Wye valley restores him 'when the fretful stir / Unprofitable, and the fever of the world, / Have hung upon the beatings of my heart' (52). 'Unprofitable' obtrudes as a long and awkward word, sounding materialistic in an otherwise emotional vocabulary. What is it doing, if not alluding to its own most famous occurrence in earlier poetry? 'O God, God, / How weary, stale, flat, and unprofitable / Seem to me all the uses of this world!' (*Ham* I. ii. 132). As Wordsworth gives extra emphasis to Shakespeare's 'hangs' by putting it at the end of a line, so he gives 'unprofitable' prominence by placing it at the beginning of a line, preceded by strong enjambement and followed by a syntactic break. But Wordsworth's ennui is not only that of Hamlet; the 'fretful'/'fever' alliteration echoes Macbeth's 'life's fitful fever' (III. ii. 23), thus completing a composite context of Shakespearean melancholy for the later poet's musings.

In this section of the poem, Wordsworth also remembers how as a child he fled to nature from something dreaded, and then nature herself came to haunt him. The phrase 'all in all' in this passage— 'For Nature then . . . To me was all in all'—is one used by Hamlet immediately after he tells Horatio that he has seen his father in his mind's eye: ' 'A was a man, take him for all in all, / I shall not look upon his like again' (*Ham* I. ii. 187). Hamlet is haunted by the ghost of his father; Wordsworth flees, perhaps from the memory of his father's death, only to find himself haunted by nature. Has nature become a substitute for his father? Wordsworth does, after all, write of the 'filial bond' between man and nature (*Prel.* ii. 263). The parallel here is slight, but the ghost of Hamlet's father will return at other crucial moments.

That the question of using the words of earlier poets was in Wordsworth's mind as he wrote 'Tintern Abbey' is shown by his footnote to the phrase 'what they half-create, / And what perceive': 'This line has a close resemblance to an admirable line of Young, the exact expression of which I cannot recollect.' The allusion to Young is marked by a footnote; this is not necessary for those to *Lear* and *Hamlet*, because the original contexts would have been so well known.

The footnote is symptomatic of Wordsworth's defensiveness about inherited poetic language. He would have been even more wary after the publication of the preface to the second edition of the *Lyrical Ballads*, with its condemnation of stock poeticisms. It is perhaps for this reason that he tampers with those parts of 'Hart-Leap Well' which are indebted to Shakespeare. One of Sir Walter's dogs is called 'Brach' in 1800 and in editions up to 1820, but 'Blanch' from 1827 onwards (*WPW* ii. 249). The change is slight, from one part of *Lear* to another ('Brach': I. iv. 112; 'Blanch': III. vi. 63), but is indicative of uneasiness. The second part of the poem begins 'The moving accident is not my trade': as in *The Ruined Cottage*, Wordsworth distances his kind of tragedy from Shakespeare's. Shakespearean phrases often occur in groups: the next line contains another echo, 'To curl the blood I have no ready arts'. But in the second errata this is changed to 'To freeze the blood', the reading retained in all subsequent editions (*WPW* ii. 252). Why did Wordsworth make this change? Perhaps he decided that 'curl the blood' was not close enough to the original scene he wished to conjure up, Old Hamlet's description of the murder. 'Freeze the blood' manifestly echoes 'I could a tale unfold whose lightest word / Would harrow up thy soul, freeze thy young blood' while 'curl the blood' only gestures glancingly at 'curd, like eager droppings into milk, / The thin and wholesome blood' (*Ham* I. v. 15, 69). The original version is too like the limp inheritance of a 'poetic' phrase; the emended one does not attempt to obscure its origin, it is an allusion which is put to work. Revision shows Wordsworth in the process of working out his relationship with Shakespearean language; sometimes a later version will make an allusion more explicit, on other occasions a verbal debt will be obscured or removed.

In 'Hart-Leap Well' Wordsworth uses allusion to tell his reader that his story is unlike *Othello* or *Hamlet*. But not all his tragedies in lyrical ballad form are distant from Shakespeare; in its economy of characterization, use of dialogue in fluid, conversational blank verse, and tragic irony of non-recognition, I find 'The Brothers' profoundly Shakespearean. Equally, Wordsworth's Michael takes on the proportions of a Shakespearean tragic hero.

'I have attempted to give a picture of a man, of strong mind and lively sensibility, agitated by two of the most powerful affections of the human heart; the parental affection, and the love of property, *landed* property, including the feelings of inheritance, home, and personal and family independence' (*EY* 322). This is Wordsworth writing about 'Michael', but it could as well be an account of *King Lear*. Dorothy's description of the sheepfold that inspired the poem is suggestive in this respect: 'it is built nearly in the form of *a heart unequally divided*' (*Journals*, 45, my italics). Beside these references some hints from the poem itself may be placed: 'blind love'; 'instinctive tenderness' working 'blindly'; 'The Old Man's grief broke from him, to his heart / He press'd his Son, he kissed him and wept'; Michael alone with the wind and storms; and, above all, the lines 'There is a comfort in the strength of love; / 'Twill make a thing endurable, which else / Would break the heart:—Old Michael found it so' (*WPW* ii. 83–93). In editions from 1820 onwards, the last of these lines was brought closer to the mood of *Lear*: 'Would *overset the brain*, or break the heart' (my italics). (Echoes in poems such as 'Invocation to the Earth' suggest that Shakespeare took on renewed importance for Wordsworth in the period 1815–20, after the publication of the more Miltonic *Excursion*.) However much or little weight is attached to the specific parallels, as a tale of an old man enduring all until he is released by death, told partly by means of powerful simplicity and understatement, and with an emphasis on the intensity of familial bonds, 'Michael' is in a line of descent from *King Lear*.

Another figure who might possibly be seen as a Lear of rural life is the shepherd in 'The Last of the Flock' who is stripped of his fifty sheep as Lear is stripped of his hundred knights (weeping, he carries in his arms the body of the last of his flock: a visual allusion to Lear and Cordelia?). 'Michael' and 'The Brothers' were written, Wordsworth claimed, 'with a view to shew that men who do not wear fine cloaths can feel deeply' (*EY* 315). Or, to put it another way, that ordinary men may suffer as profoundly as the kings and nobles of traditional tragedy. This is equally true of 'Simon Lee' and 'Matthew'.

Simon Lee 'says he is three score and ten, / But others say he's eighty' (*WPW* iv. 60); Lear speaks of his four score years—furthermore, both poem and play tell a man's age in terms of years upon his back. Simon and Lear are men once strong, now reduced, who have enjoyed riding and hunting; Simon has lost one eye, while Gloucester loses two. The parallels would be incidental but for the fact that kindness and kinship, gratitude and mourning, are vital to both the tragedy and the ballad. Lear and Simon each have to learn to say 'thank you' for a very simple deed. On the heath Lear commands, 'Come, unbutton here' (III. iv. 109); in the final scene he requests and thanks, 'Pray you undo this button. Thank you, sir' (V. iii. 310). Simon thanks 'Wordsworth' for helping him to dig up his root, an act of kindness that expresses human kinship. Lear hopes to set his rest on Cordelia's 'kind nursery' (I. i. 124); he becomes the victim of 'sharp-tooth'd unkindness' (II. iv. 135), and, at that moment which Wordsworth picked out as paradigmatic of the human and dramatic imagination, is led by his daughters' unkindness to express kinship with the elements, 'I tax not you, you elements, with unkindness'. At the end of 'Simon Lee', Wordsworth says that he has heard of 'hearts unkind', but 'Alas! the gratitude of men / Has oftner left me mourning'. At the end of *Lear* our mourning is more for the gratitude Lear has learnt in the last moments of life than it is for the suffering caused by 'hearts unkind'.

The final stanza of 'The Two April Mornings' reads

> Matthew is in his grave, yet now
> Methinks I see him stand,
> As at that moment, with his bough
> Of wilding in his hand.

> (*WPW* iv. 71)

This stanza evokes two passages in Shakespeare that Wordsworth knew well. Macbeth's 'life's fitful fever', which I have suggested is a presence behind 'Tintern Abbey', occurs in a clause subordinate to 'Duncan is in his grave' (*Mac* III. ii. 22); as in the Lucy poem, 'She dwelt among th' untrodden ways', with its penultimate line 'But she is in her Grave', Wordsworth gives profound elegiac power to a simple monosyllabic statement. Secondly, the bough of wilding suggests the lyrical scene that opens the final act of *The Merchant of Venice*, 'In such a night / Stood Dido with a willow in her hand'.[16] The implicit comparisons give Matthew, the village schoolmaster, the dignity of the regal figures of tragedy and mythology. Allusion enables Wordsworth to show that in his poetry the ordinary man has taken the place of the high-born characters who traditionally people the higher poetic genres. Hazlitt noted that to make such a substitution was a political, a revolutionary act: 'kings and queens were dethroned from their rank and station in legitimate tragedy or epic poetry, as they were decapitated elsewhere' (*HW* v. 162).

It is as if Shakespeare has been rewritten with his shepherds and servants as central rather than secondary characters. Thus it is Michael and Matthew who speak an authentically Shakespearean language. In a rejected passage of 'Michael', the old shepherd is said to look 'as with a Poet's eye' (*WPW* ii. 482). In 'Expostulation and Reply', 'Matthew' recommends William to read more ('drink the spirit breath'd / From dead men to their kind', *WPW* iv. 56); then in 'The Two April Mornings' he speaks with the poetry of Florizel: 'She seem'd as happy as a wave / That dances on the sea' echoes 'When you do dance, I wish you / A wave o' th' sea' (*WPW* iv. 71; *Wint* IV. iv. 140). Florizel is a prince in shepherd's clothing; Matthew is a low-born man with a princely nature. Perhaps the best evocation of him is in an elegy which Wordsworth did not publish: now that the schoolmaster is dead, the classroom will no longer be 'like a playhouse in a barn / Where Punch and Hamlet play together' (*WPW* iv. 454). The yoking of popular, 'low' tradition and the tragic character who appealed most strongly to the Romantic imagination demonstrates beautifully what the 'Matthew' figure (regardless of the extent to which he represented William Taylor) meant to Wordsworth.

To place Hamlet beside Punch is to accommodate him. In the best of the *Lyrical Ballads*, Wordsworth is conscious of but unalarmed by Shakespeare. The failure of *The Borderers* had shown that to borrow from Shakespeare was insufficient; there also had to be what Coleridge would have called an 'acknowledged difference'. Lear dies shortly after his daughters, while Michael lives on; Lear rages, while Michael's emotion is internalized. Perdita is in motion, is lost and found in a world where time is benevolent; the girl with the basket on her head is frozen in the past, the irreparable loss of Matthew's daughter pervades the second April morning in a world where time is remorseless.

Paradoxically it is Wordsworth's ordinary men rather than his poet-figures who are seen as the true guardians of Shakespearean values. In 'Resolution and Independence', the Leech Gatherer stands firm linguistically as well as philosophically. While 'Wordsworth' is stultified by 'fleshly ills' (Hamlet's 'shocks That flesh is heir to') and the thought of 'mighty Poets in their misery dead', the Leech Gatherer speaks with 'lofty utterance', 'Choice word, and measured phrase': he is the special kind of man that the poet ought to be. In the penultimate stanza Wordsworth writes, 'In my mind's eye I seem'd to see him pace / About the weary moors continually' (*WPW* ii. 238–40). Hamlet tells Horatio that he sees the figure of his father 'In my mind's eye' (I. ii. 185). Whenever Hazlitt quotes the phrase he marks it off with quotation marks or italics; this suggests that it had not become merely proverbial by the early nineteenth century.[17] In 'Resolution and Independence' it still has the pressure of its original context. As the ghost will come to whet Hamlet's almost blunted purpose, so the figure of the Leech Gatherer admonishes Wordsworth for his Hamlet-like self-absorption. It is testimony to the range of responses elicited in the Romantics by Hamlet that here Wordsworth uses him as a negative example, while in the 'Matthew' elegy he is a positive figure.

The echo in 'Resolution and Independence' is faint, but the fact remains that many of Wordsworth's more teasing Shakespearean allusions are to the first act of *Hamlet*. Like Coleridge, he found the ghost scenes 'incomparable' among Shakespeare's openings, and 'full of exhausting interest' (*Memoirs*, ii. 471). But why was Hamlet's confrontation with his dead father of such interest to Wordsworth as poet as well as reader?

In the 1812 manuscript of *The Waggoner*, Wordsworth introduces a digression concerning his Muse, 'who scents the morning air'.[18] In *Hamlet* it is the ghost who 'scent[s] the morning air' (I. v. 58): is Hamlet's father therefore a figure for Wordsworth's Muse? The Romantic poet's identification of himself as Hamlet—the Wilhelm Meister strategy—has often been remarked upon. But what happens if the poet also accepts the tradition, commonplace since Rowe's biographical sketch of 1709, that Shakespeare played the part of the ghost of Hamlet's father (shortly after the death of his own son, Hamnet)? Then, surely, Shakespeare himself is cast as the Romantic poet's father—and, in the case of this particular allusion, his Muse as well.

Harold Rosenberg defines allusion as 'the most profound, the true *ghostly* principle of historical revival, since by allusion the thing alluded to is both there and not there.'[19] We might add that it is seen by some and not others, by Hamlet readers and not Gertrude readers. If the Romantics saw themselves as Hamlets and Shakespeare as the father of English poetry, there could be no more apposite ghostly presence in their poems than allusions to Hamlet and his dead father. Such allusions, furthermore, are not illicit appropriations: 'to take a phrase or an

inspiriting line from the great fathers of poetry, even though no marks
of quotation should be added, carries with it no charge of plagiarism',
writes De Quincey in his 1831 *Blackwood's* reminiscence of Coleridge
(*DQW* ii. 144). When applied to allusion at its best, the word 'inspiriting' needs to be given its full weight: inspirational, ghostly, an
answering to the spirit of the father-poet.

It is astonishing how frequently Wordsworth's poems on questions
of the poetic tradition, of ghostliness and fathering, bring Shakespeare
into play. The sonnet 'A volant Tribe of Bards' takes a phrase, *with
what De Quincey calls 'marks of quotation', from *the* Bard: ' "coignes
of vantage" ' (*WPW* iii. 19; *Mac* I. vi. 7). A late sonnet called 'Spon-
sors', which begins 'Father! to God himself we cannot give / A holier
name!', also lifts a phrase from *Macbeth*: 'to make assurance doubly
sure' (*WPW* iii. 395; *Mac* IV. i. 83). Wordsworth, then, adopts Shakespeare as his god-father to assure his own place in the English pantheon.

Poets do not, however, have single precursor-figures. Wordsworth
echoes the language of Hamlet and his father on other occasions: one
of the sonnets on King's College chapel, Cambridge, conjoins the
idea of 'sound, or ghost of sound' and the phrase 'list! O list!', which
readers would associate with the ghost; the Spirit at the beginning of
'Invocation to the Earth', otherwise known as 'Elegiac Verses,
February 1816', sings 'Rest, rest, perturbed Earth!', echoing 'Rest,
rest, perturbed spirit!' (*WPW* iii. 406; iv. 267; *Ham* I. v. 22, 182).
But his imagination is also haunted by other ghosts. A sonnet that
includes the pregnant line on the poet's dilemma, 'Haunts him
belated on the silent plains', begins with an italicized quotation from
Cowper ('*There is a pleasure in poetic pains*', *WPW* iii. 29).

Wordsworth's Shakespearean allusions are frequently less overt
than his Miltonic ones. An 1816 poem to Dora provides a case in
point:

> '*A little onward lend thy guiding hand*
> *To these dark steps, a little further on!*'
> —What trick of memory to *my* voice hath brought,
> This mournful iteration?

(*WPW* iv. 92)

Wordsworth finds himself quoting from *Samson Agonistes*; a poem on
the interplay of self-expression and allusive 'iteration' begins with the
language of Milton. If there is another obvious precursor-text, it is
Oedipus at Colonus with its child leading a blinded father: in the manu-

script and the first published text of 1820, the line that eventually becomes 'O my own Dora, my belovèd child!' reads 'O my Antigone, beloved child!' (iv. 92 t.a.). Another possible influence is Coleridge's *The Wanderings of Cain*, the poem on which he and Wordsworth worked in 1798. According to Coleridge, the scheme to collaborate 'broke up in a laugh: and the Ancient Mariner was written instead'—but not before he had drafted a prose sketch of canto two which begins, ' " A little further, O my father, yet a little further, and we shall come into the open moonlight" ' (*CPW* i. 287–8).

But Geoffrey Hartman draws attention to such phrases as 'brink precipitous' and the image of the circling birds; a father 'poorly led' to a cliff must reach back to *King Lear*.[20] The 'trick of memory' which we call *allusion* thus takes on additional complexity: 'The trick of that voice I do well remember' says Gloucester (*Lr* IV. vi. 106), the pun linking the idea of a characteristic trait with that of a deceitful device. Allusion is a trick of speech in that the words of the earlier poet are reiterated with altered voice ('Methinks thy voice is alter'd', says Gloucester a little earlier in the Dover Cliff scene, anticipating the 'altered voice' of 'Christabel'). They are both the same and different, distinctive yet tricked out in the dress of the later poet and—as in this case—sometimes inextricable from the words of other earlier poets. In the Dora poem, 'abrupt abyss' is placed in quotation marks, implicitly ascribed to Milton, yet it is not an accurate quotation—it elides 'The dark unbottomed infinite abyss' with 'the vast abrupt' (*PL* ii. 405, 409)—and it can be said to originate as much with Shakespeare's Dover Cliff as anything in Milton. Perhaps Mary Wordsworth understood the importance of *Lear* to her husband's reflections on fathers and children, blindness and vision: when she writes to Dora in April 1839 of William and his son, Willy, she makes a most thought-provoking juxtaposition: 'Willy is reading King Lear beside me—Father's eyes keep well.'[21]

Wordsworth's Shakespearean allusions are not schematic enough for us to speak of precise correspondences or implied narratives. The identifications of poet-figure as Hamlet, ghostly father as Shakespeare, the older Wordsworth as a self-conscious Lear, are suggestive rather than definitive. Allusions frequently form no more than a subliminal thread running through poems which can be read, entered into, and interpreted without any significance being attached to their presence. But their presence is one aspect of the many-faceted, infinitely suggestive nature of poetic language. How conscious they may be and how much weight may be attached to them will vary and will never be easy to determine. Sometimes, however, we are assisted by external evidence. Consider, for example, some of the circumstances surrounding an allusion in Wordsworth's 'Ode: Intimations of Immortality'.

In a letter to Coleridge dated 6 March 1804, Dorothy writes that Wordsworth 'is sitting beside me reading Hamlet' (*EY* 451). Mark Reed dates the 'Immortality' Ode as follows: 'Most of last seven stanzas probably composed, and the poem completed, probably early 1804, by 6 Mar.'[22] On finishing, or on putting the finishing touches to, his Ode, Wordsworth returns to a play that is full of meditations on mortality and ghostly intimations of immortality. His own poem becomes inextricable from the matter of *Hamlet*.

Thus in the ninth stanza he establishes an analogy between the supernatural encounter in *Hamlet* and his own heightened state when he senses other-worldly 'High instincts, before which our mortal Nature / Did tremble like a guilty Thing surpriz'd' (*WPW* iv. 283). The ghost of Hamlet's father 'started like a guilty thing' (I. i. 148) and 'faded', not 'into the light of common day', but 'on the crowing of the cock'. 'Like a guilty Thing' is not the only shadowy recollection in this passage of Hamlet and the ghost: that encounter is also characterized by 'vanishings' and 'obstinate questionings' ('Thou com'st in such a questionable shape'). Immortality in the Ode as a whole is paradoxically associated with the past rather than the future, a before-life rather than an after-life. By summoning up the ghost, Wordsworth is able simultaneously to stress man's mortality and to make a link with the more conventional sense of immortality, the idea of life beyond the grave.

These associative processes may explain why the verbal echo is there, but whether or not it has any effect on the reader is a different question. De Quincey said that on his advice Wordsworth went back on his intention to put the phrase 'like a guilty Thing' in quotation marks in the published text of the Ode, 'for that this reference to a book had the effect of breaking the current of the passion' (*DQW* v. 101). At first sight, this information suggests an attempt to obscure the allusion. But the absence of a specific signal does not stop the reader who is familiar with *Hamlet* (that is to say, nearly all Wordsworth's readers) recognizing it. In some ways, the effect of embedding the allusion is to intensify it, to make the comparison with the atmosphere of the ghost scene not incidental but integral to this moment in the Ode. It is for this reason more successful than the quotation from the dedicatory sonnet of Samuel Daniel's *Musophilus* in the seventh stanza. ' "Humorous stage" ' is doubly ineffective, first because of its reliance on quotations marks, and second because in the context of a 'little Actor' conning his parts 'down to palsied Age', if there is to be a quotation at all, it should be from *As You Like it*, not *Musophilus* (perhaps by a trick of memory Wordsworth thought that he *was* quoting from Jaques's Seven Ages).

That De Quincey believed in the added power of an embedded allusion is implied by his eschewal of inverted commas when using the phrase 'like a guilty thing' at certain key moments of almost supernatural intensity in his own autobiographical prose. It occurs when he imagines hearing the footsteps of God as he kisses his dead sister (in this context, one thinks not only of the 'guilty thing' but also of Wordsworth's 'like a living thing' in the boat-stealing scene of *Prel.* i. 411), and in his account of when he first approached Grasmere. In the latter case, the word 'surprised' suggests the influence of the Ode rather than *Hamlet*: 'I retreated like a guilty thing, for fear I might be surprised by Wordsworth' (*DQW* i. 42; ii. 231).

This grouping—Shakespearean allusion, Wordsworth at the time of the 'Ode', De Quincey—leads us to a remark that does much to explain the importance for Wordsworth of the use of previous poets. In a letter to De Quincey, also dated 6 March 1804, Wordsworth writes, 'love Nature and Books; seek these and you will be happy; for virtuous friendship, and love, and knowledge of mankind, must inevitably accompany these, all things ripening in their own due season' (*EY* 454). Wordsworth seeks a maturity of vision that corresponds to what we understand by Hamlet's 'readiness' and sense of 'due season' in the final act of the play, or indeed to the 'ripeness' of which Edgar speaks in *Lear*. It may be accomplished, Wordsworth believes, under the dual influence of 'Nature and Books'. Allusion—as distinct from self-serving plagiarism, a practice he attacks in the same letter (*EY* 455)—is one method of acknowledging the ripening influence of books. That influence is charted in Wordsworth's poem on the growth of his own mind, at which he was also working in early March 1804. It is now necessary to consider Shakespeare's presence in that poem.

Shakespeare is not always used creatively in *The Prelude*; the borrowing of phrases is sometimes a mark of slackness. One symptom of

Wordsworth's decline is the fact that loose 'Shakespearean' diction is more prominent in the text published in 1850 than the thirteen-book *Prelude* of 1805. The very first lines of the poem provide an example: 'Oh there is blessing in this gentle breeze, / That blows from the green fields and from the clouds' is changed to 'O there is blessing in this gentle breeze, / A visitant that while he fans my cheek' (i. 1). 'Fans my cheek' is not an allusion to Enobarbus' description of Cleopatra's barge, but it is a borrowing of the elevated diction we find there, which is out of place in the context of Wordsworth's solitary meditation.

The more telling appropriations are those where Shakespeare is actively brought into play as a point of reference or source of authority. Sometimes specific allusions will have the slackness of borrowed poeticisms. When Wordsworth uses the formulation 'If this be error, and . . . ' (ii. 435), the echo of Sonnet 116 does no more than give a vague rhetorical authority (the authenticity of my emotion is underwritten by the fact that I am speaking with the voice of Shakespeare in one of his most personal sonnets). But since the tonal and contextual weight of the precursor text is not brought into play, the allusion is hollow. Such weak effects show that allusion is not *necessarily* a device to be applauded. More frequently, though, there is greater richness about Wordsworth's choices of Shakespearean texts.

In the first book, Wordsworth recounts how, before he decided to write a poem on the growth of his own mind, he considered a variety of possible themes,

> But deadening admonitions will succeed,
> And the whole beauteous fabric seems to lack
> Foundation, and withal appears throughout
> Shadowy and unsubstantial.

> (i. 225)

This sense of a 'baseless fabric', an 'insubstantial pageant' which has 'melted into air', establishes a parallel between the poet's visions and the masque conjured by Prospero. In the 1850 text, the echo is made stronger by the introduction of the phrases 'the unsubstantial structure melts' and 'Mist into air dissolving' (i. 225–7). The image is transformed in the very final lines of the poem when the mind of man is seen as something that need not be transient, that is 'Of substance and of fabric more divine' (xiii. 452).

Allusions to *The Tempest* recur at many key moments in *The Prelude*. Again and again, Wordsworth's invocations to nature echo Prospero's 'Ye elves of hills, brooks, standing lakes, and groves' (V. i. 33). Miltonic and eighteenth-century invocations, other catalogues of 'ye's, have intervened between Shakespeare and *The Prelude*, but there are several occasions on which close parallels of phraseology inevitably make the reader recall Prospero: 'to bury those two books', 'ye brooks . . . And you, ye groves, whose ministry it is / To interpose the covert of your shades' (V. 103; xi. 12–16, compare 'you whose pastime / Is to make . . .', *Tp* V. i. 38). The first invocation in the 1805 text, 'Ye presences of Nature' (i. 490–2) does not call up *The Tempest*. This may be a reaction on Wordsworth's part against the extreme allusiveness of this invocation as it is first drafted in the two-part *Prelude*: 'ye that are familiars of the lakes / And of the standing pools' (*1799* i. 188).

If the poet Wordsworth is a Prospero, we would expect him to have a magic island. So it is that in the second book we see him out on Windermere, rowing to 'an island musical with birds / That sang for ever' (ii. 59), his version of 'the isle is full of noises, / Sounds, and sweet airs, that give delight and hurt not' (*Tp* III. ii. 135). On this occasion the allusion is insufficiently explicit, so the line is subsequently revised to echo the rhythm and syntax of Caliban more closely: 'sang for ever' is changed to 'sang and ceased not' (*1850* ii. 59).

There are further parallels with *The Tempest*; the idea, for example, of the poet 'clothed in priestly robe' (i. 61) suggests the robe of a Prospero-figure or magus, as well as a priest. But the image of the world as an 'insubstantial pageant' does not only summon up Prospero. Where it occurs in the context of ennui rather than creative power, it brings to the reader's mind that other favourite figure for the poet, Hamlet. In book four, Wordsworth is sidetracked from the benign influence of 'books and Nature'; his inner 'falling off' [23] leads to a sense that

> man, a creature great and good,
> Seems but a pageant plaything with vile claws,
> And this great frame of breathing elements
> A senseless idol.
>
> (iv. 301)

The echo here is of Hamlet's 'this goodly frame, the earth, seems to me a sterile promontory' and his recognition that man is potentially the noblest of creatures but also mere 'quintessence of dust' (II. ii. 295–308).

Wordsworth's 'sadness', his grieving for the state of man, 'Thou paramount creature', is still apparent at the beginning of book five (1–10). He speaks of the works of man which are 'worthy of unconquerable life', then laments that 'we feel—we cannot choose but feel— / That these must perish' (19–21). The 'choose but' construction leads him to the couplet of Shakespeare's great sonnet on time and decay: 'This thought is as a death, which cannot choose / But weep to have that which it fears to lose' (*Sonn* 64). He then alerts his reader to his source by using quotation marks: man, 'As long as he shall be the child of earth, / Might almost "weep to have" what he may lose' (v. 24).

Shakespeare is thus brought into the reader's mind at the beginning of the book on 'Books'. Wordsworth then goes on to name him, along with the other mighty poet whose books are especially influential: 'Shakespeare or Milton, labourers divine' (v. 165). Despite the preponderance of Miltonisms and Miltonic allusions throughout *The Prelude*, when Wordsworth comes at the climax of book five to speak of the power in the language of 'mighty poets', it is to Shakespeare that he looks. 'Visionary power', he writes,

> Attends upon the motions of the winds
> Embodied in the mystery of words;
> There darkness makes abode, and all the host
> Of shadowy things do work their changes there
>
> (v. 619).

Wordsworth associated that word 'motion' with *Measure for Measure*. Not only does he allude to Claudio's 'sensible warm motion' in the Windy Brow additions to *An Evening Walk* and a manuscript revision to 'Salisbury Plain',[24] but earlier in *The Prelude* we find him inverting 'The wanton stings and motions of the sense' (*Meas* I. iv. 59) in 'These hallowed and pure motions of the sense' (i. 578). 'Motions of the winds' faintly suggests a conflation of 'motions of the sense' with a line that comes in the same speech as 'sensible warm motion', 'To be imprison'd in the viewless winds' (III. i. 123). 'Viewless' is an influential Shakespearean coinage. In his revised text, Wordsworth makes the allusion more explicit: 'Visionary power / Attends upon the motions of the viewless winds' (*1850* v. 595). 'The viewless winds' provide a powerful metaphor for the inspiration of poetic language, one to set beside the 'correspondent breeze' that recurs in several key Romantic poems. The allusion to Claudio is made powerfully by Keats in his 'Nightingale' ode, and deflected by Shelley when he writes in 'Mont Blanc' of 'viewless *gales*' (*SPW* 533). But even in the 1805 *Prelude*, where the echo of *Measure for Measure* is muted, Wordsworth's crucial passage has its Shakespearean resonance. 'There darkness makes abode' and the 'shadowy things' working their changes are in the spirit of *A Midsummer Night's Dream*, not only Shakespeare's most magical and 'poetic' play, but the one in which he offers what was taken to be his definition of the poet's imaginative power.

In the following book, immediately after the crossing of the Alps, Wordsworth addresses the imagination directly. Here, he raises the issue of spontaneous inspiration as against the influence of the mighty poets:

> Imagination!—lifting up itself
> Before the eye and progress of my song
> Like an unfathered vapour
>
> (vi. 525).

But can the imagination be 'unfathered' when Wordsworth's imaginative utterance is shaped by his poetic fathers? The use of invocation and the self-conscious reference to his 'song' proclaim the epic nature of his poem, its filiation from Milton,[25] while the use of a doublet in a discussion of the imagination is Shakespearean: the Friar in *Much Ado* equates 'imagination' with 'the eye and prospect of [the] soul' (IV. i. 225, 229).

The imagination is the eye of the mind or the soul; its transforming vision goes beyond that of the senses, the literal eye. Believing this, Wordsworth would rather read Shakespeare, enact the plays in his own imagination, than see them on stage. In the seventh book of *The Prelude*, he recalls his visits to the London theatres. He appears to have attended both the suburban ones, with their musical entertainments, and the patent theatres, where he witnessed 'tragic sufferings'. But not even the latter passed 'beyond the suburbs of the mind' (vii. 436–507). The allusion to *Julius Caesar* (II. i. 285) implies that on stage Shakespeare dwelt 'but in the suburbs' of Wordsworth's 'good pleasure'. His only satisfaction came when the 'gross realities' of the stage, 'The incarnation of the spirits that moved / Amid the poet's beauteous world', enabled him to 'glimpse' by sheer force of contrast

> the things which I had shaped
> And yet not shaped, had seen and scarcely seen,
> Had felt, and thought of in my solitude.
>
> (vii. 514)

The 1850 version leaves us in no doubt as to whose plays he is talking about, for the line 'When, having closed the mighty Shakespear's page' is inserted (*1850* vii. 484).

The effect of what Wordsworth calls 'incarnation' was the major difficulty faced by the Romantics on seeing Shakespeare in the theatre. Certain plays were of such importance to their conceptions of imagination and the 'spirit' of poetry that stage representation was limiting. Wordsworth's response to Shakespeare is private, meditative, rich, and many-layered ('seen and scarcely seen', 'shaped And yet not shaped'), a combination of musing, thinking, and feeling that is altogether characteristic of the man and by its very nature far removed from public performance and the grandiloquence of the early nineteenth-century theatre.

In the 1850 *Prelude*, Wordsworth has a little more respect for the stage. He opens his section on actors by calling them ' "forms and pressures of the time" ' (*1850* vii. 288); the (inaccurate) quotation is an acknowledgement of the potential social power of the actor who lives up to the ideals expressed by Hamlet (III. ii. 16–28). Wordsworth also introduces a reference to Siddons 'in the fulness of her power' (*1850* vii. 406). Whether or not he actually saw Siddons in his youth —we cannot be sure that he accompanied Dorothy to Drury Lane in December 1797—the later Wordsworth looks back to her years as a golden age in the English theatre. But as I showed in my previous chapter, during those years he had little time for it.

These two additions slightly modify rather than significantly alter the attitude expressed in *The Prelude* to the staging of Shakespeare; it is essentially the same as that implied by the 1805 letter to Beaumont. Indeed, in book seven Wordsworth seems to be against any public appropriation of Shakespeare, any attempt to remove him from the individual imagination. From the stage, he goes on to attack a fashionable parson who gilds his sermons with 'ornaments and flowers' from the poets, Shakespeare among them (547–66).

There are occasions, then, on which Wordsworth resists the tendency, so widespread at this time, to make Shakespeare contemporary. He is careful to distinguish his Lakeland shepherds from those of literary Arcadias, the golden worlds of Spenser, *As You Like it*, and *A Winter's Tale* (*Prel.* viii. 183–91). Here again, he slightly modifies his position in the later text. By referring to 'Shakespeare's genius' and increasing the number of lines paraphrasing the plot of *As You Like it*, he draws more attention to the Shakespearean pastoral than is quite commensurate with its status as a negative point of reference (*1850* viii. 136–41).[26]

There is another implied rejection of contemporary reductions of Shakespeare when Wordsworth attacks the practice of making 'the tragic super-tragic' (viii. 532). The widow of the gothic tale is an inflated revivified Lear, 'Wetting the turf with never-ending tears, / And all the storms of heaven must beat on her' (540). Equally, in the 'Vaudracour and Julia' episode, he remarks that any attempt to write love poetry will be inferior to that of the 'darling bard / Who told of Juliet and her Romeo' (ix. 638). In mentioning Romeo and Juliet Wordsworth is not only evading the difficulties posed for him by love poetry, but also implying that the love of Vaudracour and Julia is a *grande passion*, like that of Romeo and Juliet (the choice of name for the beloved may not be coincidental). Such self-conscious use of Shakespeare is usually more successful than the imitative practice of gothic tales, including Wordsworth's own *Borderers*, but here the strategy is insufficient to redeem Wordsworth's vapid versification of his love-affair in France. Love is merely described from the outside; we do not grasp the inner turmoil and excitement of Vaudracour and Julia as we do with Romeo and Juliet. The language is prosaic, where that of *Romeo* reveals Shakespeare at his most heightened and lyrical.

Wordsworth alludes more creatively in the public part of the books concerning his 'Residence in France'. In book ten Shakespearean figures of disorder and guilt are used to strengthen an attack on the Terror, which destroyed Wordsworth's faith in the French Revolution. As he meditates on the September massacres, he writes 'The horse is taught his manage' (x. 70). The phrase seems curious until it is placed in its original context, Orlando's reflections at the beginning of *As You Like it* on the iniquitous way in which he is being treated by his brother (I. i. 12).

Brother against brother, the end of Fraternité, is one apposite context for this moment in French history; killing a king is another. 'A

little month' (x. 65) is another phrase derived from the first act of
Hamlet (I. ii. 147). Hamlet telescopes to 'a little month' the time between the death of the king and Gertrude's remarriage; Wordsworth's
retrospective narrative plays on his readers' knowledge that the French
monarchy was formally abolished in the same month as the massacres,
and that the King himself was executed within a few little months.
The imagined voice crying out 'To the whole city, "Sleep no more!" '
(x. 77) further emphasizes the connection between the massacres and
the subsequent regicide by summoning up the voice that haunts
Macbeth immediately after he murders the sleeping Duncan (II. ii.
32–40).[27] Jonathan Wordsworth has pointed out that there may also
be an intermediate allusion in 'Sleep no more', to Godwin's 'The
voice of an irresistible necessity had commanded me to "sleep no
more" '.[28] Contextually, however, *Macbeth* is the more powerful influence; the allusion expresses Wordsworth's own guilt at his involvement in the revolutionary fervour. Richard Onorato puts it well: 'did
Wordsworth himself feel that in some way he had "murther'd sleep"?
What the patriots have done, has the youthful partisan not willed?'[29]

Another phrase from the first act of *Hamlet* is used with reference to
the reign of Robespierre: 'Blasts / From hell came sanctified like airs
from heaven' (x. 313; cf. *Ham* I. iv. 41). This is a good example of the
strong co-presence of Shakespeare and Milton in Wordsworth, for a
few lines earlier Robespierre and his crew have been compared to
Satan and his: 'Tyrants, strong before / In devilish pleas' (309) closely
echoes Milton's 'So spake the fiend, and with necessity, / The
tyrant's plea, excused his devilish deeds' (*PL* iv. 393; 'necessity' ties
in with the Godwinian context of 'sleep no more').

There is a similar conjunction in the lines on Arras, 'place from
which / Issued that Robespierre, who afterwards / Wielded the sceptre
of the atheist crew' (x. 455). In view of Robespierre's deism, 'athiest
crew' is mildly unfortunate; accuracy has been sacrificed to the desire
to make a comparison with Milton's devils ('The atheist crew', *PL* vi.
370). More effective are the image of Arras groaning 'Under the
vengeance of her cruel son, / As Lear reproached the winds' (x. 461,
Robespierre implicitly compared to Goneril and Regan) and the allusion at line 468 to 'Moloch, horrid king besmeared with blood / Of
human sacrifice' (*PL* i. 392). There is fine ironic propriety in setting
up Robespierre as a Moloch, a tyrannical king, since the whole point
of the Revolution had been to overthrow the autocracy of the *ancien
régime*.

It is in the following book to 'Residence in France and French Revolution' that Wordsworth finally places the crucial 'spots of time' passage, followed by the recollection of his father's death. In the two-part *Prelude* of 1799, this section had been more tellingly placed closer to the major 'spots of time' of Wordsworth's childhood. There, it occurs immediately after the episode of the drowned man, linked by some lines not included in the full *Prelude*:

> I might advert
> To numerous accidents in flood or field,
> Quarry or moor, or 'mid the winter snows,
> Distresses and disasters, tragic facts
> Of rural history, that impressed my mind
> With images to which in following years
> Far other feelings were attached—with forms
> That yet exist with independent life,
> And, like their archetypes, know no decay.

> (*1799* i. 279)

Not only do these lines reveal Wordsworth's conception of the 'spots' and of the relationship between memory and imagination, they also include another echo of Othello's 'moving accidents by flood and field',[30] which we have seen to be important in other poems on which Wordsworth was working between 1798 and 1800. In *The Ruined Cottage* and 'Hart-Leap Well', the allusion is couched in negative terms as Wordsworth seeks to distinguish his kind of tragedy from Shakespeare's. Here, the phrase from *Othello* is used differently, for it serves to give authority to 'tragic facts / Of rural history'. Wordsworth's rural histories might seem to be below the dignity of tragedy, but the allusion raises them to the level of Othello's heroic early life. There is also a contextual parallel: the phrase refers to Othello weaving stories from his past, captivating Desdemona with a combination of memory and imagination which seems to amount to witchcraft. Othello's—and, by extension, Shakespeare's—magical power with words is a fitting analogue to the process Wordsworth is describing, whereby incidents from the past take on a life and a permanence of their own in the imagination and the memory. Furthermore, the act of alluding is singularly appropriate at this moment since allusions recover past voices, those of previous poets, just as spots of time recover the individual's own past.

At the climax of book eleven, his final account of how the imagination is restored by 'spots of time', Wordsworth places the incident when he stood at a cross-roads waiting for the horses that would take him and his brother home for the Christmas holidays. Ten days later his father died. Whenever Wordsworth experiences a storm or is 'in the woods' (xi. 387, suggesting a Dantesque 'selva oscura' in the middle way of life), his spirit is revived by the memory of the cross-roads, which seems to act as a barrier between him and the harsher memory of his father's death. But at the same time, the ghost of his father comes to him with the memory, for the phrase with which he describes the images of the scene is yet another recollection of Hamlet and the ghost: the elements, the sheep, the tree, the wall, 'The noise of wood and water', the mist, 'Advanced in such indisputable shapes' (xi. 375–81). Hamlet says to the ghost 'Thou com'st in such a questionable shape' (I. iv. 43). Wordsworth misreads 'questionable' (as 'dubious' instead of 'inviting talk') as powerfully as Blake does 'sightless' when in *Pity* he makes Macbeth's 'couriers of the air' blind instead of invisible. Although one would expect objects to be perceived shadowily in the mist and 'sleety rain', the shapes that come to Wordsworth are *indisputable*; but more than this, because of the allusion it is indisputable that his father lies at the root of the memory.[31] And, at another level, Shakespeare himself becomes a ghostly substitute father-figure for Wordsworth-Hamlet. Allusion has offered an intimation of the poet's immortality.

In writing about Wordsworth, one always comes back to Coleridge. His summing up of Wordsworth's pre-eminent gift remains definitive: 'in imaginative power, he stands nearest of all modern writers to Shakespear and Milton; and yet in a kind perfectly unborrowed and his own' (*BL* ii. 151). But 'perfectly unborrowed' is wrong, for Wordsworth at his best borrows creatively. Certain inherited phrases, especially those associated with passages that exemplify or circumscribe 'imaginative power', are far from 'piddling': they are powerful ghostly presences that enable Wordsworth to *stand near* to Shakespeare and Milton in a different way from that meant by Coleridge.

6

Shakespeare and Blake's Imagination

WILLIAM BLAKE still intimidates some readers. He used to be regarded with suspicion because of his association with eighteenth-century mystical traditions; his later and longer poems remain the preserve of the initiated few. Most of us prefer not to penetrate beyond the 'pure' poetry of the songs into the wild terrain of the late prophetic books. Perhaps because they are read only by those whom Shelley, referring to difficult poems of his own such as *Epipsychidion*, called the *synetoi*, Blake's longer works are often approached by way of their esoteric sources. Recondite allusions are emphasized at the expense of obvious ones.

Take the following passage from *The Marriage of Heaven and Hell*: 'Any man of mechanical talents may, from the writings of Paracelsus or Jacob Behmen, produce ten thousand volumes of equal value with Swedenborg's, and from those of Dante or Shakespear an infinite number. But when he has done this, let him not say that he knows better than his master, for he only holds a candle in sunshine' (K 158). Faced with this, the scholar will probably respond by elucidating the history of the metaphor in the second sentence. Since it is a crucial image in the work of several seventeenth-century neo-platonists,[1] we may easily be led into a learned discourse on the relationship between Blake and Nathanael Culverwell—a worthwhile project, but one that will rapidly take us away from what Blake is actually saying. He may well have admired Culverwell more than Swedenborg—that would cohere with the assertion that Paracelsus and Boehme are superior to the Swedish mystic—but the names ranked highest here are those of Dante and Shakespeare. Swedenborg merely offers intellectualized abstractions about the centrality of imagination to true vision; Dante and Shakespeare provide imaginative creations that exemplify the power of the faculty.[2] Whether he is personified as Shakespeare, Los, or the first person singular, the poet with his visionary power is at the centre of Blake's work.

Shakespeare's status as exemplary poet is suggested by a passage in Akenside's *The Pleasures of Imagination* which is another possible source

for Blake's candle in sunshine. First the two sources of light are contrasted,

> Who but rather turns
> To Heaven's broad fire his unconstrained view,
> Than to the glimmering of a waxen flame?

Then in the following lines there is an implicit appeal to the authority
of Theseus on the poet's rolling eye that glances from heaven to earth:

> Who that, from Alpine heights, his labouring eye
> Shoots round the wide horizon, to survey
> The Nile or Ganges roll his wasteful tide

> (1744 edn., i. 174 ff.).

Like Akenside, Blake will allude to *A Midsummer Night's Dream* in
discussions of the imagination, a practice which we have already seen
at work in Coleridge and Wordsworth. In this chapter and the next
one, we will see Blake assimilating Shakespeare into a theory of
imagination and persistently alluding to the plays that were also
favoured by Coleridge and Wordsworth. For all Blake's idiosyn-
crasies, his interpretations and appropriations of Shakespeare are
very similar to those of the other major poets of the 1790s. A consideration of Blake's Shakespeare therefore provides a way of coming to
terms with some of the most difficult poems of the period, and
demonstrating the unity of English Romanticism.

Throughout his scathing annotations to Sir Joshua Reynolds's *Dis-
courses* Blake emphasizes the insufficiency of imitation and memory,
and the need for inspiration, vision, and genius. A passage like the
one I have quoted from *The Marriage of Heaven and Hell* provides a
valuable reminder that this emphasis does not mean that Blake wholly
rejects the imitation of great models, or that he has no time for recollection and re-creation of their works. He specifically uses the figure
of *producing* volumes from those of one's predecessors. The later
poet's works are multiplications of Dante and Shakespeare. He is a
pupil, they are his masters; later poems are only candles in the bright
sunshine of the skyey influences.

We must, however, be wary of treating a metaphor in one of
Blake's illuminated books as if it were a personal critical judgement of
the sort we find in his annotations to Reynolds. Nothing in the *Marriage*
should be taken at face value. Nevertheless, plate twenty-one, where
this remark occurs, is not one of those headed 'The voice of the Devil'

or 'Proverbs of Hell', nor does the comment come in a light-hearted 'Note' at the end of a plate, as the famous pronouncement on the true meaning of *Paradise Lost* does. It may therefore be assumed that Blake is not being ironic in giving supremacy to Dante and Shakespeare.

Sometimes, however, he adopts contrary voices and plays devil's advocate. The language of Quid the Cynic in the early unfinished prose satire *An Island in the Moon* is in that eighteenth-century tradition of rationally and sceptically questioning the geniuses of the past. Dr Johnson complained that in *Paradise Lost* 'the want of human interest is always felt'; Hugh Blair accused Shakespeare of 'genius shooting wild; deficient in just taste, and altogether unassisted by knowledge or art'.[3] Blake's Quid is unequivocal: 'I think that Homer is bombast, and Shakespeare is too wild, and Milton has no feelings: they might be easily outdone' (K 51). That Shakespeare is too wild is an eighteenth-century commonplace; that Homer is bombast is as much the opinion of Blake the visionary in certain moods as it is of Quid the Cynic (the whole of *An Island in the Moon* is open to ironic reading, but if one character comes closest to Blake's own position, it is Quid). Blake frequently extolled the biblical tradition and condemned the classical. The preface to *Milton* sets out to provoke: 'The Stolen and Perverted Writings of Homer and Ovid, of Plato and Cicero, which all Men ought to contemn, are set up by artifice against the Sublime of the Bible; but when the New Age is at leisure to Pronounce, all will be set right' (K 480).

The Shakespeare attacked in *An Island in the Moon* keeps company with Homer and Milton. We need to distinguish between this Shakespeare and the lyric poet who, with his fellow Elizabethans and their eighteenth-century imitators such as Collins, presides over the diction of the *Poetical Sketches* written in the years preceding the prose satire. Blake's approach to Shakespeare underwent radical transformation in the years between *King Edward the Third*, with its servile imitation, and *Jerusalem*, with its subtle allusiveness. Just as Romantic conceptions of Shakespeare differ from poet to poet, so they change within the body of a single poet's work. Different attributes and different plays are emphasized at different times. The Shakespeare of the songs and early works is accorded the praise implied by imitation in the *Poetical Sketches*, but he is clearly not the Shakespeare who, beside Milton, is yoked to the classics in the preface to *Milton*: 'Shakespeare and Milton were both curb'd by the general malady and infection from the silly Greek and Latin slaves of the Sword' (K 480). In the sentence preceding this, Blake has looked forward to the day when 'the Daughters of Memory shall become the Daughters of Inspiration', that is to say, when the poetry of mimesis will give way to the poetry of vision. The inspired Shakespeare was himself an inspiration to Blake; the Shakespeare who, like nearly all other English poets, wrote in iambic pentameter derived from classical hexameter was rejected. The preface to *Jerusalem* makes this clear:

When this Verse was first dictated to me, I consider'd a Monotonous Cadence, like that used by Milton and Shakspeare and all writers of English Blank Verse, derived from the modern bondage of Rhyming, to be a necessary and indispensible part of Verse. But I soon found that in the mouth of a true Orator such monotony was not only awkward, but as much a bondage as rhyme itself. I therefore have produced a variety in every line, both of cadences and number of syllables. (K 621)

Yet the rhetorical effect of this rejection of Miltonic cadence depends on an allusion to Milton. It is a reply to the note prefacing the second edition of *Paradise Lost* with its claim that the poem 'is to be esteemed an example set, the first in English, of ancient liberty recovered from the troublesome and modern bondage of rhyming' (*PL* p. 39). And Blake is still very much bound to Milton when he begins his epic:

> Of the Sleep of Ulro! and of the passage through
> Eternal Death! and of the awaking to Eternal Life.
> This theme calls me in sleep night after night, and ev'ry morn
> Awakes me at sun-rise.[4]

Although Blake may have escaped from iambic pentameter, the language of this opening is clearly derived from 'Of man's first disobedience, and the fruit . . .' and 'while thou / Visit'st my slumbers nightly, or when morn / Purples the east' (*PL* i. 1, vii. 28).

This way of implicitly assimilating Milton while at the same time reacting against him is very typical of Blake. In his case we cannot speak only of the praise implied by imitation. Influence is always at work, but Blake's relationship with his predecessors is usually revisionary. I make no apology for using Harold Bloom's word, for Blake is the poet of this era about whom he writes best and to whom his theory of influence is most applicable. After all, Blake's annotation to the passage in Reynolds's first *Discourse* on how the 'great Masters' should be 'perfect and infallible guides' to young artists, 'subjects for their imitation, not their criticism', was an incisive 'Imitation is Criticism' (K 453).

It was the prosody of Milton and Shakespeare that Blake said he wished to reject. This was partly because of his desire to introduce biblical rhythms into English verse, but also because he realized that there was no future in the surface imitation of Shakespearean and Miltonic styles. The preface to *Jerusalem* is dated 1805: the lifeless, derivative nature of late eighteenth-century English verse drama had shown that the attempt to imitate Shakespeare was doomed to failure. Southey's *Joan of Arc* (1796) suggested that the same was true of Miltonic epic—Blake was not to know that at this time Wordsworth was working on *The Prelude*, the nearest thing to a successful assimilation of Miltonic style and Romantic sensibility. What he needed was a form of imitation that was also a form of criticism. In *Jerusalem*, with its 'variety in every line', stylistic influence is eschewed but, as we shall see, intuitive filiations remain.

Blake's most overt statement of his debt to Shakespeare occurs in a poem that was not intended for publication. To call a poem *Milton* is to engage publicly with the influence of Milton; Blake works out his relationship with Shakespeare more privately. The second half of a letter to John Flaxman, dated 12 September 1800, is written in verse. Blake thanks God for his friends on earth, Flaxman, Henry Fuseli, and William Hayley—all of them, incidentally, ardent admirers of Shakespeare who included moments from the plays among the raw materials for their own creative works.[5] He then considers his 'lot in the Heavens', the company he keeps among the mighty dead:

> Now my lot in the Heavens is this, Milton lov'd me
>   in childhood and shew'd me his face.
> Ezra came with Isaiah the Prophet, but Shakespeare
>   in riper years gave me his hand;
> Paracelsus and Behmen appear'd to me
>
>   (K 799).

As we have seen from the reference in *The Marriage of Heaven and Hell*, highly as Blake valued Paracelsus and Boehme, their influence was less important than that of past geniuses among poets. The Old Testament prophets are fundamental in view of Blake's desire to write poetry of biblical sublimity. Ezra is especially important because it is a book about rebuilding the temple at Jerusalem; Blake wished to build Jerusalem in England's green and pleasant land (it is, incidentally, fitting that his most English lyric, 'And did those feet', should begin by adapting an image belonging to England's national poet, 'Over whose acres walk'd those blessed feet'—*1H4* I. i. 25). In a letter to Dr Trusler written just over a year before, Blake had been more explicit about his identification with Milton; with reference to some of his designs, he wrote 'And tho' I call them Mine, I know that they are not Mine, being of the same opinion with Milton when he says That the Muse visits his slumbers and awakes and governs his Song when Morn purples the East' (K 792). Beside the biblical and Miltonic influences, so manifest throughout Blake's major writings, that of Shakespeare is hard to pin down; perhaps that is why modern criticism has neglected it.[6] Yet in this list Shakespeare is given as much weight as the others.

The reference in the letter to Dr Trusler is to the passage in the seventh book of *Paradise Lost*, also echoed in the preface and opening lines of *Jerusalem*, in which Milton imagines being visited by his Muse. Blake makes similar statements on several other occasions. Crabb Robinson records the following remark: 'I write when commanded by the spirits, and the moment I have written I see the words fly about the room in all directions—It is then published and the Spirits can read.'[7] In successive letters of summer 1803 to Thomas Butts, Blake states 'I have written this Poem from immediate Dictation, twelve or sometimes twenty or thirty lines at a time, without Premeditation and even against my Will' and, with reference to *Milton* or possibly *The Four Zoas*, 'I may praise it, since I dare not pretend to be any other than the Secretary; the Authors are in Eternity' (K 823, 825). Blake imagines his hand to be guided by ancestral voices; Crabb Robinson identifies some of these 'Authors' in a letter to Dorothy Wordsworth when he describes the poet in his later years 'enjoying constant intercourse with the world of spirits—He receives visits from Shakespeare Milton Dante Voltaire etc., etc., etc. And has given me repeatedly their very words in their conversations . . . his books . . . are dictations from the Spirits' (*Records*, 324). Voltaire, representative of the Enlightenment, is an odd man out, but otherwise the list suggests that Blake's equivalents of the 'Muse' who visited Milton nightly were the great poets of the past. To judge from a 'spiritual conversation' recorded by his friend John Varley in 1819, Blake was visited by Shakespeare's characters as well as the dramatist himself:

> Hotspur said
> any and we shou[l]d have had the Battle
> had it not been for those cursd Stars

Hotspur Said he was indignant to have been killd
through the Stars Influence by such a Person
as Prince Henry who was so much his
inferior.[8]

Blake seemed to treat his spiritual conversations lightly, but there is no irony in the passages concerning inspiration in the letters to Butts; Crabb Robinson's account must therefore be as valid for the poet's productive years as his old age.

The specifically physical nature of the metaphors in the poem to Flaxman bears out this interpretation. Milton shows his face, the prophets come, the hermeticists appear, Shakespeare offers his hand. Blake is the 'Secretary'; 'the Authors are in Eternity'—they are at once the authors who make up the tradition, the authors of Blake's own words, and the authorities who give his works their weight. If Blake really understood his creative processes in this way, it is right that the voices of those 'Authors' should sometimes make themselves heard in the form of verbal echoes. He allows his poetic forefathers to speak through him; in so doing, he both revives and revises them. We will see, for example, that he often revives a Shakespearean familial conflict or encounter, but alters the roles played by different generations.

With regard to the relative influence of the ever-living dead English poets, that of Milton has always been seen as more important than that of Shakespeare. But the lines sent to Flaxman in 1800 make an interesting chronological distinction: 'Milton lov'd me in childhood . . . but Shakespeare in riper years gave me his hand'. In the preface to *A Father's Memoirs of his Child* (1806, repr. in *Records*, 421–31), for which Blake designed the frontispiece, B. H. Malkin testifies that as a young man the poet had a taste—unfashionable in the 1770s—for Shakespeare's sonnets and narrative poems. The early *Poetical Sketches* are steeped in the language of Shakespeare and the Elizabethans; Alexander Gilchrist discerned that a lyric such as 'To the Evening Star', with its 'then the wolf rages wide, / And the lion glares thro' the dun forest', was 'a reminiscence, but not a slavish one' of Puck's night song, 'Now the hungry lion roars, / And the wolf behowls the moon',[9] a pairing to which Blake returned much later when he wrote in *The Four Zoas*, 'Why howl the Lion and the Wolf? why do they roam abroad?' (K 276).

There are, however, few traces of Milton in the *Sketches*. 'Protect them with thine influence' Blake says to the evening star; in the later works, the prophetic books, such a plea will always evoke the biblical and Miltonic Pleiades 'shedding sweet influence',[10] but the influences protecting the early works are Elizabethan (as Keats will, Blake includes an 'Imitation of Spenser' in his first collection). It is hard to detect the 'childhood' influence of Milton; if he is not present in the *Poetical Sketches* written between the ages of twelve and twenty, his power must have dissipated rather quickly. The 'riper years' are presumably the 1780s and '90s, the crucial period of Blake's poetic development; that Shakespeare guides him in this period poses a question mark over the accepted notion that Milton was Blake's chief mentor among English poets. The image of Shakespeare taking the hand of the poet to lead him forward implies a touchingly personal relationship. Milton may be the star shedding blinding influence from the *Paradiso* of his massive achievement, but Shakespeare is the fellow-traveller guiding the poet through the *Inferno* of the 1790s, Virgil to his Dante. Or to use another metaphor, Milton is like the vapour which represents God in 'The Little Boy lost', Shakespeare like the father holding the child's hand in 'The Little Boy found'.[11]

It is perhaps unwise to cite Virgil in a metaphor. In accordance with his argument that 'Shakespeare and Milton were both curb'd by the general malady and infection from the silly Greek and Latin slaves of the Sword', Blake reacted violently against the Shakespeare who could in any way be seen as part of the 'classical' tradition; in his savage satirical paraphrase of the classically learned Dr Thornton's translation of the Lord's Prayer, he wrote 'lead us not to read the Bible, but let our Bible be Virgil and Shakspeare' (K 789). The Shakespeare who held sway over Blake in the early part of his career stood in opposition to the 'classical'. He was the Shakespeare of the magical plays and, above all, of the songs which departed from pentameter. This Shakespeare is as important for Blake's songs as Milton is for his prophetic books.

Blake's particular interest in the magical and supernatural Shakespeare is demonstrated by the range of subjects he chose to illustrate: again and again he returned to *Macbeth* and *A Midsummer Night's Dream*, or to dreams and visions in other plays. I do not intend to enter here into a discussion of Blake as an artist; I shall do so in the sequel to this book, in the context of an account of Shakespearean illustration in the Romantic age.[12] But it is revealing to list some typical subjects: *Hecate*; *Macbeth and the Ghost of Banquo*; *Oberon, Titania and Puck with*

Fairies Dancing; *Oberon and Titania on a Lily*; *Oberon and Titania, preceded by Puck*; *Hamlet Administering the Oath to his Friends*; *Hamlet and his Father's Ghost*; and four versions of *The Vision of Queen Katharine* in *Henry VIII*.[13]

The well-known large colour print of 1795, *Pity* (Fig. 1; Butlin, Nos. 310–15), is the Shakespearean design that has most relevance to a study of Blake's poetry. The lines it illustrates struck a deep chord in Blake's sensibility, which was so influenced by the traditions of sympathy and sentiment:

> And pity, like a naked new-born babe,
> Striding the blast, or heaven's cherubin, hors'd
> Upon the sightless couriers of the air,
> Shall blow the horrid deed in every eye,
> That tears shall drown the wind.
>
> (I. vii. 21)

It is unusual for Shakespeare to expand a simile into three lines—that is more the prerogative of Milton—which is perhaps why Blake found the image especially fruitful. Notoriously, he misinterprets 'sightless' by making his horses blind—Shakespeare meant 'invisible'—but this does not matter, for the originality of *Pity* lies in the way that it evokes the outrageous vividness of Macbeth's image and at the same time assimilates it into a Blakean frame of reference. There could be no better example of the tendency simultaneously to revive and revise Shakespeare.

Blake frequently associated pity with tears and the wind, as in plate twenty-five of *The First Book of Urizen*, printed at the time he was working towards his image from *Macbeth*: 'And he wept and he called it Pity, / And his tears flowed down on the winds' (K 235). 'Pitying tears' are also linked with a 'new born babe' in a *Notebook* lyric of 1793 (K 186) and in the song of innocence concerning sympathy, 'On Anothers Sorrow': 'Pouring pity in their breast . . . Weeping tear on infants tear' (K 122). In *The Four Zoas* 'two little Infants wept upon the desolate wind' (K 269). Blake's attitude to pity was double-edged. On the one hand, 'Pity must join together those whom wrath has torn in sunder' (*Jerusalem*, 7: 62, K 626), but on the other, 'pity divides the soul / In pangs, eternity on eternity' (*Urizen*, 13: 53, K 230). That notion of division is crucial, for *Pity*, with its hint of a mother dying in childbirth, draws together a sense of Macbeth's murderous breaking of human bonds, the bloody children in the play (Lady Macbeth's

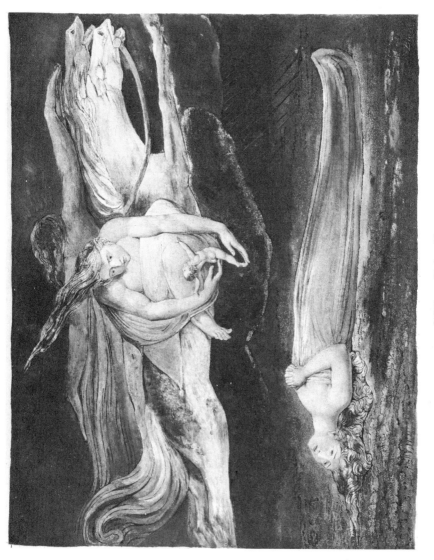

1. William Blake, *Pity*

threat to dash out the brains of her babe; Macduff's murdered 'chicks'; the apparition of a bloody babe), and the Blakean belief that the self is divided on entering mortal life.

'I should have remember'd that pity divides the soul / And man unmans', laments Los in *Milton* (8: 19, K 488). The influence of *Macbeth* is manifest here since 'And man unmans' echoes Lady Macbeth's persistent taunts, which first occur immediately after the 'pity' soliloquy, that Macbeth is 'quite unmann'd'. The association between a thread of imagery in the play, Blake's colour print of horses stretching across the sky, as if possessed, and Los's discussion of pity in *Milton* is reinforced by the preceding lines: 'Palamabron is also in sad dilemma: / *His horses are mad*' (8: 17, my italics).

Because of its exploration of the visionary power of imagination, *Macbeth* is one of the Shakespearean plays that most preoccupied Blake. The two incidents he chose to depict in his portrait of Shakespeare were Banquo's show of kings and the first appearance of the witches (Butlin, No. 343.10). The seriousness Blake attached to the witches is demonstrated by an aside in his catalogue description of the painting, *Sir Jeffery Chaucer and the nine and twenty Pilgrims on their Journey to Canterbury*:

By way of illustration, I instance Shakspeare's Witches in Macbeth. Those who dress them for the stage, consider them as wretched old women, and not as Shakspeare intended, the Goddesses of Destiny; this shews how Chaucer has been misunderstood in his sublime work. Shakspeare's Fairies also are the rulers of the vegetable world, and so are Chaucer's; let them be so considered, and then the poet will be understood, and not else.

(K 569–70)

This shows that Blake knew something of Shakespeare on stage. He took a keen interest in the theatrical world: *An Island in the Moon* seems to be indebted to the theatrical entertainments of Samuel Foote;[14] Blake was a friend of the dramatist and theatrical impresario Prince Hoare; he is known to have attended productions at Drury Lane (see *Records*, 272–3), and he criticized Master Betty in such a way as to suggest that, despite his reservations about the staging of the Shakespearean supernatural, he treated the art of acting very seriously— 'The Town is Mad. Young Roscius like all Prodigies is the talk of Every Body. I have not seen him and perhaps never may. I have no curiosity to see him, as I well know what is within the compass of a boy of 14, and as to Real Acting it is Like Historical Painting, No Boy's Work' (K 859).

Like so many of his contemporaries, Blake posited a close connection between the supernatural and the visionary imagination. He
saw both the *Macbeth* witches and the fairies in *A Midsummer Night's
Dream* as especially powerful forces who were travestied when embodied on stage. The two plays were crucial for both his theory and
practice of imagination. *A Midsummer Night's Dream* offered not only a
fairy-world that he took to be the product of imagination in its highest
sense, but also Theseus' definition of the imagination. His response
to the latter is recorded on the half-title page of his copy of Swedenborg's *Heaven and Hell*. An earlier reader had (inaccurately) quoted
Theseus: '"And as Imagination bodies forth is [*sic*] forms of things
unseen turns them to / "shape and gives to airy Nothing a local
habitation and a Name."' Blake annotated the annotation: 'Thus
Fools quote Shakespeare; the above is Theseus' opinion Not Shakespear's. You might as well quote Satan's blasphemies from Milton
and give them as Milton's Opinions' (K 929). Is Blake thus distancing himself from the tendency to treat Theseus' view of the poetic
imagination as Shakespeare's?

The comparison is ambivalent in that Blake wrote this around 1790
as he was first coming to terms with Milton in *The Marriage of Heaven
and Hell*, a text that, from title onwards, engaged with Swedenborg's
Heaven and Hell. At this time, Blake was provocatively arguing that
Paradise Lost was flawed; he wanted to throw off the chains of Reason
that had restricted Milton, in whom 'the Father is Destiny, the Son a
Ratio of the five senses, and the Holy-ghost Vacuum!' (*MHH* pl. 6,
K 150). Whatever the possible tonal ironies, this is a serious critique
in a well-established tradition. The poet in Milton is seen to be in
opposition to the rationalist in whose hands, as Pope put it, 'God the
Father turns a School-Divine'.[15] The *poet* is in unconscious sympathy
with Satan. It is therefore possible to argue that Blake was being
ironic in drawing a distinction between Theseus and Shakespeare: as
Satan voices the opinions of the poet Milton, so Theseus speaks for
the poet Shakespeare.

But this interpretation is unsatisfactory in that it makes 'Thus
Fools quote Shakespeare' redundant. Clarification is provided by
Gilchrist; some years later Blake discussed with him the lines from
A Midsummer Night's Dream and was reported as saying that 'the things
imagination saw were as much realities as were gross and tangible
facts'. It was to Theseus' 'aery nothing' that he objected (Gilchrist,
318). This explains matters: Theseus is a rational man, under

Urizen,[16] whose account of the poet's power is therefore inadequate. For Shakespeare himself, Blake implies, the imaginative world—the fairy world of the wood with which Blake is in sympathy—is the one that endures. Blake's position is closer to that of Hippolyta: 'fancy's images' grow to 'something of great constancy' (v. i. 25—Blake makes no Coleridgean distinction between imagination and fancy). In one of the best modern accounts of *A Midsummer Night's Dream*, C. L. Barber contends that Theseus' lines are not simply a glorification of the poet, as they are often taken to be when quoted out of context: 'In his comment there is wonder, wonderfully expressed, at the power of the mind to create from airy nothing; but also recognition that the creation may be founded, after all, merely on airy nothing.'[17] Blake, too, senses that Theseus restricts the world of imagination, makes it into an airy nothing without power in everyday material existence (in Blake's language, the 'vegetable' world; in Barber's, the 'working-day' as opposed to 'festive' world). This is why Blake insists on distancing Shakespeare from Theseus; he would have Shakespeare accord eternal and universal power to the imagination. 'Shakspeare's Fairies' are not restricted to the magical but evanescent night: they 'also are the rulers of the vegetable world'.

Shakespeare, then, was of great value to Blake as he thought out his conception of imagination. But what of his imaginative practice? An examination of certain jottings and sketches in the *Notebook* which he inherited in 1787 on the death of his brother, Robert, will reveal some of the ways in which Shakespeare worked on Blake's imagination in the crucial years around the time he was composing *Songs of Innocence and of Experience*.

Four of its captioned emblems have Shakespearean associations. Emblem five shows a couple in the blossom of an anemone; it is inscribed 'Every thing that grows / Holds in perfection but a little / moment'.[18] Robert Blake had already sketched in the *Notebook* (N5) an ink and wash drawing of Oberon and Titania reclining on a flower, with fairies dancing above. This is the source for Blake's watercolour of *Oberon and Titania on a Lily*, which is reproduced, though with left to right reversal, as the fifth plate of *The Song of Los*. What begins as a Shakespearean illustration becomes an archetypal Blakean image: the design that heads the second chapter of *Jerusalem* shows two lovers in the heart of a lily, as does the title-page to *The Book of Thel*. 'The Blossom' in *Songs of Innocence* includes an embracing couple among other tiny figures on a flower, and 'Infant Joy' provides a

variation where a different kind of love, maternal as opposed to sexual, is held within an anemone. Both these lyrics are illuminated by
the lines from sonnet fifteen quoted underneath the *Notebook* sketch,
'When I consider every thing that grows / Holds in perfection but a
little moment'. A Blakean song of innocence is a crystallization of a
single, momentary image of perfection.

But to freeze an image is to deprive it of energy, even of life. So it is
that a song of innocence is likely to be answered by a song of experience. The fifty-third emblem in Blake's *Notebook* shows a mother with
a child 'untimely pluckd' by death. The faint inscription beneath it
reads 'Sweet rose fair flower untimely pluckd soon faded / Pluckd in
the bud and faded in the Spring / Shakespeare' (N83). The quotation
is from the tenth poem of *The Passionate Pilgrim*. Blake has no reason to
question the then commonly accepted attribution of that series of
poems to Shakespeare. Here his lyric poetry is associated with the
image of life as a flower that only endures for a moment, that is all too
quickly tainted by 'experience', cut off by death.

Another group of emblems testifies to Blake's interest in a different
aspect of Shakespeare. The legend to the pencil drawing of a man on
page ninety-five of the *Notebook* reads 'O that the Everlasting had not
fixd / His canon gainst Self slaughter / Shakespeare'. Contemplation
of suicide leads to Hamlet's 'To be, or not to be' soliloquy. Erdman
describes one of the sketches on page seventy-five as 'Theotormon
(perhaps), on a rock or mound, acting the part of Hamlet' (N75 n.).
This may appear to be a tenuous connection, but Erdman goes on to
show that 'The Hamlet figure, with minor alterations, changes into
King David in *The Gates of Paradise* 8 or, more exactly, was drawn
upon when Blake revised Emblem 15 into *GP* 8'. (Emblem fifteen
shows a father and son, perhaps related to Hamlet and the ghost.)

This is only one of several associations between Shakespeare and
The Gates of Paradise, that curious brief work first engraved in 1793 in
which Blake juxtaposed visual and verbal emblems in a manner
related to, though far cruder than, that of the *Songs*. The title of the
first *Gate* is lifted directly from *As You Like it*, 'I found him beneath a
Tree' (K 761, quoting III. ii. 235); the spiritual body in the thirteenth
is in a position identical to that of the ghost in Blake's drawing, *Brutus
and Caesar's Ghost* (K 768; Butlin, No. 547.4). Most interestingly, the
third emblem, 'Earth' (K 762), reproduces emblem fifty-nine of the
Notebook, a figure with arms clasped over top of the head, inscribed
'Rest rest perturbed Spirit / Shakespeare' (N93, quoting *Ham* I. v.

182). Blake may have made the association with 'Earth' because Hamlet says to the perturbed spirit of his father, 'Well said, old mole, canst work i' th' earth so fast' (I. v. 162). On page seventy-four of the *Notebook* there are two sketches of figures in the same position, arms curled round the head, expression anguished. It is the expression of these heads, with their long noses, large eyes and aggressively open mouths, that appears on the face of the self-clutching, bat-winged head at the foot of the first page of the Preludium to *Europe*.[19] This figure seems to represent the agonized Louis XVI. Through the associated drawings in the *Notebook*, it is possible to see Blake treating Old Hamlet and the French king as comparable monarchs, each having been abruptly removed from his throne. The parallel should not be pushed so far as to suggest that Blake by implication condemns the perpetrators of the French Revolution as self-interested Claudiuses, but it is instructive to see an image moving from the status of commentary on Shakespeare to commentary on Europe in the 1790s.

This account of the transformations of *Notebook* emblems and inscriptions has dwelt on minutiae, but by examining such processes in Blake's imagination one becomes more acutely aware of Shakespeare's hitherto under-estimated place in the writings and drawings in which he worked towards the *Songs* and shorter prophetic books. It is now time to consider Shakespeare's presence in the poems themselves.

7

Blake's Poetry and the Auspices of Shakespeare

IN his first collection, *Poetical Sketches,* Blake strives to find a voice; in doing so, he imitates a range of models, both Elizabethan and eighteenth century. Shakespeare's presence is thus visible on the surface; he is not assimilated and transformed as he will be by the more mature Blake.

'To Spring', the first poem in the collection, reveals Blake's debt to the language of Elizabethan verse. When he asks 'dewy' spring to 'Come o'er the eastern hills' (K 1), he may not be indebted specifically to Horatio's description of the morn walking 'o'er the dew of yon high eastward hill' (*Ham* I. i. 167), but he is clearly imitating the lyrical language of Shakespeare and his contemporaries. There are further quasi-Elizabethan aubades in the song 'When early morn walks forth in sober grey' (Horatio, too, emphasizes dawn's dress) and at the beginning of scene three of *King Edward the Third* (K 10, 21).

'Fair Elenor' (K 4–6) is Blake's attempt at a gothic horror poem. Its principal affinities are with the 'graveyard' school of eighteenth-century poetry, but the phrase 'The deed is done' evokes *Macbeth*, the play that appealed most strongly to the gothic imagination. 'I am thy husband's head', though it sounds like a line out of *The Castle of Otranto*, rhythmically suggests Old Hamlet's 'I am thy father's spirit' (I. v. 9), a possible parallel that is strengthened by the injunction to Elenor not to give her hand to the 'cursed duke' who murdered her husband as he slept—and indeed by the fact that as an illustrator Blake returned on several occasions to the encounter between Hamlet and the ghost. But then there is a 'bloody napkin' that intrudes incongruously from *As You Like it* (IV. iii. 93, 138): 'Fair Elenor' is a farrago of insufficiently thought out or organized borrowings.

Since the *Songs of Innocence and of Experience* are Blake's most perfect and intricately crafted works, the most interesting pieces in *Poetical Sketches* are the early songs. They reveal that Blake's conception of song originates in Elizabethan, and especially Shakespearean, lyric. 'My silks and fine array' (K 6) is a beautifully finished exercise in the

manner of the songs in the plays. Its axe, spade, and winding sheet
come from the *Hamlet* gravedigger (V. i. 94–5); the dying lover, yew
tree, and the idea of weeping over a grave from Feste's 'Come away,
come away, death'; and the female point of view—most Elizabethan
lyrics have a male voice complaining about a cruel mistress—from
Ophelia. Similarly, 'Memory, hither come' (K 8) is under the sway
of the 'Come hither' song in *As You Like it*, and 'Blind-man's Buff',
with its jolly tetrameter, warm down-to-earth tone, and opening
image 'When silver Snow decks Susan's cloaths, / And jewel hangs at
th' shepherd's nose' (K 15) is manifestly derived from the song at the
end of *Love's Labour's Lost*, 'When icicles hang by the wall, / And Dick
the shepherd blows his nail'. The connection with Shakespeare is
compounded when Blake echoes the opening of 'Blind-man's Buff' in
a later 'Song by an Old Shepherd', composed about 1787 and written
into a copy of the *Sketches*:

> When silver snow decks Sylvio's clothes
> And jewel hangs at shepherd's nose,
> We can abide life's pelting storm
> That makes our limbs quake, if our hearts be warm.

(K 64)

This results in an unlikely conjunction of *Love's Labour's Lost* and *King
Lear*, with its 'pelting of this pitiless storm' that was to be echoed by
Wordsworth and Coleridge. Then in the third stanza, 'Blow, boisterous wind, stern winter frown', another song from *As You Like it* is
introduced, 'Blow, blow, thou winter wind'. Again, Blake borrows
Shakespearean language without thinking through the consequences
of his juxtapositions.

Blake's first echo of *King Lear* is in his 'Mad Song' (K 8) where the
phrase 'a-cold' is a recollection of Edgar's 'Tom's a-cold'. The tone
of the 'Mad Song' is that of Lear on the heath: the speaker of the
poem cries out to 'the vault / Of paved heaven', his brain seized
'With frantic panic'. This is a first intimation that the image of Lear
in the storm captured the imagination of Blake as poet as well as
painter (*Lear Grasping his Sword* on the heath is one of his early
Shakespearean character-heads: Butlin, No. 84.5). There is a further
connection between this early poem and *Lear*. Blake probably owed
the idea of writing a 'Mad Song' to Percy's *Reliques of Ancient English
Poetry*, which included six of them. Their context in Percy is the
section devoted to ballads related to Shakespeare's plays—and this is

the most well-thumbed section in Blake's copy of the *Reliques*. Percy collected 'Mad Songs' in order to illustrate the character of Poor Tom in *Lear*; Blake went to Percy and found illuminations of Shakespeare, which he then turned to his own account.

As most students of *Poetical Sketches* have noted, Shakespeare's influence is at its greatest when Blake tried to write a play. The chief influence on *King Edward the Third* is the second historical tetralogy, *Henry V* in particular. The balancing of phrases, the use of enjambment and the occasional substitution of anapaest for iamb suggest that Blake had been studying the metre of *Henry V* in some detail. That play would also have provided him with some of the clearest examples of Shakespeare's movement from verse to prose when the social scale is descended. When Blake's Sir Thomas Dagworth disguises himself and treats the common soldiers—including his man William who, like Williams in *Henry V*, questions the morality of war —to a little touch of Dagworth in the night, he turns to prose. Peter Blunt is supposed to be a choric Shakespearean clown, while the Black Prince is a crudely drawn Hotspur ('It is my sin to love the noise of war': K 26), and the King, like Henry V, dedicates the battle to God, then, like Henry IV, compares princes to the sun. There are numerous verbal echoes and Shakespearean cadences.[1]

When Blake moved on from the *Poetical Sketches* to *Tiriel*, he borrowed more extensively from the matter of *Lear*. The poem begins with an aged king cursing his children; that is enough to alert us to the influence, despite the fact that Tiriel carries in his arms his dying wife rather than his youngest daughter. 'Serpents, not sons' says Tiriel (1: 22, K 99), combining Lear's 'Tigers, not daughters' with his 'How sharper than a serpent's tooth it is / To have a thankless child' (IV. ii. 40, I. iv. 288). Not recognizing the exiled Tiriel, his brother Ijim calls him 'foul fiend', just as Edgar when playing Poor Tom calls his father Gloucester 'the foul fiend Flibbertigibbet'. The innocent Har and Heva possess 'singing birds' and Har 'sing[s] in the great cage', a lyrical vision as violence rages around, in the same way that Lear's dream of restored innocence with Cordelia conceives that 'We two alone will sing like birds i' th' cage' (*Tiriel*, 4: 8, 3: 22, K 103; *Lr* III. iv. 115, V. iii. 9). As in *Lear*, there is a world of belching thunder and imprecations, a repeated image of 'eyes' seeing 'folly', and a youngest daughter who comes to the aid of her father after the other children have rejected him. But in this last instance there are two variations. Hela eventually abandons Tiriel and he curses her again, a twist very different from the end of *Lear*; Blake, whose visionary imagination is fundamentally optimistic, often resists the tragic in his approaches to Shakespeare. Secondly, the idea of the youngest daughter leading the aged king suggests not only Shakespeare but also Sophocles' *Oedipus at Colonus*[2] and the opening of *Samson Agonistes*. Earlier, however, Ijim has said to Tiriel 'I will lead thee', reinforcing the link between them and the pair of Edgar and Gloucester in the sub-plot of *Lear* (4: 23, K 104; cf. 'Poor Tom shall lead thee', IV. i. 79).

I think that Blake was aware of his extensive debt to *Lear* and sometimes tried to curb the influence, to escape the overbearing power of Shakespeare's handling of a similar story. Thus he deletes the lines 'The aged Tiriel could not speak, his heart was full of grief; / He strove against his rising passions, but still he could not speak' (2: 44, K 101). The idea of *not speaking*, the rising heart filled with grief: these are so fundamental to *Lear*, used so resonantly and inimitably by Shakespeare, that Blake perhaps felt that it was going too far to borrow them. Similarly, when he summarizes his poem in Tiriel's last speech, he deletes a line that is equally a summing up—if such a thing were possible—of *King Lear*: 'Such was Tiriel, / Hypocrisy, the idiot's wisdom and the wise man's folly' (8: 36, K 110). It is almost as if he has momentarily forgotten which work he is talking about; 'the idiot's wisdom' is a fine description of the Fool in *Lear*, but it is hard to find anything in *Tiriel* to which it might refer.

It is clear, then, that Blake's handling of Shakespeare in *Tiriel* is not entirely satisfactory. He has not progressed from unreconstituted borrowing of the sort that pervades the *Poetical Sketches*. Later, instead of simply borrowing the matter of *King Lear*, he will *transform* images from the play, incorporating them into his own vision. That very distinctive manuscript poem 'Auguries of Innocence' provides a case in point: the bleakness of Gloucester's 'As flies to wanton boys are we to th' gods, / They kill us for their sport' (IV. i. 36) becomes a proverbial couplet about nature's power to rebound on human cruelty, 'The wanton Boy that kills the Fly / Shall feel the Spider's enmity' (K 431).[3] The comparison of man's mortality to the fly's in *Songs of Experience* ('The Fly', K 213) may be another distant transformation of Gloucester's lines, although the image is not Shakespeare's alone.

At what stage does Blake begin actively to recast Shakespeare in this way, to transform instead of borrow? The overt Shakespearean references that inform the *Notebook* show him at work on the process. The first poem in which he achieves some measure of success in this

respect is *The Book of Thel*, dated 1789 though probably not completed
that year. Consider its flower, which is related to the watercolour,
Oberon and Titania on a Lily, and the *Notebook* sketch with its inscription
from Shakespeare's fifteenth sonnet, which was discussed in the
previous chapter. Since the title-page uses the image of lovers in an
anemone, the inscription which accompanies that image in the *Notebook* may be applied to the poem: it is about the precariousness of the
state of innocence. Thel descends into the world of experience and the
moment of her beauty and perfection is shattered. The Shakespearean
parallel is, however, drawn without explicit reference.

The poem begins 'by the river of Adona' (1: 4, K 127), a setting
lifted from Milton (*PL* i. 450–2) but also evoking Spenser's Garden of
Adonis and the fate of Adonis in Shakespeare's poem—his perfection,
too, lasts but a moment, and he ends by being transformed into an
anemone. A further intimation that the paradise of innocence cannot
endure the world of generation is provided by the presence there of a
'gilded butterfly' (i. 18). Blake frequently turned to the scene in
which King Lear constructs a world of innocence in which he and his
daughter 'laugh At gilded butterflies' (v. iii. 12), a world destroyed
by the harsh realities of 'vegetable' nature.

Thel is rudely awakened by a Cloud, a Worm, and a Clod of Clay.
Claudio's speech to the Duke in *Measure for Measure* had memorably
associated death with a 'clod', as Blake was to do on several subsequent occasions (e.g. at *First Book of Urizen*, 6: 11, K 226). The
worm is the canker in the bud of which Blake would have learnt in
Shakespeare's sonnets and other Elizabethan poems; in *Thel*, he uses
it with the richness of *Antony and Cleopatra*, as a symbol of both sexual
generation and death. It is another image that must to some extent be
indebted to Blake's early reading of Shakespeare; he uses it again and
again, for example on the lily in the uncorrected opening plate of
Jerusalem chapter two, where it is both a phallic symbol and a
reminder that this lily too will be 'Pluckd in the bud'.

Thel is finally confronted by a 'voice of sorrow', speaking the knowing language of the fallen world that predominates in so many of
Shakespeare's sonnets—'the poison of a smile', 'gifts and graces
show'ring fruits and coined gold', 'a Tongue impressed with honey
from every wind' (6: 12–16, K 130). These are not specific allusions
to or echoes of the sonnets; it is rather a case of Blake having adapted
the tone of Shakespeare and fitted it to a poem written in a very different form.

The themes of civil war, mad monarchs, tyranny, and unnatural family division kept sending Blake back to *King Lear*. In the *Notebook* there is an equivocal little pair of couplets, apparently written in the early 1790s, entitled 'Merlin's Prophecy' (K 177). They serve as a reminder that Lear's Fool, the topsy-turvy prophet with his jingling paradoxes, is as considerable an influence on Blake as the grander prophets, Ezekiel and Milton. In its social, sexual, and spiritual vision, the Fool's rhyme in the storm is quintessentially Blakean:

> When priests are more in word than matter;
> When brewers mar their malt with water;
> When nobles are their tailors' tutors;
> No heretics burn'd, but wenches' suitors;
> Then shall the realm of Albion
> Come to great confusion. . . .
> This prophecy Merlin shall make, for I live before his time.

> (*Lr* III. ii. 81–95)

Here are Blake's concerns of hypocrisy in the upper echelons of society, priests who do not practise what they preach—a theme most power-fully and concisely expressed in the lyric 'The Garden of Love' —and an established church that has made herself a harlot ('And bawds and whores do churches build', says the Fool). For Blake, 'the realm of Albion' has indeed 'Come to great confusion'.

'Merlin's Prophecy', which owes more to *Lear* than the pseudo-Chaucerian poem of that title which Shakespeare is parodying, is only the most obvious example of Blake's debt to the manner of the Fool. Like many radical writers of the 1790s, he owes much of his trenchancy and prophetic power to his capacity to hold Miltonic or biblical strains of rhetoric together with the Fool's technique of dropping into an almost nursery-rhyme manner which is all the more bitterly satiric —and memorable to the reader—for being so simple. His use of the Fool's prophecy is a particularly striking example of the way that Shakespeare is not of an age but for all time; *King Lear* may be set in the dark early days of British history, but it speaks irresistibly to Shakespeare's own society, to Blake's, and to ours.

The question of simplicity, or rather density within a framework of simplicity, brings us to Blake's lyrics. There are few obvious verbal echoes in *Songs of Innocence and of Experience* and the related *Notebook* lyrics, but they could not have been written without the example of

Shakespeare's songs. We are, however, presented with considerable difficulties in writing critically about this relationship. It is easier felt than explained; that is why accounts of it have tended to be vague and emotive.

A. E. Housman, who pondered much on the music of verse, believed that these songs stood alone in the language: 'For me the most poetical of all poets is Blake. I find his lyrical note as beautiful as Shakespeare's and more beautiful than anyone else's.' He went on to quote from the two poets' songs examples of 'poetry neat, or adulterated with so little meaning that nothing except poetical emotion is perceived and matters'.[4] His terms, so unfashionable now, perhaps derive from Pater's argument in 'The School of Giorgione' that lyric is the highest and most complete form of poetry 'because in it we are least able to detach the matter from the form, without a deduction of something from that matter itself'. Pater continues,

And the very perfection of such poetry often appears to depend, in part, on a certain suppression or vagueness of mere subject, so that the meaning reaches us through ways not distinctly traceable by the understanding, as in some of the most imaginative compositions of William Blake, and often in Shakespeare's songs, as pre-eminently in that song of Mariana's page in *Measure for Measure*, in which the kindling force and poetry of the whole play seems to pass for a moment into an actual strain of music.[5]

This is a very helpful account of Blake's songs, which so frequently convey meanings 'not distinctly traceable by the understanding'. But are we to conclude that an attempt to explicate the ways in which they are like Shakespeare's songs is destined to lead nowhere?

Difficult as it is to prove the relationship, some shreds of evidence may be gathered. There is, for example, Blake's persistent use in connection with *Innocence* of the lark image that occurs in the *Cymbeline* song 'Hark, hark, the lark' (II. iii. 20–6). Blake does, after all, use other images from that song: Kathleen Raine relates the 'Marygold' at the beginning of *Visions of the Daughters of Albion* to Shakespeare's 'Mary-buds', and the 'golden springs' in *Thel* to his 'springs', 'chalic'd flow'rs', and 'golden eyes' (*Blake and Tradition*, i. 169). But then the figurative value of the lark in English poetry is hardly the unique property of Shakespeare.

There is also the fact that some lines which occur shortly after the song 'Come away, come away, death' in *Twelfth Night* are alluded to in a *Notebook* lyric sandwiched between the first drafts of two *Songs of*

Experience. 'Never pain to tell thy love' (K 161) establishes a dialogue with Viola's 'she never told her love, / But let concealment like a worm i' th' bud / Feed on her damask cheek' (II. iv. 110), lines which have been transformed into song by composers as varied as Haydn in Blake's time and Britten in ours. Viola's image of what happens if love is not told is answered by Blake's equally bleak 'I told my love, I told my love . . . Ah, she doth depart'. Wordsworth's 'I will dare to tell' in 'Strange fits of passion I have known' also works within this tradition. 'A Poison Tree' in *Songs of Experience* provides a further variation on the dangers of *not telling* an emotion (K 218). The appropriation of Viola's 'worm i' th' bud' brings us back to Blake's use of Shakespeare's cankered flowers; in this context it could be argued that Viola's lines lie behind the 'invisible worm' of 'The Sick Rose', also drafted in the *Notebook* at this time. But again, it is a traditional image; commentators have adduced other equally plausible sources.[6]

John Beer touches on the problem inherent in this kind of discussion in his article 'Influence and Independence in Blake'. One richness of the lyric 'London' (K 216) lies in the multiple significance of the words 'charter'd' and 'mark'. 'Charter'd' means both mapped, confined by reason, and licenced to be hired out for commercial interest. E. P. Thompson has shown how 'marks of woe' implies the mark of the Beast in the Book of Revelation, making London into Babylon.[7] Beer demonstrates that Shakespeare sometimes uses 'mark' in the sense of a mark on the face, and that he puns on the word's function as both verb and noun; his essay examines the various meanings of 'charter' in Shakespeare and finds an especially resonant pre-echo of Blake in the 'charter'd libertine' of *Henry V* (I. i. 48). Is this a case of allusion or affinity? Blake's types of ambiguity are in no way dependent on Shakespeare's, but he must have learnt his trade from the master.

'London' also includes a negative allusion that constitutes Blake's richest adaptation of the *Pity* image. In the final stanza, 'Blasts the new-born Infants tear' imports several elements of Macbeth's epic simile—the blast, the babe, the tear—but activates it in a new and terrible way by transforming 'Blasts' into a verb and omitting the key word 'pity'. The chartered streets of London are thus shown to be marked by the absence of pity.[8] The point is forced home by the poem with which 'London' is most frequently juxtaposed in *Songs of Experience*, 'The Human Abstract', which begins 'Pity would be no more, / If we did not make somebody Poor' (K 217).[9] Blake's attitude to those who hold the view that poverty is necessary so that charity can be exercised is made clear by the fact that there is no 'Pity' for the poor of 'London'.

But these specific parallels prove little. Metrical evidence is equally insufficient: it would be possible to compare the rhythmic and rhyme patterns of a pair of songs, but this would inevitably be inconclusive. We are left with intangibles, with Pater's and Housman's intuitive pairing. What can we say about these two songs?

> Fear no more the heat o' th' sun,
> Nor the furious winter's rages,
> Thou thy worldly task has done,
> Home art gone and ta'en thy wages.
> Golden lads and girls all must,
> As chimney-sweepers, come to dust.
>
>   .   .   .   .
>
> Quiet consummation have,
> And renowned be thy grave.
>
> > (*Cym* IV. ii. 258)

> Ah Sun-flower! weary of time,
> Who countest the steps of the Sun:
> Seeking after that sweet golden clime,
> Where the travellers journey is done.
>
> Where the Youth pined away with desire,
> And the pale Virgin shrouded in snow:
> Arise from their graves and aspire,
> Where my Sun-flower wishes to go.
>
> > (K 215)

We could examine the ways in which each song exploits syllabic variation and syntactic complexity. Which clause is in apposition to which? Blake in particular makes astonishing use of parataxis. We could make comparisons of rhyme schemes and particular rhymes, or of metrical effects such as the way each song begins with a strong dactyl. But such similarities could be found in numerous other Elizabethan lyrics which we know Blake read in his youth.

Comparison of imagery takes us slightly further. Each song is characterized by its distinctive use of traditional emblematic language. Each depends on certain powerful contrasts: in Blake, the sun and the golden clime are played off against the pale virgin and the pining youth, shrouded in snow and associated with winter; in Shakespeare, the hot sun is implicitly golden, like the lads and girls, while winter is pale, as they will be when they come to dust. Each poem exploits not only the 'sun'/'done' rhyme, but also a further internal echo which links that pairing to the idea of a journey (Shakespeare: 'done', 'gone'; Blake: 'is done', 'wishes to go'). The journey is towards death (Blake's 'travellers journey'; Shakespeare's 'Home art gone'). The sunflower follows the sun until it dies; it also loses its petals: it comes to dust in two senses. 'Chimney-sweepers' in Shakespeare may be Warwickshire dialect for ribwort, another plant whose seeds come to dust and travel on the wind.

The author of 'The Chimney Sweeper' must have been especially attracted to a Shakespearean song containing that image. A series of contextual parallels suggest that *Cymbeline* might have been at the back of his mind as he wrote 'Ah! Sun-flower'. The 'pale Virgin shrouded in snow': Posthumus of Imogen, 'As chaste as unsunn'd snow' (II. v. 13—notice how the sun is negatively present here). That 'sweet golden clime': the golden world of *Cymbeline*'s pastoral. The 'travellers journey': the many journeys that take place in the play. Pining youths: Arviragus and Guiderius. The virgin: Imogen (but here there is a sharp distinction between Shakespeare's ideal of chastity and Blake's critique of virginity's life-denying coldness). Furthermore, Imogen does arise from the grave to which the youths are taking her as they sing 'Fear no more'.

But we are still far from a definitive statement. The real similarity is one of tone, something notoriously difficult to describe. It would be tempting to say that each song is itself a 'Quiet consummation', except that Blake's strongly avoids consummation, offers only aspiration (contrast his 'wishes to go' with Shakespeare's conclusive 'Home art gone'). Ultimately a definitive statement is not what we want of poems such as these: it is of their very nature that they cannot be de-fined, that they are not statements. A comparison is something that must be left to the ear and the imagination of the individual reader. Pater sensed that language in Blake's and Shakespeare's songs is becoming music. Although music can be described analytically, its only meaning is itself (when asked what he *meant* by a piece of music, Schumann played it again). The relationship between 'Ah! Sun-flower' and 'Fear no more' is evident to me when I read them, but in the end I can only account obliquely for what joins them. Hazlitt wrote in *Characters of Shakespear's Plays*, 'Shakespear alone could describe the effect of his own poetry' (*HW* iv. 315); he then quoted some lines

from the opening of *Twelfth Night*. I think they say more about the
songs of Shakespeare and Blake than would be possible in critical
prose:

> That strain again, it had a dying fall;
> O, it came o'er my ear like the sweet sound
> That breathes upon a bank of violets,
> Stealing and giving odour.
>
> (I. i. 4)

There is remarkable variety in Blake's uses of Shakespeare. Sometimes, as in 'London', with its investing of several meanings in single
words, it is a matter of absorbing certain techniques which intensify
the texture of a poem. An exchange in *Lear* that must have attracted
Blake, with his neo-platonic interest in 'shadows', is the following:

> *Lear.* Who is it that can tell me who I am?
> *Fool.* Lear's shadow.
>
> (I. iv. 230)

The richness of this is that the Fool answers both questions at once: it
is the Fool, Lear's shadow, who can tell Lear what he has become, his
own shadow (a very Blakean concept). We find a similar effect near
the beginning of *The Book of Urizen*:

> what Demon
> Hath form'd this abominable void,
> This soul-shudd'ring vacuum? Some said
> 'It is Urizen.'
>
> (K 222)

Urizen *formed* the soul-shuddering vacuum or Urizen *is* the soul-
shuddering vacuum? Both, of course.

On other occasions, Blake echoes particular phrases that speak
especially strongly to his conception of the poetic imagination. His
late poem *The Ghost of Abel*, etched in 1822 as a response to Byron's
Cain of the previous year, sets out as one of its premises that 'Nature
has no Supernatural and dissolves: Imagination is Eternity' (K 779).
The close association for Blake between imaginative vision, poetry,
and the supernatural is emphasized by a Shakespearean allusion at
the end of the first plate. The ghost of Abel appears; Adam says 'It is
all a Vain delusion of the all creative Imagination'; Eve replies 'I see

him plainly with my Mind's Eye' (K 780). In the context of a family ghost's appearance, there is no denying the pressure of:

> *Hamlet.* My father—methinks I see my father.
> *Horatio.* Where, my lord?
> *Hamlet.*   In my mind's eye, Horatio.
>
>   (I. ii. 184)

Hamlet is summoned in order to give authority to Blake's belief that the eye of the imagination is endowed with 'Supernatural', eternal vision where the eye of the body is not.

A third use of Shakespeare might be termed 'analogical'. The plays sometimes provide verbal parallels to Blake's emblematic designs. We have seen this happening in the *Notebook*; Blake's friend George Cumberland employs the device in order to bring *Europe, A Prophecy* into relation with Shakespeare. Copy D of *Europe*, now in the Print Room of the British Museum, has extensive quotations from authors as diverse as Dryden and Mrs Radcliffe inscribed by hand on many of the plates; the hand has been identified as Cumberland's.[10] Many of the quotations are culled from Bysshe's *Art of English Poetry*, which provided Cumberland with a convenient store of literary analogues that helped him to read Blake's imagery.

The poem proper, as opposed to its Preludium, begins on plate three, headed 'A Prophecy' (pl. 4 in K), which shows what Erdman calls a 'scroll-garmented, huge-winged Cassandra' flying from left to right (*Illuminated Blake*, 161–2). Cumberland sees this figure as 'A Comet' and inscribes on the plate passages about the prophetic power of comets from Homer, Milton, Rowe, and Shakespeare. Since Blake's figure clutches at her hair, the most apposite of these, possibly even an image that was in Blake's mind, is 'Comets importing change to times and states / Brandish your golden tresses in the Skies' (*1H6* I. i. 2, slightly misquoted). By comparing the first image in the main body of the text of *Europe* to the first image in Shakespeare's first tetralogy, Cumberland implies a broader comparison: Blake's poem will follow Shakespeare's histories in exploring the apocalyptic effects of war, taking war between England and France as a starting-point. Blake's use of the phrase 'The youth of England' (at 12: 5, K 242, they are 'hid in gloom' rather than 'on fire') bears out this interpretation. Thus plate five, which shows Rintrah—at once a symbol for war and an image of Pitt—grasping a sword, is inscribed with another quotation from *Henry VI*, 'O war! thou Son of Hell, / Whom angry heavens do make their minister!' (*2H6* v. ii. 33; Pitt, of course, was prime *minister*). Whatever Blake's intentions may have been, one reader at least finds assistance in Shakespearean analogues as he attempts to interpret the prophetic books.

One is presented with special problems when talking about Blake's 'reader', since his works were hand-produced in such tiny editions. As epigraph for the advertisement of his 1809 exhibition Blake chose Milton's 'Fit audience find tho' few' (K 560). It is fair to assume that if he thought of his readers at all when writing the long prophetic books, he would have assumed that one element of their fitness would have been the ability to recognize his biblical, mythological, and literary allusions. The putative reader of *Milton* would be expected to know his Milton. From its title and epigraph ('To Justify the Ways of God to Men') to the many verbal parallels and the casting of Milton himself as protagonist in the action of the second book, *Milton*—perhaps more than any other poem in the language—is essentially about the later poet's struggle with Milton. But this does not mean that Shakespeare's influence necessarily diminishes in importance for the later Blake; it is rather a case of that influence becoming more covert, more dependent on the reader's fitness to discern allusions and echoes.

Although it is essentially Miltonic, *Milton* is incidentally Shakespearean. For the eighteenth century, *Lear*, with its storm, heath, cliff, frenzy, and blindness, was the great drama of the sublime, comparable to Milton's epic sublime; the discord of the first thirteen plates of Blake's sublime allegory is often mediated through the language of *Lear*. When Los plays off 'Wisdom' and 'Folly' against each other, addresses Satan as his 'youngest born' and says 'leave me to my wrath', then rolls 'his loud thunders' (4: 7–15, K 483), we begin to associate him with Lear, who refers to his 'youngest born' (II. iv. 213) and silences Kent with 'Come not between the dragon and his wrath' (I. i. 122), before being forced out into the thunder. Like the first act of *Lear*, the first part of *Milton* turns on anger, silence, and folly. Plate five describes the Daughters of Albion with their threefold nature, 'Head and Heart and Reins' (K 484); the action of *Lear* pivots on conflicts between reason, emotion, and sexuality. 'Their Loins / Surrounded with fires unapproachable' (5: 8, K 484) is a version of Lear's terrifying description of women's genitals, 'There is the sulphurous pit, burning, scalding, / Stench, consumption' (IV. vi. 128), a further recollection of which possibly occurs a few lines later in the daughter's song: 'fill'd with the vapours of the yawning pit' (5: 30, K 485).

Blake's network of faint allusions to *Lear* is complicated a little later when Palamabron, another of the sons of Los, speaks of Satan, again in the language of Shakespeare's exploration of family discord and its cosmic counterpart: 'seeming a brother, being a tyrant . . . darkness and despair . . . pretence of pity and love' (7: 24–8, K 487). If Los was Lear cursing his child, Satan is certainly no Cordelia; in Palamabron's terms, he is a Goneril or a Regan. Lear's daughters certainly seem to be in Blake's mind, for Palamabron goes on to speak of how Satan injures his servants, a variation on the confrontation between Kent, Oswald, Lear, and Regan. Satan then accuses Palamabron of 'crimes / Himself had wrought' (7: 36), another trope with which we are familiar from the play.

There is no conscious coherent parallelism, but when Blake addresses certain themes he is guided by Shakespeare. Satan works at the mill (line forty-one of *Samson Agonistes*, 'Eyeless in Gaza at the mill with slaves', keeps recurring in Blake). He wishes to change places with Palamabron, who works at the plough. The consequence of this upsetting of the natural order is that Palamabron's horses are maddened: the figure is reminiscent of *Macbeth*, where Duncan's horses go wild as part of the universal upsetting of natural order on the night of the king's murder. [11]

Despite excursions into *Macbeth*, it is *Lear* that recurs most persistently in Blake's account of the fractious goings-on in the house of Los. We see Satan 'Himself exculpating with mildest speech' (8: 2) very much in the manner of those simpering dames, Goneril and Regan, as well as his own forebear in *Paradise Lost*, and Los admitting that he the father is responsible for what has happened. Like Lear, he comes to the recognition 'Mine is the fault!' (8: 19, K 488). Los says that the day of discord in his family makes 'a blank in Nature', just as the tragic events in *Lear* and *Macbeth* constitute a 'breach in nature' (8: 21; *Mac* II. iii. 113; *Lr* IV. vii. 14). An autocratic father accuses his children of 'ingratitude' and 'in his wrath curs'd heaven and earth' (9: 13, 20, K 489): it is a familiar pattern. The movement from curse to benediction, which lies at the heart of *Lear*, has a profound effect on many of Blake's works. Similarly, both Shakespeare's tragedy and Blake's short epic make frequent use of the contrast between wrath and pity; both employ images of serpent and dragon, of Dover cliff and the dividing of nations.

But once we reach the fourteenth plate, when the voice of the 'Bard' takes refuge in Milton's bosom and Milton himself arises to begin his journey through eternal death into a new life of imagination, the echoes of *Lear* all but die out. The next plate shows a star, representing Milton, about to enter Blake's left foot (see *Illuminated Blake*, 233). In the next section of the poem, Milton becomes the major character; the language of *Paradise Lost* assumes far greater significance for the whole. Ultimately, the parallels with *Lear* are merely incidental. To find them taking on the kind of centrality that those with *Paradise Lost* have in *Milton*, we must turn to Blake's last substantial and in some senses his climactic work, *Jerusalem*.

The two major themes of *Jerusalem* are England, personified in the giant Albion, and the creative imagination, exemplified in the figure of Los. Since Shakespeare was seen in Blake's time as both the national poet and the poet with the most original creative imagination, it is fitting that he should be among the figures who preside over *Jerusalem*. Again, the pre-eminent influence is *King Lear*, with its ancient English setting (it is helpful to recall James Barry's painting of Lear and the dead Cordelia, which has a Stonehenge-like structure as background).

In Shakespeare's play, Lear is king of Albion; in Blake's poem, Cordella, Gonorill, and Ragan are among the daughters of Albion. Blake would have derived his names and his plot from a variety of sources, notably Milton's *History of Britain*, but the broad movement of his poem follows Shakespeare. In the first chapter Vala, representative of 'nature' in Edmund's sense, jealously causes Albion to reject Jerusalem; love is overthrown and only restored in the final chapter when Albion arises. Positive, creative values are recovered, as they are when Lear awakens in the final scene of Shakespeare's fourth act; since the ending of *Jerusalem* is anything but tragic, there is nothing of the fifth act of *Lear*.

The first chapter turns on the *Lear* themes: division and wrath, 'War and deadly contention Between / Father and Son' (18: 20, K 640), curses and, conversely, the hope of forgiveness and regeneration. Los struggles against the perverted vision of Albion's children, among whom 'Ragan is wholly cruel' and even Cordella, whom Albion 'thought pure as the heavens in innocence and fear', is 'broken' (11: 21, 21: 20, K 631, 644). Los accuses the daughters of 'a pretence of love to destroy love, / Cruel hipocrisy. . . . Calling that Holy Love which is Envy, Revenge and Cruelty', with the result that man is reduced to 'a little grovelling Root' (17: 26–32, K 639). In *Lear* the cruelty, hypocrisy, and love-destroying pretence of love that characterize Goneril, Regan, and Edmund reduce man to 'a poor, bare, fork'd animal' (III. iv. 107). As Lear recognizes this, he strips off his clothes; the contrast between the nakedness of 'the thing itself: unaccommodated man' and the way that 'Robes and furr'd gowns hide all' is a crucial one. In *Jerusalem*, Albion says that because they are not pure Gwendolen and Ragan need to be covered 'with costly Robes / Of Natural Virtue' (21: 14, K 643), then at plate sixty-six there is a stripping down for sacrifice.

Blake unites his two concerns, England and the imagination, by bringing both Albion and Los into relation with King Lear. Albion follows Lear in yoking his children with the savagery of the elements: 'I see their piteous faces gleam out upon the cruel winds' (21: 38, K 644—'piteous' alerts us to Albion's greater sympathy for his daughters, and to the pervasive influence of Macbeth's 'Pity'). Like Lear, Tiriel, Urizen in *The Four Zoas*, and Los in *Milton*, Albion comes to recognize his own fault: 'I have erred! I am ashamed! and will never return more. / I have taught my children sacrifices of cruelty' (23: 16, K 646). But it is *Los* who divides Britain among Albion's children. Here again the parallel with *King Lear* must be put into perspective, treated as one among several analogues, for behind Blake's image of Los dividing Britain there is also a parallel with the division of Israel into twelve tribes; this brings home his point that Britain was 'the Primitive Seat of the Patriarchal Religion' (pl. 27, K 649).

The two middle chapters of *Jerusalem* continue to echo the matter of *Lear*. Albion speaks of 'ingratitude' but regrets that he has cursed his daughters (K 669–70). The parallels are not developed in an ordered way—it is Los whom Albion denounces at this point, not his daughters—but there is no more powerful statement of the theme than Lear's 'monster ingratitude' and 'filial ingratitude', so whatever parallels of his own or anyone else's may or may not have been in Blake's mind, it is Shakespeare's play that forces itself into the reader's. I think it is unconscious association that leads Blake from his reference to ingratitude to the lines 'So spoke Albion in gloomy majesty, and deepest night / Of Ulro roll'd round his skirts from Dover to Cornwall' (42: 17, K 670). Dover and Cornwall do their work of representing the extremes of the south coast, but they are also names deeply implicated in the tragedy of *King Lear*.

There is a recurring pattern in poets who are steeped in Shakespeare whereby one echo is followed closely by another, sometimes fainter one. In plate sixty-three the word 'Multitudinous', which can never be isolated from its famous context in *Macbeth*, comes into conjunction with a vision of a knife that only exists, Los thinks, in the imagination: 'He saw in Vala's hand the Druid Knife of Revenge and the Poison Cup / Of Jealousy, and thought it a Poetic Vision of the Atmospheres' (63: 21, 39, K 697–8). The allusion is diffused here, in that it simultaneously engages with another tradition crucial to Blake, the Druidic, and by introducing the 'Poison Cup' makes us think of tragic drama in general, not *Macbeth* in particular. But Macbeth's vision of the dagger fascinated Blake because it provided a prime example of the way in which something imagined can be more potent than material 'reality', to the extent that it controls the character's actions, as when Macbeth is led on to murder Duncan.

Early in *Jerusalem* imagination is contrasted with rationalism and equated with Christ: 'Abstract Philosophy warring in enmity against Imagination / (Which is the Divine Body of the Lord Jesus, blessed for ever)' (5: 58, K 624). Later, Jerusalem asks of Imagination-Jesus ('O Lord and Saviour . . . O Human Imagination, O Divine Body'), 'Art thou alive, and livest thou for evermore? or art thou / Not but a delusive shadow, a thought that liveth not?' (60: 54, K 693). Close correspondence of phrasing conjures up Macbeth's

> Art thou not, fatal vision, sensible
> To feeling as to sight? or art thou but
> A dagger of the mind, a false creation,
> Proceeding from the heat-oppressed brain?
>
> (II. i. 36)

('heat-oppressed brain' may have influenced a phrase earlier in *Jerusalem*, 'Phantom of the over heated brain!', 4: 24, K 622). Macbeth's words have provided Blake with what he needs at this point in the poem, a circumspect interrogatory formulation that asks whether imaginative vision is genuine or 'delusive'. For authority on the matter of the imagination's supremacy, Blake has turned not to a purveyor of abstract philosophy, but to Shakespeare, supreme poet of the imagination.

It was because Blake located truth, eternal 'reality', in the world of imagination, not the so-called 'vegetable' world of nature and appearance, that he was especially attracted to the supernatural in

Shakespeare and in particular to those passages where a character conceives in his imagination and gives vivid life to something not visible on stage. Macbeth's dagger is one such conception; Edgar's monster on Dover cliff is another,

> As I stood here below, methought his eyes
> Were two full moons; he had a thousand noses,
> Horns welk'd and waved like the enridged sea.
> It was some fiend
>
> (*Lr* IV. vi. 69)

Blake describes as follows 'the form of mighty Hand sitting on Albion's cliffs':

> His bosom wide and shoulders huge, overspreading wondrous,
> Bear Three strong sinewy Necks and Three awful and terrible Heads,
> Three Brains, in contradictory council brooding incessantly
>
> (70: 1, K 708)

The Shakespearean image is transformed into a new creation that is wholly Blakean (the threefold form is especially distinctive); the assimilation is so complete that the connection with Shakespeare is far from obtrusive and cannot even be proved to exist. It is the richest, though most elusive, way of using previous poets, the one most deeply bound up with the creative process itself. Interesting as it is to draw together Blake's and Shakespeare's respective treatments of 'terrible Family Contentions' and 'The silent broodings of deadly revenge springing from the / All powerful parental affection' (43: 38, K 672; 54: 9, K 685), Shakespeare's real significance for Blake lay in his capacity to create a world in and through the imagination.

In a crucial passage in the prose preface to the fourth book of *Jerusalem*, Blake writes of 'Imagination, the real and eternal World of which this Vegetable Universe is but a faint shadow' (K 717). The prose preface, addressed 'To the Christians', is framed by two poems. It is preceded by the short lyric,

> I give you the end of a golden string,
>   Only wind it into a ball,
> It will lead you in at Heaven's gate
>   Built in Jerusalem's wall.
>
> (pl. 77, K 716)

and followed by a longer piece which begins,

> I stood among my valleys of the south
> And saw a flame of fire, even as a Wheel
> Of fire surrounding all the heavens . . .

(K 717)

John Beer points to the connection between the first lyric and 'Hark, hark, the lark', the song in *Cymbeline* which, as we have seen, furnished Blake with a number of images. 'I give you the end of a golden string' contains within its compact four lines an 'oblique reference to dawn revelation furnished by the Shakespearean context of "Heaven's gate"'.[12]

The 'flame of fire' at the beginning of the second prefatory poem ultimately derives from the vision at the start of the Book of the Prophet Ezekiel, but the phrase 'a Wheel Of fire' also alludes to Lear's vision of himself, 'Bound Upon a wheel of fire' (IV. vii. 45). Between them, the allusions to *Cymbeline* and *Lear* set the discussion of imagination in the address 'To the Christians' in a context of Shakespearean inspiration (the lark at heaven's gate) and vision (Lear's dream of Cordelia's 'bliss' and his own purgatory). A further summoning of the awakening scene in *Lear* seems to occur shortly afterwards, on plate eighty-one, which shows the daughters of Albion arguing, one of them pointing to a caption written in reversed writing. Held to a mirror, it reads 'In Heaven the only Art of Living / Is Forgetting and Forgiving' (K 724). That perverse word-order (once sin has been forgotten, what remains to be forgiven?) follows Lear's delicate 'Pray you now forget, and forgive' (IV. vii. 83). Blake's word-order may be determined by the fact that he is writing in reverse, or simply the exigencies of rhyme, but since he has already evoked the 'wheel of fire' and we know from both his own illustrations and his admiration of George Romney's painting, *King Lear awakened by his daughter Cordelia*, that this scene is very important to him, the case for a specific allusion is strong.[13]

When he wakes, Lear sees Cordelia's point of view for the first time; the principle of sympathy is at work. In the fifth act, he makes the imaginative leap that enables him to invert the expected order of things ('When thou dost ask me blessing, I'll kneel down / And ask of thee forgiveness', V. iii. 10); he dies half imagining that Cordelia lives. The rational man will say that he is deluded; Blake, with his faith in the supremacy of the imagination, would not have been so sure. For him, the imagination is the real and eternal world 'in which we'—and Cordelia in Shakespeare's play—'shall live in our Eternal or Imaginative Bodies when these Vegetable Mortal Bodies are no more' (K 717).

The idea of an 'imaginative leap' brings us to the essence of Blake's Shakespeare. In the *Descriptive Catalogue*, Blake describes one of his designs as follows: 'A Spirit vaulting from a cloud to turn and wind a fiery Pegasus.—Shakspeare. The Horse of Intellect is leaping from the cliffs of Memory and Reasoning; it is a barren Rock: it is also called the Barren Waste of Locke and Newton' (K 581). Among Blake's extra-illustrated Second Folio designs there is a watercolour of a horse leaping from a rock towards a dazzling sun, which must be a version of this (Fig. 2; Butlin, No. 547.6). Blake's inspiration is Vernon's description in *1 Henry IV* of the transformed Hal who vaulted into his saddle with such ease

> As if an angel dropp'd down from the clouds
> To turn and wind a fiery Pegasus,
> And witch the world with noble horsemanship.

(IV. i. 108)

Anthony Blunt noted that Vernon's speech is the only Shakespearean example used by Edmund Burke in his *Philosophical Enquiry into the Origin of our Ideas of the Sublime and Beautiful*; Blake's design is thus read as an allegory of the poetic sublime.[14] This argument is strengthened if 'leaping from the cliffs' is taken to be a quiet allusion to Gloucester's imaginary leap in Shakespeare's sublime tragedy. But even if these connections are admitted, Vernon's image is no more than a point from which Blake makes a leap to imaginative concerns of his own. I take this design to be a central image of Blake's conception of the imagination and consequently powerful testimony of Shakespeare's importance in determining that conception. The barren rock, the corner of which protrudes at the bottom of the picture, represents the restricted material or vegetable world of Newtonian and Lockean reason. Blake prefers a higher, imaginative world, that of dazzling sun, leaping animal energy, and graceful visionary beings. The magic and energy of Hal is like that of Shakespeare himself, who witches the world with noble poetry—not least in Vernon's wonderful speech. Blake changes Vernon's angel to 'A Spirit vaulting from a cloud', perhaps because his own understanding of angels involved moral ambiguities of the sort that inform such lyrics as 'I asked a

2. William Blake, design for an extra-illustrated Shakespeare Second Folio

thief', which would be out of place in this context. The 'Spirit' is the imaginative power—embodied most fully in Shakespeare—that turns and guides the 'Horse of Intellect' in its proper direction, away from the shackles of 'Memory and Reasoning', up, and 'into Eternity / Ever expanding in the Bosom of God, the Human Imagination' (*Jerusalem*, 5: 19, K 623).

There are many Shakespearean echoes and points of contact in *Jerusalem*.[15] But I would attach special significance to the allusions in the prefatory address to the final chapter, for they enable us to see Shakespeare's place in Blake's prose passage on the eternity of imagination. It is Shakespeare's imagination that leads to 'Heaven's gate' and that releases Lear from his 'wheel of fire' into eternity. So it is as it should be that Shakespeare takes his place in the final apotheosis of the imagination at the end of the poem, an apotheosis so complete that even abstract philosophers are redeemed: 'The innumerable Chariots of the Almighty appear'd in Heaven, / And Bacon and Newton and Locke, and Milton and Shakspear and Chaucer' (98: 9, K 745).

It is important to remember that Shakespeare does not appear in isolation here; he is one of several English geniuses who exert their influence on Blake, who appear together in a bright red sun. Blake often sees visions in the sun. One thinks of those marvellous lines at the climax of *A Vision of the Last Judgment* which take us to the very core of his way of seeing the world:

'What,' it will be Question'd, 'When the Sun rises, do you not see a round disk of fire somewhat like a Guinea?' O no, no, I see an Innumerable company of the Heavenly host crying 'Holy, Holy, Holy is the Lord God Almighty.' I question not my Corporeal or Vegetative Eye any more than I would Question a Window concerning a Sight. I look thro' it and not with it. (K 617)

Some time after writing this, Blake illustrated Milton's 'L'Allegro' and 'Il Penseroso'. The climactic illustration to 'L'Allegro' (Fig. 3; Butlin, No. 543.6) is inspired by Milton's 'Such sights as youthful poets dream . . .' (lines 125–34). Blake describes it as follows: 'The youthful Poet, sleeping on a bank by the Haunted Stream by Sun Set, sees in his dream the more bright Sun of Imagination under the auspices of Shakespeare and Johnson, in which is Hymen at a Marriage and the Antique Pageantry attending it' (K 618).

3. William Blake, *The Youthful Poet's Dream*, design for Milton's 'L'Allegro'

The association of sun and imagination suggests that the illustration could as well be of Blake himself seeing an 'Innumerable company' within the sun, as at the end of *Jerusalem* and *A Vision of the Last Judgment*. If the youthful poet is Blake, who presides over him? He does not seem to be paying much attention to his book, the property of 'Jonson's learned sock'. His robe has the same laced collar as Shakespeare's,[16] and his left hand is not only in a similar position to Shakespeare's but actually gestures up towards him. Blake had already associated Shakespeare's inspiration with the sun: his illustration to the section of Gray's 'Progress of Poesy' that described Shakespeare as 'Nature's darling' showed 'the mighty mother' encircled in the sun, cradling the infant Bard of Avon in her arms with his river below (Butlin, No. 335.49). For Blake, then, the poet's dream, mediated through Milton, is of 'the more bright Sun of Imagination' which exists eternally 'under the auspices of Shakespeare'.

Blake has many Shakespeares. Among them are the national poet, whose Lear is king of Albion, and the dramatic poet, whose command of the interplay of characters presides over Blake's own 'Visionary forms dramatic' (*Jerusalem*, 98: 28, K 746). It is essential to conceive of Blake's prophetic books as giant cosmic *dramas*; earlier in *Jerusalem*, perhaps as a response to seeing *Hamlet* or *Macbeth* in the theatre, he employs his own vivid theatrical image: 'Drinking and eating, and pitying and weeping as at a trajic scene / The soul drinks murder and revenge and applauds its own holiness' (41: 29, K 669).

But above all, there is the master of the imagination. 'Prospero had One Caliban and I have Two' (K 538) writes Blake, with reference to Flaxman and Stothard. He looks at the artists around him, claiming that he found them blind and taught them to see but 'now they know neither themselves nor me' (K 543), and comes to the conclusion that he himself is the only one with true vision, with the Shakespearean Prospero-spirit of magical creativity.

As epigraph for his essay on Blake written in 1811, Henry Crabb Robinson chose Theseus' 'The lunatic, the lover, and the poet / Are of imagination all compact'; Frederick Tatham said that the 'best and only likeness' of Blake's most striking feature was 'Shakespeare's description of the Eye of the Inspired Poet, in his midsummer nights Dream' (*Records*, 432, 529). The quotations are the right ones for, although his subtle differentiation between Theseus and Shakespeare must be taken into account, Blake's own conception of 'the power of inspiration', even when voiced in the context of *Milton*, is cast in the form of allusive homage to these lines. Some sons of Shakespeare, Blake among them, conceive of the poetic imagination

> Creating form and beauty around the dark regions of sorrow,
> Giving to airy nothing a name and a habitation
> Delightful, with bounds to the Infinite putting off the Indefinite
> Into most holy forms of Thought.

(28: 2, K 514)

8

Shakespeare to Hazlitt to Keats

IF we are to believe Charles Cowden Clarke, when John Keats was a
schoolboy he was so moved by the image in *Cymbeline* of the departing
Posthumus melting 'from The smallness of a gnat to air' that his eyes,
like Imogen's, filled with tears (CCC 126). This story may, however,
be apocryphal or exaggerated; Clarke's memory and his accuracy as
a biographer may have been overcome by a desire to show that his
friend was intuitively responsive to Shakespeare at an early age, and
perhaps even to hint at a distant Shakespearean provenance for the
gnats in the final stanza of Keats's last great ode. Everyone knows
that there are 'constant indications through the memoirs and in the
letters of Keats of his profound reverence for Shakespeare', but as
Clarke himself admits, Keats knew little of the plays until he became
an author himself.[1] Then 'his own intensity of thought and expression visibly strengthened with the study of his idol' (CCC 156).[2]

Keats began to read Shakespeare in detail on his visit to the Isle of
Wight in spring 1817, a crucial time in his poetic development;
Clarke's suggestion that there was a causal relationship between the
study of Shakespeare and the maturing of the young poet is therefore
highly plausible. In the extant letters of Keats before this trip there
have been only a few incidental references to Shakespeare. But when
he wakes in Southampton feeling rather lonely, he comforts himself
by unboxing the pocket edition of Shakespeare that is now in the
Houghton Library at Harvard.[3] Like so many of his contemporaries,
Keats spices his letters with quotations from the plays, adapted to his
own situation; the letter to his brothers from Southampton is the first
in which he does so repeatedly. Thus ' "There's my Comfort" ' is a
quotation from *The Tempest*: Caliban was referring to alcohol, Keats
drowns his sorrows in Shakespeare (*Tp* II. ii. 45, 55; *KL* i. 128).

Once he has made the crossing to Carisbrooke, fate comes to his
aid. In the house where he is lodging he finds a print of Shakespeare's
head and hangs it over his books: 'Now this alone is a good morning's
work', he writes to his friend Reynolds in a letter that returns again
and again to Shakespeare. It is here that Keats speaks of *Lear* and

writes his sonnet on the sea, here that he eagerly anticipates
Shakespeare's birthday the following week and says 'Whenever you
write say a Word or two on some Passage in Shakespeare that may
have come rather new to you; which must be continually happening,
notwithstanding that we read the same Play forty times' (17, 18 April
1817, *KL* i. 130–4). He then says a word or two about a passage in
The Tempest, a play in which he has immersed himself to such an
extent that his own choice of phrase, 'new to you', is a verbal
echo—' 'Tis new to thee' (v. i. 184). For Keats at this moment,
Shakespearean drama is a brave new world.

Keats wrote his name and the date, April 1817, in the first two
volumes of his pocket edition; he must have bought it especially to
study while alone and able to concentrate in the Isle of Wight. Why
did he decide to explore the plays at this time? How does one account
for the sense of excitement and discovery in the letter he sent from
Carisbrooke to Reynolds back in London? Throughout his short life
Keats was very impressionable; I think that the inspirational influence
of three men accounted for the sudden stepping up of his interest in
Shakespeare.

The painter Benjamin Robert Haydon was so ardent a Bardolater
that his diary began with a rhapsody on 'Shakespeare's cliff' at Dover
and ended with a suicide note in the form of a quotation from *King
Lear*, ' "Stretch me no longer on this tough World"—Lear. End—'.[4]
A month before Keats left London, he received a letter from Haydon.
To judge from its beginning ('Consider this letter a sacred secret')
and ending ('let our hearts be buried in each other'), and its extrava-
gant praise of the early poem 'Sleep and Poetry', he must have
treasured it. It is in this letter that Haydon first articulates to Keats an
aesthetic of benign influence. He describes how after a day's work he
would often sit and muse on what he has achieved and what he hopes
to achieve,

till filled with fury I have seen the faces of the mighty dead crowd into my
room, and I have sunk down and prayed the great Spirit that I might be
worthy to accompany these immortal beings in their immortal glories, and
then I have seen each smile as it passed over me, and each shake his hand in
awful encouragement. (*KL* i. 124)

The young artist's prayer that he may be worthy to join the ranks of
the mighty dead, his fear that he may not, that he may die too soon,
the notion of 'awful encouragement': these become constant Keatsian

preoccupations. There is awe, but in Haydon's vision there is no sense of prohibition, of a clash of wills between poet and precursor. Harold Bloom's tropes, shaped as they are by fierce Judaic and Freudian myths, are out of place here. Haydon speaks the language of Christian supplication and his immortals respond in a gentle, very English way with a smile and a gesture of the hand (one recalls Blake's 'Shakespeare gave me his hand').

This is not to say that influence is always unproblematic for Haydon and Keats; there will sometimes be occasions on which the young Romantic feels that he is not even worthy to gather up the crumbs from under the table of the immortals. This biblical figure—one of many possible metaphors for picking up the language of past poets—draws attention to another problem, the conflicting demands of religious and poetic faith. Haydon was a dedicated Christian, so in speaking of his artistic gods he has to be evasive and say 'prayed the great Spirit'. Wordsworth's withdrawal from Shakespeare in his later years went together with his movement towards established religion. Keats was less certain about belief in God and ultimately fell back on faith in art: 'in the Name of Shakespeare Raphael and all our Saints' (*KL* i. 145). The idea of Shakespeare as the god of our idolatry which began with Garrick in the eighteenth century as a hyperbole proclaiming the supremacy of popular sentiment over the narrowness of neo-classical criticism was becoming something far more deep-seated. We are on the road traced by Matthew Arnold: art is taking over from religion, the poets are becoming the priests.

Shakespeare's own religious views are another issue at stake here: could one have faith in someone who himself lacked Christian faith? Haydon, Keats, Leigh Hunt, and Shelley engaged in a heated discussion on Christianity at a dinner party of Horace Smith's on 20 January 1817; Haydon and Shelley sought to strengthen their opposing cases by invoking Shakespeare, quoting from the plays to prove that he was or was not a Christian.[5] Keats recalled the discussion when he wrote to Hunt on 10 May and adduced one passage for and one against Shakespeare's Christianity; he realized that it was the characters who spoke, not the dramatist himself. The latter's strength was to see both sides of the question, to remain in uncertainties, doubts.

These are some of the wider questions raised by Haydon's vision. More locally, his letter led Keats to meditate on his own relationship with 'the mighty dead'. Towards the end of April, after spending only a week or so at Carisbrooke, he moved round the coast from the

Isle of Wight to Margate. There he soon received a letter from
Haydon with the exhortation 'go on, dont despair, collect incidents,
study characters, read Shakespeare and trust in Providence—and you
will do—you must, you shall—' (*KL* i. 135). This reminder of the
relationship between reading Shakespeare and doing great things led
Keats to reply to the earlier letter: 'I remember your saying that you
had notions of a good Genius presiding over you—I have of late had
the same thought. . . . Is it too daring to Fancy Shakspeare this
Presider?' (*KL* i. 141–2). The delicate combination of modesty and
confidence is wholly convincing, wholly characteristic.

   In one sense at least it is not too daring, for the letter as a whole
(*KL* i. 140–5) is presided over by Shakespeare. Keats begins by
quoting the opening lines of *Love's Labour's Lost*, transforming the
King's affected rhetoric (typified by the figure 'grace us in the disgrace') into a personal plea for 'Fame'. Keats is not concerned with
the context or the dramatic irony of the lines; he achieves instead a
rhetorical effect of his own, whereby the act of quotation implicitly
makes him and his friend 'heirs' not only 'of all eternity' but also of
Shakespeare. Both Keats and Haydon veer between the hope that
Shakespeare might underpin their own work, that his achievement
could be regarded as an ideal out of which they might create anew,
and the fear that his genius could be neither ignored nor surpassed.
Keats moves rapidly from self-doubt ('There is no greater Sin after
the 7 deadly than to flatter oneself into an idea of being a great Poet')
to hope and faith in Shakespeare ('I never quite despair and I read
Shakspeare'). One moment he speaks of the 'Trumpet of Fame' as a
'tower of Strength', the next he professes to 'hate' his own work and
describes himself as ' "one that gathers Samphire dreadful trade" the
Cliff of Poesy Towers above me'. Keats has a vertical imagination—
one thinks of stout Cortez looking down from the 'peak in Darien', the
poet ascending the steps to the temple in *The Fall of Hyperion*, and
the figure of the 'mountaineer' (*KL* i. 342). In the letter to Haydon,
the image of the man-made tower, denoting the poet's own strength,
gives way to the towering cliff, suggesting his insignificance beside
the force of earlier poesy. This particular cliff denotes the Presider,
for it is that of *King Lear*, which was also such a potent image for
Wordsworth. Keats's comparison of himself to the samphire-gatherer
is especially effective because it is both a quotation and a figure for the
act of quotation, which may be seen as the gathering of choice phrases
from the Shakespearean cliff. The intuitions and metaphors of this

letter provide a model which in my next chapter I will apply to Keats at work in his own poems.

The second figure to whom Keats owed his intensified awareness of Shakespeare at this time, and by far the most important of the three, is also mentioned in the letter to Haydon: 'I am very near Agreeing with Hazlit that Shakspeare is enough for us' (i. 143). Close kinship in response to Shakespeare is revealed by the way that Keats in this letter and Hazlitt in both his *Life of Napoleon Buonaparte* and *Conversations of Northcote* apply Enobarbus' lines on allegiance to a fallen lord to Napoleon's confidant, Bertrand.[6] 'But how differently does Buonap bear his fate from Antony!' continues Keats, for whom a combination of sameness with difference makes a parallel between Shakespeare and the contemporary world interesting.

Keats's familiarity with Hazlitt's turns of mind and phrase by this time is apparent in a letter to Reynolds of 9 March 1817, 'It's the finest thing by God—as Hazlitt wo^d say' (*KL* i. 123). Keats met Hazlitt in the first few months of 1817; awareness of Shakespeare grew together with that of Hazlitt as a critic of the first order. The following autumn Keats read and admired Hazlitt's collection of essays, *The Round Table* (*KL* i. 166). He would have found in the volume a synthesis of many of the ideas Hazlitt had already shared with him in conversation. He may well have been familiar with some of the essays from their original publication in *The Examiner*; that he already knew at least one of them well is suggested by his borrowing in 'Sleep and Poetry', written in late 1816, of an image from 'On Milton's Versification', published the previous year: 'Dr Johnson and Pope would have converted his vaulting Pegasus into a rocking-horse' (*HW* iv. 40).

Hazlitt seems to have provided a springboard for the crucial series of letters to Benjamin Bailey written in October and November 1817, in which Keats goes further than he has done before in exploring and defining his conceptions of imagination and his poetic aspirations. In the first of these letters, he applies to the vicissitudes of his friends a line which Hazlitt quotes on numerous occasions, 'The web of our life is of a mingled yarn';[7] in the next, he refers to Hazlitt's essay 'On Common-place Critics' and to the discussion of Wordsworth's poem 'Gipsies' in the essay 'On Manner', which confronts him with a conflict between an admired poet and an admired critic ('I think Hazlitt is right and yet I think Wordsworth is rightest', *KL* i. 173–4).[8]

Although many of Hazlitt's ideas about poets and poetry had been prefigured in the eighteenth century, *The Round Table* was the direct source for many concepts Keats was to make his own. 'On Classical Education', the second essay in the collection, went straight to some of his own chief preoccupations. The study of classical literature—Keats and Hazlitt would both have thought of the English classics as well as the ancients—is seen as the fundamental 'discipline of humanity': 'It gives men liberal views; it accustoms the mind to take an interest in things foreign to itself; to love virtue for its own sake; to prefer fame to life, and glory to riches; and to fix our thoughts on the remote and permanent, instead of narrow and fleeting objects' (*HW* iv. 4). The ideas of schooling the soul and of the pursuit of poetic fame were especially compelling for Keats; those of disinterestedness and of going outside oneself exercise a formative influence on the conception of sympathy, of partaking in the life of another (even of a sparrow or a billiard ball), that is so crucial to his later letters. Whether or not Keats actually read Hazlitt's early philosophical *Essay on the Principles of Human Action*,[9] he would have assimilated via essays such as this its central idea, its anti-Hobbesian argument that the mind is naturally disinterested and sympathetic. 'On Classical Education' would also have cohered with Haydon's vision of benign artistic influence. One passage begins with Hazlitt's favourite allusion to Thomson's 'hold high converse with the mighty dead', which also occurs in Haydon's letter:

By conversing with the *mighty dead*, we imbibe sentiment with knowledge; we become strongly attached to those who can no longer either hurt or serve us, except through the influence which they exert over the mind. We feel the presence of that power which gives immortality to human thoughts and actions, and catch the flame of enthusiasm from all nations and ages. (*HW* iv. 5)

For Keats, disinterestedness could be learned from the example of Shakespeare and the other writers whom he admired—the figure of conversation again suggests an approach on equal terms, an entering into a brotherhood of immortals.

To converse with and participate in the great works of the past was Hazlitt's constant ambition:

We complain that this is a Critical age; and that no great works of Genius appear, because so much is said and written about them; while we ought to reverse the argument, and say, that it is because so many works of genius *have appeared*, that they have left us little or nothing to do, but to think and talk about them—that if we did not do that, we should do nothing so good—and if we do this well, we cannot be said to do amiss! (*HW* xvi. 212)

Hazlitt, the critic and journalist, was content to 'think and talk about' the great writers of the past. For Keats, the practising poet, this was insufficient; he sought to produce 'works of Genius' himself. A subsequent *Round Table* essay, 'On Modern Comedy', would have brought him face to face with the problem of belatedness. 'It is because so many excellent Comedies have been written, that there are none written at present' (*HW* iv. 10). Hazlitt goes on to apply his argument to tragedy: 'the materials of Tragedy cannot be found among a people, who are the habitual spectators of Tragedy . . . Shakspeare, with all his genius, could not have written as he did, if he had lived in the present times' (iv. 13); in a critical age, the freshness and vigour of nature are dulled. Keats cannot wholly agree with Hazlitt's feeling that 'We have not, neither do we want, two Shakspeares, two Miltons, two Raphaels, any more than we require two suns in the same sphere' (iv. 156). At the height of his Bardolatry he can only be *very near* agreeing with Hazlitt that Shakespeare is enough. Despite the fact that Shakespeare 'has left nothing to say about nothing or any thing' (*KL* i. 189), the young poet cannot repose in that achievement as the critic can; he must strive to prove that it is still possible to create anew, if not in comedy and tragedy, then at least in certain lyric forms.

The very fact of the younger writer's awareness of his predecessors marks him off from the great originals. Shakespeare was conceived of as a writer unaffected by anxiety over competition or posthumous fame. This is a questionable assumption; that Shakespeare felt the need to parody Marlowe suggests that he feared him and might in some ways have been relieved at his early death. And the sonnets are full of reflections on endurance and the poet's after-life in his works. But Hazlitt, for whom Shakespeare only became himself by representing others, pays little attention to the sonnets; the conclusion of the essay 'On Posthumous Fame,—Whether Shakspeare was influenced by a Love of it?' is that he was not. Hazlitt argues that a writer's concern for his future fame is directly related to his idolatry of his predecessors: 'The love of fame is a species of emulation; or, in other words, the love of admiration is in proportion to the admiration with which the works of the highest genius have inspired us' (iv. 22). This brings us back to the intimate connection between Keats's growing idolatry of Shakespeare and his own poetic aspirations, a connection that is clear from such remarks as 'I have been very idle lately, very averse to writing; both from the overpowering idea of our dead poets and from abatement of my love of fame' (*KL* ii. 116). For Keats, the question 'How will posterity take what I am writing?' cannot be separated from the thought 'What would Shakespeare have said here?'; his ambition is that posterity might ask 'What would Keats have said here?'[10]

But Keats is far more self-conscious than Shakespeare. Although we must not fall into the old trap of regarding Shakespeare as a spontaneous genius devoid of self-examination, it may confidently be asserted that if a bundle of his letters were to be found, they would not be full of reflections on self and poetry as those of Keats are. The Romantic age longed for biographical information about Shakespeare —the Ireland family's forgeries attracted such interest because the 1790s needed them; Haydon wrote to Keats wild with joy when he heard that a ring and seal claimed to be Shakespeare's had been found in a field at Stratford (*KL* i. 239). Had more been known about Shakespeare, the Romantics would have been disappointed: there simply would not have been a case for transforming him into a poet whose whole life and work was an overt exploration of the self. Hazlitt was grateful for the lack of biographical information precisely because it reinforced his own conception, itself to some extent another myth, of Shakespeare as the impersonal genius who exposed the limitations of contemporary egotists.

Keats learns most from Hazlitt in matters of artistic process, not of self-examination. Indeed, it is to Hazlitt that he owes the aspiration to 'annihilate' the self, as he later put it, for the purposes of artistic creation. In *The Round Table,* Hazlitt defines *gusto,* a key term in his criticism, as 'power or passion defining any object' (*HW* iv. 77). W. J. Bate glosses usefully: gusto is 'an excitement of the imagination in which the perceptive identification with the object is almost complete, and the living character of the object is caught and shared in its full diversity and given vital expression in art.'[11] Within months of reading the essay 'On *Gusto*' Keats was using the term himself and writing of negative capability, the willingness to be in uncertainties and doubts that renders the mind open to acts of sympathetic identification.

One reason why Shakespeare was seen as the great poet of sympathy was that he wrote plays, the form most conducive to impersonality. In the first of his two *Round Table* essays 'On Actors and Acting' Hazlitt argues that actors have the power to become others, to annihilate self: 'The height of their ambition is to be *beside themselves*' (iv. 153).[12] The best actors enter into their roles in performance just as Shakespeare entered into his characters in writing—it is not often noted that the image of a Proteus was applied to Burbage long before it was to Shakespeare.[13] On perusing *The Round Table*, Keats would have found not only Hazlitt's general reflections on acting and its relationship to the concept of sympathy, but also an essay on a particular actor, Edmund Kean. It had been as much due to Hazlitt's favourable reviews as anything else that Kean had risen to stardom so quickly after his first appearance as Shylock at Drury Lane in January 1814, and that his advent had come to be seen as 'the first gleam of genius breaking athwart the gloom of the Stage' (*HW* v. 175). Kean at his best made Hazlitt and other Romantic critics modify their scepticism about the possibility of doing justice to Shakespearean tragedy on stage.[14]

According to Charles Cowden Clarke, Keats 'idolized' Kean (CCC 123). We do not know how frequently he saw him on stage,[15] but many of the letters hint at Keats's love of the theatre. In a letter to Clarke of 25 March 1817 he jokingly alludes to *Macbeth*, 'When shall we see each other again? . . . jumbled together at Drury Lane Door?' (*KL* i. 126). Kean had appeared as Macbeth at Drury Lane earlier that month;[16] it is quite possible that Keats and Clarke had seen a performance. This was a time of great theatrical excitement in London because Junius Brutus Booth had appeared as a possible rival to Kean and on an electrical evening at Drury Lane the two actors had played opposite each other in *Othello*. Cowden Clarke records that 'the most eminent among literary men and critics' were present; 'This is a night to be remembered!' said William Godwin as he came out of the performance (CCC 15). Hazlitt reviewed the performance and one imagines that it must have been discussed in the Keats circle.

After Hazlitt and Haydon, Kean was the third major impulse behind Keats's intense study of Shakespeare from April 1817 onwards. He later expressed the desire 'to make as great a revolution in modern dramatic writing as Kean has done in acting' (*KL* ii. 139), in other words to enter into his characters as Kean entered into his roles and to revive Shakespearean dramatic poetry as Kean had revived Shakespearean acting.

Testimony to Kean's importance for Keats is provided by his place in the famous letter on 'negative capability', written at the end of

1817. Taken in isolation, a remark such as 'the excellence of every Art is its intensity, capable of making all disagreeables evaporate, from their being in close relationship with Beauty and Truth—Examine King Lear and you will find this examplified throughout' (*KL* i. 192) will seem to idealize the play and remove Shakespeare from the theatre. But the letter begins with Keats's account of seeing Kean as Richard III and the news that at the request of Reynolds he has written a critique of Kean for *The Champion*. The letter and the review should be read as complementary texts. To use the terms of the review, Keats's own response to Shakespeare is 'spiritual', it finds in the plays 'hieroglyphics of beauty:—the mysterious signs of an immortal freemasonry'.[17] The conception of an immortal brotherhood of poets, mysteriously in touch with the principles of beauty and truth, is altogether characteristic. But he recognizes that 'the sensual life of verse springs warm from the lips of Kean'. For Keats, poetry must be both spiritual and sensual; his approach to Shakespeare involves not only an immersion of the spirit, as recounted in the sonnet 'On Sitting Down to Read *King Lear* Once Again', but also a receptivity in the theatre that would have made him agree with Byron: 'I am acquainted with no *im*material sensuality so delightful as good acting' (*LJ* iv. 115).

'Mr Kean', published in *The Champion* on 21 December 1817, is indebted to Hazlitt both stylistically and in its perception of Kean. For instance, Shakespearean quotation is used to describe Kean's acting and the word 'gusto' applied to his voice. Keats also follows Hazlitt in arguing that Kean is at his best in certain heightened moments of intense brilliance, which are rarely sustained throughout a performance: 'Other actors are continually thinking of their sumtotal effect throughout a play. Kean delivers himself up to the instant feeling, without the shadow of a thought about any thing else.' 'Delivers himself up' implies a sympathetic going out from the self, analogous to Keats's 'I wish to give myself up to other sensations'.

Parallels with Hazlitt's dramatic criticism extend to the letter begun on the day of the article's publication. For Keats, 'the excellence of every Art is its intensity', a quality Hazlitt looked for in the actor; in order to be negatively capable a writer must be sympathetic and unegotistic, qualities Hazlitt associated particularly with Shakespeare and dramatic form. That Keats's deliberations arise partly from a theatrical context is further suggested by a remark between the passage on intensity and that on negative capability,

'They talked of Kean and his low company—Would I were with that company instead of yours said I to myself!' (*KL* i. 193).

I would argue, then, that a response to Kean was one of the things that 'dovetailed' in Keats's mind and led to the formulation on negative capability. The review of Kean is also important because it provides the occasion on which Keats first expresses his belief, reiterated at Haydon's dinner party a week later, then in 'Lamia', that Newton and mechanic physics had destroyed the rainbow: 'Kean! Kean! . . . Cheer us a little in the failure of our days! for romance lives but in books. The goblin is driven from the heath, and the rainbow is robbed of its mystery!' Kean is made into a representative of 'genius' and 'romance' in a coldly rational age. Keats's attack on the Enlightenment in 'Lamia' combines the spoiled rainbow and banished goblin with Hazlitt's statement in his lecture 'On Poetry in General' that 'the progress of knowledge and refinement has a tendency to circumscribe the limits of the imagination, and to clip the wings of poetry':[18]

> There was an awful rainbow once in heaven:
> We know her woof, her texture; she is given
> In the dull catalogue of common things.
> Philosophy will clip an Angel's wings,
> Conquer all mysteries by rule and line,
> Empty the haunted air, and gnomed mine.
>
> ('Lamia', ii. 231)

The example of Kean should not, however, be over-emphasized simply because it has often been neglected. He is important not so much in himself but because he was so important to Hazlitt; it is through the latter that Keats learns how to read Kean's performances. Not only is Keats's review of Kean deeply indebted to Hazlitt, but when Keats had the idea in 1819 of making a living as a journalist, 'endeavouring, for a beginning, to get the theatricals of some paper', his immediate thought was 'I shall apply to Hazlitt, who knows the market as well as any one, for something to bring me in a few pounds as soon as possible' (*KL* ii. 176–7). In his review, Keats had drawn a contrast between the sensual grandeur with which Kean spoke Shakespearean verse and the same words on the page, 'the very letters and points of charactered language' which 'show like the hieroglyphics of beauty'. Hazlitt's strength was that he responded to Shakespeare on the stage, to Kean especially, yet also in his reading of the plays in the closet had, as Keats put it, 'hieroglyphic visioning'.[19]

There is no association between Kean and the specific play mentioned by Keats in the letter to his brothers of 21 and 27 December 1817. Because of the King's apparent madness, *King Lear* was not performed on the London stage in the Regency years. Unable to see the play on stage, Keats read it intensely, responding not only with his sonnet but also with such impassioned marginal annotations as

How finely is the brief of Lear's character sketched in this conference—from this point does Shakspeare spur him out to the mighty grapple: 'the seeded pride that hath to this maturity blowne up' Shakspeare doth scatter abroad on the winds of Passion, where the germs take boyant root in stormy Air, suck lightning sap, and become voiced dragons—self-will and pride and wrath are taken at a rebound by his giant hand and mounted to the Clouds—there to remain and thunder evermore.[20]

This extraordinary series of images, almost a poem itself, is not a description of the text but a creative improvisation on the text. Of all the plays, *Lear* was the one to inspire Keats most directly to create anew out of Shakespearean materials: the sonnet 'On the Sea' was written under the influence of Edgar's lines on the sea; that written on sitting down to re-read the play was actually transcribed by Keats into his Folio edition (Fig. 4), and here a miniature text is produced in the margin of that edition. This, then, is one response to Shakespeare's superiority and the fact that he has left nothing to say about nothing or anything: to produce new writing in various forms of marginalia to his plays.

In addition, with the exception of a single witty comparison of Hazlitt to Ferdinand in *The Tempest*,[21] the only annotations Keats made to his copy of *Characters of Shakespear's Plays* were in the chapter on *King Lear*. We do not know precisely when Keats read and marked Hazlitt's book, but since Hazlitt exerted such a strong influence on him, one imagines that it would have been soon after its publication in April or May 1817, and certainly before the letter on *King Lear*, imaginative intensity, and negative capability.

Keats's underscorings and marginal markings to Hazlitt's chapter on *Lear* are concentrated on passages which emphasize those key terms imagination, sympathy, passion, and the heart: 'a style of pathos, where the extremest resources of the imagination are called in

That *Rosincrance* and *Guildensterne* are dead :
Where should we haue our thankes ?
   Hor. Not from his mouth,
Had it th'abilitie of life to thanke you :
He neuer gaue command'ment for their death.
But since so iumpe vpon this bloodie question,
You from the Polake warres, and you from England
Are heere arriued. Giue order that these bodies
High on a stage be placed to the view,
And let me speake to th'yet vnknowing world,
How these things came about. So shall you heare
Of carnall, bloudie, and vnnaturall acts,
Of accidentall iudgements, casuall slaughters
Of death's put on by cunning, and forc'd cause,
And in this vpshot, purposes mistooke,
Falne on the Inuentors heads.   All this can I
Truly deliuer.
   For. Let vs hast to heare it,
And call the Noblest to the Audience.
For me, with sorrow, I embrace my Fortune,
I haue some Rites of memory in this Kingdome,

Which are ro claime, my vantage doth
Inuite me,
   Hor. Of that I shall haue alwayes cause to speake,
And from his mouth
Whose voyce will draw on more :
But let this same be presently perform'd,
Euen whiles mens mindes are wilde,
Lest more mischance
On plots, and errors happen.
   For. Let foure Captaines
Beare *Hamlet* like a Soldier to the Stage,
For he was likely, had he beene put on
To haue prou'd most royally :
And for his passage,
The Souldiours Musicke, and the rites of Warre
Speake lowdly for him.
Take vp the body ; Such a sight as this
Becomes the Field, but heere shewes much amis.
Go, bid the Souldiers shoote.
     *Exeunt Marching : after the which, a Peale of
     Ordenance are shot off.*

FINIS.

On sitting down to read King Lear once again.

O Golden-tongued Romance, with serene Lute!
  Fair plumed Syren, Queen of far-away!
  Leave melodizing on this wintry day
Shut up thine olden Pages and be mute.
Adieu! for once again, the fierce dispute,
  Betwixt Damnation and impassion'd clay
  Must I burn through; once more humbly assay
The bitter-sweet of this Shaksperean fruit.

Chief Poet! and ye Clouds of Albion,
  Begetters of our deep eternal theme!
When through the old oak forest I am gone,
  Let me not wander in a barren dream:
But, when I am consumed in the fire,
  Give me new Phœnix wings to fly at my desire.

Jany. 22. 1818.

4. John Keats, 'On sitting down to read King Lear once again',
in his facsimile Shakespeare First Folio

to lay open the deepest movements of the heart, which was peculiar to Shakespear'; 'our sympathy with actual suffering is lost in the strong impulse given to our natural affections, and carried away with the swelling tide of passion, that gushes from and relieves the heart' (*Characters*, 171, 177). The latter observation clearly prefigures Keats's idea of disagreeables evaporating in *Lear* through their close relationship with beauty and truth. The collocation of the imagination and the heart in the former passage leads us to the letter to Bailey of 22 November 1817, 'I am certain of nothing but of the holiness of the Heart's affections and the truth of Imagination' (*KL* i. 184), a statement immediately followed by the assertion 'What the imagination seizes as Beauty must be truth', Keats's first yoking of the terms that he will use to describe *Lear* the following month (and, of course, put into the mouth of the Grecian urn in 1819).

Keats's conception of beauty is also illuminated by reference to Hazlitt and Shakespeare. In a letter to Haydon, written on 8 April 1818, he speaks of the 'innumerable compositions and decompositions which take place between the intellect and its thousand materials before it arrives at that trembling delicate and snail-horn perception of Beauty' (*KL* i. 265). This description of the creative process in the artist's mind fuses a remark in Hazlitt's lecture on Shakespeare and Milton—'In Shakspeare there is a continual composition and decomposition of its elements, a fermentation of every particle in the whole mass' (*HW* v. 51)—with Keats's own earlier reflections on the 'beauties' in Shakespeare's non-dramatic verse in a letter to Reynolds where he quotes the line from *Venus and Adonis*, 'As the snail, whose tender horns being hit' (*KL* i. 189). A specific beauty in Shakespeare is combined with Hazlitt's account of Shakespeare's mind at work and leads to Keats's insight concerning the way in which the poet perceives, and in perceiving creates, beauty.[22]

Keats's most substantial note to *Characters* is next to the third of Hazlitt's four generalizations arising from his reading of *Lear*, 'That the greatest strength of genius is shewn in describing the strongest passions' (p. 177). Keats writes in the margin, 'If we compare the Passions to different tuns and hogsheads of wine in a vast cellar—thus it is—the poet by one cup should know the scope of any particular wine without getting intoxicated—this is the highest exertion of Power, and the next step is to paint from memory of gone self storms'. Here we have in embryo the idea of negative capability: the poet must be content to taste of the different passions, to know the scope of them without getting intoxicated by any one of them. According to Keats, Coleridge lacked negative capability because he was incapable of remaining content with this kind of 'half knowledge'.

But Keats's second step brings us back to the problem of the self. The idea of painting 'from memory of gone self storms' is an essentially Romantic, egotistic one. Negative capability is not synonymous with sympathy, but it is closely related to it in that each quality involves suppression of any irritable reaching or obtrusion of the self. The relationship between the two ideas is brought out by the fact that shortly before making his marginal note to *Characters* that has within it the germ of 'negative capability', Keats underlines a phrase Hazlitt quotes from Lamb which turns on the ideal of sympathetic identification in the act of reading: 'we see not Lear, but we are Lear' (p. 176).

But what of the self's role in the act of writing? Early in 1818, Keats attended most of Hazlitt's lectures on the English poets.[23] In the lecture on Shakespeare and Milton, he would have heard Hazlitt attack the modern 'experiment to reduce poetry to a mere effusion of natural sensibility' and 'to surround the meanest objects with the morbid feelings and devouring egotism of the writers' own minds' (*HW* v. 53). Shakespeare, on the other hand, was praised as 'the least of an egotist that it was possible to be': 'He was nothing in himself; but he was all that others were, or that they could become' (*HW* v. 47). This stands behind Keats's distinction in his letter to Woodhouse on the poetical character (27 October 1818, *KL* i. 386–8) between 'the wordsworthian or egotistical sublime; which is a thing per se and stands alone' and the kind of poet Shakespeare is and Keats himself would like to be:

it has no self—it is every thing and nothing—It has no character . . . it lives in gusto . . . It has as much delight in conceiving an Iago as an Imogen. . . . A Poet is the most unpoetical of any thing in existence; because he has no identity—he is continually in for [informing?]—and filling some other Body.

Woodhouse's gloss on this passage, in a letter to Keats's publisher John Taylor, seeks to show not only that Keats is a Shakespearean poet but also that his idea of the poet falls in with Shakespeare's own:

Shaksp^r was a poet of the kind above ment^d—and he was perhaps the only one besides Keats who possessed this power in an extr^y degree, so as to be a

feature in his works. He gives a descr^n of his idea of a poet
   The Poets eye etc. (*KL* i. 390).

As so often in the period, Theseus' playful lines are treated as if they were Shakespeare's *Poetics*: the poet's glancing eye and the imagination's bodying forth of things unknown are appropriated into the philosophical tradition of sympathy.

   The debt to Hazlitt in Keats's description of the poetical character is stylistic as well as substantive, as we see from his choice of the word 'gusto' and his adoption of Hazlitt's strategy of weaving a phrase from Shakespeare into his prose ('he is a very man *per se* and stands alone', *Troil* i. ii. 15). The idea of the poet conceiving an Iago as well as an Imogen was probably suggested not by the lecture on Shakespeare and Milton, but by the *Round Table* essay 'On Posthumous Fame'. Hazlitt had written there of the ideal poet's lack of an individual existence and Shakespeare's capacity to animate very different characters: 'He seemed scarcely to have an individual existence of his own, but to borrow that of others at will, and to pass successively through "every variety of untried being,"'—to be now *Hamlet*, now *Othello*, now *Lear*, now *Falstaff*, now *Ariel*' (*HW* iv. 23). In writing to Reynolds of the mind's associative processes, Keats made the progression from 'Hogarth to Shakespeare Shakespeare to Hazlitt— Hazlitt to Shakespeare' (*KL* i. 280).[24] An analogous formulation can be made: the idea of sympathy travelled from a variety of eighteenth-century philosophers and writers on aesthetics to Hazlitt's Shakespearean criticism to Keats.

   But the kind of empathy Keats achieved in his own poems was very different from that of Shakespearean drama. Keats aspired to be a dramatic writer; one recalls the remark, with its telling invocation of Kean, that he wished to make a revolution in modern dramatic writing. The importance he attached to the drama is apparent from his remarks about the lines in *Endymion* that begin 'Wherein lies happiness?' (i. 777–842): they are seen as both 'a regular stepping of the Imagination towards a Truth' and 'my first Step towards the chief Attempt in the Drama' (30 January 1818, *KL* i. 218). 'Imagination', 'Truth', and 'the Drama' are linked to describe a passage that turns on the idea of sympathy ('fellowship divine, / A fellowship with essence').

   But when he did make an attempt in the drama, Keats failed lamentably to grasp the organizing principles or the tonal qualities of

Shakespearean tragedy. On the matter of entering into his creations, Keats was least Shakespearean in his plays and most empathetic in his least Shakespearean form, the ode. There is certainly a sense of dramatic engagement and dialogue in the odes—Keats throws himself into the nightingale and the urn more fully than into Otho the Great and Ludolph—but 'To Autumn' is a masterpiece of impersonality in a lyrical-descriptive, not a dramatic vein. The engagement in Keats is frequently between himself, or a poet-figure, and a character, property, or personification; the complete impersonality afforded to the poet in Shakespeare's plays is rarely available to him. This is partly a question of genre—like all his contemporaries, Keats is essentially a lyric not a dramatic poet—but it is also one of self-consciousness.

For all his remarks about creating half at random, Keats is always conscious of himself as a poet; the very existence and nature of the letters is proof of that. Where Shakespeare got on with the business of making money out of writing plays, Keats meditated obsessively on Shakespeare and the possibility of ever writing plays like Shakespeare's; where Shakespeare created characters for the stage, Keats identified with those characters, refusing to separate art from life: 'I throw my whole being into Triolus [sic]', 'Hamlet's heart was full of such Misery as mine is when he said to Ophelia "Go to a Nunnery, go, go!"' (*KL* i. 404, ii. 312). Keats criticized Byron for cutting a figure, while he praised Shakespeare for living not as an individual but allegorically through his works (*KL* ii. 67). Whatever he may have said about the poetical character, Keats himself was closer to Byron than he would have wished—of all English poets they are the two whose lives and personalities are remembered as well as, if not better than, their works.

The letter on the poetical character arose out of a discussion with Woodhouse in which Keats said that 'there was now nothing original to be written in poetry; that its riches were already exhausted' (*KL* i. 380). Woodhouse disagreed, arguing that the potential beauties of poetry were inexhaustible and that new combinations of perceptions were always available to the poet. He contrasted the imitator, *Poeta factus*, who says nothing new, with the son of Genius, *Poeta natus*, who creates an imaginative world of his own (*KL* i. 380). But Keats knew that he could not create in isolation; he had to be a son not only of genius but also of the great English poets. By 27 February 1818, soon after the end of Hazlitt's lecture course, he could say 'I have great reason to be content, for thank God I can read and perhaps understand Shakspeare to his depths' (*KL* i. 239). But precisely because he had come to know and understand Shakespeare, he could not ignore him when he came to write his own poems. How could he avoid being *overpowered* by the 'idea of our dead poets'? How was he to respond to his presider?

9

Keats and his Presider

ACCORDING to Charles Brown, the genius of Keats was awakened by *The Faerie Queene*; the young poet's 'earliest attempt' was an 'Imitation of Spenser' subsequently published in his 1817 collection (*KC* ii. 55–6). Richard Woodhouse, who frequently compared Keats with Shakespeare, believed that a Shakespearean influence was already at work in this first poem; he pointed to the line 'Or rob from aged Lear his bitter teen' (22) and cited occurrences of the word 'teen' in *The Tempest, Richard III*, and *Venus and Adonis*.[1] But the story of Lear is told in *The Faerie Queene* and 'teen' is simply an example of archaic, 'Elizabethan' diction, not a specific borrowing from Shakespeare. The young Keats was under the auspices not of Shakespeare but of Spenser, or more specifically Spenser mediated through Leigh Hunt. What he wrote of Hunt, he could as well have written of himself: 'In Spenser's halls he strayed, and bowers fair, / Culling enchanted flowers' ('On the Day that Mr Leigh Hunt Left Prison'). The early poems are fragrant with flowers of language culled from Spenser and the world of faery.

In the 'Ode to Apollo', Keats's first formal invocation of his poetic forefathers, Shakespeare occupies no more than a conventional place as master of the passions and inspired original genius. One could as well be reading Hunt's *The Feast of the Poets*, or indeed an eighteenth-century catalogue of poets, such as Gray's 'The Progress of Poesy'. Nor can a special debt to Shakespeare be adduced from 'On Receiving a Curious Shell', for the King Oberon who presides over the romance world of that poem is derived not from *A Midsummer Night's Dream*, but from William Sotheby's popular translation of Wieland's *Oberon*.[2]

The first poem in which Keats meditates at length on his own status in relation to earlier poets is 'To George Felton Mathew'. It is a reply to Mathew's 'To a Poetical Friend', published in October 1816, in which Keats is praised as a budding Shakespeare or Milton: 'As thine is, I ween was the spring of their powers; / Like theirs, is the cast of thine earlier lay.'[3] Keats includes in his response quotations from

'L'Allegro' and *The Faerie Queene*; he thus proclaims his allegiance to Milton and Spenser. Mathew said later that the borrowing of Spenser's 'made a sunshine in the shadie place' was 'singularly felicitous in its adaptation'; he took Keats to be adept in the art of quotation even this early in his career (*KC* ii. 181). Keats's plea that he will be responsive to Mathew's poem is cast in the form of a metaphor that will recur when he learns to answer other poets in such a way that their utterances no longer have to be appropriated bodily as quotations: 'Fain would I echo back each pleasant note' (13). But a more prominent image is that which begins the poem: 'a brotherhood in song', 'the brother Poets', 'this great partnership' (2–8). The specific exemplars here are Beaumont and Fletcher, 'Who with combined powers, their wit employ'd / To raise a trophy to the drama's muses', but Keats implies that there can be a brotherhood between all poets. When Shakespeare is introduced he is a more companionable figure than he was in the 'Ode to Apollo', 'warm-hearted Shakspeare' sent to meet Chatterton and welcome him to heaven (56–8). Keats will often invoke Chatterton as an intermediary between himself and Shakespeare, for example in the original dedication to *Endymion* ('To the memory of The most english of Poets except Shakspeare, Thomas Chatterton'). 'To Autumn' will be conceived in an idiom of naturalness and Englishness which Keats believed Chatterton had inherited from Shakespeare. But already in this early ode there is a certain closeness to Shakespeare and none of Wordsworth's feeling that his genius is *unapproachable*.

The 1817 volume begins with 'I stood tip-toe upon a little hill', in which Keats reflects on the relationship between poetry and mythology; it ends with 'Sleep and Poetry', not only the longest of his early poems but the one in which he gives fullest consideration to the poet's task. We remember 'Sleep and Poetry' for its account of the progression of genres, the need to go beyond the romantic realm 'Of Flora, and old Pan' in which Keats had begun, and its attack, influenced by Hazlitt's essay 'On Milton's Versification', on Augustan poets who 'sway'd about upon a rocking horse, / And thought it Pegasus' (186). Less frequently remarked upon is the poem's first invocation:

> O Poesy! for thee I hold my pen
> That am not yet a glorious denizen
> Of thy wide heaven—Should I rather kneel
> Upon some mountain-top until I feel

A glowing splendour round about me hung,
And echo back the voice of thine own tongue?

(47)

The young poet—the ephebe, as Harold Bloom would have it—must be open to the 'strange influence' (69) of Poesy. He must kneel reverentially on the mountain-tops, perhaps go to what Coleridge called 'the two glory-smitten summits of the poetic mountain', the works of Shakespeare and Milton. Then he will eventually be able to 'echo back' their voices.

Of all the Romantic poets Keats is the one for whom the idea of *echo* is most potent. Where allusion provided Wordsworth and Coleridge with a partial solution to the difficulties raised by Shakespeare's priority, echo provided Keats—Keats at his best, that is—with a complete one. Some metaphors in the letter to Reynolds of 19 February 1818 provide a particularly suggestive frame of reference for a discussion of Keats and echo (*KL* i. 231–3).

Keats begins by proposing that a man might 'pass a very pleasant life' in reading 'a certain Page of full Poesy or distilled Prose': 'let him wander with it, and muse upon it, and reflect from it, and bring home to it, and prophesy upon it, and dream upon it'. One's own thoughts, he implies, should be improvisations on certain passages from past writers; individual passages in his predecessors are a 'starting post' for the later poet's own 'voyage of conception'. The process may be facilitated by sensual perceptions; in Keats's example, external sounds lead to internal reminiscences of Shakespeare—'a strain of musick conducts to "an odd angle of the Isle" and when the leaves whisper it puts a "girdle round the earth["]'. Keats then introduces an image of the spider, itself an improvisation on a theme of Swift or one of his classical precursors. The bee collecting nectar from a variety of flowers is a traditional image of poetic borrowing, with a history going back to Seneca.[4] Keats inverts the traditional preference for the bee by likening creativity to the weaving of the spider, whose material is more circumscribed than that of the bee. 'The points of leaves and twigs on which the Spider begins her work are few and she fills the Air with a beautiful circuiting: man should be content with as few points to tip with the fine Webb of his Soul and weave a tapestry empyrean'; 'by every germ of Spirit sucking the Sap from mould ethereal'. May we legitimately conceive of Keats the poet sucking the sap from the mould ethereal of a few mighty forebears, weaving a tapestry empyrean out of leaves and twigs from the 'old oak forest' of Shakespeare? If Keats is a spider, not a bee, we should emphasize not the variety of his borrowings, but the completeness with which he weaves a web from a few canonical sources. The image of beginning work on 'the points of leaves and twigs' is especially apposite in view of Keats's taste for woodland imagery when describing the works of past poets in such sonnets as 'On Sitting Down to Read *King Lear* Once Again' and 'Spenser, a jealous honourer of thine, / A forester deep in thy midmost trees'.

Later in his letter Keats shifts his emphasis from insect to flower. 'Let us open our leaves like a flower and be passive and receptive'. Keats is thinking of receptivity specifically to nature—these meditations were inspired, he says, 'by the beauty of the morning'—but ultimately to all kinds of experience. A poet's reading is part of his experience of nature, so he should be receptive to the words of past poets; we have seen that Keats's list of 'Things real' includes 'passages of Shakspeare' beside 'Sun Moon and Stars'. Passivity is suggested nicely not only by Keats's preference for the flower over the bee, but also by the way that the poet is the object not the subject of the verb in a remark like 'the following, from the Tempest, never struck me so forcibly as at present' (*KL* i. 133). Some lines from the sonnet 'Four seasons fill the measure of the year', written within a month of the letter to Reynolds, provide an excellent metaphor for Keats's appropriations of the thoughts and language of past poets:

> He chews the honied cud of fair spring thoughts,
> Till, in his soul dissolv'd, they come to be
> Part of himself.[5]

In some cases 'appropriation' is too violent a term. Often it is the words of the past poet that take possession of the later poet, not vice-versa. Wordsworth was surprised to find himself quoting the beginning of *Samson Agonistes* ('A little onward lend thy guiding hand'). When Keats wrote to Haydon in May 1817, he said that he dared to fancy Shakespeare his 'Presider' because the propriety of things he did 'half at Random' was afterwards confirmed by his judgement. This notion of randomness helps us to perceive the lack of conscious control in Keats's echoes; to adapt one of his poetic axioms, Shakespearean language comes to him 'as naturally as the Leaves to a tree' (*KL* i. 238). The words of Shakespeare become a part of Keats's self. They do not often obtrude on a first reading; their presence is only confirmed when the analytical mind sets to work and the judgement is brought into play.

It is noticeable that Keats lists among 'Things real' sun, moon, stars, and *passages of* Shakespeare, not 'Shakespeare' *in toto*. Similarly, he says 'Shakspeare and the paradise Lost every day become greater wonders to me—I look upon fine Phrases like a Lover' (*KL* ii. 139). It is phrases, not scenes or poems or plays, that 'like a Lover' he wishes to possess. On first reading *The Faerie Queene* he 'especially singled out epithets, for that felicity and power in which Spenser is so eminent' (CCC 126). The markings in his pocket edition reveal a similar approach in his reading of Shakespeare: many of the underlinings draw attention to striking images. When Richard Woodhouse read and annotated Keats, he kept a special ear open for 'fine phrases' that recalled those of the mighty dead. Often a single word could cue a parallel in Woodhouse's mind; beside 'each sting / Thrown by the pitiless world' in the epistle to Mathew (64), he writes that phrase in *Lear* which also spoke to Wordsworth, Coleridge, and Blake, 'bide the pelting of this pitiless storm' (Sperry, 145). As George Cumberland's reading of Blake's *Europe* was facilitated by analogous images in Shakespeare, so for Woodhouse Keats's language is characterized by its extreme responsiveness to the words of his predecessors.

Certain figures and conceptions in other letters provide metaphors for this process. Keats writes to Bailey of being 'surprised with an old Melody' and of 'redigestion' (i. 185–6), to Reynolds of associations that 'chime': 'This crossing a letter is not without its association—for chequer work leads us naturally to a Milkmaid, a Milkmaid to Hogarth Hogarth to Shakespeare Shakespear to Hazlitt—Hazlitt to Shakespeare and thus by merely pulling an apron string we set a pretty peal of Chimes at work' (*KL* i. 280). The initial association hinges on the yoking of two 'fine Phrases' in Milton, 'many a maid, / Dancing in the chequered shade' and 'the milkmaid singeth blithe';[6] the figure is completed by another kind of association, the pun that leads from an apron string to a bell-ringer's rope. This setting of 'a pretty peal of Chimes at work' provides us with a wonderful image of Romantic *echo*, that kind of allusion in which a range of phrases and associations are heard, but the text is not directly dependent on a single earlier text, as it is when a poem includes a 'quotation'. Furthermore, it is a process that works in the poetic imagination, below the level of conscious intention; echoes can therefore be integrated more fully into a poem than more overt forms of allusions can—one recalls De

Quincey's concern about the interruption of the flow of the Immortality Ode occasioned by Wordsworth's quotation marks around 'like a guilty thing'.

Thomas McFarland's words about Coleridge's plagiarisms may be adapted and applied to Keats's echoes. Every poet echoes the words of others, English poets those of Shakespeare in particular, but Keats does so more frequently and more creatively than others—to such an extent that echo, Shakespearean echo especially, forms virtually a mode of composition in his poems. The poems themselves sometimes manifest an awareness of their own nature as echoes or of the literary tradition as an echo-chamber. In 'How many bards gild the lapses of time!' Keats refers to past poets as the 'food' of his fancy; this is another traditional image for the process by which poets are nourished by scraps from their predecessors, which are then metabolized in the body of the later poem (Seneca, *Ad Lucilium*, ii. 278–81). Keats broods over poetic 'beauties' and the bards 'intrude' into his mind, providing him with a 'pleasing chime' (1–8). In 'Isabella' he describes as follows his relationship with Boccaccio, the 'honied cud' on which he is chewing:

> To honour thee, and thy gone spirit greet;
> To stead thee as a verse in English tongue,
> An echo of thee in the north-wind sung.

> (stanza 20)

Each echo of Shakespeare we hear in Keats is an honouring of the 'Presider', a greeting of his gone spirit.

The sonnet 'On the Sea' provides an especially fruitful example of Shakespearean echo because there is external evidence to connect it with one of the plays. It appears in the letter to Reynolds from Carisbrooke in which Keats speaks of finding 'a head of Shakspeare' and hanging it, like a presiding deity, over his books. The sonnet is inspired by a combination of Shakespeare and nature, a walk on the cliffs and 'the passage in Lear—"Do you not hear the Sea?"' (*KL* i. 132; *Lr* IV. vi. 11–24). It is a characteristic Romantic strategy to perceive nature through Shakespeare in this way. In 'My First Acquaintance with Poets', Hazlitt recalls an occasion on which Wordsworth looked out of the window and said 'How beautifully the sun sets on that yellow bank!'; 'I thought within myself', Hazlitt remarks, ' "With what eyes these poets see nature!" ' (*HW* xvii. 118).

But in fact Wordsworth is adapting the line from *The Merchant of Venice*, 'How sweet the moonlight sleeps upon this bank!' (v. i. 54); it is with Shakespeare's eyes that he sees nature.

Keats says that the passage in *Lear* has 'haunted' him 'intensely'; his sonnet is consequently haunted by echoes of this and other moments in the play. His 'eternal whisperings' parallel Shakespeare's 'murmuring surge', his motionless shell on the shore, Shakespeare's 'idle pebble'. There is an echo in the strictly aural sense when the sibilance of 'scarcely will the very smallest shell' matches that of 'Show scarce so gross as beetles'. Edgar is describing the cliff to Gloucester, who has had his 'eyeballs' plucked out; the presence of the word in the sonnet moves us out from the passage on the sea to the world of *Lear* generally.[7] This movement is enhanced by 'vext', the first of the two past participles used as adjectives to qualify 'eyeballs', for shortly before the scene on the cliff, Cordelia speaks of Lear 'As mad as the vex'd *sea*' (IV. iv. 2, my italics, whole line underscored by Keats in his Folio). Here Keats has brought about a characteristic transformation of his original. In Shakespeare, the sea and the wind tempestuously mirror the passions. In Keats, we are feasted with 'the wideness of the sea' where we might expect its wildness: 'wideness' suggests a vast, flat surface; nature is a source of repose for man's 'eyeballs vext and tir'd'. There is a similar contrast in the preceding line, where Keats's seascape is calm, for it is some time since 'last the winds of heaven were unbound' and before there will be another storm; but in *Lear*, the unbinding of the 'winds of heaven' is at the centre of a play pervaded by bonds and bindings, emotional and physical.

Keats probably made the association, with its attendant contrasts, between *Lear* and the sea 'half at Random'. He would have found it afterwards confirmed by his judgement 'in a dozen features of Propriety' when he read *Characters of Shakespear's Plays*. In his copy of Hazlitt's book he marked the phrases in the chapter on *Lear* 'that rich sea, [Lear's] mind, with all its vast riches', 'the ebb and flow of the feeling', and 'the swelling tide of passion' (*Characters*, 175, 157, 177). Johnson had used a similar metaphor when he wrote of the 'current of the poet's imagination' in his note on *King Lear* (*SJS* 703); for once, Keats would have agreed with him. Elsewhere, he went further than Johnson or Hazlitt, and introduced the sea as a metaphor for Shakespeare's plays in general, not just *King Lear*: 'Which is the best of Shakspeare's Plays?—I mean in what mood and with what accompenament do you like the Sea best?' (to Jane Reynolds, *KL* i. 158). That nonchalant 'I mean' makes Shakespeare synonymous with the natural power and variety of the sea. It is a poet's intuition— one is reminded of W. B. Yeats's description, with its quiet allusion to *The Tempest*, of his response to Shakespearean drama at Stratford-upon-Avon: 'I have felt as I have sometimes felt on grey days on the Galway shore, when a faint mist has hung over the grey sea and the grey stones, as if the world might suddenly vanish and leave nothing behind.'[8]

Though a sonnet, 'On the Sea' is a response to *King Lear*, not the Sonnets; one area in which it does not echo Shakespeare is that of form. All Keats's earlier sonnets are either Petrarchan or irregular; this is another symptom of his indebtedness to Leigh Hunt, a well-known apologist for the Petrarchan form.[9] But in January 1818, when he reread *King Lear* and rededicated himself to his art, Keats began imitating the Shakespearean form. The 'Lear' sonnet is the first in which he did so, though it still has the vestiges of Petrarchan form in that the octave is rhymed 'abba abba'. His next poem, 'When I have fears that I may cease to be', can only be described as an imitation or highly accomplished pastiche of a Shakespearean sonnet.

Its debt is thematic as well as formal. 'When I have fears' is a meditation on love, fame, and time, in which each quatrain begins with the same temporal clause. The two sonnets in which Shakespeare repeats 'When I . . .' most memorably are the twelfth and the sixty-fourth. Keats takes his image of the 'shore' from the latter and combines it with a phrase which had also attracted Wordsworth, 'Of the wide world' (Sonnet 107). The image-cluster 'glean'd', 'rich garners', 'the full ripen'd grain' is derived from the second quatrain of sonnet twelve, which he had quoted in a letter to Reynolds two months earlier ('I neer found so many beauties in the sonnets'):

> When lofty trees I see barren of leaves
> Which erst from heat did canopy the herd
> And Summer's green all girded up in sheaves,
> Borne on the bier with white and bristly beard.
>
> (*KL* i. 188)

These are lines which, crucially, will echo again in Keats's mind when he comes to write 'To Autumn'.

The influence of Shakespeare on 'When I have fears' is not confined to vocabulary, rhetorical structure, and subject-matter (the latter is the common stuff of sonnets). Jackson Bate showed forty years ago that the later sonnets of Keats bear other Shakespearean hallmarks: the use of balanced lines; the repetition of phrases from line to line; the answering of the first line in the last; patterns of alliteration, assonance, and antithesis (*Stylistic Development*, 118–25). In addition, there are occasional signs of a Shakespearean mastery of ambiguity and conceit—the phrase 'fair creature of an hour' has no single referent; the final image of sinking turns around that of standing on the shore.

With 'When I have fears that I may cease to be', the Shakespearean sonnet is actively revived, both formally and tonally, by a major English poet for the first time in two hundred years. But to reproduce certain effects in the Sonnets, elegantly as Keats does so here (less persuasive is 'Time's sea hath been five years at its slow ebb', an undistinguished version of sonnet sixty), is in no way to *go beyond* Shakespeare. To do that, Keats would have to find a language that, while still responsive to Shakespeare, did not rely on the crude borrowing of phrases.

In terms of their relationship with Shakespearean language, the sonnets are no great advance on *Endymion*. In that poem, the marks of Keats's reading of the magical plays, *A Midsummer Night's Dream* and *The Tempest*, are visible in phrases borrowed but not given new life. Secondhand epithets, the kind of poetic phrases handed down from father to son which Wordsworth condemned in his preface, add to the opulence but also the looseness of *Endymion*: 'rain-scented eglantine', 'spangly light', 'Night-swollen mushrooms', 'Whose eyelids curtain'd up their jewels dim'. And the following are indicative of a servile, not a creative, approach to Shakespeare: 'Who dives three fathoms where the waters run / Gurgling in beds of coral'; 'Old ditties sigh above their father's grave'; 'that fine element that visions, dreams, / And fitful whims of sleep are made of'; 'Swift as a fathoming plummet down he fell'.[10] Similarly, John Jones shows that the line 'How tiptoe Night holds back her dark-grey hood' (i. 831) combines several images from *Romeo and Juliet*, thus producing a top-heavy effect; 'such Shakespearian farragos are common in bad Keats', he justly remarks (*Dream of Truth*, 52 n.).

Endymion is sub-titled 'A Poetic Romance'. It is in a letter to his brothers written after sending the first book to his publishers and preparing the second for the press, that Keats speaks of 'a very gradual ripening of the intellectual powers' and transcribes the sonnet he has just written 'On sitting down to King Lear once Again' (*KL* i. 214–15). The word 'ripening' shows that the language of the play has been at work on him ('Ripeness is all'). In the sonnet Keats proposes that the path to maturity lies in rejecting 'golden-tongued Romance' in favour of the 'bitter-sweet' experience of Shakespearean tragedy. By burning through *King Lear* he will purify himself of the fripperies of *Endymion*; only when he has been consumed in the fire will he be reborn, phoenix-like, as a writer. He is beginning to be true to *King Lear* as he was not in his early 'Imitation of Spenser', where he imagined that a tale of a romantic isle had power to rob Lear of his bitterness. 'So you see I am getting at it, with a sort of determination and strength', he writes to George and Tom after copying the sonnet for them.

What he is getting at is the need to grapple in his poetry with human suffering. The sonnets he then writes show him turning from the mythological world to the individual consciousness, loving, desiring, fearing. But it is also at this time that he is attending Hazlitt's lectures on the English Poets where he was reminded that full engagement with human suffering could only come in the impersonal, sympathetic form of tragedy. Keats's next major poems are 'Isabella' and 'The Eve of St Agnes'; in retrospect he saw them, the latter especially, as steps on the path to Shakespearean drama:

> The little dramatic skill I may as yet have however badly it might show in a Drama would I think be sufficient for a Poem—I wish to diffuse the colouring of St Agnes eve throughout a Poem in which Character and Sentiment would be the figures to such drapery—Two or three such Poems, if God should spare me, written in the course of the next six years, would be a famous gradus ad Parnassum altissimum—I mean they would nerve me up to the writing of a few fine Plays—my greatest ambition (*KL* ii. 234).

'Isabella' is an intermediate step. Keats was not yet ready for the drama, or even the dramatic, but he needed to advance from the sonnet; after all, in *Characters of Shakespear's Plays*, which he had read by this time, Hazlitt had condemned the Sonnets for their lack of dramatic impersonality. Coleridge's *Biographia Literaria*, which he might also have read by early 1818, or at least discussed with Hazlitt,[11] described Shakespeare's narrative poems in such a way as to make them into the perfect model for Keats at this stage of his development:

I think, I should have conjectured from these poems, that even then the great instinct, which impelled the poet to the drama, was secretly working in him, prompting him by a series and never broken chain of imagery, always vivid and because unbroken, often minute; by the highest effort of the picturesque in words, of which words are capable . . . to provide a substitute for that visual language, that constant intervention and running comment by tone, look and gesture, which in his dramatic works he was entitled to expect from the players. His 'Venus and Adonis' seem at once the characters themselves, and the whole representation of those characters by the most consummate actors. You seem to be *told* nothing, but to see and hear every thing. (*BL* ii. 21)

Whether or not Keats knew the passage, he would have agreed with this reading of Shakespeare's poems; in 'Isabella' and 'The Eve of St Agnes' he strives after the effects described by Coleridge.

In 'Isabella' he employs the Shakespearean device of reworking in verse a story from an old prose romance. His choice of metre, *ottava rima*, is not strictly Shakespearean, but its precedents are Renaissance ones, and it bears close resemblance to the stanza of *Lucrece* (Shakespeare: ababbcc; Keats: abababcc). Some of the imagery, notably recurrent effects of colour (the white of chastity, fear, and death contrasted with the red of passion, shame, and blood), and the rhetorical formality (excessive use of anaphora and other varieties of balance and repetition) could have been learnt from either poem. Specific parallels with *Venus and Adonis* are more noticeable. Many of Keats's departures from his original in Boccaccio are explained by the influence of Shakespeare's poem. Isabella, like Venus, is seen as a mother-figure as well as a lover for the young Lorenzo; like Adonis, the latter is a hunter who ends up being gored to death in the forest (Isabella's brothers, who are compared to animals, play the role of Shakespeare's boar). Like Venus, Isabella finds the place where her lover fell; she almost seems to undergo a metamorphosis analogous to Adonis's, 'Upon the murderous spot she seem'd to grow, / Like to a native lily of the dell' (st. 46). Certain key images are borrowed—veiling hair, the moist lips and palm of passion—as is a tendency to digress. The most famous digression in *Venus and Adonis* is that concerning the hunted hare; the digression in which Keats addresses Boccaccio is cued by the phrase 'as doth the hunted hare' (st. 18). Keats would have read in Lemprière's *Dictionary* that Venus was sometimes known as Basilea; he might even have been familiar with the tradition that basil was planted in pots and used in the worship of Adonis. He would certainly have known that Adonis was associated with the spring, which may account for the structural role of the seasons in his poem: the love of Lorenzo and Isabella grows in the spring and flowers in the summer, then Isabella decays in the autumn and winter (this progression is not emphasized in Boccaccio).[12] But the most creative aspect of Shakespeare's influence on 'Isabella' may be summarized in Coleridge's terms: the figures in the poem are both characters and actors; the picturesque language of look, gesture, and backdrop provides a running commentary on the action. The best strokes in the poem are certain minute details, such as Isabella throwing back her hair as it gets in her eyes while she digs up Lorenzo's body (st. 47), a gesture which enables us to see her emotional state without being *told* about it.

In 'The Eve of St Agnes' Keats goes further in developing an art that is at once pictorial and dramatic. He reverts to the Spenserian stanza and a Spenserian combination of gorgeousness and dangerousness,[13] but by echoing Shakespeare's plays achieves a much stronger dramatic structure than that of 'Isabella'. It has frequently been pointed out that *Romeo and Juliet* is the principal Shakespearean influence.[14] Porphyro enters the house of his beloved during an evening of revelry, although his family is at odds with hers; he is assisted by the aged Angela, who thus plays the role of Juliet's nurse, Angelica (though she is also descended from the attendants and retainers of the gothic novel).[15] As in *Romeo and Juliet*, the erotic and the religious are closely linked, though the beadsman is a figure who contrasts with the love-plot and is not involved with it as Friar Lawrence is. Keats introduces other tonal changes: the bedroom scene is sinisterly re-written as that in *Cymbeline*, where Iachimo lasciviously watches the sleeping Imogen; the conception that things are better in a dream than in reality is introduced from *The Tempest*. Madeline prefers the Porphyro of her dream to the real one: 'How chang'd thou art! how pallid, chill, and drear! / Give me that voice again, my Porphyro' (st. 35); in one of his transcriptions of the poem Richard Woodhouse, guided by his sense of Keats's affinity with Shakespeare, wrote 'Give me that voice again *sweet Prospero*', a recollection of Caliban crying 'to dream again'. Woodhouse might also have associated Porphyro with Prospero in that each of them produces from nowhere an exotic feast.

Echoes of the drunken revelry at Claudius's court provide a backdrop for the quasi-supernatural encounter between Madeline and Porphyro: compare 'The boisterous, midnight, festive clarion, / The kettle-drum, and far-heard clarionet. . . . The bloated wassaillers . . .

Drown'd all in Rhenish' with 'Keeps wassail . . . And as he drains his draughts of Rhenish down, / The kettle-drum and trumpet thus bray out' ('St Agnes', 258–9, 346–9; *Ham* I. iv. 9–11). But tragedy is avoided. The parallel with *Hamlet* is only an atmospheric effect; the lovers run off into the night. An element of the grotesque is introduced in the final stanza, but it is as if *Romeo and Juliet* were to end with the lovers reunited and the nurse dying. And although the poem has dramatic elements it could never have been a play; it is dramatic in the way that a series of narrative tapestries can be dramatic. Keats realized as much when he wrote later of the poem's 'colouring' and 'drapery', of how his dramatic skill was sufficient for a poem but would show badly in a drama.

Just how badly it shows in a drama can be seen in *Otho the Great*. Keats cannot be blamed for the construction of his only complete play, since he worked it up from plot-synopses by Charles Brown. But its language reveals that in writing for the stage, like Wordsworth and Coleridge before him, he reproduced Shakespearean phraseology without breathing new life into it. It would be tedious to rehearse the debts in detail.[16] They are apparent from the very first speech, in which the villain, Conrad, soliloquizes in the manner of Richard III. Many of the borrowings are extremely casual; 'thwart spleen' is used in the context of anger (I. iii. 91) merely because that is the vocabulary of Lear's anger. Often a pair of phrases from different plays are combined, perhaps in order to avoid any impression of a specific debt. 'How dar'st thou lift those beetle brows at me?' (III. ii. 77) is an awkward combination of Macbeth addressing Banquo's ghost and Mercutio's 'beetle brows' (*Rom* I. iv. 32); Ludolph's 'vanish'd? melted into air? / She's gone! I cannot clutch her!' (V. i. 24) at least has the merit of yoking two examples of imaginative power, Prospero's masque and Macbeth's dagger, though both tonally and contextually the former is an irrelevance. Keats wrote the part of his hero, Ludolph, with Kean in mind, so his speeches in particular are farragos out of the major Shakespearean roles with which Kean had made his name. But the relationship with Shakespeare is not organized; when Ludolph speaks of a 'bright sword' (IV. ii. 106) we think of *Othello* but then there is a confusing reference a few lines later to *Otho*, not a hero but a father. Only occasionally is there an understanding, as opposed to an imitation, of Shakespearean language: an image of fawning spaniels (I. iii. 82—Shakespeare's favourite

metaphor for flatterers), a transformation of a noun into a verb
('medicin'd', 'fever'd': II. i. 9, 51). In 'To Autumn', written a
month after the completion of *Otho*, Keats will exploit syntactic con-
version to the full. An understanding of the energy of the Shakespearean verb is also apparent in the fragment of *King Stephen*,
another work written shortly after *Otho*; its brisk sequence of scenes
has some of the gusto of Shakespeare's early history plays, as does a
line like 'How like a comet he goes streaming on' (I. i. 17).

John Jones writes that 'Shakespeare is always a bad sign in Keats'
(*Dream of Truth*, 81). He could easily have said this of *Otho the Great*,
but in fact the context of his remark is an account of Saturn's 'hector-
ing spate of command and question' in the first book of *Hyperion*. The
debt to Lear in the portrayal of Saturn is not confined to the former's
'Does any here know me? . . .' (I. iv. 226 ff.; cf. *Hyperion*, i. 98 ff.).
There is a more general influence in that Saturn feels that he has lost
his whole self once he is 'Unsceptred' and 'realmless' (i. 19); the
following is a re-writing of Lear's predicament in Keatsian language:

> I have left
> My strong identity, my real self,
> Somewhere between the throne, and where I sit
> Here on this spot of earth.
>
> (i. 113)

For Jones the influence of Lear on Saturn is bad because it is 'a
mark of knowingness and strain'. The problem is one of tone; after
all, *Hyperion* is not a tragedy. But I think his generalization needs to
be recast: the *obtrusive* presence of Shakespeare is always a bad sign in
Keats, but where Shakespeare is genuinely embodied and reconsti-
tuted, Keats is often at his best.

Near the end of his self-questioning address to Thea, Saturn speaks
of 'ripe progress' towards the repossession of heaven and his own re-
enthronement (i. 125). The conception of 'ripeness' is picked up in
Oceanus' great speech in the second book:

> And first, as thou wast not the first of powers,
> So art thou not the last; it cannot be:
> Thou art not the beginning nor the end.
> From Chaos and parental Darkness came
> Light, the first fruits of that intestine broil,
> That sullen ferment, which for wondrous ends
> Was ripening in itself. The ripe hour came,

And with it Light, and Light, engendering
Upon its own producer, forthwith touch'd
The whole enormous matter into life.

(ii. 188)

True 'ripeness', argues Oceanus, lies in the acceptance of change, in giving way to the future, in the realization that as one was not the first one cannot be the last. Edgar's 'Ripeness is all'[17] and the idea, so fundamental to *Lear* and Shakespeare's last plays, of handing over power and life to the next generation have been transmuted beyond recognition—there is no correspondence between the three younger gods and Lear's three daughters. The transformation is so powerful that, along with other tendencies in the Romantic reading of Shakespeare, we are no longer able to read the original lines as they would have been read or heard when the play was written. J. V. Cunningham has shown that for Shakespeare and his contemporaries 'ripeness' simply meant readiness for death; Edgar's lines, like Hamlet's on the special providence in the fall of a sparrow, would originally have been comprehended in Christian terms: 'By "Ripeness is all," then, Shakespeare means that the fruit will fall in its time, and man dies when God is ready.'[18] But we now read the phrase as though it looked towards life, not death; 'all would agree that "Ripeness is all" gathers into a phrase something of the ultimate value of this life; it reassures us that maturity of experience is a final good, and that there is a fulness of feeling, an inner and emotional completion in life that is attainable and that will resolve our tragedies' (Cunningham, 7). For Cunningham, this reading has its locus in modern psychology; I think it has its origins in Keats—in the letters, where a reading of Shakespeare and an understanding of the poet's self come to fruition together, and in *Hyperion*. 'Ripeness' in *Lear* is bound up with tragedy as finality, as a movement towards death. But as I have said, *Hyperion* is not a tragedy; it moves away from the fallen gods towards life, breaking off at a moment not of destruction but of creation, with Apollo about to be transformed into a god.

It is possible to reconstruct Shakespeare's meaning historically, as Cunningham does, but a living reading of 'Ripeness is all' cannot but be a misreading influenced by Keats. Two remarks in Eliot's 'Tradition and the Individual Talent', an essay much influenced by Keatsian notions of impersonality, are especially apposite: 'We shall often find that not only the best, but the most individual parts of [a poet's] work

may be those in which the dead poets, his ancestors, assert their immortality most vigorously'; 'The existing monuments form an ideal
order among themselves, which is modified by the introduction of the
new (the really new) work of art among them.'[19] Shakespeare is
modified by Keats.

This reading of *Hyperion* is a selective one. A glance at Oceanus'
rhetoric, with its biblical vocabulary, its reference to 'Chaos and
parental Darkness', its 'intestine broil', will reveal the influence of
Milton. It was the burden of Milton's language that led Keats to give
up his second version of *Hyperion* in 1819: 'there were too many
Miltonic inversions in it—Miltonic verse cannot be written but in an
artful or rather artist's humour. I wish to give myself up to other sensations. English ought to be kept up' (*KL* ii. 167). 'Give myself up to
other sensations' suggests a preference for Shakespearean negative
capability over the Miltonic egotistical sublime, but Milton's influence on Keats in 1818 and 1819 is as powerful as Shakespeare's.
The re-dedication in January 1818 took place under twin presiders:
the day before 'Sitting Down to Read *King Lear* Once Again', Keats
wrote his 'Lines on Seeing a Lock of Milton's Hair' (the play and the
relic: Milton the man is visible, while Shakespeare is subsumed in his
works). Structurally, *Hyperion* is an imitation of *Paradise Lost*: book
one introduces fallen gods who debate their course of action in book
two; book three begins with an invocation of the Muse and moves to a
new realm of light. The poem stands in a similar relation to Milton as
Otho the Great does to Shakespeare, though in itself Keats's unfinished
epic is much more successful than his completed tragedy. It is to be
regretted that *The Fall of Hyperion* is also unfinished, for at certain
moments in that poem Keats works tragic intuitions into his epic
structure; one thinks, for example, of Moneta's words on how none
can climb to the shrine 'But those to whom the miseries of the
world / Are misery, and will not let them rest' (148). Had it been
completed, *The Fall of Hyperion* might have been Keats's richest synthesis of Milton and Shakespeare.

In the odes, by eschewing direct imitation of Shakespearean or
Miltonic form Keats wrote poetry that was responsive to both but servile to neither. I say 'direct' imitation because Shakespeare and
Milton had an indirect influence on the form of the odes. To call them
'odes' was to engage with an eighteenth-century tradition of vatic
utterance that derived much of its language from Milton.[20] The stanza

of the odes which were probably written in May 1819—'Indolence', 'Nightingale', 'Grecian Urn', and 'Melancholy'—grew out of Keats's dissatisfaction with both Shakespearean and Petrarchan sonnet forms. At the beginning of that month Keats wrote, 'The legitimate [Petrarchan] does not suit the language over-well from the pouncing rhymes—the other kind appears too elegaic—and the couplet at the end of it has seldom a pleasing effect' (*KL* ii. 108). In place of the un-English Petrarchan octave and the uncertain combination of elegiac and epigrammatic he detected in the Shakespearean sonnet, Keats produces a single Shakespearean quatrain followed by a Petrarchan sestet. All four odes are rhymed ababcdecde (with occasional variation of order in the last three lines); the stanza is both more leisured and more closely-knit than any of Keats's experiments with the sonnet.[21]

Keats's six odes are not all intimately related to Shakespeare. 'Psyche' needs to be read in a context of Keats and mythology; it seeks to recover the pagan gods banished by Milton in his 'Nativity' ode. Its relationship with Milton is apparent from line two: 'sweet enforcement and remembrance dear' is itself a partially inverted remembrance of *Lycidas*, 'Bitter constraint, and sad occasion dear' (6). The 'Grecian Urn' is classical where the 'Nightingale' is romantic, concerned with the visual and plastic arts, not the music of Shakespearean song.[22] If there is an influence on this ode, it is that of Shakespeare's most classical poem, 'The Phoenix and Turtle', which Keats read and marked in his copy of the *Poems*. In the 'Threnos' Beauty and Truth are seen enclosed in an urn; there is also a reference to 'married chastity', which might be a source for Keats's 'unravish'd bride'. Howard Felperin summarizes well: both 'The Phoenix and Turtle' and the 'Ode on a Grecian Urn' 'celebrate paradoxically an ideal of love; both attempt to transcend the mutability inherent in human love by purging it of sexual consummation; and both recognize the price at which this ideal state is purchased—the impossibility of fruition and generation.'[23] The two poems are also about art: they themselves give new life and movement to what is dead and static. Shakespeare emphasizes the uniqueness of the phoenix, but for Keats all poetry has within it potential phoenix-wings, the capacity to make its writer immortal.

The interplay of mortal fears and immortal longings is the stuff of the odes 'on Indolence' and 'to a Nightingale'. In the former, the poet is approached three times by three shadowy figures who first seem to be Graces or Muses and are then specifically identified as Love,

Ambition, and Poesy. The language describing their apparition echoes the first act of *Hamlet*—where the ghost appears three times. The word 'fade' or 'faded' is used three times; by the third, readers may have been jogged into remembering that the ghost of old Hamlet 'faded on the crowing of the cock' (I. i. 157), especially as Keats writes 'So, ye three ghosts, adieu!', a variation upon the moment in *Hamlet* where the one ghost says 'adieu' three times and Hamlet himself echoes the word twice (I. v. 91, 111). The language of Hamlet's melancholy soliloquies is also suggested by words like 'melt' and 'ache' ('O that this too too solid flesh would melt'; 'the heart-ache and the thousand natural shocks / That flesh is heir to'). As the ghost comes to chide Hamlet into action, so the ghostly figures come to chide the indolent Keats into Poesy. The pattern is familiar from those Wordsworthian encounters discussed in chapter five; it also alerts us to a similar set of echoes in the 'Nightingale' ode.

 Keats only met Coleridge once, when they walked together on 11 April 1819; in his long journal-letter to his brother and sister-in-law, the younger poet listed the topics of conversation broached by the older one. That list begins 'Nightingales, Poetry—on Poetical sensation' (ii. 88). Within a month, Keats was to write a poem about 'Poesy' in which the nightingale is an image of the ideal poet, singing in 'full-throated ease'. Like Wordsworth's and Coleridge's nightingale poems, with their quotations of Shakespeare's 'fiery heart' and Milton's 'Most musical, most melancholy', this ode is a highly literary construct; it constitutes the densest example in Keats of echo, considered as that technique whereby a poem is made with the language of previous poets but does not allude self-consciously to those poets. This form of pre-conscious allusion is especially fitting in an ode in which the first-person poet-figure strives to share in the spontaneous song of the nightingale.

 Critics have detected the quiet presence in the ode of the language of Milton, Wordsworth, Coleridge, Hazlitt's lectures, and other works read by Keats, including sources as diverse as Horace's fourteenth Epode and *Tristram Shandy*.[24] But the number of Shakespearean analogues is most remarkable: there are about fifty of them in this eighty-line lyric.[25] Two passages may have led Keats to draw on Shakespeare when writing about a nightingale. According to Haydon (*Diary*, ii. 318), the line 'Where youth grows pale, and spectre-thin, and dies' alluded to Keats's brother Tom, who died of tuberculosis in December 1818; in his Folio *Lear* Keats underlined the words 'poore

Tom' at III. iv. 38 and wrote in the margin 'Sunday Evening Oct. 4. 1818'. When he read *Lear* in his pocket edition, he would have come across one of poor Tom's lines in the arraignment scene which is omitted from the Folio: 'The foul fiend haunts poor Tom in the voice of a nightingale' (III. vi. 29). Is there a sense in which Tom haunts Keats in the voice of the nightingale? Even if any biographical reading is eschewed, the idea of the poem being *haunted* by a Shakespearean voice remains powerful—after all, Keats himself had once spoken of being 'haunted' by *King Lear*.

The second nightingale is that of *The Passionate Pilgrim*, which, as I have said, was still attributed to Shakespeare in the early nineteenth century; Keats marked it up in his copy of the *Poems*. In the final poem of that collection, there is a 'forlorn' nightingale in a bower (xx.9); this may be why Keats emphasizes so strongly the word 'forlorn' which ends the seventh stanza of the ode and is echoed at the beginning of the eighth.[26] The nightingale of *The Passionate Pilgrim* is a sorrowful bird like that of 'Il Penseroso'; we saw in chapter two that Coleridge questioned this attribute and in his 'Conversation Poem' made the nightingale joyful. Keats is on Coleridge's side of this debate, but retains the melancholy mood by giving it to the poet, who is contrasted with the bird; the ode derives its dramatic force from the dialogue between the two states. That emphasis on 'the very word' *forlorn*, with its suggestion of the power in the very sound of words, shows that this is a poem in which words and their resonances will have peculiar weight.

The allusion to poor Tom Keats in the third stanza contrasts with the embracing of death in the sixth ('Now more than ever seems it rich to die'). These stanzas are improvisations on two of the most famous speeches in *Measure for Measure*, both marked extensively by Keats in his pocket edition, the Duke's 'Be absolute for death' and Claudio's 'Ay, but to die'. The picture of youth and 'palsied' age in the third stanza belongs to the Duke; the highly physical consciousness of death in the sixth is shared by Claudio. There is a particularly striking aural echo of 'to become A kneaded clod' in 'To thy high requiem become a sod'; the image of wooing death ('half in love with easeful Death, / Call'd him soft names') parallels Claudio's 'I will encounter darkness as a bride' (*Meas* III. i. 119, 83; 'Nightingale', 60, 52)—but here Keats changes the gender in his image, perhaps in an attempt to get away from his usual figure of a 'belle dame sans merci'. The tension between these two stanzas of the ode is similar to that in the conflicting attitudes of the Duke and Claudio; 'the "Ode" pits an abstract summary of the ills to which mortal flesh is heir against a vividly felt sense of the same mortal life as humanity's most valuable possession' (Grennan, 290). The comparison should not, however, lead us to ignore the profound differences between ode and play—the Christian context which is absent in Keats, and the fact that in *Measure for Measure* both the Duke and Claudio are very suspect characters whose words and motives cannot be trusted as those of 'Keats' can in the ode.

The Duke's vision of youth and age may be mediated via Wordsworth's *The Excursion*, which was much admired by Keats; the imagery of the third stanza and the subsequent yoking of 'generations' and the verb to 'tread' echo

> While man grows old, and dwindles, and decays;
> And countless generations of mankind
> Depart; and leave no vestige where they trod.
>
> (*Excursion*, iv. 760)

Poets, however, do leave vestiges where they tread; later poets then follow in their footsteps—as Keats said with regard to *Hamlet*, 'We read fine things but never feel them to [the] full until we have gone the same steps as the Author' (*KL* i. 279). In verbal echoes we may sometimes discern the vestiges of more than one precursor. Helen Vendler argues that the fifth is the greatest stanza of the ode, the bower described there Keats's greatest bower, decked not from nature but from art: 'the violets and musk-roses and eglantine are borrowed from Titania's bower in *A Midsummer Night's Dream*, described by Oberon (as this bower is described by Keats) from memory, not sight.'[27] The choice of flowers suggests that Keats is remembering Oberon's 'I know a bank . . .' (*MND* ii. i. 249 ff.), which he marked in his Shakespeare, but in a larger sense he is entering into a tradition of English poetic bowers which includes those of Spenser (the Garden of Adonis) and Milton (the bower in the fourth book of *Paradise Lost*, presided over by a nightingale).

For Keats's friend Reynolds the greatest catalogue of flowers in the language is that of the early Milton writing under the sway of Shakespeare and Spenser:

The following passage of Milton is so beautifully descriptive of the most attractive flowers and shrubs, that fancy could not imagine a more exquisite selection.

'Bring the rathe primrose that forsaken dies,
'The tufted crow-toe, and pale jessamine,
'The white pink, and the pansy freakt with jet,
'The glowing violet,
'The musk-rose, and the well-attired woodbine,
'With cowslips wan that hang the pensive head.'

Lycidas [142 ff.].

This quotation is from one of Reynolds's footnotes to his poem *The Eden of Imagination*, published in 1814. Considering the closeness of Keats and Reynolds, it is hard to imagine that Keats did not know the poem. It is especially relevant to the ode because in Reynolds's vision the imagination is activated by the song of the nightingale and 'the spirits of our bards' are then released.[28] Reynolds writes of the nightingale in another footnote, 'This beautiful songster is the promoter as well as the performer of exquisite music, for we are indebted to it for one of Wordsworth's best poems' (*Eden*, 32 n.); he is referring to Coleridge's nightingale poem, but has confused the authorship since it was published in *Lyrical Ballads*. For both Keats and Reynolds, the song of the nightingale and the catalogue of flowers are means of establishing continuity between English poets past and present. Reynolds's explicit references and Keats's embedded echoes sustain a tradition that runs from Spenser to Shakespeare to Milton to Wordsworth and Coleridge.

Shakespeare, Milton, and Reynolds all lie behind the fifth stanza of the 'Ode to a Nightingale', but none of them is visible in it—their Poesy is *viewless*. If echo enables Keats to allude to several writers simultaneously, is it possible to say that any particular reminiscence is more important than any other? I think we can make such distinctions: more weight may be attached to the sustained series of echoes than the incidental parallel. In the 'Nightingale' there are a dozen or more phrases reminiscent of *Hamlet*, only one of *Othello* (and the parallel between stanza six and 'If it were now to die, / 'Twere now to be most happy', *Oth* II. i. 189, is probably merely a coincidence of thought). The most fascinating aspect of echo in the 'Nightingale' concerns the way in which, like the 'Ode on Indolence', it is a poem haunted by the language of *Hamlet*.[29]

The very first line may alert us to the influence. 'My heart aches, and a drowsy . . .' chimes with 'The heart-ache and the thousand . . .' of Hamlet's 'To be or not to be' soliloquy (III. i. 61), announcing that the poem will have its Hamlet-like intonations and reflections on mortality. (This is not the only example of Keats echoing the rhythms of Hamlet's soliloquies in summer 1819: Albert's soliloquy at the beginning of the third act of *Otho the Great*, with its 'O that . . . Or that', is modelled on 'O that this too too solid flesh would melt'.) As 'drowsy' evokes 'thousand' by assonance, so 'Lethe-wards' summons up 'Lethe wharf', a phrase used by the ghost of Hamlet's father (I. v. 33). The drinking of poisonous 'hemlock' parallels the 'hebona' that is poured in the ear of the king (I. v. 62), whose manner of death is perhaps suggested by the gradual paralysis that creeps over the poet in the opening lines of the ode. Is Keats, then, murdering his poetic father in order to escape his influence? Doubtless Harold Bloom would like to think so, but the parallel is tonal rather than narrative.

If Keats casts himself as anybody, it is not Claudius but Hamlet. At the beginning of the second stanza the poet calls for a 'draught of vintage'; Hamlet speaks of 'draughts of Rhenish' (I. iv. 10). Keats wishes to 'fade away' with the nightingale; initially, the direct parallel disappears, for it is the ghost who 'faded on the crowing of the cock', but when the word 'fade' is picked up at the beginning of the third stanza—the ode echoes itself as well as other poems—Keats begins to play Hamlet in earnest. 'Fade far away, dissolve, and quite forget . . . The weariness, the fever, and the fret' is a version of Hamlet's desire for his flesh to 'melt, / Thaw, and resolve itself into a dew' in order that he might escape the 'weary, stale, flat, and unprofitable' world (I. ii. 129). Keats's weariness, fever, and fret also refer back to 'the fretful stir / Unprofitable, and the fever of the world', that key phrase in 'Tintern Abbey' which combines the language of Hamlet's soliloquy with Macbeth's 'life's fitful fever', another speech central to Romantic ennui ('fever-fit' in the 'Ode on Indolence' is also relevant here).

'Away! away! for I will fly to thee' cries Keats to the nightingale at the beginning of the fourth stanza. But this is also Hamlet to the ghost: 'I say away!—Go on, I'll follow thee' (I. iv. 86). If the third stanza has shown Keats to be Hamlet, we can now only assume that the nightingale is Shakespeare (warbling his native wood-notes wild, as Milton's 'L'Allegro' would have it). Keats flies to his poetic father 'on the viewless wings of Poesy': the phrase itself summons up the exemplars of English poesy, for it combines Milton's 'viewless wing' ('The Passion', 50) with Shakespeare's 'viewless winds' from that speech of Claudio's in *Measure for Measure* to which Keats, like Wordsworth and Hazlitt, adverted on several key occasions.[30] There may also be a hint of Troilus's lines on how night 'flies the grasps of love / With wings more momentary-swift than thought' and Hamlet's 'wings as swift / As meditation, or the thoughts of love' (*Troil* IV. ii. 13; *Ham* I. v. 29).

Keats pitches his own mortality against the nightingale's voice: 'Still wouldst thou sing, and I have ears in vain'. The line conflates Hamlet's 'Still am I call'd' with the comment after his death, 'The ears are senseless that should give us hearing' (I. iv. 84; V. ii. 369). The 'high requiem' of the following line echoes the 'sage requiem' that Ophelia cannot have (V. i. 237). Hamlet is called to re-establish the claims of his father, but is interrupted in his task by death; Keats wished to re-introduce Shakespearean qualities into English poetry, but feared that he would die before doing so (tell Shelley, he wrote to Leigh Hunt, that 'there are strange Stories of the death of Poets—some have died before they were conceived').[31]

In the final stanza Keats is tolled back 'to [his] sole self'; Hamlet is conscious of the fact that he is his father's only child, 'I, his sole son' (III. iii. 77). Keats, Shakespeare's poetic son, is himself solely when he answers to his father, his presider. He finally bids a triple 'Adieu!' to the nightingale. This is a momentary inversion, for it is the ghost who says to Hamlet 'Adieu, adieu, adieu! remember me' (I. v. 91), though, as I pointed out with respect to the 'Ode on Indolence', these are words that Hamlet echoes. The placing of 'thy' in the line 'Adieu! adieu! thy plaintive anthem fades' suggests that 'Adieu, adieu' is itself the plaintive anthem of the nightingale (the sound is not far from the bird's traditional cry 'Tereu, tereu', used in *The Passionate Pilgrim*). If this is the case, we may take the farewell to be that of Shakespeare, leaving Keats to face the waking world. Leaving him, however, with the implied injunction 'Remember me'. Keats is left enriched by the voice of Shakespeare, the 'immortal bird'; as at the end of the *Lear* sonnet, the poet returns from Shakespeare to the world refreshed, given 'new phoenix wings'.

Since Hamlet is the most melancholy of Shakespeare's tragic heroes, one would also expect him to preside over the 'Ode on Melancholy'. But although there is a tonal similarity to Hamlet in soliloquy, there are few verbal echoes.[32] If we remember that Keats's remark about beauty and the evaporation of disagreeables was made with respect to *King Lear*, we might associate the images of Beauty, Melancholy, and the bursting of Joy's grape with the death of Gloucester: 'his flaw'd heart . . . 'Twixt two extremes of passion, joy and grief, / Burst smilingly' (V. iii. 197). But I think that the play which is

most important for this ode is *Antony and Cleopatra*. In Shakespeare's
Egypt melancholy, anger, and erotic love are all indulged to the full.
Antony and Cleopatra 'stand up peerless' (I. i. 40), as the eyes of the
mistress in the ode are 'peerless'. Feeding is a crucial image in both
play and poem; 'burst Joy's grape against his palate fine' catches the
vitality of Cleopatra's 'Now no more / The juice of Egypt's grape
shall moist this lip' (v. ii. 281). In each case, the 'st' sound bursts in
the mouth as we speak the line.

But the 'cloudy trophies' that end the poem are trophies lifted from
a Shakespearean sonnet, not a tragedy: 'Hung with the trophies of
my lovers gone' (*Sonn* 31). This line is marked in Keats's copy of the
poems, with the word 'conceit' written beside it, possibly by Reynolds.
It was to Reynolds that Keats had written of the 'beauties in the
sonnets—they seem to be full of fine things said unintentionally—in
the intensity of working out conceits'. We will remember that after
saying this Keats quoted the lines from sonnet twelve on 'Summer's
green all girded up in sheaves'. In her scrupulous analysis of 'To
Autumn', Helen Vendler uses this passage to show how in this final
ode Keats has developed a Shakespearean intensity of image and consequently no longer needs to use the abstract language of allegory that
had pervaded the earlier odes, with their addresses to Love, Poesy,
Youth, Melancholy, and so on.

The silent, nameless concrete symbolic system of *Autumn* springs direct . . .
from Shakespeare's 'intensity of working out conceits' . . . Keats's study of
Shakespeare's images in the sonnets led him to see that 'intention' could be
left unsaid, that he no longer had to draw explicit parallels, as he had in
When I have fears, between his pen and a gleaner, between rich garners and
high-pilèd books, between feelings and full-ripened grain. (*Odes of Keats*,
275–6)

This is a much more valuable account of why 'To Autumn' is
Shakespearean than Middleton Murry's rhapsodic 'it need not be
pointed out with the finger how deeply Shakespearean that perfect
poem is—Shakespearean in its rich and opulent serenity of mood,
Shakespearean in its lovely and large periodic movement, like the
drawing of a deep, full breath. . . . It is the perfect and unforced
utterance of the truth contained in the magic words: "Ripeness is
all"' (*Keats and Shakespeare*, 189; a classic case of reading Edgar's line
as if it were written by Keats).

But 'To Autumn' is also Keats's most Shakespearean poem in terms of its echoes; although there are not as many echoes as there are in the 'Nightingale', they have unsurpassed intensity. As with the allegorical framework, there are no explicit parallels; 'To Autumn' is full of fine things taken unintentionally out of Shakespeare. A comparison with the masque of Ceres in *The Tempest* (IV. i. 60–138) will make the point. That Keats associated this part of *The Tempest* with autumn is suggested by the echo of Iris's 'sunburn'd sicklemen, of August weary' (IV. i. 134) in a couplet in *Endymion*, the tone of which foreshadows his final ode, 'When last the sun his autumn tresses shook, / And the tann'd harvesters rich armfuls took' (i. 440).

There are similarities of tonal effect and verbal technique. Not only do masque and ode each brim over with a vocabulary of fullness, but they each have a fullness of vocabulary, of adjective especially. That is to say, their vocabulary is enriched by copious compounds and adjectives formed from nouns. Examples of the former include 'pole-clipt', 'honey-drops', 'grass-plot' in Shakespeare, 'thatch-eves', 'soft-lifted', 'stubble-plains' in Keats; of the latter, 'sedg'd crowns' in Shakespeare and 'moss'd cottage-trees' in Keats. I am not arguing that words like 'thatch'd' and 'brims' (IV. i. 63–4) are actually sources for Keats's 'thatch-eves' and 'o'er-brimm'd', even though much of the masque is underlined in Keats's Shakespeare (*KS* 79–80). But it does seem to me that, for all the differences of rhyme and rhythm, Keats's voice in 'To Autumn' echoes, answers to, and is in a line of descent from Shakespeare's in such lines as

> Earth's increase, foison plenty,
> Barns and garners never empty;
> Vines with clust'ring bunches growing,
> Plants with goodly burthen bowing;
> Spring come to you at the farthest
> In the very end of harvest!

(IV. i. 110)

Since the echo of these lines is not explicit—it does not have to be located and analysed for the poem to be effective—the ode is free from what De Quincey referred to as references to books that break the current of the passion. 'To Autumn' is self-sufficient in a way that it would not have been had it used overt allusion, yet its echoes provide a subliminal dialogue with the great tradition of English poetic language.

Keats at his best uses a language that is both inherited and fully his own. However, his emphasis on 'fine Phrases' and *passages* of Shakespeare is potentially damaging. It may damage a reading of Shakespeare by resulting in a return to the 'select beauties' approach of William Dodd and the compilers of collections like *The Speaker* and *Elegant Extracts*. It may also damage the work of the later poet.

In the preface to the first edition of his *Poems* (1853), Matthew Arnold argues that the young poet needs to be guided through the confusion of the many models available to him. In the absence of a commanding living voice, he must penetrate the works of his predecessors, 'catching their spirit'.[33] 'Foremost among these models for the English writer stands Shakespeare'; Arnold goes on to argue that his influence has shaped and to some extent limited the poetry of the early nineteenth century. He follows Shakespeare's own contemporaries in suggesting that the distinctive quality of the plays is a gift of 'happy, abundant, and ingenious expression, eminent and unrivalled'. The problem is that 'what distinguishes the artist from the mere amateur, says Goethe, is *Architectonicè* in the highest sense; that power of execution, which creates, forms, and constitutes: not the profoundness of single thoughts, not the richness of imagery, not the abundance of illustration'. But it is these 'attractive accessories' rather than the spirit of the whole that the young poet can most readily grasp: 'Of this preponderating quality of Shakespeare's genius, accordingly, almost the whole of modern English poetry has, it appears to me, felt the influence. To the exclusive attention on the part of his imitators to this it is in a great degree owing, that of the majority of modern poetical works the details alone are valuable, the composition worthless.'

Arnold tests his case on Keats's 'Isabella'. He finds it 'a perfect treasure-house of graceful and felicitous words and images: almost in every stanza there occurs one of those vivid and picturesque turns of expression, by which the object is made to flash upon the eye of the mind, and which thrill the reader with a sudden delight'. But the construction of the poem, the unfolding of the action, is feeble, especially when compared with Boccaccio's original. Arnold makes a similar point in his essay on Keats. In 'natural magic', 'rounded perfection' of phrase and beauty of image, 'he is with Shakespeare', but in both 'architectonics' and 'moral interpretation', he 'was not ripe'.[34]

I find Arnold's reading of Keats wholly convincing. In local effect, Keats not only echoes, but he is *with* Shakespeare, as he hoped to be ('I think I shall be among the English Poets after my death'—*KL* i.

394). But partly because of the influence of one aspect of Shakespeare, the felicity of his language, many of Keats's poems lack organization and discrimination on a larger scale. It is only certain *passages*, in the odes above all, that have placed him among the English poets.

10

Shelley and the Lion in the Path

IN his *Records of Shelley, Byron, and the Author*, E. J. Trelawny tells of an occasion when Mary Shelley was transcribing one of Byron's plays and read out some lines. Shelley said, ' "They are excellent, but he fails in the drama. He is too abstract and diffuse. We all must fail. Shakespeare is the lion in the path; he has done for the drama what the Greeks had done for sculpture—perfected it." ' Mary Shelley replied, laughing, 'Byron has the vanity to be jealous of Shakespeare'.[1] The exchange may have been embroidered by Trelawny, but we will see that Byron's supposed jealousy of Shakespeare is well authenticated elsewhere. The case of Byron will be considered in the next chapter; in this one, I shall discuss Shelley's encounter with 'the lion in the path', particularly in *The Cenci*, his only complete drama written for the stage.

The popular conception of Shelley is that he was like his own skylark, pouring out his full heart 'In profuse strains of unpremeditated art' (*SPW* 602). But he was the most learned and widely read of the younger Romantic poets. His poems were rarely 'unpremeditated'. Indeed, to introduce that long, latinate word in the otherwise mainly monosyllabic first stanza of 'To a Skylark' is to be not spontaneous but Miltonic. We do not believe the claim in the invocation to book nine of *Paradise Lost* that nocturnal visits from the muse gave easy inspiration to Milton's 'unpremeditated verse' (*PL* ix. 24). *Paradise Lost* is the product of many years' premeditation; the image of inspiration is strictly conventional. Shelley's allusive adjective neatly informs us that his art cannot be as 'unpremeditated' as the skylark's. Similarly, when he writes towards the end of the poem that mankind is not like the skylark because 'We look before and after', the point proves itself, for Shelley is looking before, recalling that phrase of Hamlet's in the preface to *Lyrical Ballads* which was discussed in chapter four, 'Emphatically may it be said of the Poet, as Shakspeare hath said of man, "that he looks before and after" '.

A glance through the journals of Mary Shelley and Claire Clairmont reveals what an immense amount of time Shelley and his circle spent reading—often reading aloud, often reading Shakespeare. Their response to Shakespeare is the quintessential Romantic one: living, vibrant, careless. The landscape of *As You Like it* is not exactly Alpine, but that is made irrelevant:

> we hastened away and climbed some wild rocks and sat there reading till the sun went down. I read As you like it which Shelley lent me, for though he forgot to bring his watch, he put in his pocket three small volumes of Shakespeare and carries them about everywhere with him. The wild scene in which this romantic drama is laid, accorded wonderfully with the scene before us—Shelley said that poetry read in a room never came so near the soul as if read in a beautiful spot, in the wide open air and under the wide open Heaven.[2]

Shelley's absorption of Shakespeare from an early age was such that phraseology from the plays is to be found throughout his poetry, prose, and letters.[3] In many of his lyrics he arrives at a highly successful accommodation of Shakespeare, appropriating and transforming his language in ways that ensure it does not become a burden. Ahasuerus' lines on transience in *Hellas* patently borrow from Prospero's 'Our revels now are ended . . .' and Hamlet on the illusoriness of the firmament 'fretted with golden fire', but they are wholly characteristic of Shelley's idealism and, indeed, his distinctive diction:

>   Earth and ocean,
> Space, and the isles of life or light that gem
> The sapphire floods of interstellar air,
> This firmament pavilioned upon chaos,
> With all its cressets of immortal fire,
>   . . . this Whole
> Of suns, and worlds, and men, and beasts, and flowers,
> With all the silent or tempestuous workings
> By which they have been, are, or cease to be,
> Is but a vision;—all that it inherits
> Are motes of a sick eye, bubbles and dreams;
> Thought is its cradle and its grave, nor less
> The Future and the Past are idle shadows
> Of thought's eternal flight—they have no being:
> Nought is but that which feels itself to be.

>   (*SPW* 470-1)

Perhaps because his main concern is to revivify Greek tragedy, such Shakespearean touches as there are in Shelley's 'lyrical dramas' seem untroubled. The Furies in act one of *Prometheus Unbound* have the rhythmic power of the weird sisters, while the song of spirits in act two scene three has the mysteriousness of Ariel's 'Full fathom five' (*SPW* 219–20, 235–6). The play touches both the sublimity of *Lear* and the ethereal music of *The Tempest*; the second act in particular evokes the atmosphere of Shakespeare's last play.

The Tempest is also a source for the enchanted islands in 'Fragments of an Unfinished Drama' and *Epipsychidion*;[4] in several other poems, Prospero-like, Shelley invokes 'Spirits of the Air' (there is a good example near the end of 'Lines written among the Euganean Hills'). The play was especially important for his later works. Rousseau's vision in 'The Triumph of Life' uses language from the masque of Ceres.[5] A magic circle is traced in 'To Jane: the Recollection'; a fragment is entitled 'Life rounded with Sleep'. 'With a Guitar, to Jane' begins with the striking

> Ariel to Miranda:—Take
> This slave of Music, for the sake
> Of him who is the slave of thee
>
> (*SPW* 672).

The poem is as fine an improvisation on *The Tempest* as Browning's 'Caliban upon Setebos' or Auden's *The Sea and the Mirror*. It turns on a parallel, as beautifully executed as it is conceived, between Ariel and a guitar. Each is the instrument of an artist, each has been imprisoned in a tree and then transformed into the embodiment of music.[6]

To Trelawny, Shelley 'seemed as gentle a spirit as Ariel' (*Records*, 124). The identification was partly a reaction against the portrayal in the popular press of the radical young poet as 'a monster more hideous than Caliban', but the iconography has stuck. The title of the biography by André Maurois is only the most obvious instance. Ironically, Shelley in fact had as much sympathy with Caliban: his idealization of the noble savage in part eight of *Queen Mab* suggests not only Rousseauesque primitivism, but also a political interpretation of *The Tempest* that reads Caliban as dispossessed native.

Shelley undertook several political appropriations of Shakespeare. As its title indicates, his early radical polemic in verse builds its vision on Mercutio's Queen Mab.[7] 'England in 1819' makes George III into Lear, or rather a combination of Lear and Gloucester: 'An old, mad, blind, despised, and dying king' (*SPW* 574). The potency of the comparison is clear if we recall that *Lear* was considered too politically sensitive to be staged during the Regency years. Trelawny records another scheme: 'He thought a play founded on Shakespeare's "Timon" would be an excellent mode of discussing our present social and political evils dramatically, and of descanting on them' (*Records*, 122); but Shelley got no further than planning in his notebook the first act of a 'Modern Timon'.[8]

If Trelawny can be believed (he often cannot), Shelley made this suggestion shortly after referring to his attempt at an English republican drama, *Charles the First*.[9] In this unfinished play, he had descanted on contemporary politics while attempting in style and manner to 'approach as near our great dramatist' as his 'feeble powers' would permit. ' "King Lear" is my model, for that is nearly perfect. I am amazed at my presumption. Poets should be modest. My audacity savours of madness' (*Records*, 121–2). The problem with perfection is that it implies completion. Translator, reviser, and imitator all face impossible tasks—'What is a translation of Homer into English? A person who is ignorant of Greek need only look at "Paradise Lost," or the tragedy of "Lear" translated into French, to obtain an analogical conception of its worthless and miserable inadequacy' (*SL* ii. 277–8).[10]

Shelley was well aware of the difficulty inherent in the attempt to imitate Shakespeare. Some two years before starting *Charles the First* he wrote in the preface to *The Revolt of Islam*, 'I have adopted the stanza of Spenser (a measure inexpressibly beautiful), not because I consider it a finer model of poetical harmony than the blank verse of Shakespeare and Milton, but because in the latter there is no shelter for mediocrity; you must either succeed or fail' (*SPW* 35). He may have succeeded in translating certain elements of Shakespeare into lyric but in the case of *Charles the First* he failed in the drama. The blank verse is flaccid; image has no relation to character; action is retarded by ornamentation. For our purposes, the play is most interesting for its fool, since Romantic neo-Shakespearean drama is notable for its lack of fools and comic touches. In accordance with his belief, expressed in the *Defence of Poetry*, that the perfection of *Lear* lay in its capacity to embrace comedy, above all in the character of the Fool, Shelley gives a substantial part to Archy, King Charles's jester.

Archy is not the most original of fools. Like his counterpart in *Lear*, he talks of seeing 'everything upside down' and asks 'Will you hear Merlin's prophecy' (ii. 37, 368). His resemblance to Lear's fool makes the Queen say, 'Have you not noted that the Fool of late / Has lost his careless mirth', and the King irrelevantly mouth Lear-like phrases, such as 'To bring news how the world goes there'—particularly unfortunate is his transformation of Lear and Cordelia in prison laughing at 'gilded butterflies' into the simile 'like a parrot / Hung in his gilded prison' (ii. 446, 106, 98). Sometimes Archy borrows from other plays, such as *Hamlet* ('setting springes to catch woodcocks'—ii. 38), and on one occasion he alludes overtly to *The Tempest* while also referring anachronistically to Coleridge and Southey's pantisocratic scheme:

> Where they think to found
> A commonwealth like Gonzalo's in the play,
> Gynaecocoenic and pantisocratic
>
> (ii. 360)

But derivative as he is, Archy's is a welcome presence; the song with which he ends the fragment of *Charles the First* is a particularly delicate touch. Shelley, always the lyricist, found it easier to write songs for plays than to complete plays themselves: in addition to those in *Prometheus*, we have a song for *Tasso* (which remained unwritten but for one short scene)[11] and the fine hymns of Apollo and Pan, written for Mary Shelley's play, *Midas*. Shelley also contributed two songs to his wife's other play, *Proserpine*. He seems to have had a high opinion of her dramatic potential: before doing so himself, he suggested that she might write plays on the Cenci family and on Charles I.

Even had they been completed, it is likely that *Charles the First* and *Tasso* would have remained among the Romantic neo-Elizabethan dramas that are now—quite justifiably—read only by the most dedicated of scholars and enthusiasts. *The Cenci*, however, is another matter. George Steiner contends that here 'pastiche is carried to the level of art';[12] I share his belief that it is the best play in its tradition and that its only possible rival is the strange, intense *Death's Jest-Book*, written some years later by Thomas Lovell Beddoes, another poet who was aware that the drama had become a 'ruin' haunted by the ghosts of the Elizabethan and Jacobean dramatists. Beddoes saw that the contemporary dramatist was 'peculiarly liable to involuntary plagiarism' of the Elizabethans, but he felt that in *The Cenci* Shelley had written the best play since the time of Shakespeare (he also expressed interest in *Charles the First* because he had been told that it contained a Shakespearean clown).[13] While *The Borderers, Remorse,* and *Otho the Great* are among the less successful works of their authors, *Death's Jest-Book* is probably Beddoes's best and *The Cenci* is among Shelley's best. Mary Shelley went so far as to assert that it was universally praised as 'the best tragedy of modern times' and that its fifth act was 'the finest thing he ever wrote, and may claim proud comparison not only with any contemporary, but preceding, poet' (*SPW* 337). She is challenging us to make the comparison with Shakespeare.

Shelley engaged more directly with Shakespeare than he had done before simply by the act of writing for an English stage dominated by blank verse dramas such as Milman's *Fazio*—farragos of the gothic and the pseudo-Elizabethan which he rightly condemned as 'miserable trash' (letter to Byron, *SL* ii. 290). Another indication that his drama would aspire to be in the Shakespearean tradition is that the actors he had in mind to play the leading roles (see *SL* ii. 102) were Eliza O'Neill, whose Juliet was seen by Hazlitt as the nearest thing to Mrs Siddons's ideal interpretations of Shakespearean tragedy (*HW* v. 198–9), and Edmund Kean, who since 1814 had been the leading interpreter of the major Shakespearean roles.[14]

In his dedication to the play, dated 29 May 1819, Shelley acknowledged that his earlier writings had been 'little else than visions which impersonate my own apprehensions of the beautiful and the just' (*SPW* 274). They are seen as subjective visions of a better future, as 'dreams of what ought to be' which partake of the ideal and are removed from 'sad reality'. In approaching the objective and the real, he trod in the footsteps of Shakespeare. Putting down his visionary style, he turned to the past in order to illuminate the present; in Jacobean fashion, he took as his material a bloody story of Renaissance Italy. That *The Cenci* is shot through with traditional notions of Italy— machiavels, intrigue, blood, incest—suggests that in some respects it is more Jacobean than Shakespearean.

Nevertheless, by adapting this kind of inherited material, Shelley came much closer to Shakespeare's method than Wordsworth and Coleridge had done in their plays. In *Charles the First* he made use of Hume's and Catherine Macaulay's very different histories of England, in addition to a seventeenth-century source, Whitelocke's *Memorials of the English Affairs*.[15] In *The Cenci* he gradually refined his material, producing first a translation of the original Italian manuscript containing the story, then a compressed account in his notebook, and finally the play itself (for which an additional source was the painting supposedly of Beatrice Cenci attributed to Guido Reni).[16] He made free with his material, as Shakespeare had done with his: the Count became a Catholic instead of the atheist he had been in the 'Relation of the Death of the Family of the Cenci'; Bernardo was made an innocent boy instead of a man in his twenties; and the characters of Orsino and Camillo were introduced. Shelley seems to have realized intuitively that Shakespeare's originality was achieved through the transmutation of disparate source-material. In his preface he also pointed out that the 'deepest and the sublimest tragic compositions', *Lear* and the Oedipus plays, were based on stories already existing in popular tradition —tragic effect thus derives from the audience's knowledge of the outcome, their sense that there is no escape from the received ending.

For Shelley, like Hazlitt, tragedy is distinguished by its capacity to awaken sympathy. By doing so, it fulfils art's highest moral purpose of teaching the human heart 'knowledge of itself' (*SPW* 276). Shelley argues that drama should not be made subservient 'to what is vulgarly termed a moral purpose'; he contends that morality is to be found in education of the heart, not in dogma imposed from without. Johnson had criticized Shakespeare for occasionally sacrificing virtue to convenience and therefore seeming to write without any moral purpose. Shelley would have agreed with Hazlitt in his essay on *Measure for Measure*: 'Shakespear was in one sense the least moral of all writers; for morality (commonly so called) is made up of antipathies; and his talent consisted in sympathy with human nature, in all its shapes, degrees, depressions, and elevations'—but his knowledge of the heart and 'fellow-feeling' for humanity make him in a fuller sense 'the greatest of all moralists' (*HW* iv. 346–7).

Shelley's account of his aims in *The Cenci* implies that he has tried to live up to Shakespearean ideals. Although Shakespeare is not mentioned by name at this point in the preface, he had been cited so frequently as the exemplar of sympathy and disinterestedness that he would inevitably have come to the nineteenth-century reader's mind when Shelley wrote of his attempt to portray the characters as they probably were, to avoid making them mere projections of his own self and his own beliefs, 'thus under a thin veil converting names and actions of the sixteenth century into cold impersonations of my own mind' (*SPW* 277). The implication is that Shelley wishes to be like Shakespeare rather than, say, Byron, whose characters were so frequently seen as impersonations of his own mind. Hazlitt's complaint about a passage in *Marino Faliero*, written a year after *The Cenci*, is typical: 'it is Lord Byron speaking in the nineteenth century, and not the Doge of Venice in the fourteenth' (*HW* xix. 49).

Shelley continues his preface with the assertion that he has also sought to avoid 'what is commonly called mere poetry', by which he means detached similes and isolated descriptions that bear no relation to the action. He makes the Coleridgean point that in dramatic composition 'the imagery and the passion should interpenetrate one another' (*SPW* 277). In the notebook draft of this passage there is a sentence omitted in the published preface: 'The finest Works of Shakespeare are a perpetual illustration of this doctrine' (*Note Books*, ii. 95; a note here provides an illustration from Sonnet 111). *The Cenci* has a unity of feeling that is absent from the other plays which I have discussed; certain images, such as those of lamp and flame, recur in a truly organic fashion.[17]

Shelley says that he has used both remote and familiar imagery to illustrate strong feeling. The choice of adjectives suggests that again he has Shakespeare in mind here: he seems to be recalling Johnson's remark that Shakespeare 'approximates the remote, and familiarizes the wonderful' (*SJS* 65). Shakespeare's use of the familiar and the colloquial was ignored in most eighteenth- and nineteenth-century imitations; Shelley attempts to match this aspect of Shakespeare in his play, as Wordsworth had done in the *Lyrical Ballads*. The preface to *The Cenci* takes up the theme of Wordsworth's more famous preface: 'I entirely agree with those modern critics who assert that in order to move men to true sympathy we must use the familiar language of men, and that our great ancestors the ancient English poets are the writers, a study of whom might incite us to do that for our own age which they have done for theirs' (*SPW* 278). Shelley takes issue with Wordsworth's use of Cumberland shepherds, arguing that 'it must be the real language of men in general and not that of any particular class to whose society the writer happens to belong'. But the two poets are in fundamental agreement: the aim of poetry is 'to move men to true sympathy', the method is to 'use the familiar language of men', and the exemplars are 'our great ancestors the ancient English poets'. Of those poets it was Ben Jonson who used the phrase 'language, such as men do use', but it was Shakespeare who forged tragedy from what Coleridge called the *lingua communis*. We have seen how Wordsworth adjusted to Shakespearean language and Shakespearean sympathy by working in forms which were not Shakespearean; Shelley came closer to success actually in the drama.

Shelley claims in the preface that his only detachable description is
that of the chasm appointed for Cenci's murder (III. i. 243 ff.). It is a
familiar Romantic *topos*, one always likely to lean on similar descriptions in Shakespeare, Milton, and such eighteenth-century poets of
the sublime as Young. But the influence acknowledged by Shelley is
that of the Spanish dramatic poet whom he saw as 'a kind of Shakespeare' (*SL* ii. 115): 'An idea in this speech was suggested by a most
sublime passage in *El Purgatorio de San Patricio* of Calderon; the only
plagiarism which I have intentionally committed in the whole piece'
(*SPW* 277 n.). This plagiarism is, however, far less noticeable to most
readers than are many Shakespearean ones. The exchange in the
murder scene,

> Did you not call?
>> When?
>>> Now.
>>> (IV. iii. 8),

cannot but be plagiarized from that at a similar moment in *Macbeth*,

> Did you not speak?
>> When?
>>> Now.
>>> (II. ii. 16)

Is Shelley, then, adopting the strategy of acknowledging a minor
debt in order to obscure the major one? For every person—in both his
own day and ours—who reads *The Cenci* and thinks 'Calderon', there
must be hundreds who read it and think 'Shakespeare'. I do not,
however, think that Shelley is being devious about his debts in the
way that Coleridge and Byron, for their own good (and sometimes
not so good) reasons, are about theirs. We should believe Shelley
when he says that the borrowing from Calderon was 'the only plagiarism which I have intentionally committed in the whole piece'. The
important word here is 'intentionally'. Shakespeare's influence is so
pervasive that to plagiarize him is inevitable. It is something in the
very nature of writing blank verse drama in England in the early
nineteenth century; it is not like the borrowing from Calderon which
involves the conscious thought, 'I wish to write a sublime description
of a chasm—I know of such a description in Calderon—I shall make
use of it.' In chapter two I argued that in the case of the Romantics
and Shakespeare it is not a solecism to speak of an unintentional

allusion. In the case of *The Cenci* and Shakespearean tragedy, we will find numerous unintentional plagiarisms. They are, however, qualitatively different from the unintentional plagiarisms in most other Romantic drama, for they exercise a revisionary function. Where those in the plays of Wordsworth, Keats, and the rest are local and stultifying, Shelley's borrowings are structurally significant and thematically enriching.

The comparative success of *The Cenci* as a neo-Shakespearean play lies principally in the way similarity is compounded with difference. It appropriates as freely, and frequently as crudely, as other Romantic plays do, but uniquely it sometimes does so only to work against the grain of the original. When *The Cenci* is unshakespearean that is often because it means to be unshakespearean, not because it fails to be Shakespearean. I say 'it means' rather than 'Shelley means' because the revisionary process is not consciously articulated. In the preface Shelley enumerates Shakespearean principles without continually citing Shakespeare as exemplar; indeed, the removal of one such citation from the manuscript draft possibly suggests that he tried to push aside the thought that Shakespeare was his model. The choice of actors, attitude to sources, preface, quasi-Jacobean characters and subject matter, dramatic form (act and scene divisions, stage directions, and layout of speeches conform to those in eighteenth-century editions of Shakespeare): all conspire to demonstrate that *The Cenci* was a confrontation with the lion in the path. But nowhere does Shelley actually say that Shakespeare was his model, as he said that *Charles the First* was modelled on Lear. Conscious imitation would prove an impossible task; *Charles the First* was left unfinished. *The Cenci* was completed successfully because Shelley did not drive himself into a corner by worrying about models and borrowings. The conscious mind left well alone; the creative imagination worked its alchemy.

Inevitably the imaginative recreation sometimes involved mere pilfering. Throughout the play there are the usual clusters of Shakespearean phraseology.[18] Towards the end of act four scene one, Cenci moves in the space of a few lines from the giddy expectation of Troilus (he is a Troilus whose desire is illicit),

> I feel a giddy sickness of strange awe;
> My heart is beating with an expectation
> Of horrid joy

(IV. i. 165)

to the tone of Lear—'It were safer / To come between the tiger and his prey' (173)—to an apostrophe to 'Conscience' in the language of Macbeth:

> They say that sleep, that healing dew of Heaven,
> Steeps not in balm the foldings of the brain
> Which thinks thee an imposter.

(178)

In the final scene, Beatrice borrows from *Measure for Measure* one moment, and *Lear* the next, as her Claudio-like 'To die so suddenly? So young to go / Under the obscure, cold, rotting, wormy ground!' is swiftly followed by 'Let me not go mad!' (V. iv. 49–56). Pseudo-Shakespearean metaphors obtrude at various points. 'How slow', exclaims Beatrice, 'Behind the course of thought, even sick with speed, / Lags leaden-footed time!' (IV. ii. 2); 'We can escape even now', exhorts Orsino, 'So we take fleet occasion by the hair' (V. i. 37). And so on. Certain verbal effects learned from Shakespeare are more rewarding: the use of a seemingly unpoetic verb ('her awe-inspiring gaze, / Whose beams anatomize me nerve by nerve'—I. ii. 84), a moment of gallows-humour as the tension is at its height (rack-humour in fact: 'To stretch a point against the criminals'—V. ii. 74). But most interesting are the moments where Shelley adapts Shakespearean material in ways that achieve effects which Shakespeare did not attempt.

The first scene ends with a crude borrowing of Macbeth's image of the stones on which he walks prating of his fell intent (*Mac* II. i. 57–8, *Cenci* I. i. 141–4). But the scene has also included an encounter that is reminiscent of, yet very different from, *Macbeth*. Count Cenci tells Cardinal Camillo how he enjoys inflicting pain; Camillo, a moderating force akin to his namesake in *The Winter's Tale* (though one with less power to influence events), does not believe him. The scene is comparable to that at the English court where Malcolm tests Macduff with a catalogue of his vices. But we never take Malcolm wholly seriously; we are less convinced by his performance than Macduff is. With Cenci, on the other hand, we are left in no doubt that he is in deadly earnest. He has—and Shelley seems to share—a relish and intensity in the description of sadism and suffering that never occurs in Shakespeare. As so often in this play, we think of the other Jacobean dramatists who were being rediscovered at this time. Coleridge sought to imitate Shakespeare but found himself tracking Beaumont and Fletcher and Massinger instead; in *The Cenci*, Shelley often tracks the feeling of Webster, Middleton, and Ford. Perhaps such a compromise, an approach to the lesser luminaries in place of the star himself, was all one could reasonably expect. Captain Medwin had no doubts about the influence:

Among English plays he was a great admirer of *The Duchess of Malfy*, and thought the dungeon scene . . . as equal to anything in Shakspeare, indeed he was continually reading the Old Dramatists—Middleton, and Webster, Ford and Massinger, and Beaumont and Fletcher, were the mines from which he drew the pure and vigorous style that so highly distinguishes *The Cenci*.[19]

When Shelley introduces a man called Orsino who is in love with the heroine and speaks to her by a cypress, we expect to see a stock figure out of Shakespearean romantic comedy. But he turns out to be a treacherous prelate; the hypocrisies of Italian Catholicism, which Shelley saw at first hand, were not a Shakespearean concern. Yet for Shelley, author of *The Necessity of Atheism*, to write convincingly about 'Catholics deeply tinged with religion' (Preface, *SPW* 277) reveals what Coleridge had defined in chapter fifteen of the *Biographia* as a Shakespearean ability to write about things remote from the self.

Act one scene three is a bold variation on the broken banquet in *Macbeth*. In Shakespeare the protagonist's hysteria, the consequence of the assassination he has instigated, leads to the breaking up of the feast. In Shelley, the protagonist confidently says that his wish regarding his sons has been fulfilled—they are dead. He remains calm and in control of himself; others become hysterical and the banquet breaks up. Cenci hands round the drinking bowl where in *Macbeth* the apparition of Banquo interrupts the toast. Beatrice says that the ghosts of her dead brothers ought to haunt her father—but they do not. In the world of Shelley's play, vice thrives and Cenci is remorseless. He actually says to Beatrice that *she* has spoilt the feast with her insanity; he says to *her* words like Macbeth's to the ghost, 'get thee from my sight!' (I. iii. 168).

In the first scene of the second act, Cenci invokes darkness with much more confidence than Macbeth does. His 'Would that it were done!' (II. i. 193) has none of the indecision, the need to whip the self up to the deed, of Macbeth's 'If it were done, when 'tis done . . .'. Cenci's tone in 'Come darkness!' (II. i. 181) approximates more to that of Lady Macbeth in her unsexing invocation; Macbeth's self-exploratory soliloquy is given over to Orsino. It is the latter who asks a series of questions beginning 'if . . .', who starts and stops in his tracks, and who echoes Macbeth's lines on the dagger seen in the imagination:

> I clasp the phantom of unfelt delights
> Till weak imagination half possesses
> The self-created shadow.
>
> (II. ii. 141)

Orsino's 'Weak imagination' inverts Theseus' 'strong imagination' in that other much favoured source for such passages, the final act of *A Midsummer Night's Dream*. There is another characteristic echo a little earlier in the scene when the indecisive Giacomo speaks of trusting imagination with terrible thoughts, 'phantasies' whose 'horror makes them dim / To the mind's eye' (II. ii. 86). The tone is that of Macbeth's 'My thought, whose murther yet is but fantastical' (I. iii. 139), but in writing of imagination Shelley, like the other Romantics, turns to Hamlet's 'mind's eye'.

Giacomo's character is revealed by his language. Even as he participates in the overthrow of his father, he is a victim. In the course of the first scene in which he appears, he defines himself through two similes, one conventional ('I am as one lost in a midnight wood'— II. ii. 93), the other memorable: 'And we are left, as scorpions ringed with fire. / What should we do but strike ourselves to death?' (II. ii. 70). This image, probably created from Byron's comparison of the brooding mind to a 'Scorpion girt by fire' (*The Giaour*, 423 ff.), is richer than Macbeth's 'O, full of scorpions is my mind' (III. ii. 36). The allusion to the popular belief that a scorpion stings itself when surrounded by fire wonderfully compresses the image that runs through the play of life as a flame all too easily extinguished, and the idea that for this character there is no way to turn. Giacomo will not even achieve mental freedom after the murder of Cenci, as Beatrice does.

Given the relationship of language to character, Shelley goes badly wrong when Giacomo makes a sustained comparison of the flesh to an unreplenished lamp, culminating in the lines 'And yet once quenched I cannot thus relume / My father's life' (III. ii. 51). The metaphoric structure and such words as 'quench' and 'relume' are manifestly derived from Othello's 'Put out the light, and then put out the light . . .' (V. ii. 7–13). There is some interest in the inversion of context:

the life to be destroyed is that of Cenci, not a Desdemona (would Othello have expressed such sentiments if he were about to kill Iago?); Shelley suggests that all life is sacred, that parricide is parricide even if the father is a Cenci. But Shelley's handling of the image is both imprecise and overblown; in F. R. Leavis's words, he offers 'insistence, elaboration, and explicitness' in place of Shakespeare's 'concrete realization'.[20] And as far as character is concerned, to think of Giacomo and Othello together would be preposterous.

Macbeth is among Shakespeare's most tightly controlled plays in the distribution of its dramatic climaxes, more especially in the positioning of those before the final act—the murder of Duncan and its aftermath, and the banquet scene. Shelley's scenic form is less fluid than Shakespeare's, but he too establishes a compelling pattern of lull and climax. The banquet in act one scene three is the first high point, the murder in act four scene three the final one (as in *Prometheus*, the last act is a kind of coda). At the centre of the play is the longest and most intense scene, where Beatrice enters distracted having been raped by her father. It begins in Shelley's most Websterian manner, with lines such as

> I am choked! There creeps
> A clinging, black, contaminating mist
> About me
>
> (III. i. 16).

But although we think primarily of *The Duchess of Malfi*, there are certain Shakespearean touches: the charnel-house language owes something to *Romeo and Juliet*, as does the repetition of exclamations almost to the point of absurdity in 'O, world! O, life! O, day! O, misery!' (III. i. 32).[21] Even where the influence of *The Duchess* is most marked, in the lines 'O blood, which art my father's blood, / Circling through these contaminated veins', the image is combined with a Macbeth-like sense of being unable to 'wash away the crime' (III. i. 95–9). For a moment, Shelley seems able to compound Webster and Shakespeare.

The Cenci frequently combines the idiosyncratic with the Shakespearean. Throughout the play, and in act three scene one especially, there are references to 'shadows' which bespeak Shelley's platonic inheritance (the figure of death as a 'double-visaged shadow' is especially striking—III. i. 178). But when Beatrice speaks of exercising

a vengeance that will make her suffering 'but a shadow', she does so
in the unmistakable manner of Lear:

> If I try to speak
> I shall go mad. Ay, something must be done;
> What, yet I know not . . .

(III. i. 85, Shelley's ellipsis)

She is like Lear in not only the sense of impending madness, but also
the expression of an intention that cannot fully be articulated, such is
the stress on the mind: 'I will do such things— / What they are yet
I know not' (*Lr* II. iv. 280). The difference is that Lear has been
abused by his children, Beatrice by her father. Shelley, in keeping
with his distaste for authority, attempts what Shakespeare did not, a
tragedy of parental tyranny. *Romeo and Juliet* is the closest the latter
comes to such a tragedy, but old Capulet is hardly a Cenci; most of
Shakespeare's cruel fathers are confined to the comedies, where they
can be overcome or won round.

An early reviewer noted the most striking parallel between Shelley's
play and the tragedy which, in *The Defence of Poetry*, he judged the
most perfect specimen of the dramatic art: 'Cenci's imprecation on
his daughter, though an imitation of Lear, and one of a multitude of
direct plagiarisms, is absolutely too shocking for perusal'.[22] There is a
double standard in this judgement: what is allowed in the classic is not
countenanced in the morally dangerous contemporary work. At least
the *Literary Gazette* reviewer does not exercise his prudery on Shakespeare himself, as Thomas Bowdler was doing at this time (the *Family
Shakespeare* was published in 1818).

Cenci's invectives, which contain as many exclamation marks as
Lear's, are shot through with such words as 'infects', 'blistering',
'parch', 'strike', and 'blinding' (IV. i. 115 ff.). The language is that of
Lear as he calls the elements down on Goneril in act two (II. iv.
162 ff.). Cenci then takes Lear's curse in the previous act, 'Hear,
Nature, hear . . . If she must teem, / Create her child of spleen'
(I. iv. 275 ff.), and converts it into

> That if she ever have a child; and thou,
> Quick Nature! I adjure thee by thy God,
> That thou be fruitful in her, and increase
> And multiply, fulfilling his command,
> And my deep imprecation! May it be

A hideous likeness of herself, that as
From a distorting mirror, she may see
Her image mixed with what she most abhors,
Smiling upon her from her nursing breast.

(IV. i. 141)

This is different from the run-of-the mill excursion into Shakespeare
in Romantic drama because the source material is transformed in
such a way as to make it contextually relevant. The invocation to
nature has ironic power in view of Cenci's utter unnaturalness. That
'distorting mirror' is the most memorable among the mirrors and
reflections which constitute one thread of the play's imagery; it is also
an excellent simile with which to conceive the imagined child of an
incestuous union.

Although it stands in its own right, the borrowing inevitably raises
the question of correspondence between characters. If not consciously, then in the depths of his imagination, Shelley is associating
Cenci and Lear. The parallel is not immediately apparent. We do not
accept Lear unreservedly; something in us may admire Cenci's
brazenness. Lear sets himself up as a figure of authority and Shelley is
the questioner of authority, whether parental, social, or religious
(Beatrice has to face not only her father but also the Pope). Shelley
may therefore be showing us that there is a thin dividing line between
Lear's wilfulness and Cenci's tyranny. But this is not sufficient to
make Cenci into a tragic victim or Lear a villain of the blackest hue.
What is most likely to strike us about the identification is that it is a
perverse one. It accords with that reversal of moral perspective which
leads to the Romantic interest in Iago, Macbeth, and Milton's Satan.
Shelley's tragedy comes to a very different conclusion from Shakespeare's. For all the bleakness of *Lear*, at least some good characters
are left at the end to sustain the gored state; in *The Cenci*, however, the
social order is seen to be wholly rotten. Good is powerless in the face
of evil; the bad win out. It is hardly surprising that morally minded
reviewers were outraged.

Lear has some justification for his curse; Cenci has none. Beatrice
is no Goneril; if anything, she is a Cordelia—capable of gentleness,
integrity, and love, but with a streak of her father's stubbornness.
Shelley raises the horrible possibility that Lear might have brought
down his curse upon *Cordelia*; had he done so, the love and forgiveness
of act four scene seven would have been far more difficult, if not

impossible, to achieve. Although Cordelia leads an army, on stage she strikes us as a passive figure; like many virtuous characters in literature, she is rather boring. Shelley avoids this problem by making Beatrice into an active heroine. She partakes of the nature of several Shakespearean women—of their nature, not merely of a handful of their words and attitudes as is the case with, say, Coleridge's Osorio in his relationship with Shakespeare's male tragic protagonists. When she gently sings in the penultimate scene we recognize her as a Desdemona, but in the murder scene in act four she is a Lady Macbeth. At one point her action precisely echoes her forebear's 'Give me the daggers' (*Mac* II. ii. 50, *Cenci* IV. iii. 31 s.d.).

The murder is a sustained variation on that of Duncan; the pace and structure of Shelley's scenes show that he must have paid unusually close attention to Shakespeare's dramatic technique in the second act of *Macbeth*. Night-sounds, staccato exchanges and half-lines, words such as 'equivocation', 'deed', 'done', and 'undone': all contribute to the effect. What is more, the key phrases have been prepared for by earlier uses and variations (such as 'deeds / Which have no form' at III. i. 141). There is even that authentic touch whereby the moment of death is imagined as apocalyptic: the castle horn, which fulfils the role of the knocking at the gate in *Macbeth*, 'sounds / Like the last trump' (IV. iii. 57).

But Shelley effects a series of reversals. Most obviously in our sympathies: we want the murder to take place. More locally, there are the two murderers, Olimpio and Marzio. When first described, they are like the assassins in *Macbeth*:

> two dull, fierce outlaws,
> Who think man's spirit as a worm's, and they
> Would trample out, for any slight caprice,
> The meanest or the noblest life.

> (III. i. 233)

Yet they are employed not by Cenci, as the parallel might suggest, but in order to kill Cenci. And it is one of them who combines the hesitancies of Macbeth and Lady Macbeth. Like Macbeth with the grooms, he sees the old man stirring in his sleep and hears him speaking to God (though not in the most pious fashion); like Lady Macbeth, he thinks of his own father,

> I knew it was the ghost
> Of my dead father speaking through his lips,
> And could not kill him.
>
> (IV. iii. 20)

This is one of the play's many mirror effects; the most touching of them is that in act five when Camillo sees in Beatrice the image of a dead nephew (V. ii. 63–6).

Beatrice herself is another version of both Macbeth and Lady Macbeth, a far more profound one than Marzio. But she reaches the state for which Macbeth strives in vain. He is a kind of Romantic idealist, restlessly in pursuit of the absolute, the completion of his deed. In the imperfect material world, he is confined; when the second assassination is botched and Fleance escapes, he says,

> I had else been perfect,
> Whole as the marble, founded as the rock,
> As broad and general as the casing air;
> But now I am cabin'd, cribb'd, confin'd, bound in
> To saucy doubts and fears.
>
> (III. iv. 20)

Beatrice, however, is freed by her action. She proclaims that 'The deed is done', that she is now founded as the rock, free as the casing air:

> I am as universal as the light;
> Free as the earth-surrounding air; as firm
> As the world's centre. Consequence, to me,
> Is as the wind which strikes the solid rock
> But shakes it not.
>
> (IV. iv. 48)

The strength of these lines is that they are wholly in Beatrice's character, wholly Shelleyan (who else could have written 'I am as universal as the light'?), yet also provokingly allusive in the reversal of Macbeth's images. Nowhere else in Romantic drama is the relationship with Shakespeare more genuinely creative.

The matter of allusion apart, the play has many other strengths which make it Shakespearean. Its diction is unusually immediate for Shelley; the imagery is unified; the characters sound like human beings, interrupting each other or stopping in mid-sentence as a new thought occurs to them. Shelley recognizes the supreme dramatic power of simplicity, especially at the very end of a tragedy. Beatrice's

> Here, Mother, tie
> My girdle for me, and bind up this hair
> In any simple knot; ay, that does well.
>
> (v. iv. 159)

has the austere dignity of Lear's 'Pray you undo this button' (v. iii. 310) and Cleopatra's 'Give me my robe' (v. ii. 280).

The Cenci is not afflicted by what Shelley called the 'faults of youthful composition'; unlike most who attempted poetic drama in the early nineteenth century, he manages to avoid 'diffuseness, a profusion of inapplicable imagery, vagueness, generality, and, as Hamlet says, *words, words*' (*SPW* 337). Shelley felt himself incapable of forming and following-up a plot and 'asserted that he was too metaphysical and abstract, too fond of the theoretical and the ideal, to succeed as a tragedian' (*SPW* 335). These doubts about his aptitude as a dramatist, mentioned by Mary in her note on the play, are applicable to most Romantic drama, but not to *The Cenci*. Byron's praise is justified: it is 'a play,—not a poem, like "Remorse" and "Fazio" '.[23]

There are nevertheless long speeches, scenes of inaction, and passages that depart from the immediate matter of the drama, which, along with the play's unity of action, suggest that there is some justification in Beddoes's judgement that Shelley's model was Greek, not Shakespearean tragedy (Donner, 578). Part of the play's strength is its avoidance of Shakespeare: there is no stultifying Hamlet-figure; the heroine is in some ways more Greek than Elizabethan, more a combination of Electra and Antigone than one of Lady Macbeth and Cordelia. Shelley's twin aims in writing *The Cenci* are apparent from a letter to Medwin: 'My chief endeavour was to produce a delineation of passions which I had never participated in, in chaste language, and according to the rules of enlightened art' (*SL* ii. 189). The latter ideal is neo-classical, but the former is Shakespearean—not only was he traditionally seen as unsurpassed in the delineation of passions, but the year before starting the play Shelley had read the *Biographia*, where Coleridge praised Shakespeare for entering the minds of his characters 'himself meanwhile unparticipating in the passions'.[24]

In her note on the play Mary Shelley points out that it is difficult for a young writer, egotistic and lacking in experience of the world, to be a dramatist (*SPW* 334); this is especially true of a young writer

obsessed with Shakespeare, as her husband was. *The Cenci*, by simultaneously rejecting and borrowing creatively from Shakespeare,
comes closer to successful English poetic tragedy than any other play
of the age. Leigh Hunt was not praising his dead friend excessively
when he made the bold claim that 'assuredly, had he lived, he would
have been the greatest dramatic writer since the days of Elizabeth, if
indeed he has not abundantly proved himself such in his tragedy of
the *Cenci*.'[25]

11

Byron's Pose

> The time is out of joint: O cursed spite,
> That ever I was born to set it right!

'In these words, I imagine, will be found the key to Hamlet's whole procedure. To me it is clear that Shakspeare meant, in the present case, to represent the effects of a great action laid upon a soul unfit for the performance of it. In this view the whole piece seems to me to be composed. There is an oak-tree planted in a costly jar, which should have borne only pleasant flowers in its bosom; the roots expand, the jar is shivered.

'A lovely, pure, noble and most moral nature, without the strength of nerve which forms a hero, sinks beneath a burden which it cannot bear and must not cast away. All duties are holy for him; the present is too hard. Impossibilities have been required of him, not in themselves impossibilities, but such for him. He winds, and turns, and torments himself; he advances and recoils; is ever put in mind, puts himself in mind; at last does all but lose his purpose from his thoughts; yet still without recovering his peace of mind.'[1]

ROMANTIC readings of *Hamlet* and Romantic images of the artistic temperament owe much to Wilhelm Meister. This famous passage touches upon many preoccupations shared by the English Romantics: Hamlet is read as if he were a human being, not a dramatic character; the chosen metaphor is organic; heroism is set up as an ideal, but one of which the sensitive, reflective, self-tormenting mind falls short.

With the possible exception of Goethe himself, Byron was the strongest critic of Romanticism among the exponents of Romanticism. In the ninth canto of *Don Juan*, he catches himself descanting on those perennial Romantic topics, the cyclical nature of history and man's loss of paradise. He stops in his tracks:

> But I am apt to grow too metaphysical.
> 'The time is out of joint', and so am I.
> I quite forget this poem's merely quizzical
> And deviate into matters rather dry.

> (ix. 41)

By playfully quoting 'The time is out of joint', Byron offers a quizzical view of his age, himself, and Hamlet—and the use of Shakespearean quotation. Byron's critique in matters Shakespearean is an important part of his wider critique of Romanticism; it is also an essential anti-dote to the attitudes and practices which I have been examining.

In 1830 the *New Monthly Magazine* published an unsigned article, attributable to Mary Shelley, entitled 'Byron and Shelley on the Character of Hamlet'.[2] Shelley's interpretation of Hamlet, as recorded by his wife, is explicitly indebted to Goethe and Schlegel. It is the con-ventional Romantic reading: the character of Hamlet is the 'central germ' from which the play is conceived and organized; he 'represents the profound philosopher; or, rather, the errors to which a contem-plative and ideal mind is liable'; the supernatural is 'an outward and visible sign of the sudden apparitions of the mysterious world within us'; Hamlet's problem (Shelley's problem, that is) arises from the 'mysterious contradiction between reality and ideality' or 'the excess of an over-ingenious intellect'; 'Whenever he does any thing, he seems astonished at himself, and calls it rashness'. Shelley supports his argument with the favourite quotations—'my mind's eye', 'The pangs of despised love', 'sicklied o'er with th[e] pale cast [of thought], and lose the name of action'—and comes to the conclusion that the play is 'a complete and reasonable whole, composed in an harmonious proportion of difference and similitude, into one expressive unity'. The argument bears the distinctive marks of Shelley's ontology ('the mysterious world within us'), but the interpretation of Hamlet's character could as well have belonged to Coleridge.

Byron's reading is more equivocal. He admits to the Romantic identification with Hamlet, saying, very much in the manner of Hazlitt's 'It is *we* who are Hamlet' (*HW* iv. 232), 'We love Hamlet even as we love ourselves.' But he also finds the prince cold towards Ophelia, inexplicably insulting to Laertes, and 'fiend-like in cruelty' when without compunction he sends his old companions, Rosencrantz and Guildenstern, to their deaths with no time for repentance. Byron continues in Johnsonian vein: the same 'diabolical refinement of revenge' leads Hamlet not to kill the King while he is at prayer—something explained away by Shelley and other Romantic critics as the prevarication of a tender soul that is unaccustomed to action. Byron sums up his attack on Romantic Hamlet with the expostu-lation, 'I am sick of this most lame and impotent hero'; physically lame himself, he has no time for lameness of spirit. He then proceeds to find fault with the other characters and with the logic of introducing that creature so admired by his contemporaries, the ghost (this last gesture is consistent with the attitudes to the gothic and the super- natural revealed by the final cantos of *Don Juan*). Byron expresses the old-fashioned opinion that 'Shakspeare was a man of great genius but no art'; he responds to Shelley's painstaking analysis of the internal coherence of *Hamlet* by falling asleep.

In accordance with his broader opinions on poetry, Byron adopts a neo-classical attitude towards Shakespeare and loves to undercut the uncritical Bardolatry of his contemporaries. However, his ironic manner is such that we can rarely take his pronouncements at face value. Is his 'attitude' in fact a pose? Consider his most extended assault on the Bard, which occurs in a letter to James Hogg. It was a reply to a request for a contribution to a proposed anthology of all the major poets of the day; in the event, Hogg ended up writing parodies of them all, including Byron and himself, an indication that he was no stranger to irony. That Byron's letter is to some extent a perfor- mance, a piece of role-playing, may be judged from the tone of 'You seem to be a plain spoken man, Mr Hogg, and I really do not like you the worse for it. I can't write verses, and yet you want a bit of my poetry for your book' (*LJ* iv. 84). The condemnation of Shakespeare is equally bluff, but more ambivalent than it first appears.

Byron begins by saying that Shakespeare had 'no invention as to stories' and threw together his plots from old novels 'at as little ex- pense of thought as you or I could turn his plays back again into prose tales' (*LJ* iv. 84–5). Seven years earlier, Charles and Mary Lamb *had* turned Shakespeare's best-known plays back into prose tales; 'at as little expense of thought' could as well be directed at their labours as Shakespeare's. Byron then argues that Shakespeare's felicities 'are taken all but *verbatim* out of the old affairs': 'You think, no doubt, that *A horse, a horse, my kingdom for a horse!* is Shakespeare's. Not a syllable of it. You will find it all in the old nameless dramatist.' But if he knew that Richard's line had an analogue in the old plays, would he not have known what the original was? In *The True Tragedie of Richard III* it is 'A horse, a horse, a fresh horse'; the parallel in Peele's *The Battle of Alcazar* (*c.*1589) is 'A horse, a horse, villain a horse.' Neither of these exclamations has anything like the force of 'my kingdom for a horse'. Byron's 'all but' gives the game away: all is taken from the old plays *but* 'my kingdom for', the image that gives the line its dramatic power. 'Not a syllable of it' Shakespeare's? The line's strength and originality are wholly his.

Byron then offers a comparison: 'Could not one take up Tom Jones and improve it, without being a greater genius than Fielding?' The rhetorical question is phrased in such a way that at first glance the reader will assent to it, but on reflection he is likely to think 'No, one could not improve *Tom Jones* without being a greater genius than Fielding.' Whether Byron intended Hogg to see the irony is open to question, but it is quite possible in view of his admiration for Fielding, whom he called 'The *prose* Homer of human nature' (*LJ* viii. 11). Far from believing that anyone could improve *Tom Jones*, Byron may well have agreed with Coleridge that it had one of the 'most perfect plots ever planned' (*TT* 5 July 1834). We should therefore also be suspicious of the parallel claim that 'Shakespeare's plays might be improved', especially since in support of his contention Byron points to the popularity of 'improvements' by Cibber and others—about as equivocal a piece of evidence as one could ask for. Such phrases as 'you may depend on it' and 'no doubt' are further signs that the persona who attacks Shakespeare has more rhetoric than reason at his disposal. Byron himself refuses to be pinned down.

In a curious way, Byron is as much of a chameleon as Shakespeare. He is a master of the occasion: when he needs to adopt a new style or attitude, he will do so. The ironic critique of Shakespeare is right for his letter to Hogg, but when called upon to write an address for the re-opening of Drury Lane in October 1812, he can produce the traditional encomiums—'A shrine for Shakspeare', 'the magic of that name / Defies the scythe of time', and so on (*BPW* iii. 18).[3] But then in a letter to Tom Moore, he speaks of 'the barbarian himself', and in one to Octavius Gilchrist, a fellow-pamphleteer against Bowles, of entertaining the 'heterodox notion' that Shakespeare was not 'without the grossest of faults' (*LJ* viii. 188, 200). Byron's private letters are full of incidental provocations of this sort; glancing and off-the-cuff, they must always be treated lightly.

Byron's public position is also calculated to provoke. In his reply to Bowles's *Strictures on the Life and Writings of Pope*, he sets up Pope as a truly international figure, the poet of civilization, and argues that the inflated reputations of Shakespeare and Milton rest on nationalistic grounds: 'an Englishman, anxious that the posterity of strangers should know that there had been such a thing as a British Epic and Tragedy, might wish for the preservation of Shakespeare and Milton;

but the surviving World would snatch Pope from the Wreck, and let the rest sink with the people.'[4] Byron's cosmopolitan perspective and his commitment to the Horatian ideal of poetry as civilized discourse are important correctives to the literary nationalism and the emphasis on poetry as self-expression that pervade the early nineteenth century.

Another letter to Moore, also written at the time of the Bowles controversy, recasts the distinction between Pope on the one hand, Shakespeare and Milton on the other, in the form of metaphors:

As to Pope, I have always regarded him as the greatest name in our poetry. Depend upon it, the rest are barbarians. He is a Greek Temple, with a Gothic Cathedral on one hand, and a Turkish Mosque and all sorts of fantastic pagodas and conventicles about him. You may call Shakespeare and Milton pyramids, if you please, but I prefer the Temple of Theseus or the Parthenon to a mountain of burnt brickwork. (*LJ* viii. 109)

Byron, then, attacks Shakespeare out of a desire to defend Pope and classical form. His allegiance to the eighteenth century is proclaimed by style as well as content, for the extended metaphor is in the tradition of Johnson's comparison of Shakespeare to a forest, the works of more correct and regular writers to landscaped gardens. Byron is shrewd not to use the same metaphor as Johnson, for the latter was praising Shakespeare; Byron's architectural imagery is more favourable to Pope. Lady Blessington offered a romantic version of Johnson's figure when she said that any comparison between Shakespeare and Pope was 'as absurd as comparing some magnificent feudal castle, surrounded by mountains and forests, with foaming cataracts, and boundless lakes, to the pretty villa of Pope, with its sheen lawn, artificial grotto, stunted trees, and trim exotics'; Byron replied that the simile was 'more ingenious than just' and held fast to Pope.[5]

The emphasis is different in each comparison: Johnson aims to praise Shakespeare without deriding more 'correct' writers, Lady Blessington resorts to clichés and the stock properties of the sublime ('foaming cataracts'), while Byron's rejection of 'Turkish Mosques' and eastern fancies is an ironic touch in view of how, more than any other poet except perhaps Moore in *Lalla Rookh*, he made capital out of the fashion for Turkish tales. According to George Bancroft, Byron said that Johnson's preface 'expressed his opinion of Shakespeare exactly' (*HVSV* 293). In this respect, he is diametrically opposed to Keats, who expressed his opinion of Johnson by scoring out some of the summary judgements on individual plays reprinted in his pocket edition of Shakespeare, and wittily turning the words of the poet against the critic ('The clamorous Owl that hoots at our quaint Spirits'; 'Newts and blind worms do no wrong / Come not near our faery queen'—*KS* 30).

Byron's *obiter dicta*, like Wordsworth's, need to be used with caution because they may sometimes consist of what the acquaintance would have liked the great man to say, not what he did say. But as a record of the attitudes of the exiled poet's public persona, as opposed to the private musings of his formative years, the conversations remain invaluable. A remark recorded by Thomas Smith accords with the dialogue in the *New Monthly Magazine*: 'I do not admire [Hamlet] to the extent of the common opinion' (*HVSV* 423). But is Byron really dissociating himself from the tendency to play Hamlet? He made the remark to Smith immediately after lying full length on his back in an open sarcophagus muttering lines from the graveyard scene. As George Finlay wryly observed, 'it was curious that Lord B. was so strangely conversant in an author of such inferior merit, and that he should so continually have the most melodious lines of Shakspeare in his mouth' (*HVSV* 551-2). Lady Blessington says something similar: 'I have rarely met with a person more conversant with the works of Shakspeare than was Byron. I have heard him quote passages from them repeatedly . . . Could there be a less equivocal proof of his admiration of our immortal bard than the tenacity with which his memory retained the finest passages of all his works?' (Blessington, 358). Her observation may be tested against the letters and journals.

It could only have been perversity that led Byron to profess disdain for Shakespeare while quoting from him with such facility. He always quotes from memory, often making slight slips; he must therefore have had a remarkable knowledge of the twenty-eight plays from which he culls phrases in his letters and journals. *Macbeth* is his favourite source, then *Hamlet*, *Othello*, and *1 Henry IV*. The last of these appealed to the Falstaffian side of his character; *Othello* was a particular favourite in 1814-15, the years of his disastrous marriage. In a letter to Murray, and again in *Childe Harold*, he wrote of the literary associations of Venice—Othello, Shylock, and Otway's Pierre (*LJ* v. 131, *BPW* ii. 125). Despite the claim, 'I hate things *all fiction* and therefore the *Merchant* and *Othello*—have no great associations to me' (*LJ* v. 203), he has frequent recourse to *Othello* and *The Merchant of Venice* when describing his Venetian experiences. Here he is, jostling in the queue as he leaves the opera on Boxing Day 1816:

The crowd was enormous—and in coming out—having a lady under my arm—I was obliged in making way to 'beat a Venetian and traduce the state' being compelled to regale a person with an English punch in the guts—which sent him as far back as the squeeze and the passage would admit—he did not ask for another (*LJ* v. 152).

He is for ever exercising such comic turns on his originals. Hamlet's 'Man delights not me—nor woman neither' (II. ii. 309) would appeal to a gloomy Romantic egotist; one could imagine Coleridge or Keats saying 'man delights not me—and only one woman' (Sara, Fanny); but Byron has a sting in the tail: ' "Man delights not me" ', he quotes in his journal during February 1814, 'and only one woman—at a time' (*LJ* iii. 246). The dash is timed to perfection.

Many of Byron's quotations take the form of playful twists: 'The Douglas and the Hotspur both together / Are confident against the world in arms' (*1H4* v. i. 116) becomes 'the "Jeffrey and the Moore together are confident against the world in ink" ' (*LJ* iv. 323). But sometimes a simple comic effect will be followed by a more psychologically revealing quotation, as in this letter to his publisher:

I have thought as much for some time past—but you will find in the long run (though I hear that you go about talking of yourself like Dogberry 'as a fellow that hath had losses') that you will not change for the better.—I am worth any 'forty on fair ground' of the wretched stilted pretenders and parsons of your advertisements. (*LJ* ix. 213)

The first quotation is notable only for its pun (Dogberry's losses were not financial as Murray's are), while the second—from *Coriolanus*, a play from which Byron quotes with unusual frequency for the early nineteenth century—reveals something of his pride, isolation, and underlying insecurity. Byron saw himself as a Coriolanus who was rejected by his own people and had to go to the 'world elsewhere' of Italy and Greece (see *LJ* iv. 61, v. 25).

While most of Byron's quotations from the comedies and histories serve to provide his addressees with analogues, often ironic or incongruous, for the situations he describes, those from the tragedies, *Macbeth* especially, often define his own state of mind. Partly because of his own Scottish ancestry, Byron felt a special affinity with the world of *Macbeth*; in a letter to Lady Melbourne, he even claimed to be descended from Banquo (*LJ* iii. 38). Some of his quotations from the play are marked by bravado; he writes of his financial plight at the age of eighteen, 'since like Macbeth, "they've tied me to a Stake, I cannot fly" I shall imitate that *valorous* Tyrant, and "Bear-like fight the Course" ' (*LJ* i. 96). But more of them are stoical. One of the most emotionally charged occurs on the death of the boy he loved, John Edleston: ' "I have almost forgot the taste of grief," and "supped full of horrors" till I have become callous, nor have I a tear left for an event which five years ago would have bowed down my head to the earth' (*LJ* ii. 110). Byron would have expected the context of the quotation to be remembered: it refers to the death of a loved one and is in close proximity to 'To-morrow, and to-morrow, and to-morrow', Macbeth's speech on human transience, which must have struck a deep chord in the author of *Childe Harold's Pilgrimage*. Here, the quotation, with its quiet substitution of 'grief' for Macbeth's 'fear', helps Byron to take control of his emotions.

There are a number of equally intense quotations in the 1813–14 journal. Typical phrases from the final act of *Macbeth* are ' "that perilous stuff which weighs upon the heart" ' and ' "I 'gin to be a-weary of the sun" ' (*LJ* iii. 243, 246). On another occasion, after a night of bad dreams, Byron quotes Richard III on being tormented by the ghosts, then the next day he records a better night: 'No dreams last night of the dead nor the living—so—I am "firm as the marble, founded as the rock"—till the next earthquake' (iii. 216, 219). The same crucial speech from *Macbeth*, which I discussed at the end of chapter ten, will recur in the poetry.[6] The strong identification implied by such quotations should not lead us to conclude with Wilson Knight that Byron was in touch with Shakespeare's spirit and somehow incarnated the greatest Shakespearean characters; it should, however, lead us to question his professed indifference to the plays.

Not only do George Finlay and Lady Blessington both advance Byron's use of quotation as evidence that he did not really despise Shakespeare, they also both explain his position in social terms. Finlay recounts that on one occasion when Byron attacked Shakespeare, a gentleman rushed out of the room in disgust 'and afterwards entered his protest most anxiously against such doctrines. Lord B. was quite delighted with this, and redoubled the severity of his criticism.' His motive, then, is the desire to unsettle; more specifically, to annoy the English by setting himself up as a European: 'He said once, when we were alone, "I like to astonish Englishmen: they come abroad full of Shakspeare, and contempt for the dramatic literature of other nations; they think it blasphemy to find a fault in his writings, which are full of them["]' (*HVSV* 551–2). Lady Blessington also comes to the conclusion that 'A wish of vexing or astonishing the English is, I am persuaded, the motive that induces him to attack Shakspeare; and he is highly gratified when he succeeds in doing either, and enjoys it like a child' (Blessington, 310). Her simile opens up the possibility that Byron's bravado may be a mark of insecurity. A remark of Shelley's, recorded by Finlay, suggests that there was more to the matter than a desire to blaspheme against English values: ' "B. you are a most wonderful man." "How?" "You are envious of Shakspeare" ' (*HVSV* 551, a version of the opinion attributed by Trelawny to Mrs Shelley).

On one level, then, Byron's professions of disdain for Shakespeare are the product of a desire to entertain 'heterodox notions'. But on another, they are intimations of uneasiness about his own status as a poet. It is telling that while people from high society emphasize Byron's tendency 'to talk for effect, and to assert what he does not believe' (Blessington, 358), writers who themselves had to grapple with Shakespeare's influence discuss the matter of inferiority. In 'Lord Byron en Italie', Stendhal writes 'He was the least dramatic poet who ever lived; he was incapable of entering into another character. This was the cause of his marked hatred of Shakespeare' (*HVSV* 201). And, definitively, there is Goethe:

He is a great talent, a born talent, and I never saw the true poetical power greater in any man. In the apprehension of external objects, and a clear penetration into past situations, he is quite as great as Shakespeare. But, as a pure individuality, Shakespeare is his superior. This was felt by Byron; and on this account he does not say much of Shakespeare, although he knows whole passages by heart. He would willingly have denied him altogether; for Shakespeare's cheerfulness is in his way, and he feels that he is no match for it. Pope he does not deny, for he had no cause to fear him: on the contrary, he mentions him, and shows him respect when he can; for he knows well enough that Pope is a mere foil to himself. (Eckermann, 89)

'Cheerfulness' is a poor translation of Eckermann's 'Heiterkeit'. It does not refer to, say, Shakespeare's comic genius—among the Romantics, Byron was unusually responsive to that. Goethe partly has in mind the way that Byron peoples his poems with brooding exiles who could never have been created by the flexible and down-to-earth Shakespeare. But he is also thinking of the common accusation that all Byron's heroes are in fact Byron himself. A better translation of 'Heiterkeit' would be 'serenity' or 'clearness': Shakespeare's works are not clouded by his own emotions; his impersonality and willingness to be 'in uncertainties' are the qualities lacking in the egotistic and volatile Byron. *Don Juan* is the great exception to all this: there Byron not only created a counter-hero who was a cheerful exile, but also adopted a sceptical yet life-asserting tone that was more authentically Shakespearean than anything else in the age. And it was also in *Don Juan* that he finally solved the problem of what to do with Shakespeare's language.

Byron's approaches to Shakespeare in his poems are as various as his quotations in the letters. In *Hints from Horace*, he invokes Shakespeare as the ideal to which the contemporary stage should aspire; but he also makes him into a classical dramatist, who obeys the rules of art: 'Not on the stage, the regicide Macbeth / Appals an audience with a monarch's death' (*BPW* i. 299). In *English Bards and Scotch Reviewers*, Byron is himself neo-classical: one element of his homage to Pope is his use of allusion to strengthen his satiric argument, the device on which Reuben Brower dwelt in his study of the Augustan poet.[7] Towards the end of the poem, there is a group of Shakespearean allusions, beginning with 'Our men in buckram shall have blows enough, / And feel, they too are "penetrable stuff" ' (*BPW* i. 262). The 'men in buckram' are those who attack Falstaff at Gadshill: the allusion places the critics who are Byron's subjects—they are imaginary opponents, whose strength is greatly exaggerated. ' "Penetrable stuff" ' is Hamlet adopting the critic's practice of chastising in order to correct (*Ham* III. iv. 36); Byron turns the phrase on critics and implies that they are as susceptible to attack as authors are. A few lines later, Byron continues

> The time hath been, when no harsh sound would fall
> From lips that now may seem imbued with gall . . .
> But now, so callous grown, so changed since youth,
> I've learned to think, and sternly speak the truth;
> Learned to deride the critic's starch decree,
> And break him on the wheel he meant for me
>
> (1053–60).

Here he is alluding to Macbeth's 'time has been', which Wordsworth and Coleridge evoked in very different contexts; the line occurs shortly before 'I have supp'd full with horrors', that phrase which Byron

adapted on several occasions, most movingly on the death of John
Edleston, but more relevantly for this allusion when he said in another
letter, ' "I have supp'd full of" Criticism' (*LJ* ii. 76). The educated
reader of *English Bards* will see that Byron imagines himself to be
hardened by harsh reviews and literary isolation, as Macbeth is
hardened by familiarity with death and literal isolation.

A neo-classical allusion such as this is intended to be recognized; it
works towards the ideal of poetry as cultivated discourse, conversation
between educated writer and educated reader. A Romantic allusion is
more for the benefit of the poet himself; it serves to enrich his language
and secure his relationship with his admired forebear. This kind of
allusion frequently occurs when Byron adopts his Romantic style. In
Childe Harold's Pilgrimage, he produces a typical image of the Romantic
soul chained and tormented in the material world: 'Though from our
birth the faculty divine / Is chain'd and tortured—cabin'd, cribb'd,
confined' (iv. 127, *BPW* ii. 166). The two Romantic spirits invoked
here are Wordsworth, with his 'The vision and the faculty divine'
(*Excursion*, i. 79, a line applied to Wordsworth himself by Coleridge,
BL ii. 60), and the Macbeth who is 'cabin'd, cribb'd, confin'd,
bound in / To saucy doubts and fears'. Similarly, when early in the
poem Childe Harold is said to be 'sick at heart', we recall the beginning of *Hamlet* or the end of *Macbeth* (i. 6, *BPW* ii. 10; *Ham* I. i. 9, *Mac*
V. iii. 19).

Byron also has the Romantic capacity of turning Shakespearean
images to his own account. In his description of the Falls of Terni, he
produces a flight as sublime as Wordsworth's description of crossing
the Alps—'cleaves', 'Crushing the cliffs', 'Lo! where it comes like an
eternity' (*Childe Harold*, iv. 69 ff., *BPW* ii. 147–8); he then effects a
wonderful transition to the serenity of the rainbow across the water-
fall, which is compared to 'Hope upon a death-bed'. The simile may
derive from Pericles' awakening, where Marina looks 'Like Patience
gazing on king's graves, and smiling / Extremity out of act' (V. i.
138), but the broader comparison which Byron goes on to make conjures up Shakespeare's other great scene of awakening: 'Resembling,
'mid the torture of the scene, / Love watching Madness with unalter-
able mien'. The natural scene is elided with a dramatic one: the love
and peace of Cordelia and Lear when they are reunited after nearly
four acts of torture, storm, and madness. Wilson Knight, for all his
rhapsodies and eccentricities, is very sensitive to moments such as
this. 'Generally Byron expands Shakespeare; here we watch the

reverse', he writes in *Byron and Shakespeare* (285–6). 'The concluding line is an amazing compression, perfect in lucidity and final in tragic conquest, of Lear's reunion with Cordelia. . . . Such is the high peace attainable, or imaginable, beyond conflict; it may be touched for a while, *within* tragedy, as it is in *King Lear* and Byron's lines.'

Byron's Romantic appropriations of Shakespeare are not restricted to *Childe Harold's Pilgrimage*; there are also many instances in his Turkish tales. One could explore, say, parallels of character and action between *The Bride of Abydos* and *Hamlet*,[8] but since my primary concern is with poetic language, my example is a single image in *The Corsair*. A lot of gazing goes on in Byron's poems; in *The Corsair*, Medora watches her beloved Conrad as he departs from her view: 'The tender blue of that large loving eye / Grew frozen with its gaze on vacancy' (493, *BPW* iii. 167). This is a beautiful image, not a pastiche, because Byron takes his idea from one moment in Shakespeare— Imogen watching the departure of Posthumus' ship—and his language from another, Gertrude's 'you do bend your eye on vacancy' as Hamlet looks at the ghost (III. iv. 117). The combination is such that Byron achieves a Shakespearean feel without introducing an obtrusive Shakespearean presence. In this case, the Countess of Blessington's judgement on his borrowings is just: 'he seizes thoughts which, in passing through the glowing alembic of his mind, become so embellished as to lose all identity with the original crude embryos he had adopted' (Blessington, 130). The originals are not crude embryos, but the metaphors of adoption and alchemic transformation are apt.

The more problematic occasions are those on which Byron does not embellish his borrowings. We have seen with other poets that various forms of allusion and echo provide one solution: the original is acknowledged and turned to commodity. But we have also seen that this will not do when the form is dramatic; an *author* may express his admiration for Shakespeare by revivifying his words, but a *character* who is supposed to have lived before those words were written is another matter. When Byron began writing plays, the problem of plagiarism became acute.

He attempted to deal with the matter in a variety of ways. The following contains a characteristic mixture of self-defensiveness and aggression towards contemporary fashion: 'He was anxious to show you that he possessed no Shakspeare and Milton; "because," he said, "he had been accused of borrowing from them!" He affected to doubt whether Shakspeare was so great a genius as he has been taken for, and whether fashion had not a great deal to do with it'.[9] There are two defences here: 'I do not know Shakespeare, therefore I cannot plagiarize him' and 'I do not admire Shakespeare, therefore I would not want to plagiarize him.' The first was hardly tenable in view of the fact that so many of Byron's letters, poems, prefaces, and annotations included Shakespearean quotations; the second is related to his frequently reiterated claim that his plays were not modelled on Shakespeare's.

What alternatives were available to the defence 'I do not know Shakespeare'? One was to go to the opposite extreme: Tom Moore noticed a volume in Byron's gondola with a number of paper marks between its leaves; he asked what it was, and Byron replied, 'Only a book from which I am trying to *crib*, as I do wherever I can;—and that's the way I get the character of an original poet' (*HVSV* 238). Another strategy was to praise the plagiarist as a 'modern Proteus' who 'seems to identify himself' with the genius from whom he borrows (Blessington, 239–40). Nearest to the truth is the claim that every author is a plagiarist: Byron told Medwin that when he read Lamb's *Specimens of English Dramatic Poets*, he was surprised to find in Webster and others many ideas that he thought exclusively his own, but that it was also apparent that the old dramatists themselves, including Shakespeare, plagiarized each other—only in those days they were less worried about such matters (Medwin, 139–40). The healthiest attitude in this respect was that of Goethe, who said with regard to his *Faust*, a play from which Byron was accused of plagiarizing in *Manfred*, 'my Mephistopheles sings a song from Shakespeare, and why should he not? Why should I give myself the trouble of inventing one of my own, when this said just what was wanted?' (Eckermann, 83).

There is also the question of intention. The following comment, recorded by Lady Blessington, offers a sane account of unintentional plagiarism, and in so doing makes effective use of familial metaphor:

'But,' said Byron, 'who is the author that is not, intentionally or unintentionally, a plagiarist? Many more, I am persuaded, are the latter than the former; for if one has read much, it is difficult, if not impossible, to avoid adopting, not only the thoughts, but the expressions of others, which, after they have been some time stored in our minds, appear to us to come forth ready formed . . . and we fancy them our own progeny, instead of being those of adoption.' (Blessington, 363–4)

It may have been a distinction along these lines that the editor of *The Literary Gazette* had in mind in his introduction to a series of six articles by Alaric Watts on 'Lord Byron's Plagiarisms', which appeared between February and May 1821; he asks his readers to decide 'Whether the following exposition may exhibit Lord Byron as an authorized spoliator of other men's goods, or as a culpable pilferer.'[10] It is not quite clear what is meant by an 'authorized spoliator'— perhaps that it is acceptable for a writer unconsciously to gather spoils from his predecessors, and that his piracy may be authorized if he stamps his own mark on the goods and creates anew from them (without *spoiling* them?). Culpability is attached to the author who deliberately pilfers small phrases and fails to obscure the fact that he has done so. Watts felt that Byron was especially culpable in his plays. He condemned *Marino Faliero* for 'want of originality', arguing that it contained only 'a little of the noble author's own' and was largely a 'mere compound' of *Venice Preserved*, *Othello*, *Measure for Measure*, *Julius Caesar*, 'and other plays, so well known, that we suppose Lord Byron thinks them common property, and therefore that it is no harm to pillage them.'[11]

A list of the more prominent Shakespearean parallels will show that in *Marino Faliero* Byron did little to transform or recast his originals. The Doge addresses the heavy crown in the manner of Bolingbroke, and frequently uses the language of Macbeth—'There's blood upon thy face', 'It is our knell', 'And calmly wash those hands incarnadine', 'I am settled and bound up'. The play from which Byron quotes most frequently in his letters is without question the major influence on the language of *Marino*: 'But if we fail—', 'Make our assurance doubly sure', 'we will not scotch, / But kill', 'look to the lady!' There are strong structural parallels with not only *Macbeth* but also *Julius Caesar*, for example in the scene where Bertram tells Lioni not to go out on the morrow, and in the explicit comparison of Calendaro and Bertuccio to Brutus and Cassius. The play being set in Venice, *Othello* is also used liberally: 'It is the cause', 'and then farewell! / Farewell all social memory! all thoughts . . .'.[12]

When Wordsworth alludes to Shakespeare in his epic or Byron in his satires, they are manifestly doing something other than imitating him. But unregenerated Shakespearean phraseology in a blank verse drama inevitably sounds like lame imitation. Byron creates a variety of dramatic situations, more or less similar to ones in Shakespeare, but is unable to find a language of his own to render them in verse.

Even where there is no direct verbal debt, the verse often has the feel of pastiche. In the *New Monthly Magazine* dialogue on *Hamlet*, Shelley praises the music of the letters *s*, *l*, *b*, and *p* in the line 'How sweet the moonlight sleeps upon this bank' (p. 330, *MerV* v. i. 54); in Byron's 'I cannot shape my tongue / To syllable black deeds into smooth names' (*Marino*, iii. i. 57), the proximity of *b* to *d*, *m* to *n*, and *ee* to *oo* is too patently mimetic of the hollow loquaciousness the lines describe —this is one of those occasions on which Byron's facility is such that he becomes facile.

In his review of *Marino Faliero*, Hazlitt refers to Byron's 'unaccountable pilfering of single phrases from Shakspeare' (*HW* xix. 47). There is no greater pilferer of Shakespearean phrases than Hazlitt, but while the effect is often a strength in Hazlitt's essays, it is invariably a weakness in Byron's plays. As Hazlitt also points out in his review, 'allusion to Shakspeare' is incongruous in the mouth of a fourteenth-century Doge (xix. 49). When the later poet speaks in his own voice, he can, to use a phrase of Hazlitt's which was quoted earlier, 'do nothing so good' as to allude to Shakespeare—and if he does this well, he cannot be said to do amiss. But when he speaks in the voice of a historical character, the poet's personal dialogue with Shakespeare becomes an encumbrance; the failure to escape Shakespeare is another symptom of the Romantic's inability to stand apart from his own preoccupations and enter into his characters—'it is Lord Byron speaking in the nineteenth century, and not the Doge of Venice in the fourteenth.'

Sardanapalus, the tragedy of an emperor who bears a distinct resemblance to Mark Antony, is probably the best of Byron's plays,[13] not least because it eschews direct verbal borrowings. Wilson Knight summarizes the similarity with *Antony and Cleopatra*: 'The hero's position as imperial master criticized for sexual laxity and irresponsible hedonism closely corresponds to Antony's. In both dramas the conventional warrior and governmental values are in opposition to sexual and related enticements' (*Byron and Shakespeare*, 258). But *Sardanapalus* is an active re-working, whereas *Marino* was characterized by mere passive borrowings. Byron's position is more explicit than Shakespeare's: where judgements are singularly slippery in *Antony and Cleopatra*, there is no doubt about them in *Sardanapalus*. Despite his effeminacy, our sympathies are with the magnanimous emperor; for one thing, his tenderness towards his estranged wife, Zarina, contrasts sharply with Antony's attitude to Fulvia and

Octavia. Sardanapalus' favourite, Myrrha, is a slave with a wholly noble nature, while Cleopatra is a queen who resorts to anger and cunning. Antony and Cleopatra not only die at different times; their idealization of each other is counterpoised by the way that Antony botches his suicide and Cleopatra pragmatically breaks off her apotheosis to make arrangements with her treasurer. Sardanapalus and Myrrha, on the other hand, go to death together; the play ends as they mount and light their own funeral pyre in a triumphant *Liebestod*.[14] Sardanapalus falls from power because he tries to build an earthly paradise; if 'love' is understood to mean not merely individual love, but the principle that would govern the ideal society, then the title of Dryden's version of Shakespeare's play is applicable to Byron's—*All for Love or The World Well Lost.*

In view of the Shakespearean parallels in all Byron's plays, a few of them enriching, but most of them debilitating, one is taken aback by the vociferous denials of any influence. *The Two Foscari* is a neo-Elizabethan tragedy of the conflict between family and state, with an Iago-like villain in the character of Loredano. But Byron wrote of it, 'You will find all this very *un*like Shakespeare—and so much the better in one sense—for I look upon him to be the *worst* of models— though the most extraordinary of writers' (*LJ* viii. 152). He claimed that he had been influenced by Alfieri and the Greeks, not the Elizabethans and Jacobeans, and criticized *The Cenci* because he thought that it was modelled on earlier English drama: 'I am not an admirer of the old dramatists *as models*', he wrote to Shelley (*LJ* viii. 103).[15] 'Do not judge me by your mad old dramatists', he requested in a letter to Murray, emphasizing that the classical unity, clarity, and simplicity of plot at which he had aimed in *Marino Faliero* set him apart from 'those turbid mountebanks—always excepting B. Jonson—who was a Scholar and a Classic' (*LJ* viii. 57).

In his reply to the letter about *The Cenci*, Shelley said that Byron was the one to whom he looked for something worthy of the English stage, a play in the true Shakespearean tradition (*SL* ii. 290). Another of Byron's counter-Shakespearean claims was that his plays were not written for the stage. This, however, is belied by his involvement with the management of Drury Lane, his role-player's love of the theatre, and his high regard for the leading English actors, notably Kean.[16] Like Keats and so many others, he particularly admired Kean's *Richard III*: 'Just returned from seeing Kean in Richard. By Jove, he is a soul! Life—nature—truth—without exaggeration or diminution

. . . Richard is a man; and Kean is Richard' (*LJ* iii. 244). The energy of the character, as well as the actor, fascinated Byron. The day after recording this opinion in his journal, he made some comparative judgements in a letter to James Wedderburn Webster: 'There is a new Actor named Kean come out—he is a wonder—and we are yet wise enough to admire him—he is superior to Cooke certainly in many points—and will run Kemble hard—his style is quite new—or rather *renewed*—being that of Nature.—Nobody knows as yet what is to become of Bonaparte . . .' (*LJ* iv. 67). Byron's scorn for contemporary taste is behind the implication that admiration for Kean is unusually discriminating for the age and may therefore not last much longer. The association of Kean with nature and the conception of him as a rival to John Kemble and a superior G. F. Cooke are conventional responses. In *Detached Thoughts* Byron wrote 'Of Actors—Cooke was the most natural—Kemble the most supernatural—Kean a medium between the two—but Mrs Siddons worth them all put together' (*LJ* ix. 31). This is a characteristic combination of convention (Mrs Siddons as the ideal synthesis) and idiosyncrasy (Kemble associated with the supernatural).[17] Most distinctively Byronic in the letter to Webster is the progression from Kean to Napoleon. There is another suggestive parallel in *Detached Thoughts*, when Byron muses on all the people to whom he has been compared; in addition to 'Kean the Actor', the list includes those other embodiments of energy '[Milton's] Satan—Shakespeare—Buonaparte' (*LJ* ix. 11).

B. W. Procter discerned that 'some of the fine passages of Kean's acting suggested as fine passages in Byron's poetry'; *passages* takes us back to the problem that both Romantic actor and Romantic poet produce bursts of genius, but neither can sustain a performance. Procter offers the much admired moment in *Richard III* when Kean drew distractedly with his sword on the ground while he stood outside his tent on the eve of Bosworth Field as a source for the lines in the 'Ode to Napoleon Buonaparte',

> Or trace with thine all idle hand
> In loitering mood upon the sand
> That Earth is now as free!
>
> (*BPW* iii. 264)

'The ode was written on the 10th of April, 1814, and Kean had first appeared in *Richard* in the February previous. The actor was, therefore, in all his *Richard* glory at this moment.'[18] Kean's business was probably also the source for the following stage direction: 'ULRIC, who has unbuckled his sabre, and is drawing lines with it on the floor —still in its sheath' (*Werner*, v. i. 206). T. C. Grattan went so far as to assert that Byron, Kean, and Napoleon were all 'stage-players', that they were three geniuses of the 'same species of mind'; he compared Napoleon in Egypt, Byron in Greece, and Kean in North America, 'each at the head of his wild and half-savage tribe'.[19]

Byron's identification with, and debts to, Edmund Kean show that we should be taken in no more by his professions of detachment from the English stage than by his supposed avoidance of Shakespeare. In his less provocative moods, he is capable of recognizing that what he is really looking for in his plays is some middle path, 'neither a servile following of the old drama—which is a grossly erronious one—nor yet *too French*'. He says that he is seeking a combination of 'good English —and a severer approach to the rules' (*LJ* viii. 78), by which he may mean responsiveness to both Shakespearean language and classical form.

The problem with combining 'good English' and 'a severer approach to the rules' was that the influence of Shakespeare's English remained, even when any formal imitation was eschewed. Immediately after *Sardanapalus* and *The Two Foscari*, Byron wrote *Cain*, the play in which he came closest to the programme outlined in a letter to Murray of August 1821: 'my dramatic Simplicity is *studiously* Greek', 'I admire the old English dramatists—but this is quite another field— and has nothing to do with theirs.—I want to make a *regular* English drama—no matter whether for the Stage or not . . . but a *mental theatre*' (*LJ* viii. 186–7). But not even in *Cain* does Byron escape Shakespeare's language—Cain's encounter with Lucifer inappropriately suggests Hamlet's with the ghost; the opening exchanges establish an altogether irrelevant parallel between Cain and Cordelia,

> *Adam.*   Son Cain, my first-born, wherefore art thou silent?
> *Cain.*   Why should I speak?
>
> (I. i. 21)

By turning to the tradition of burlesque *ottava rima*, which J. H. Frere had Englished in his 'Whistlecraft' cantos, Byron was able to evade this problem. By writing in a form totally different from anything in Shakespeare, he avoided rivalry; he was able to recapture the Shakespearean virtues of variety, vitality, and magnanimity without having to worry about the weight of Shakespearean language. He would inevitably find himself speaking Shakespearean phrases, but he could do so openly and unashamedly. His Italian models, such as Pulci, gave him a precedent for the casual, unanxious use of quotations.[20] Furthermore, the retention of quotations on the surface of the text contributed to his implied attack on the Coleridgean ideal of a unified, organic work of art. Romantic poems strive to echo instead of quote because, as De Quincey put it, overt references to books interrupt the current of the feeling; as *Don Juan* as a whole is an accumulative, disparate, unorganic work,[21] so its quotations are not integrated. Byron makes a virtue of the incidental, the momentary, the superficial. Overt quotations and adaptations could also be used to demonstrate the vulnerability of the English classics. Comic, bantering quotations are a form of affectionate mockery that render their subjects human and approachable. Byron is able simultaneously to mock Romantic awe in the face of Shakespeare and to overcome that sense of his own inferiority which was discerned by Goethe.

Thus at the beginning of canto six, a grand Shakespearean statement is modified. The first stanza opens,

> 'There is a tide in the affairs of men
>   Which taken at the flood'—you know the rest,
> And most of us have found it now and then;

the second, 'There is a tide in the affairs of women / "Which taken at the flood leads"—God knows where'. Then a Miltonic invocation is brought down to size: 'Thrones, worlds, et cetera' (*DJ* vi. 4).[22] And at the beginning of the next canto, Spenser is reversed: ' "Fierce loves and faithless wars"—I am not sure / If this be the right reading— 'tis no matter' (vii. 8). We should not be disarmed: it matters greatly that in *Don Juan* loves are fierce and wars are faithless, whereas in the first stanza of *The Faerie Queene* Spenser said that 'Fierce warres and faithfull loves shall moralize my song'.

Byron's range of styles and subjects in *Don Juan* is matched by his range of literary allusions. Alexander Pope is quoted one moment, an advertising slogan the next (i. 16, 17); Shakespeare will be quoted in both lyrical and satirical contexts. Byron's field of reference within Shakespeare is unusually wide; while his contemporaries often restrict themselves to the magical plays and the major tragedies, he is equally at home invoking Parolles (as at xiii. 84) or comparing Don Juan hidden amid the nether regions of Julia and Antonia to Clarence in his butt of malmsey (i. 166). Romanticism returns persistently to a handful of moments that underwrite theories of the imagination's creative power; Byron effortlessly extracts from Shakespeare phrases more relevant to the world of *Don Juan* (' "brain them with their lady's fan" '—i. 21, from *1H4* II. iii. 23), or deploys a much-quoted phrase in a new way—'Yet very fit to "murder sleep" ' is used with regard not to regicide, as in Wordsworth, or remorse, as in Coleridge, but to the fact that Dudù's charms are likely to turn a man's mind from sleep (vi. 42). A measure of the difference between high Romantic uses of Shakespeare and those in *Don Juan* is provided by Edgar's samphire-gatherer. For Keats, he is an image of the poet precipitately at work on the 'Cliff of Poesy'; for Byron, 'dreadful trade' acts as an image of the reduction of literature to commerce (the tyranny of the cash-nexus is a theme that recurs throughout *Don Juan*): 'the literary lower empire . . . A "dreadful trade" like his who "gathers samphire" ' (xi. 62).

The twist on 'trade' is typical of the narrator of *Don Juan*. Witty, ironic but generous in spirit, pleasure-loving and worldly-wise: there are Falstaffian elements in the rich compound of his character. So it is that in the preface to cantos one and two he is imagined with a jug of ' "right sherris" ' on the table in front of him (*DJ* p. 38, alluding to Falstaff's monologue on sherris in *2H4* IV. iii. 96 ff.). Occasionally he also reveals some of Falstaff's vulnerability, for example when he refers self-consciously to ' "us youth" ' (i. 125, quoting *1H4* II. ii. 85). The narrator's quotation from *Macbeth* early in the canto during which Haidée dies, 'Now my sere fancy "falls into the yellow / Leaf", and imagination droops her pinion' (*DJ* iv. 3), not only prepares for the sadness to come, but also suggests the coming of his own old age—something that obsessed Byron, who seemed to live so fast that he treated his middle age as old age. This feeling reaches its most intense pitch when he alludes to *Macbeth* for the last time in his lyric, 'On this day I complete my thirty-sixth year'. The constant pressure of both vitality and mortality, the bitter-sweet sensation that pervades *Don Juan*, is also suggested by the epigraph of cantos six to eight, which was reproduced on the title-pages of all the succeeding volumes published in Byron's lifetime (cantos nine to eleven, twelve to fourteen, and fifteen to sixteen): the 'cakes and ale' passage from *Twelfth Night*, the most bitter-sweet of all Shakespeare's plays.

The Shakespearean quotations in *Don Juan* run a whole gamut of Romantic and anti-Romantic practices. At the least interesting level, there is the quotation of proverbial saws, such as Hamlet's 'dog will have his day' (*DJ* ii. 166, xv. 23) or 'Full of wise saws and modern instances', the saw about saws from *As You Like it* (II. vii. 156), which is quoted with regard to a ' "modern instance" ' of Polonius's saw, ' "True 'tis a pity, pity 'tis, 'tis true" ' (*DJ* xii. 38). Early in the poem, Byron pretends to be self-conscious about using phrases that specifically summon up Shakespeare, rather than those that have become proverbial. On one occasion, he identifies his extract and apologizes for its presence:

> 'Sweets to the sweet' (I like so much to quote,
>   You must excuse this extract; 'tis where she,
> The Queen of Denmark, for Ophelia brought
>   Flowers to the grave).
>
>   (*DJ* ii. 17)

But even here he is undertaking a typical reversal. 'Sweets to the sweet' refers not to flowers but to the 'salt tears' that Juan weeps into the 'salt sea' on being parted from Julia. There is a less prominent borrowing two stanzas later, when Byron debunks the strained emotion of Julia's letter. Her 'A mind diseased no remedy can physic'—a reminiscence of Macbeth's 'Canst thou not minister to a mind diseas'd' and 'Throw physic to the dogs' (V. iii. 40, 47)—is answered with the rhyme 'Here the ship gave a lurch, and he grew seasick' (ii. 19). The realities of the body intrude upon the flights of the lovelorn spirit. Byron's flexibility is such that here he makes comic capital out of Macbeth's fifth act weariness which in other moods will speak to him of his own melancholy.

The occurrence of two allusions in quick succession, the second usually quieter than the first, is very frequent in *Don Juan*; once the mind is sent to Shakespeare, it dwells there for a moment and picks up a second treasure. Thus in canto eight the openly marked quotation of ' "aroint" ' from *Macbeth* leads to the rhyme 'His heart was out of joint', where quotation marks are not used (viii. 117); early in the next canto, one stanza begins 'You are "the best of cutthroats". Do not start; / The phrase is Shakespeare's and not misapplied',[23] and the next, 'I am no flatterer. You've supped full of flattery' (ix. 4, 5)—'supped full of' does not have the quotation marks it is usually given in the letters.

On another occasion in canto eight, an embedded allusion to *Hamlet*, 'We shall not see his likeness' (viii. 39), is framed by two overt references,

> they came
> Unto his call, unlike 'the spirits from
> The vasty deep', to whom you may exclaim,
> Says Hotspur, long ere they will leave their home

(38)

and 'Unto that rather somewhat misty bourn, / Which Hamlet tells us is a pass of dread' (41). The negative comparison, *unlike*, and the shift of tone effected by 'rather somewhat' ensure that Byron retains his independence from Shakespeare. 'Unlike' proclaims difference, in contrast to the usual Romantic striving for similarity with Shakespeare; the Byron of *Don Juan* sometimes prefigures J. Alfred Prufrock's relationship with the plays—'No! I am not Prince Hamlet, nor was meant to be'.

'Not' functions in the same way as 'unlike'. While Shelley frequently invokes Ariel-like spirits, Byron will say 'For ever and anon comes indigestion / (Not the most "dainty Ariel")' (xi. 3). He works hard to avoid the characteristic Romantic allusion to *The Tempest* in contexts of dream or human transience. With reference to dreams of former woes he first writes 'And leave like opening Hell upon the Mind / No "baseless fabric" but "a wreck behind" ', then changes the couplet to 'Unwelcome visions of our former years, / Till the eye, cheated, open thick with tears' (*DJ* ii. 134; MS variant, p. 599). The revision may have been subconsciously suggested by Caliban waking and crying to dream again, but all traces of the overt allusion are removed.

Certain revisions reveal Byron modifying the Bardolatry that, despite his claims to the contrary, came to him naturally. The sanity of *Don Juan* is marked by the way that extreme passion is always qualified. After four stanzas concerning Gulbayez's rage when Juan says he cannot love her, Byron produces a typical 'and yet': 'And yet she did not want to pluck the moon, / Like natural Shakespeare on the faultless page'. He revised this to make the quotation from Hotspur's 'To pluck bright honour from the pale-fac'd moon' (*1H4* i. iii. 202) slightly less direct, and to shift the emphasis from author to character. Shakespeare's name is removed, as are 'natural' and 'faultless': 'And yet she did not want to reach the moon, / Like moderate Hotspur on the immortal page' (v. 136; MS variant, p. 644). Byron has not only remembered his quasi-eighteenth-century public pose of thinking that Shakespeare is not faultless; since 'moderate' is about the most ironic epithet that one could apply to Hotspur, there is also an implicit questioning of the other adjective in the line, the cliché that Shakespeare's works are 'immortal'. All this thinking about Shakespeare leads him to make another revision at the end of the stanza: in accordance with the stormy nature of Gulbayez's passion, 'She only wished to sink— burn—and destroy' is changed to 'Her wish was but to "kill, kill, kill"', like Lear's'. The effect is that Shakespeare remains the yardstick of passion while clichés about his perfection are subverted.

It is not Shakespeare himself so much as the excesses of early nineteenth-century Bardolatry that Byron wishes to attack. During the first canto devoted to the siege of Ismail, Byron questions the morality of war; he adopts the manner of Falstaff, wondering 'if a man's name in a *bulletin* / May make up for a *bullet in* his body?' (vii. 21). 'I hope this little question is no sin', he asks,

> Because, though I am but a simple noddy,
>   I think one Shakespeare puts the same thought in
> The mouth of some one in his plays so doting,
> Which many people pass for wits by quoting.
>
> (vii. 21)

Shakespeare is invoked as authority while the narrator pretends he does not know that Shakespeare is an authority ('one Shakespeare' implies 'whoever he may be'); he calls the plays 'doting' in the very act of citing them as an exemplary critique of warfare.

Real scorn is reserved for those who make social capital out of quoting Shakespeare. ' "To be or not to be! That is the question," / Says Shakespeare, who just now is much in fashion' (ix. 14). Byron himself does not so much quote as question the famous question:

> 'To be or not to be?' Ere I decide,
>   I should be glad to know that which is being.
> 'Tis true we speculate both far and wide
>   And deem because we see, we are all-seeing.
> For my part, I'll enlist on neither side
>   Until I see both sides for once agreeing.
> For me, I sometimes think that life is death,
> Rather than life a mere affair of breath.
>
> (ix. 16)

Ironically, Byron's ironic handling of Hamlet's question makes him most like Shakespeare: his refusal to enlist on either side is a symptom of negative capability (the sceptical questionings early in canto fourteen also use the language of Hamlet's soliloquy).

Don Juan leaves us with an unresolved conflict between Adeline and Aurora for the heart of the hero. The socially adept Adeline 'Was weak enough to deem Pope a great poet / And what was worse was not ashamed to show it' (xvi. 47). But

> Aurora—since we are touching upon taste,
>   Which nowadays is the thermometer
> By whose degrees all characters are classed—
>   Was more Shakespearian, if I do not err.
> The worlds beyond this world's perplexing waste
>   Had more of her existence, for in her
> There was a depth of feeling to embrace
> Thoughts, boundless, deep, but silent too as space.
>
> (xvi. 48)

It is, of course, another woman who actually reaches Juan's bed-chamber—'her gracious, graceful, graceless Grace, / The full grown Hebe of Fitz-Fulke'. But since she is not 'at all poetic' (xvi. 50), she does not enter into this particular contest. Byron does not come down on the side of either Pope or Shakespeare; in canto fifteen Scott is praised as the heir of *both* Shakespeare and Voltaire (xv. 59). One does not have to choose between the witty rhyme 'poet' / 'show it' and the high Romanticism of 'a depth of feeling to embrace / Thoughts, boundless, deep, but silent too as space'. Byron is both the heir of the eighteenth-century satirists and a Romantic Shakespearean who aspires to the ideal and the infinite.

Byron's capacity to embrace the lyric and the satiric is at its most forceful in canto four, when he effects the transition from Haidée's death—where he creates some of his loveliest, saddest images ('No dirge, except the hollow sea's, / Mourns o'er the beauty of the Cyclades': iv. 72)—to the brisk continuation of Juan's odyssey. Each mood has its corresponding Shakespearean allusion. The stanza that begins 'Thus lived, thus died she' ends 'But she sleeps well / By the seashore, whereon she loved to dwell' (iv. 71). The simple mono-syllabic 'she sleeps well' echoes Macbeth's 'Duncan is in his grave; / After life's fitful fever he sleeps well': the echo has the sonority and the emotive force of Wordsworth's 'Matthew is in his grave'.[24] But this delicate Romantic allusion is followed by a vigorously unroman-tic one when Juan is discovered 'Wounded and fettered, "cabined, cribbed, confined" ' (iv. 75). We have seen both Byron and Shelley quoting Macbeth's phrase in metaphysical contexts, using it to image

the quest of the Romantic spirit confined by society and mortality.
Here, however, the context is uncompromisingly physical: Juan is
tied up and stowed below deck, literally confined in a cabin.

The robust use of quotation in *Don Juan* suits Byron's public
persona. His appropriations of Shakespeare are so brazen that they
are not problematic; like Don Juan, 'His manner was perhaps the
more seductive / Because he ne'er seemed anxious to seduce' (xv. 12).
But Byron could be as much of a Romantic as his contemporaries.
That very private last poem, 'On this day I complete my thirty-sixth
year', is marked by the quieter Shakespearean echoes that I have
shown to be distinctive of English Romanticism. Byron's valediction
echoes those of his three favourite Shakespearean tragic heroes. He
moves from Macbeth's 'My way of life / Is fall'n into the sear, the
yellow leaf' (v. iii. 22) to Othello's farewell ('The sword, the banner,
and the field') to the 'soldier's grave' that, like Hamlet, he will be
given despite the fact that he died before having the chance to prove
himself a soldier. After all the dash of *Don Juan*, Byron finally comes
to rest in Shakespeare:

> My days are in the yellow leaf;
>   The flowers and fruits of love are gone;
> The worm, the canker, and the grief
>   Are mine alone! . . .
>
> Seek out—less often sought than found—
>   A soldier's grave, for thee the best;
> Then look around, and choose thy ground,
>   And take thy rest.[25]

Byron was scathing about the self-indulgence of Keats's poetry; Keats
criticized Byron because he 'cut a figure' and did not deny his self in
order to live through his works, as Shakespeare was supposed to have
done (see *LJ* vii. 217, 225; *KL* ii. 67). But, opposites as they were,
Byron and Keats were the two Romantic poets who, in their last great
works before their premature deaths, succeeded most notably in
establishing untroubled and unselfconscious relationships with
Shakespeare. Byron's easy, playful quotations in *Don Juan* and
Keats's intense, resonant echoes in the odes show that 'the anxiety of
influence' can be overcome. The model of anxiety is based on the
Oedipus complex. But it is only the neurotic who is permanently
locked in Oedipal conflict. Most of us go through a phase of being

suffocated by, even of rejecting, our fathers, but we grow up: we are able to love our fathers and be ourselves. By speaking Shakespeare's words, each in his distinctive manner, Keats and Byron acknowledge their forefather while at the same time finding their own voices.

Furthermore, when faced with his own mortality and the world's hostility or indifference, the survival of literature may reassure the poet. I began this book by quoting a German of the Romantic age on the repressive power of Shakespeare; I shall end by quoting a Frenchman on his inspirational power—for there is a consolation of influence.

Shakespeare! Shakespeare! I feel as if he alone of all men who ever lived can understand me, must have understood us both; he alone could have pitied us, poor unhappy artists, loving yet wounding each other. Shakespeare! You were a man. You, if you still exist, must be a refuge for the wretched. It is you that are our father, our father in heaven, if there is a heaven.

God standing aloof in his infinite unconcern is revolting and absurd. Thou alone for the souls of artists art the living and loving God. Receive us, father, into thy bosom, guard us, save us! *De profundis ad te clamo.* What are death and nothingness? Genius is immortal![26]

Notes

Notes to Chapter 1

1. J. P. Eckermann, *Conversations with Goethe*, trans. John Oxenford (1850, repr. 1930), 31, 2 January 1824.
2. *The Burden of the Past and the English Poet* (Cambridge, Mass., 1970, repr. New York, 1972), 3–6.
3. *The Anxiety of Influence: A Theory of Poetry* (New York, 1973, repr. 1975), *A Map of Misreading* (New York, 1975), *Poetry and Repression* (New Haven, 1976).
4. See, for example, Leslie Brisman, *Milton's Poetry of Choice and its Romantic Heirs* (Ithaca, 1973), and *Romantic Origins* (Ithaca, 1978); *Milton and the Line of Vision*, ed. J. A. Wittreich Jr (Madison, 1975), 143–230; and the journal *Milton and the Romantics*.
5. Wittreich's introduction to *The Romantics on Milton: Formal Essays and Critical Asides* (Cleveland, Ohio, 1970), 13.
6. (Cambridge, Mass., 1922).
7. Middleton Murry, *Keats and Shakespeare* (1925); Wilson Knight, *Byron and Shakespeare* (1966).
8. Letter of 21 November 1882, quoted from *Alfred Lord Tennyson: A Memoir by his Son* (2 vols., 1897), i. 258.
9. III. i, *Dramatic Works of Sheridan*, ed. Cecil Page (2 vols., Oxford, 1973), ii. 541.
10. *England and the English*, ed. Standish Meacham (Chicago and London, 1970), 303.
11. Some of the best recent work on relationships between later 'Romantic' poets and their predecessors has shown how allusion may be a benign form of influence: Christopher Ricks, 'Tennyson Inheriting the Earth', in *Studies in Tennyson*, ed. Hallam Tennyson (1981), 66–104; Helen Vendler, 'Stevens and Keats's "To Autumn"', in *Wallace Stevens: A Celebration*, ed. F. Doggett and R. Buttel (Princeton, 1980), 171–95. See also 'Benignant Influence', Ricks's review of John Hollander's *The Figure of Echo*, *Yale Review*, lxxii (1982–3), 439–45. I discuss Hollander's book when considering quotation, allusion, and echo in chapter two.
12. Preface to *Foliage* (1818), in *Leigh Hunt's Literary Criticism*, ed. L. H. and C. W. Houtchens (1956), 129; review of Moore's life of Lord Byron, in Macaulay, *Critical and Historical Essays* (2 vols., 1907, repr. 1951), ii. 621, 629.
13. The best account of theories of the imagination and the rise of Romanticism is still M. H. Abrams, *The Mirror and the Lamp: Romantic Theory and the Critical Tradition* (New York, 1953); James Engell provides a synoptic survey in *The Creative Imagination: Enlightenment to Romanticism* (Cambridge, Mass., 1981).

14. Alison, *Essays on the Nature and Principles of Taste* (Edinburgh, 1790), 108; Dennis, *An Essay upon the Genius and Writings of Shakespeare, CH* ii. 283.

15. *Of Dramatic Poesy* (1668), in *Of Dramatic Poesy and other Critical Essays*, ed. George Watson (2 vols., 1962), i. 67.

16. Rymer's *Short View of Tragedy* was published in 1693; Gildon, *The Laws of Poetry . . . Explain'd and Illustrated* (1721), quoted in W. J. Bate, *From Classic to Romantic* (Cambridge, Mass., 1946), 45.

17. 'Some Account of the Life, etc. of Mr William Shakespeare', *CH* ii. 195.

18. 'The Hero as Poet' (1840), in *Shakespeare Criticism: A Selection 1623–1840*, ed. D. Nichol Smith (1916, repr. 1973), 368.

19. 'On Poesy or Art', in *BL* ed. J. Shawcross (2 vols., 1907), ii. 257.

20. Starting-points for the study of Shakespeare in Germany might be L. M. Price, *English Literature in Germany* (Berkeley and Los Angeles, 1953), Paul van Tieghem, *La Découverte de Shakespeare sur le Continent*, vol. iii of his *Le Préromantisme* (Paris, 1947), and the anthology of selections ed. by O. Le Winter, *Shakespeare in Europe* (Harmondsworth, 1970).

21. *A Course of Lectures on Dramatic Art and Literature*, trans. John Black (1815, rev. edn. 1846), 396.

22. *Letters on Chivalry and Romance*, in 3rd edn. of Hurd's *Moral and Political Dialogues* (3 vols., 1765), iii. 303–6.

23. (Chapel Hill, 1931).

24. For parallel passages, see A. A. Helmholtz, *The Indebtedness of Samuel Taylor Coleridge to August Wilhelm von Schlegel* (Madison, 1907); for the fact that the idea of organic form has a long history before Schlegel, see Thomas McFarland, *Coleridge and the Pantheist Tradition* (Oxford, 1969), 256–61.

25. His most detailed analysis of the structural unity of a Shakespearean play is not in the lectures but in an essay on *Romeo and Juliet* published in 1797; Coleridge might have seen it when he was in Germany, but there is no direct influence (see *SC* i. 6 n.).

26. For further examples of Coleridge's fundamental concern with the inner unity of Shakespeare's plays, see M. M. Badawi, *Coleridge: Critic of Shakespeare* (Cambridge, 1973).

27. See further Brian Vickers, 'The Emergence of Character Criticism, 1774–1800', *ShS* xxxiv (1981), 11–21.

28. Compare *TT*, 12 May 1830, where Shakespeare is described as the 'Spinozistic deity—an omnipresent creativeness', Milton as the 'deity of prescience'; Shakespeare's poetry is 'characterless' and does not reflect 'the individual Shakspeare', but 'John Milton himself is in every line of the Paradise Lost'.

29. Quoted from Sir William Forbes, *An Account of the Life and Writings of James Beattie* (2 vols., Edinburgh, 1806), i. 110–11.

30. *The Friend*, ed. Barbara E. Rooke, Collected Coleridge iv (2 vols., Princeton, 1969), i. 453.

31. In 'The Philosophical Basis of Coleridge's *Hamlet* Criticism', *ELH* vi (1939), 256–70, Roberta Morgan argues that Coleridge's early marginalia concerning Hamlet are as influenced by Hartleian associationism as his later lectures are by Kantean idealism.

32. See Wasserman, *The Subtler Language* (Baltimore, 1959); also E. L. Tuveson, *The Imagination as a Means of Grace: Locke and the Aesthetics of Romanticism* (Berkeley and Los Angeles, 1960), and the opening of E. E. Bostetter, *The Romantic Ventriloquists* (Seattle, 1963).
33. Elijah Fenton, 'An Epistle to Mr Southerne' (1711), *CH* ii. 266.
34. The Old Testament metaphor is anticipated by Dryden, in his poem 'To my Dear Friend Mr Congreve', but he is less anxious than later writers: Congreve is seen as a worthy successor to Shakespeare, 'lineal to the Throne'.
35. See Mackenzie's two essays on Hamlet in *The Mirror* (1780), *CH* vi. 272–80.

Notes to Chapter 2

1. For the influence of Longinus on 'pre-romantic' critical works, see S. H. Monk, *The Sublime* (New York, 1935), and Abrams, *Mirror*, 72–8.
2. *On Sublimity*, ch. 13, in *Ancient Literary Criticism*, ed. D. A. Russell and M. Winterbottom (Oxford, 1972), 475–6.
3. The author of the anonymous *Essay upon Milton's Imitations of the Ancients, in his Paradise Lost* (1741) argued (p. 4) that imitations give the reader double pleasure since comparison may be made with the original, but that greater pleasure still could be derived from imitations of passages that are themselves imitations (thus in parts of *PL* Milton, Virgil, and Homer could be brought into play simultaneously).
4. These are usefully collected in app. 5 of *CPW*.
5. George Watson takes up the question of imitation in *Coleridge the Poet* (1966), chs. 2–3.
6. See John Beer, 'The Languages of "Kubla Khan"', in *Coleridge's Imagination*, ed. Richard Gravil, Lucy Newlyn and Nicholas Roe (Cambridge, 1985).
7. *BL* (1907), ii. 256.
8. *Inquiring Spirit: A New Presentation of Coleridge from his Published and Unpublished Prose Writings*, ed. Kathleen Coburn (2nd edn., Toronto, 1979), 68.
9. De Quincey was the first to write about Coleridge's plagiarisms, in *Tait's Edinburgh Magazine* of September 1834; J. F. Ferrier (*Blackwood's*, March 1840) was the first to introduce the accusing tone that sours so many discussions of the topic down to Norman Fruman's *Coleridge, The Damaged Archangel* (New York, 1971) and detracts from the really interesting issue, the history of plagiarism.
10. Quoted in *Pantheist Tradition*, 30 n., and McFarland, *Originality and Imagination* (Baltimore, 1985), 27: the whole of 'The Originality Paradox', ch. 1 of this book, is relevant to my discussion.
11. See A. B. Howes, *Yorick and the Critics: Sterne's Reputation in England, 1760–1868* (New Haven, 1958), ch. 4.
12. See D. A. Russell, '*De Imitatione*', in *Creative Imitation and Latin Literature*, ed. David West and Tony Woodman (Cambridge, 1979), 1–16.
13. Quoted in E. H. Gombrich, 'The Style *all'antica*: Imitation and Assimilation', in *Norm and Form* (1966), 122–8 (p. 122). Starting-points for the

vast subject of Renaissance theories and practice of imitation are H. O. White, *Plagiarism and Imitation during the English Renaissance* (Cambridge, Mass., 1935) and T. M. Greene, *The Light in Troy: Imitation and Discovery in Renaissance Poetry* (New Haven, 1982).

14. 'Allusion: The Poet as Heir', in *Studies in the Eighteenth Century III*, ed. R. F. Brissenden and J. C. Eade (Canberra, 1976), 209–40.

15. 'Defence of the Epilogue: or an Essay on the Dramatic Poetry of the Last Age', in *Critical Essays,* ed. Watson, i. 169.

16. 'Milton', *Essays*, i. 153.

17. In 1763 Winckelmann praised the Carracci as 'Eclectici', by 1801 Fuseli was attacking the eclectic school in his Royal Academy lectures (*Lectures on Painting*, ed. R. N. Wornum, 1848, 394–8): see R. Wittkower, 'Imitation, Eclecticism, and Genius', in *Aspects of the Eighteenth Century*, ed. Earl Wasserman (1965), 143–61.

18. See Boswell's *Journal of a Tour to the Hebrides with Samuel Johnson*, Thursday 30 September [1773].

19. Young is quoted from *Conjectures*, repr. in *English Critical Essays* (*Sixteenth, Seventeenth and Eighteenth Centuries*), ed. E. D. Jones (1922), 270–311.

20. It is *Jane Shore* that Pope ridicules in *The Art of Sinking in Poetry* (1727), ch. 9: '*Imitation* is of two sorts: the first is when we force to our own purposes the thoughts of others; the second consists in copying the imperfections or blemishes of celebrated authors. I have seen a play professedly writ in the style of Shakespear; wherein the resemblance lay in one single line: *And so good morrow t'ye, good master Lieutenant.*'

21. *Miscellanies* (1755 [1759?]), 12–19, 48–60.

22. 'Shakspeare Sermons', *The Reflector*, i, no. 1, October 1810 (1811), 29–35.

23. *Alexander Pope: The Poetry of Allusion* (Oxford, 1959), p. viii.

24. *Anecdotes of Painting in England*, new edn. by R. N. Wornum (3 vols., 1849), i, p. xvii n.

25. *The Figure of Echo: A Mode of Allusion in Milton and After* (Berkeley, Los Angeles, and London, 1981), 64. As Ricks observes in his review, the title does not appear to cohere with the taxonomy: in one, echo is a mode of allusion; in the other, quotation, allusion, and echo are three modes of allusiveness.

26. See G. T. Tanselle, 'External Fact as an Editorial Problem', *Studies in Bibliography*, xxxii (1979), 1–47 (p. 13).

27. *The Poetics of Quotation in the European Novel* (Princeton, 1968), 8.

28. *The Diary of Joseph Farington*, ed. K. Garlick, A. Macintyre, K. Cave (10 vols. so far, through pagination, New Haven, 1978–), 3112, 27 August 1807.

29. C. P. Moritz, *Travels, Chiefly on Foot, through Several Parts of England, in 1782*, trans. by a Lady (London, 1795), 38.

30. See my articles 'Shakespearean Allusion in English Caricature in the Age of Gillray', *Journal of the Warburg and Courtauld Institutes*, xlix (1986), 'Hal and the Regent', *ShS* xxxviii (1985), 69–75, and '"Parodies of Shakspeare"', *Journal of Popular Culture*, xix (1985–6).

31. 'Hazlitt's Shakespearean Quotations', *Prose Studies*, vii (1984), 26–37.

32. Claes Schaar, 'Vertical Context Systems', in *Style and Text: Studies presented to Nils Erik Enkvist* (Stockholm, 1975), 146–57 (p. 146); J. K. Chandler, 'Romantic Allusiveness', *Critical Inquiry*, viii (1981–2), 461–87 (p. 463). See also Carmela Perri, 'On Alluding', *Poetics*, vii (1978), 289–307.

33. It is in fact principally a study of Shakespeare's image-clusters, especially his metaphors from theatre, masque, tapestry, and painting, that challengingly prefigures much twentieth-century criticism.

34. *A Specimen* . . ., ed. Alan Over and Mary Bell (1967), 5–6.

35. 'Romantic Allusiveness', 476.

36. See Lewis and Short, *A Latin Dictionary* (Oxford, 1879, often rev. and repr.).

37. See further, David Simpson, *Irony and Authority in Romantic Poetry* (1979), 185.

38. Occasionally a Miltonic allusion may work in this way: Wordsworth writes in *The Prelude* of how he 'sought that beauty, which as Milton sings / Hath terror in it' (xiii. 225). But the line is Satan's, not Milton's (*PL* ix. 490–1): the subtlety of the allusion enables Wordsworth, perhaps without consciously realizing what he is doing, to move towards the position of Blake and Shelley that Milton was a true poet and of the devil's party (the party of energy and compelling terror) without knowing it.

39. Peacock, *Memoirs of Shelley and other Essays and Reviews*, ed. Howard Mills (1970), 126.

40. Coleridge speaks of a 'literary aristocracy' in the *Biographia* (i. 140), an idea foreshadowing the 'clerisy' in *Church and State*, but since he is by this time a political conservative, he does not make Hazlitt's distinction between the political and the literary.

41. Roland Barthes, 'From Work to Text', in *Image—Music—Text*, trans. Stephen Heath (1977), 160, translation clarified. See also 'Presupposition and Intertextuality', ch. 5 of Jonathan Culler, *The Pursuit of Signs* (1981).

42. 'Plato', *Representative Men* (1850), *Works*, ed. George Sampson (1904), i. 377.

43. 'Lines on an Autumnal Evening', 74; *Carmen Nuptiale*, 'The Dream', lxx; *Endymion*, iv. 558; 'Ode to the West Wind', 50. See *OED*, 'Skyey'; Johnson's *Dictionary* only records Shakespeare's usage. See Hollander, 89, and John Bayley's review, 'Intimacies of Implication', *TLS* 7 May 1982, 499–500.

44. *HW* iv. 193; v. 48, 206; viii. 233; xvi. 401.

Notes to Chapter 3

1. *Leigh Hunt's Dramatic Criticism*, ed. L. H. and C. W. Houtchens (New York, 1949), 103.

2. The cadence also follows 'O Hamlet, what a falling-off was there' (i. v. 47).

3. *The Poetical Works of William Lisle Bowles*, ed. George Gilfillan (2 vols., Edinburgh, 1855), i. 46.

4. It also has obvious biblical resonances, which are discussed by Leslie
   Brisman in 'Coleridge and the Supernatural', *SIR* xxi (1982), 123–59
   (pp. 140–5).

5. See further, Harold Bloom, 'Coleridge: The Anxiety of Influence', in
   New Perspectives on Coleridge and Wordsworth, ed. Geoffrey Hartman (New
   York, 1972), 247–67, and for Coleridge's epic aspirations, see E. S. Shaf-
   fer, *'Kubla Khan' and The Fall of Jerusalem* (Cambridge, 1975).

6. The best accounts of the aesthetic consequences of the relationship
   between Wordsworth and Coleridge are Thomas McFarland, 'The Sym-
   biosis of Wordsworth and Coleridge', ch. 1 of his *Romanticism and the
   Forms of Ruin* (Princeton, 1981) and Lucy Newlyn, *Coleridge, Wordsworth,
   and the Language of Allusion* (Oxford, 1986).

7. Another was the ability to write successful tragi-comedy: he condemned
   the ludicrous talk of Butler and Gordon, the assassins in *The Death of
   Wallenstein*, as 'a most egregious misimitation of Shakespere' (*CPW* ii.
   599 n.).

8. For metaphors of political action as drama, see Mary Jacobus, ' "That
   Great Stage Where Senators Perform": *Macbeth* and the Politics of
   Romantic Theater', *SIR* xxii (1983), 353–87; this article is also germane
   to my discussion in chapter five, below, of Wordsworth's allusions to
   Macbeth in the 'French Revolution' section of *The Prelude*.

9. *Wat Tyler* is quoted from vol. ii of *The Poetical Works of Robert Southey*
   (10 vols., 1837).

10. In the climactic tent-scene of Cibber's *Richard III*, the ghost of King
    Henry is given some final lines, immediately preceding Richard's 'Give
    me a horse—bind up my wounds!', which do not appear in
    Shakespeare's original: 'Awake, *Richard*, awake, to guilty minds / A
    terrible example!' (Cibber's text, in Bell's edn. of *Richard the Third . . . as
    Performed at the Theatre-Royal, Drury Lane* (1773), v. iv, p. 64). The intro-
    duction of a moralizing tone is typical of Restoration and early
    eighteenth-century rewritings of Shakespeare. In *Wat Tyler*, John Ball's
    head is to be 'exposed upon / The city gates—a terrible example';
    furthermore, earlier in the play Ball has appropriated a better-known line
    from the same context, saying to the wounded Piers 'let me bind up thy
    wounds'.

11. Butler's introduction to his edn. of *'The Ruined Cottage' and 'The Pedlar'*
    (Ithaca and Hassocks, 1979), 3.

12. See further, Alethea Hayter, 'Coleridge, Maturin's *Bertram*, and Drury
    Lane', in *New Approaches to Coleridge*, ed. Donald Sultana (1981), 17–37.

13. The latter is first approached in the invocation 'Come, you spirits . . .',
    beside which Coleridge wrote in one of his editions the crucial phrase
    'shadows of the imagination' (*SC* i. 65).

14. E. A. Shearer and J. I. Lindsay, 'Wordsworth and Coleridge Marginalia
    in a Copy of Richard Payne Knight's *Analytical Inquiry into the Principles of
    Taste'*, *HLQ* i (1937–8), 63–99 (p. 80). The note is in Wordsworth's hand
    but was probably dictated by Coleridge, who was unwell at the time.

15. *Lectures*, 246; see also Kames, *Elements of Criticism* (1762), ch. 23.

16. Schneider, *Coleridge, Opium and 'Kubla Khan'* (Chicago, 1953), 91–105.

17. *Ancient Literary Criticism*, 6, translation clarified.

18. *The Starlit Dome* (1941, repr. 1971), 83.

19. Coleridge certainly saw at least one of Kemble's productions of *Macbeth* (*SC* ii. 230).

20. Shelley attempts to revivify the phrase in 'The Mask of Anarchy' by reversing it to 'pine and peak' (*SPW* 341).

21. James Gillman, *The Life of Samuel Taylor Coleridge* (1838), 301.

22. 'Thou journeyest onward tempest-tossed in thought': 'Lines written at the King's Arms, Ross', *CPW* i. 58.

23. *The Road to Xanadu* (1927, repr. 1978), 78.

24. John Beer reminds me that there is also a biblical resonance in this instance, 'the Sun of righteousness [shall] arise with healing in his wings' (Malachi, 4: 2, cf. 'Risen with healing in his wings' in Charles Wesley's hymn 'Hark! the herald Angels sing'). The next line in 'Dejection' perhaps makes Coleridge's characteristic jump from *Macbeth* to *The Tempest*, from the malign to the benign supernatural: 'And be this Tempest but a Mountain Birth!'.

25. Incidental parallels include the phrase early in the poem 'grey-beard loon', which echoes 'cream-faced loon', a coinage in *Macbeth* that Coleridge praised as a good vulgarism (*SC* i. 135), and the thick consonant sounds of 'Who thicks man's blood with cold' (cf. Lady Macbeth's 'Make thick my blood'); in the following stanza to this, 'The Night-mare Life-in-Death' cries, in the manner of the witches, ' "The game is done! I've won! I've won!" '.

26. The 'milk of Paradise' has many sources; it may possibly be seen as an inversion of Malcolm's 'Pour the sweet milk of concord into hell' (IV. iii. 98: milk is another leitmotif running through the play).

27. The allusion to Milton's Mount Amara in his list of false paradises (*PL* iv. 268–85) is crucial here. For the question of Milton's and Coleridge's true and false paradises, see my article ' "Kubla Khan" and "At a Solemn Music" ', *ELN* xxiv (1986–7). The best account of Miltonic echoes in 'Kubla Khan' is Schneider's in *Opium and 'Kubla Khan'*, especially 264–7.

28. *Seven Types of Ambiguity* (3rd edn., 1953), 19.

29. Noted by M. L. D'Avanzo in 'Coleridge's "This Lime-tree Bower my Prison" and *The Tempest*', *Wordsworth Circle*, i (1970), 66–8.

30. The *Morning Post* version is an awkward compromise: 'William' is removed, but 'Otway' is not yet introduced—instead there is the fictional 'Edmund', who would mean nothing to readers.

31. I am convinced by David Erdman's arguments for Coleridge's, not Wordsworth's, authorship of this poem: see S. M. Parrish and D. V. Erdman, 'Who Wrote *The Mad Monk*? A Debate', *BNYPL* lxiv (1960), 209–39.

32. In the original version of 'The Mad Monk' published in *The Morning Post* during October 1800, the leap is to Shakespeare's other magical play: the poem ends with four subsequently deleted lines in the manner of *A Midsummer Night's Dream*, 'The twilight fays came forth in dewy shoon . . .' (*CPW* i. 349 t.a.).

33. There is another movement from Prospero to Hamlet in Wordsworth's
ode: its final stanza begins with a Prospero-like invocation, 'And oh ye
Fountains, Meadows, Hills, and Groves', then turns inward to 'my heart
of hearts', a Hamlet-phrase (III. ii. 73; 'of heart' in early editions, but 'of
hearts' in the 1796 edn. owned by Wordsworth).

Notes to Chapter 4

1. Hunt, *Lord Byron and Some of his Contemporaries* (1828), 260.
2. Recorded in Carlyle's *Reminiscences*, ed. C. E. Norton (2 vols., 1887), ii.
302.
3. See, for example, *HW* iv. 113, vii. 144, ix. 5; the phrase is also picked up
by Leigh Hunt, *Literary Criticism*, 392.
4. *HW* xvii. 118, from *Mac* I. v. 62.
5. *The Prose Works of William Wordsworth*, ed. A. B. Grosart (3 vols., 1876),
iii. 488. Cited hereafter as Grosart.
6. R. P. Graves, 'Recollections of Wordsworth and the Lake Country', in
The Afternoon Lectures on Literature and Art (Dublin and London, 1869),
277–321 (p. 297).
7. Graves, 'Wordsworth and Shakspere', *The Academy*, xl (1891), 116.
8. Field's *Memoirs of Wordsworth*, ed. Geoffrey Little, Australian Academy of
the Humanities Monograph iii (Sydney, 1975), 36 n. (additional punctuation mine). Cited hereafter as Field.
9. Christopher Wordsworth, *Memoirs of William Wordsworth* (2 vols., 1851),
i. 34.
10. Bysshe and Knox are listed in C. L. and A. C. Shaver, *Wordsworth's
Library: A Catalogue* (New York and London, 1979), 44, 147. Enfield is
not, but Dorothy wrote of her brother on 15 April 1802, 'He brought out
a volume of Enfield's Speaker', *Journals of Dorothy Wordsworth*, 2nd edn.,
ed. Mary Moorman (1971), 110. Cited hereafter as *Journals*.
11. *Wordsworth's Library*, 232–3, 304.
12. During these years she read *MND, Tim, Mac, John, R2, AYL,* and *Wint:
Journals*, 17, 19, 20, 21, 23, 140, 146.
13. *EY* 196; Mark Reed, *Wordsworth: The Chronology of the Middle Years
1800–1815* (Cambridge, Mass., 1975), 495, 602, 604.
14. See, for example, *Journals*, 59, 65, 67, 74, 84, 102, 127, 137, 163. For
Wordsworth's reading of sixteenth- and seventeenth-century lyric poets
at this time, see J. R. Curtis, 'William Wordsworth and English Poetry
of the Sixteenth and Seventeenth Centuries', *Cornell Library Journal*, i
(1966), 28–39.
15. Shearer and Lindsay, 74.
16. Park, *A Greenockian's Visit to Wordsworth* [in 1842] (Greenock, 1887), 10;
de Vere, Grosart, iii. 488.
17. *WPr* i. 123; Jonson, prologue to *Every Man in his Humour*.
18. Coleridge, *Marginalia*, vol. i, ed. George Whalley, Collected Coleridge xii
(Princeton, 1980), 41.

Notes to Chapter 5

1. R. D. Havens adduces numerous piddling phrases (*Influence of Milton*, 177–200); Harold Bloom proposes Oedipal obligations (*Poetry and Repression*, 59–82).
2. See further, W. J. B. Owen, '*The Borderers* and the Aesthetics of Drama', *Wordsworth Circle*, vi (1975), 227–39.
3. Quotations from preface to *The Borderers*, in *WPr* i. 76–80.
4. In the later, published version renamed Oswald, perhaps with a glance at 'the only character of utter unredeemable *baseness* in Shakespeare' (*SC* i. 55).
5. See Robert Osborn, 'Meaningful Obscurity: The Antecedents and Character of Rivers', in *Bicentenary Wordsworth Studies*, ed. Jonathan Wordsworth (Ithaca, 1970), 393–424, and P. L. Thorslev, 'Wordsworth's *Borderers* and the Romantic Villain-Hero', *SIR* v (1966), 84–103.
6. C. J. Smith, 'The Effect of Shakespeare's Influence on Wordsworth's "The Borderers"', *SP* 1 (1953), 625–39 (p. 631).
7. John Jones considers the relationship between *The Borderers* and *Lear* in *The Egotistical Sublime* (1954), 57–61.
8. *Borderers*, i. iii. 161, 1797 MS version (1799 fair copy), ed. Robert Osborn, Cornell Wordsworth (Ithaca and London, 1982); unless otherwise stated, quotations are from this version; *Oth* iii. iii. 90.
9. *Wordsworth's Poetry 1787–1814* (New Haven and London, 1964), 125.
10. MS B, 290–5; MS D, 231–6: '*The Ruined Cottage' and 'The Pedlar'*, ed. Butler (Cornell Wordsworth), 58.
11. The decisive role of *Othello* in Wordsworth's thinking about tragedy is confirmed by some lines belonging to the Solitary in *The Excursion*. He links the 'tragic Muse' to Othello's valediction; the connection is made through an echo of the latter's farewell to the 'pomp, and circumstance of glorious war' (iii. iii. 354):

> give the pomp
> Of circumstance; and here the tragic Muse
> Shall find apt subjects for the highest art
>
> (vi. 550).

12. MS B, 953, *Home at Grasmere*, ed. Beth Darlington, Cornell Wordsworth (Ithaca and Hassocks, 1977), 98.
13. MS B, 959 ff. [variant in MS D], Cornell, 100–1. There is a more telling evocation of 'Farewell the tranquil mind! . . .' (*Oth* iii. iii. 348–57) in the 'Elegiac Stanzas' on Beaumont's picture of Peele Castle, 53 (*WPW* iv. 260); John Beer has suggested that 'Farewell . . . The royal banner' may lie behind the banner that is so central to *The White Doe of Rylstone* (*Wordsworth and the Human Heart* [1978], 177). *The White Doe* is, like 'Ruth', a poem that uses Shakespearean phraseology to establish an 'Elizabethan' atmosphere: 'which had a dying fall'; 'we sang of the green-wood shade'; 'Under the greenwood tree' (*Doe*, 400, 338, *WPW* iii. 293–5; 'Ruth', 216, *WPW* ii. 234).

14. To his brother Thomas, 6 June 1802, *The Correspondence of Henry Crabb Robinson with the Wordsworth Circle*, ed. Edith J. Morley (2 vols., Oxford, 1927), i. 43.

15. 'Salisbury Plain', st. 43, 1, *The Salisbury Plain Poems*, ed. Stephen Gill, Cornell Wordsworth (Ithaca and Hassocks, 1975), 33, 19. Wordsworth first visited Tintern Abbey in 1793 after crossing Salisbury Plain; the connection between the two poems was pointed out to me by Nick Roe. There may be an intermediate echo in 'houseless', of a *Lear*-influenced couplet in Goldsmith's 'The Traveller, or A Prospect of Society': 'Or onward, where the rude Carinthian boor / Against the houseless stranger shuts the door' (3–4). The mad woman at the beginning of *A Lover's Complaint* may also lie behind Wordsworth's distracted vagrant.

16. *MerV* v. i. 9; for Wordsworth's special admiration of this scene, see *LY* ii. 482–3, and of *MerV*'s language generally, Grosart, iii. 430. Note that in 'The Idiot Boy' there seems to be another collocation of the *MerV* bough and a phrase from *Mac*: 'And with a *hurly-burly* now / He shakes the green bough in his hand' (*WPW* ii. 69, WW's italics in editions from 1827 onwards). Christopher Ricks discusses the echo of 'Duncan is in his grave' in an unpublished lecture on Wordsworth and allusion.

17. See, for example, *HW* xi. 183, xvii. 342; but by 1838 the phrase had, according to De Quincey, 'pass[ed] into the currency of the language' (*DQW* iv. 32 n.).

18. MS 3, 680, *Benjamin the Waggoner*, ed. Paul Betz, Cornell Wordsworth (Ithaca and Hassocks, 1981), 305.

19. *Arshile Gorky* (New York, 1962), 55–6, quoted Hollander, 72 n., my italics.

20. See 'Diction and Defense in Wordsworth', in *The Literary Freud: Mechanisms of Defense and the Poetic Will*, ed. J. H. Smith, *Psychiatry and the Humanities*, iv (New Haven and London, 1980), 205–15.

21. *The Letters of Mary Wordsworth 1800–1855*, ed. Mary E. Burton (Oxford, 1958), 221.

22. *Chronology of the Middle Years*, 27.

23. iv. 270: might we say with the ghost, 'O Hamlet, what a falling-off was there'?

24. *Salisbury Plain Poems*, 28 n.; as in the Windy Brow passage, the context is death.

25. The apocalyptic climax of this episode is one of Wordsworth's weightiest Miltonic allusions: 'The types and symbols of eternity, / Of first, and last, and midst, and without end'; 'Him first, him last, him midst, and without end' (*Prel.* vi. 571; *PL* v. 165).

26. The earlier Wordsworth seems to have been tempted to set up easy parallels between his Lakeland world and that of *A YL*: the original beginning of 'Nutting' had two marked quotations from the play in its first seven lines—but the whole opening passage was rejected (see *WPW* ii. 505).

27. A number of other phrases in *Prel.* are marked by the influence of the *Macbeth* murder-scenes: 'innocent sleep' (vi. 579), 'Prate somewhat loudly of the whereabout' (vii. 461), and perhaps even the footsteps in the

woodcock-snaring episode (i. 328–32; cf. the 'steps' at *Mac* ii. i. 57, and the recurring notion of *doing the deed*).

28. *Caleb Williams*, ed. David McCracken (Oxford, 1970, repr. 1977), 138—see *William Wordsworth: The Borders of Vision* (Oxford, 1982), 254.
29. *The Character of the Poet: Wordsworth in 'The Prelude'* (Princeton, 1971), 337.
30. Does the recollection of the *Moor* of Venice lead by sub-conscious association to Wordsworth's 'Quarry or *moor*' (i.e. moorland)?
31. For a similar reading, see J. Wordsworth, *Borders of Vision*, 63–4; David Ellis also draws parallels between Hamlet's meeting with the ghost and Wordsworth's with the admonitory discharged soldier—*Wordsworth, Freud and the spots of time* (Cambridge, 1985), 54–5.

Notes to Chapter 6

1. See, for example, Nathanael Culverwell, *An Elegant and Learned Discourse of the Light of Nature*, ed. William Dillingham (1652), 122, and the discussion in C. A. Patrides's introduction to his edition of *The Cambridge Platonists* (1969, repr. Cambridge, 1980), 11 ff. Blake would certainly have been aware of the occurrence of the image in the first chapter of Locke's *Essay concerning Human Understanding*.
2. Blake's knowledge of Dante at this time was indirect and probably restricted to the Ugolino episode: see John Beer, 'Influence and Independence in Blake', in *Interpreting Blake*, ed. Michael Phillips (Cambridge, 1978), 196–261 (pp. 204–11).
3. 'John Milton' in *Lives of the Poets* (1779–81, repr. 2 vols., 1906), i. 132; Blair, *Lectures on Rhetoric and Belles Lettres* (1783), *CH* vi. 331.
4. *Jerusalem*, 4: 1, K 622; quotations from Blake's longer poems are followed by plate and line number as well as page number in K.
5. There are many Shakespearean scenes among Fuseli's paintings and drawings, a few among Flaxman's; the climax of Hayley's most successful poem, *The Triumphs of Temper* (published in 1781, it went through fourteen editions by 1809; Blake owned copies of two of them), turns on a fancy dress ball where Serena, the heroine, is dressed as Ariel, her father Sir Gilbert as Caliban, and her aunt Penelope as Sycorax.
6. John Beer's 'Blake's Interpretation of Shakespeare: A Reconstruction', app. 1 of his *Blake's Visionary Universe* (Manchester, 1969), is an attempt to read Shakespeare through Blakean eyes. I know of no detailed account of Shakespeare's influence on Blake's poetry, but there are passing references in David Erdman, *Blake: Prophet against Empire* (3rd edn., Princeton, 1977), R. F. Gleckner, *Blake's Prelude: 'Poetical Sketches'* (Baltimore, 1982), F. R. Leavis, 'Justifying one's Valuation of Blake', in *William Blake: Essays in Honour of Sir Geoffrey Keynes*, eds. M. D. Paley and Michael Phillips (Oxford, 1973), 66–85, A. K. Mellor, *Blake's Human Form Divine* (Berkeley, 1974), and Kathleen Raine, *Blake and Tradition* (2 vols., Princeton, 1968). This is scant coverage indeed when compared with the wealth of essays on Blake and Milton, many of which are cited in J. A. Wittreich Jr's full length study, *Angel of Apocalypse: Blake's Idea of Milton* (Madison, 1975).

7. G. E. Bentley Jr, *Blake Records* (Oxford, 1969), 322. Hereafter *Records*.
8. *The Blake–Varley Sketchbook of 1819*, ed. Martin Butlin (2 vols., 1969), i. 32.
9. Gilchrist, *Life of William Blake*, ed. Ruthven Todd (1942), 22; K 3; *MND* V. i. 371.
10. Job 38: 31; *PL* vii. 375; see in particular *Jerusalem*, 60: 60 (K 693).
11. There are, however, occasions on which Blake merely lists Shakespeare and Milton together as poets of genius. 'Even Milton and Shakespeare could not publish their own works' (K 207); 'Milton, Shakspeare, Michael Angelo, Rafael . . . are the extent of the human mind' (K 579)—the context here is a discussion of inspiration. The comparison of Shakespeare to Michelangelo, Milton to Raphael was a favourite of Fuseli's; in his public address, Blake links 'Fuseli and Michael Angelo, Shakespeare and Milton' shortly after protesting 'While the Works of Pope and Dryden are look'd upon as the same Art with those of Milton and Shakespeare . . . there can be no Art in a Nation but such as is Subservient to the interest of the Monopolizing Trader' (K 595). A further example of indiscriminate listing of Shakespeare with other greats is 'Homer or Shakespear or Dante' in an annotation to Boyd's translation of the *Inferno* (K 411).
12. A useful summary is provided by W. M. Merchant's essay, 'Blake's Shakespeare', *Apollo*, lxxix (1964), 318–25, repr. in *The Visionary Hand: Essays for the Study of William Blake's Art and Aesthetics*, ed. R. N. Essick (Los Angeles, 1973), 233–52.
13. Martin Butlin, *The Paintings and Drawings of William Blake*, (2 vols., New Haven, 1981), Nos. 316–19, 154, 161, 245, 246, 250, 547.5, 247, 547.3, 548, 549. Four of the six designs contributed by Blake to an extra-illustrated Second Folio belonging to Revd. Joseph Thomas involve the supernatural: as well as the visions of Hamlet and Queen Katharine, he drew *Richard III and the Ghosts* and *Brutus and Caesar's Ghost* (547.2–5).
14. See M. W. England, 'Apprenticeship at the Haymarket?', in *Blake's Visionary Forms Dramatic*, ed. D. V. Erdman and J. E. Grant (Princeton, 1970), 3–29.
15. 'The First Epistle of the Second Book of Horace Imitated', 102, in *The Poems of Alexander Pope,* ed. John Butt (1963), 639.
16. John Beer's point: *Visionary Universe*, 313.
17. *Shakespeare's Festive Comedy* (Princeton, 1959, repr. 1972), 142.
18. *The Notebook of William Blake: A Photographic and Typographic Facsimile*, ed. David Erdman (Oxford, 1973), N21. Cited hereafter as *Notebook*.
19. Pl.1, most conveniently reproduced in *The Illuminated Blake*, ed. David Erdman (New York, 1974), 159.

Notes to Chapter 7

1. See M. R. Lowery, *Windows of the Morning: A Critical Study of William Blake's 'Poetical Sketches', 1783* (New Haven, 1940), 108–31.
2. See Kathleen Raine, 'Some sources of *Tiriel*', *HLQ* xxi (1957–8), 1–36, and *Blake and Tradition*, i. 36–49.

3. The most celebrated couplet in the poem, 'A Robin Red breast in a Cage / Puts all Heaven in a Rage', has many analogues; Lear's 'We two alone will sing like birds i' th' cage' is one of them.

4. 'The Name and Nature of Poetry', *Selected Prose*, ed. John Carter (Cambridge, 1961), 189.

5. *The Renaissance: Studies in Art and Poetry* (1873, repr. 1912), 143.

6. See *Blake and Tradition*, i. 199–201 and E. H. Meyerstein on the influence of Matthew Prior, ' "*A True Maid*" and "The Sick Rose" ', *TLS* 22 June 1946, 295.

7. *Interpreting Blake*, 5–31.

8. Heather Glen writes well about this effect in *Vision and Disenchantment: Blake's 'Songs' and Wordsworth's 'Lyrical Ballads'* (Cambridge, 1983), 218–19.

9. Blake experimented with different orders of poems in different copies of *Songs*, but this pairing occurs in nine of the twenty-four copies for which we know his arrangement: see *Illuminated Blake*, 96–7.

10. See G. E. Bentley Jr, *Blake Books*, (Oxford, 1977), 159 and n.

11. Blake illustrated moments from the night scenes in *Macbeth* (Butlin, Nos. 248–9).

12. *Visionary Universe*, 291. Beer also makes an interesting comparison between *Jerusalem* and *Antony and Cleopatra*: Blake's Ancient Man 'contain'd in his mighty limbs all things in Heaven and Earth' (pl. 27, K 649), as Cleopatra dreams of an Antony whose 'face was as the heav'ns. . . . His legs bestrid the ocean . . .' (*Ant* v. ii. 76–100). Cleopatra's vision is another fine example of the superiority of the imagined over the physical ('Nature wants stuff / To vie strange forms with fancy').

13. *Cordelia and the Sleeping Lear* (Butlin, No. 84.4) was among Blake's seven Shakespearean miniatures of about 1780; he also illustrated *Lear and Cordelia in Prison* (Butlin, No. 53), a scene closely related to *Lr* iv. vii but actually derived from either Milton's *History of Britain* or Nahum Tate's version of the play—might he have seen the latter on stage? In a letter to Hayley dated 4 May 1804, Blake praised as 'an incomparable production' Romney's 'picture of *Lear and Cordelia*, when he awakes and knows her' (K 843).

14. Blunt, *The Art of William Blake* (1959), 19 n.

15. Some instances from the fourth chapter: Jerusalem's terrible image of the fate of her children, 'dash'd / Upon Egypt's iron floors' (79: 1, K 719) echoes Lady Macbeth at i. vii. 58; 'weep upon the wind' (79: 72, K 721) goes back to the *Pity* lines; the illustration (pl. 84) of London, old and blind, led by his child has affinities with Gloucester in *Lr* as well as Tiriel, Oedipus, and Milton's Samson; Albion sleeps surrounded by the violent elements we associate with Lear, 'Howling winds cover him: roaring seas dash furious against him: / In the deep darkness broad lightnings glare, long thunders roll' (94: 3, K 741—though this is also the stuff of the conventional eighteenth-century sublime); 'The Poet's Song draws to its period' (92: 8, K 739) uses the word 'period' with rich, Shakespearean ambiguity, as at *Ant* iv. xiv. 107.

16. I owe this observation to Mellor, *Human Form Divine*, 277.

Notes to Chapter 8

1. Though Monckton Milnes records another anecdote about Keats's intense response to Shakespeare as a boy: he is said to have told his schoolfellows that no one would dare read *Macbeth* alone in a house at two o'clock in the morning. *Life, Letters, and Literary Remains of John Keats* (2 vols., 1848), i. 8.

2. Most of the key remarks about Shakespeare in the letters are noted in Douglas Bush's concise essay 'Keats and Shakespeare', in *Shakespeare: Aspects of Influence*, ed. G. Blakemore Evans, Harvard English Studies vii (Cambridge, Mass., 1976), 71–89. The casual use of Shakespearean phrases in the letters is discussed by Bhabatosh Chatterjee in *John Keats: His Mind and Work* (Bombay, Calcutta, Madras, and New Delhi, 1971), ch. 3.

3. For Keats's markings in this edition, see *KS*.

4. *Diary*, ed. W. B. Pope (5 vols., Cambridge, Mass., 1960–3), i. 3; v. 553. The curious misquotation provides the impulse for the final lines of A. E. Ellis's novel *The Rack* (1958, repr. Harmondsworth, 1979):

   Something was grotesquely wrong. He opened his Shakespeare.
   '. . . O, let him pass! He hates him
   That would upon the rack of this tough world
   Stretch him out longer.'
   'The rack', he murmured. 'Haydon forgot the rack.' And his mind still exercised by the strangeness of the omission, he stared across at the half-open window. (p. 356)

5. See Haydon's full account of the evening in his *Diary*, ii. 80–7.

6. *Ant* III. xiii. 43–6; *HW* xv. 209, xi. 247; *KL* i. 144.

7. *All's W* IV. iii. 71; *KL* i. 169; *HW* iv. 158, 225, vi. 92, viii. 263, xi. 167, xx. 37, 349.

8. The best brief general account of the relationship between the two writers is Kenneth Muir, 'Keats and Hazlitt', in *John Keats: A Reassessment*, ed. Muir (Liverpool, 1969), 139–58. See also David Bromwich, *Hazlitt: The Mind of a Critic* (New York and Oxford, 1983), ch. 11.

9. There was a copy of this volume in Keats's library at his death (*KC* i. 254); in April 1818, he spoke of asking Hazlitt 'the best metaphysical road I can take' (*KL* i. 274).

10. I adapt these questions from 'Longinus', ch. 14, *Ancient Literary Criticism*, 476.

11. *John Keats* (Cambridge, Mass., 1963, repr. 1967), 244. Jackson Bate has many valuable insights concerning the influence of Hazlitt on Keats.

12. See also Hazlitt's *Table Talk* essay 'Whether Actors ought to sit in Boxes?': they should not, because then we would see them as themselves and not their characters (*HW* viii. 272–9).

13. By Richard Flecknoe in his *Short Discourse of the English Stage* (1664), repr. in E. K. Chambers, *The Elizabethan Stage* (4 vols., Oxford, 1923), iv. 370.

14. I shall develop this whole question in the sequel to this book.

15. Bernice Slote gathers what information there is about Keats's theatre-going in *Keats and the Dramatic Principle* (Lincoln, Nebraska, 1958).
16. See John Genest, *Some Account of the English Stage* (10 vols., Bath, 1832), viii. 589–90.
17. Keats's review, headed 'Mr Kean', is quoted from *The Champion*, 21 December 1817, p. 405. It is conveniently reprinted as app. 5 of *John Keats: The Complete Poems*, ed. John Barnard (Harmondsworth, 1973).
18. *HW* v. 9; see Miriam Allott's footnote in *The Poems of John Keats* (1970), 645.
19. Keats's annotation to Hazlitt's *Characters of Shakespear's Plays* (1817), 157, now in Houghton Library, Harvard University.
20. Keats's Facsimile Folio Shakespeare, p. 285, now at Keats House, Hampstead; repr. in *KS* 50.
21. 'I cannot help seeing Haslitt like Ferdinand—in an odd angle of the Isle sitting—his arms in this sad knot': Keats's copy of *Characters*, 125. Keats was fascinated by the ways in which people sat: 'it would be a great delight . . . to know in what position Shakspeare sat when he began "To be or not to be"' (*KL* ii. 73).
22. For fuller discussion of what Keats meant by the 'snail-horn perception of Beauty', see John Jones, *John Keats's Dream of Truth* (1969), 113–15.
23. 'I hear Hazlitt's Lectures regularly', he wrote on 21 February 1818 (*KL* i. 237); since on 20 January he had missed the second lecture of the course, on Chaucer and Spenser (i. 214), one may assume that he was assiduous in his attendance at subsequent ones, beginning with 'On Shakspeare and Milton' the following week.
24. Hogarth possibly because 'On Hogarth's Marriage A-la-Mode' is next to 'On Posthumous Fame,—Whether Shakspeare was influenced by a Love of it?' in Hazlitt's *Round Table*. In 1811 Lamb had made an extended comparison between Hogarth and Shakespeare in his *Reflector* essay 'On the Genius and Character of Hogarth'—see my essay 'Lamb on Shakespeare', *Charles Lamb Bulletin*, July 1985, 76–85 (pp. 82–3).

Notes to Chapter 9

1. S. M. Sperry, 'Richard Woodhouse's Interleaved and Annotated Copy of Keats's *Poems* (1817)', *Literary Monographs*, i, ed. E. Rothstein and T. K. Dunseath (Madison, 1967), 101–64 (p. 145). Woodhouse found 'more promise of excellence' in *Endymion* than in Shakespeare's *Venus and Adonis* (*KC* i. 54).
2. For Keats and *Oberon*, see W. W. Beyer, *Keats and the Daemon King* (New York, 1947).
3. *European Magazine*, lxx (1816), 365.
4. *Ad Lucilium Epistulae Morales*, letter lxxxiv, Loeb edn. (3 vols., 1917–25), ii. 276–9.
5. Quoted by Joan Grundy, 'Keats and the Elizabethans', in *Keats: A Reassessment*, 1–19 (p. 1).
6. 'L'Allegro', 95, 65, quoted in Rollins's note to *KL*.

7. Though D. G. James thinks that it comes from *Tp* I. ii. 302, 'invisible / To every eyeball else': 'Keats and *King Lear*', *ShS* xiii (1960), 58–68 (p. 61).

8. *Essays and Introductions* (1961), 97.

9. See W. J. Bate, *The Stylistic Development of Keats* (New York, 1945) and L. J. Zillman, *John Keats and the Sonnet Tradition* (Los Angeles, 1939).

10. *Endymion*, i. 100, i. 569, i. 215, i. 394, i. 639, i. 788, i. 748, ii. 662. Compare 'With sweet musk-roses and with eglantine', 'spangled starlight sheen' (*MND* II. i. 252, 29), 'midnight-mushrooms', 'The fringed curtains of thine eye advance', 'Full fathom five thy father lies, / Of his bones are coral made', 'The ditty does remember my drown'd father', 'we are such stuff / As dreams are made of', 'deeper than did ever plummet sound' (*Tp* V. i. 39, I. ii. 409, 397, 406, IV. i. 156, V. i. 56). Text quoted from Keats's seven volume edition; all examples underlined by Keats. For further parallels, see *KS* 56–65.

11. In November 1817 Keats asked the Dilkes (*KL* i. 183) to send him a copy of Coleridge's *Sibylline Leaves*, which had been published that July as one of three volumes, the other two being *Biographia Literaria*. If he read any of the *Biographia* as well as the poems in *Sibylline Leaves*, it would surely have been chapter fifteen, on Shakespeare and poetic power. Hazlitt knew *BL* well, having reviewed it for the *Edinburgh* (*HW* xvi. 115–38).

12. Most of these and other parallels are listed in B. T. Boyar's useful article, 'Keats's "Isabella": Shakespeare's *Venus and Adonis* and the Venus-Adonis Myth', *Keats–Shelley Journal*, xxi–xxii (1972–3), 160–9.

13. I think that Keats would have thought of 'The silver, snarling trumpets 'gan to chide' (31) as one of his most successful Spenserian lines; he had associated Spenser with 'A silver trumpet' in the early 'Ode to Apollo'.

14. Miriam Allott lists many verbal echoes in her footnotes to 'St Agnes' in *Poems* (1970).

15. For the name of Juliet's nurse, see my note 'A Herb by Any Other Name: *Romeo and Juliet*, IV. iv. 5–6', *SQ* xxxiii (1982), 336.

16. C. L. Finney lists many parallels of idea and plot: *The Evolution of Keats's Poetry*, (2 vols., Cambridge, Mass., 1936), ii. 655–67; borrowings of phraseology are listed in Allott's footnotes.

17. Which Keats did *not* underline in his Folio Shakespeare: there is no simple correspondence between his annotations and his appropriations of Shakespeare. The markings sometimes offer valuable supporting evidence but cannot be made the basis of an argument about allusion.

18. *Woe and Wonder: The Emotional Effect of Shakespearian Tragedy* (Denver, 1951, repr. Chicago, 1964), 12. I would question the implication that Edgar—here or anywhere else in the play—is acting as a spokesman for Shakespeare (Keats and Hazlitt, so concerned with Shakespeare's impersonality, might have done so too).

19. *Selected Essays* (1932, 2nd edn., repr. 1946), 14, 15.

20. For Keats and the apostrophes of eighteenth-century odes, see Geoffrey Hartman, 'Poem and Ideology: A Study of Keats's "To Autumn"', in his *The Fate of Reading* (Chicago, 1975), 124–46.

21. See further, *Stylistic Development*, 130–2.

22. Gillian Beer develops a contrast of this sort in 'Aesthetic Debate in Keats's Odes', *MLR* lxiv (1969), 742–8.

23. 'Keats and Shakespeare: Two New Sources', *ELN* ii (1964), 105–9 (p. 106). Felperin's second new source is the nightingale in *The Passionate Pilgrim*, discussed later in the chapter.

24. See parallels cited by Allott, especially those mentioned in Janet Spens, 'A Study of Keats's "Ode to a Nightingale" ', *RES* ns iii (1952), 234–43; also V. J. Lams Jr, 'Ruth, Milton, and Keats's "Ode to a Nightingale" ', *MLQ* xxxiv (1973), 417–35, and Irvin Ehrenpreis, 'Unheard Melodies', *New York Review of Books*, 12 April 1984, 33–4.

25. See Barry Gradman, '*Measure for Measure* and Keats's "Nightingale" Ode', *ELN* xii (1975), 177–82 and '*King Lear* and the Image of Ruth in Keats's "Nightingale" Ode', *K–SJ* xxv (1976), 15–22; Eamon Grennan, 'Keats's *Contemptus Mundi*: A Shakespearean Influence on the "Ode to a Nightingale" ', *MLQ* xxxvi (1975), 272–92; B. E. Haley, 'The Infinite Will: Shakespeare's *Troilus* and the "Ode to a Nightingale" ', *K–SJ* xxi–xxii (1972–3), 18–23; I. S. Harris, 'The Influence of Shakespeare on the Odes of Keats' (unpubl. Boston University Ph.D. diss., 1978); R. F. Rashbrook, 'Keats and Hamlet', *N&Q* cxcv (1950), 253–4; Willard Spiegelman, 'Keats's "Coming Muskrose" and Shakespeare's "Profound Verdure" ', *ELH* l (1983), 347–62; R. S. White, 'Shakespearean Music in Keats's "Ode to a Nightingale" ', *English*, xxx (1981), 217–29 and replies by James Ogden and myself, 'Shakespeare and the "Nightingale": Two Comments', *English*, xxxi (1982), 134–41.

26. The word 'forlorn' provides a further link with Poor Tom and *Lear*: Thomas McFarland argues that the source for Keats's emphatically postponed adjective is Cordelia's 'And wast thou fain, poor father, / To hovel thee with swine and rogues forlorn' (IV. vii. 37)—*Forms of Ruin*, 234–5. Milton frequently delays 'forlorn', as in Adam's 'wild woods forlorn' (*PL* ix. 910).

27. *The Odes of John Keats* (Cambridge, Mass., 1983), 84.

28. *The Eden of Imagination* (1814), 15 n., 32–4; particular mention is made of *A Midsummer Night's Dream*.

29. The key phrases from *Hamlet* cited in the ensuing discussion were marked by Keats in his pocket edition.

30. 'Darkling' is another word in the ode (51) that echoes both Shakespeare and Milton: contextually, it must derive from Milton's 'wakeful bird' that 'Sings darkling' and 'Tunes her nocturnal note' (*PL* iii. 38–40—in keeping with the ease of the nightingale and the melancholy of the poet, Keats transfers 'darkling' from the bird to himself), but, given the connections with *Lear*, it also suggests the Fool's 'Out went the candle, and we were left darkling' (I. iv. 217).

31. *KL* i. 140, adapting *R2* III. ii. 155, which Shelley was said to have quoted out of the blue in a stage-coach, startling the other passengers—a wonderful instance of the Romantic taste for Shakespearean quotation.

32. Helen Vendler argues that the imprisoning of the lover's hand is derived from Hamlet and Ophelia as well as *Troilus* and *Venus and Adonis*: *Odes of Keats*, 174, 314–15.

33. The preface is quoted from Arnold's *Selected Prose* (Harmondsworth, 1970), 48–51.
34. *Essays in Criticism: Second Series* (1888, repr. 1927), 119–20.

Notes to Chapter 10

1. *Records*, ed. David Wright (Harmondsworth, 1973), 75.
2. Expanded entry for 17 August 1814 in Claire Clairmont's journal: *Shelley and his Circle 1773–1822*, ed. K. N. Cameron and D. H. Reiman (6 vols., Cambridge, Mass., 1961–73), iii. 346. Shelley's lack of a watch puts one in mind of Orlando's 'there's no clock in the forest' (*AYL* iii. ii. 301).
3. See enumerations by D. L. Clark, 'Shelley and Shakespeare', *PMLA* liv (1939), 261–87; F. L. Jones, 'Shelley and Shakespeare: A Supplement', *PMLA* lix (1944), 591–6; Beach Langston, 'Shelley's Use of Shakespeare', *HLQ* xii (1949), 163–90; and notes to the Julian edn.
4. Also of interest is a rejected fragment of *Epipsychidion* in which Shelley uses the example of Shakespeare's sonnets to weigh against attempts at biographical reading: we should be interested in neither the identity of Emilia, nor that of the friend in the sonnets (*SPW* 428).
5. In particular, compare 'Triumph', 352–7 (*SPW* 515–16) with *Tp* iv. i. 76–83; see Carlos Baker, *Shelley's Major Poetry* (1948), 266 n.
6. There is an excellent article on this poem by Barry Weller: 'Shakespeare, Shelley, and the Binding of the Lyric', *MLN* xciii (1978), 912–37.
7. *Romeo and Juliet* remained a major influence: 'Ginevra' incorporates parental tyranny, the grief and despair of young lovers, the apparent death of the heroine, her burial alive in the family tomb, a wedding in close proximity to the supposed death, and a marriage of love to death.
8. *Note Books of Percy Bysshe Shelley*, ed. H. Buxton Forman (3 vols., St Louis, 1911), iii. 126.
9. For the play's politics, see R. B. Woodings, ' "A Devil of a Nut to Crack:" Shelley's *Charles the First*', *Studia Neophilologica*, xl (1968), 216–37; this article also has some useful remarks on its relation to Shakespeare's history plays.
10. For Shelley's translations—the art which strives to recover foreign literature as imitation and allusion strive to recover the native tradition— see Timothy Webb, *The Violet in the Crucible: Shelley and Translation* (Oxford, 1976).
11. Lunatic, lover, and poet, Tasso, already the subject of a play by Goethe and the speaker of a 'Lament' by Byron, would have been a good subject for a Romantic Shakespearean drama.
12. *The Death of Tragedy* (1961, repr. 1963), 147. Steiner's remains the best brief account of Shakespeare's debilitating influence on Romantic drama.
13. *The Works of Thomas Lovell Beddoes*, ed. H. W. Donner (1935), 595, 536, 578.
14. In October 1814 Shelley and his party had left a performance of *Hamlet* after the second act, 'Shelley displeased with what he saw of Kean'—*Mary Shelley's Journal*, ed. F. L. Jones (Norman, Oklahoma,

1947), 20. However, what really disgusted him about the Regency theatre was not Kean but 'the bad filling-up of the inferior parts' (*SPW* 336). For the importance of Miss O'Neill in shaping the character of Beatrice, see J. W. Donohue Jr, *Dramatic Character in the English Romantic Age* (Princeton, 1970), 166–72.

15. See K. N. Camcron, 'Shelley's Source Material in "Charles I" ', *MLQ* vi (1945), 197–210 and R. B. Woodings, 'Shelley's Sources for "Charles the First" ', *MLR* lxiv (1969), 267–75.

16. See Paul Smith, 'Restless Casuistry: Shelley's Composition of *The Cenci*', *K–SJ* xiii (1964), 77–85.

17. Stuart Curran offers a good study of imagery in ch. 4 of his *Shelley's 'Cenci': Scorpions Ringed with Fire* (Princeton, 1970).

18. For comprehensive listings, see E. S. Bates, *A Study of Shalley's Drama, The Cenci* (New York, 1908), 54–5, and Curran, 38. The whole of Curran's ch. 2 is relevant, though he plays down the echoes and does not consider the possibility that Shelley is responding to Shakespeare in, to use Bloom's term, a 'revisionary' way. My own argument is much closer to that of Paul A. Cantor in his fine article, ' "A Distorting Mirror": Shelley's *The Cenci* and Shakespearean Tragedy', in *Shakespeare: Aspects of Influence*, 91–108.

19. *The Life of Percy Bysshe Shelley*, ed. H. Buxton Forman (1913), 256. Medwin may be exaggerating Shelley's knowledge of Jacobean drama; it is likely to have been based principally on the scenes reprinted by Lamb in his *Specimens of English Dramatic Poets*, which Shelley and his wife both read in 1817—see Mary's *Journal*, 90.

20. *Revaluation* (1936, repr. Harmondsworth, 1972), 221.

21. In his *Indicator* review, Leigh Hunt argued that this line of exclamations was influenced by Greek tragedy—see N. I. White, *The Unextinguished Hearth: Shelley and his Contemporary Critics* (Durham, North Carolina, 1938), 202. Charnel-house language travelled from *Romeo and Juliet* to the Romantics via eighteenth-century 'graveyard' poetry, most notably Robert Blair's highly popular *The Grave*.

22. *The Literary Gazette*, 1 April 1820, 209–10, in White, 170; this was not the only review to mention Shelley's borrowings from Shakespeare—*The Monthly Review* singled out the debt to *Measure for Measure* in Beatrice's lines on death (White, 206).

23. Thomas Medwin, *Conversations of Lord Byron*, ed. E. J. Lovell Jr (Princeton, 1966), 97.

24. For Shelley's reading of *BL* in 1817, see Mary's *Journal*, 90.

25. *Imagination and Fancy* (1844, repr. 1910), 267.

Notes to Chapter 11

1. J. W. von Goethe, *Wilhelm Meister's Apprenticeship*, trans. Thomas Carlyle (1824), Bk. iv, ch. 13.

2. Quoted from *New Monthly Magazine*, NS xxix (1830), no. 2, 327–36. Earl Wasserman offers compelling reasons for the dialogue's authenticity in 'Shelley's Last Poetics: A Reconsideration', in *From Sensibility to Roman-*

ticism, ed. F. W. Hilles and Harold Bloom (New York, 1965), 487–511 (505–8); I am convinced by Charles E. Robinson's evidence for the attribution to Mary Shelley in his *Shelley and Byron: The Snake and Eagle Wreathed in Fight* (Baltimore, 1976), 270.

3. Cf. such lines as 'dare to strut an hour to Shakespeare's strain' in the manuscript poem of 1815, published for the first time in *BPW* (iii. 281), 'Epilogue to *The Merchant of Venice* Intended for a Private Theatrical'.

4. *Letter to* **** ****** [John Murray] *on the Rev. W. L. Bowles's Strictures on the Life and Writings of Pope* (1821), in *Letters and Journals*, ed. R. E. Prothero (6 vols., 1898–1901, repr. 1922–4), v. 536–66 (p. 560).

5. *Conversations of Lord Byron with the Countess of Blessington* (1834), 357.

6. Another quotation reinforces our sense of *Macbeth*'s relation to the theatricality of politics in the period: of his parliamentary career, Byron says that he has 'no intention to "strut another hour" on that stage' (*LJ* iii. 32).

7. See P. J. Manning, 'Byron's *English Bards and Scotch Reviewers*: The Art of Allusion', *KSMB* xxi (1970), 7–11.

8. As R. F. Gleckner does in *Byron and the Ruins of Paradise* (Baltimore, 1967), 133–8.

9. Hunt, *Lord Byron and Some of his Contemporaries*, *HVSV* 320.

10. *Literary Gazette*, 24 February 1821, 121.

11. Review of *Marino*, *Literary Gazette*, 28 April 1821, 259–63 (p. 263).

12. I. ii. 334, III. i 119, III. ii. 509, IV. ii. 73; II. ii. 93, II. ii. 156, III. ii. 268, V. i. 325; IV. i., V. i. 178–9; III. ii. 79, III. ii. 326 ff. See also Hazlitt's list of phrases in his review of the play (*HW* xix. 47), and that by Samuel Chew in *The Dramas of Lord Byron* (Göttingen and Baltimore, 1915), 179–81.

13. Its strengths are discussed by Anne Barton in ' "A Light to Lesson Ages": Byron's Political Plays', in *Byron: A Symposium*, ed. John Jump (1975), 138–62, and William Ruddick in 'Lord Byron's Historical Tragedies', in *Essays on Nineteenth Century British Theatre*, ed. Kenneth Richards and Peter Thomson (1971), 83–94.

14. The Wagnerian term is aptly used by Jerome J. McGann in *Fiery Dust*: *Byron's Poetic Development* (Chicago, 1968), 230.

15. Cf. 'I do not deny the natural powers of Mind of the earlier dramatists— but I think that their service as a *standard* is doing irreparable mischief' (*LJ* viii. 200).

16. David Erdman argues convincingly that Byron did in fact intend at least his three historical tragedies for the stage: 'Byron's Stage Fright: The History of his Ambition and Fear of Writing for the Stage', *ELH* vi (1939), 219–43.

17. Earlier Byron had praised Kemble's Coriolanus, the role to which his classical style was best suited (*LJ* ii. 149); for further remarks on Kemble, Siddons, and Kean, see Byron's original preface to *Marino Faliero* in *Poetical Works*, ed. E. H. Coleridge (7 vols., 1898–1904), iv. 338–9.

18. 'Death of Edmund Kean', *The Athenaeum*, 18 May 1833, 313–15.

19. *Beaten Paths; and those who trod them* (2 vols., 1862), ii. 195–6.

20. See C. M. Fuess, *Lord Byron as a Satirist in Verse* (New York, 1912, repr. 1973), 152–3.

21. There are some excellent comments on the non-organic structure of *Don Juan* in Jerome J. McGann, *Don Juan in Context* (Chicago, 1976), 107 ff.; to argue for the poem's deliberate diffuseness is not to deny the presence of recurring image-patterns, such as that of fall and the loss of paradise described by G. M. Ridenour in *The Style of Don Juan* (New Haven, 1960), ch. 2.

22. The best account of Byron's Miltonic allusions is McGann's, *Don Juan in Context*, 23–50.

23. The phrase is in fact Macbeth's; it occurs at III. iv. 16, a few lines before 'cabin'd, cribb'd, confin'd'—Byron must have known this section of the play particularly well.

24. 'She sleeps well' occurs among a group of phrases from *Macbeth* in *Childe Harold*, iv. 171, *BPW* ii. 181. After the siege of Ismail, there is another emotive Shakespearean phrase in the context of death: 'Of forty thousand who had manned the wall, / Some hundreds breathed—the rest were silent all' (*DJ* viii. 127) echoes Hamlet's dying words, 'the rest is silence'. As so often in *Don Juan*, the allusion is heightened by the dash.

25. 'On this day I complete my thirty-sixth year', *Poetical Works*, ed. Page, corr. Jump (1970), 112.

26. *The Memoirs of Hector Berlioz*, trans. David Cairns (1969), 462; 'both' refers to Berlioz and his wife, the Shakespearean actress Harriet Smithson.

Index